WORK AND WELFARE IN THE NEW RUSSIA

Work and Welfare in the New Russia

NICK MANNING
OVSEY SHKARATAN
NATALIYA TIKHONOVA

Translations by Karen George

Routledge
Taylor & Francis Group

LONDON AND NEW YORK

First published 2000 by Ashgate Publishing

Reissued 2018 by Routledge
2 Park Square, Milton Park, Abvingdon, Oxon OX14 4RN
711 Third Avenue, New York, NY 10017, USA

Routledge is an imprint of the Taylor & Francis Group, an informa business

Publisher's Note
The publisher has gone to great lengths to ensure the quality of this reprint but points out that some imperfections in the original copies may be apparent.

Disclaimer
The publisher has made every effort to trace copyright holders and welcomes correspondence from those they have been unable to contact.

A Library of Congress record exists under LC control number: 00110766

ISBN 13: 978-1-138-72914-8 (hbk)
ISBN 13: 978-1-138-72911-7 (pbk)
ISBN 13: 978-1-315-19005-1 (ebk)

Contents

List of Tables

Authors/Translator

Nick Manning has been engaged in research on social issues in Russia since 1979 (*Socialism, Social Welfare and the Soviet Union*, 1980, with Vic George; *The New Eastern Europe: past, present and future for social policy*, 1992, with B. Deacon, et al.; *Environmental and Housing Movements, grassroots experience in Hungary, Russia and Estonia*, 1997, edited with K. Lang-Pickvance, and C. Pickvance). He is also interested in medical sociology and health policy, and social theory and social policy, and has written or edited 15 books. Since 1995 he has been Professor of Social Policy and Sociology at the University of Nottingham, UK.

Ovsey Shkaratan has written or edited more than 21 books on employment and social issues in Russia (*Problems of Working Class Social Structure*, 1970; *Man at Work*, 1977; *National and Social Problems of the City*, 1986; *New Power in New Russia*, 1994; *Social Stratification*, 1995, with V. Radaev). He is an internationally renowned sociologist concerned with labour processes and social structure in Russia, and since 1992 has been editor of *Universe of Russia*. He has been Professor of Sociology since 1976 at Moscow State University, and is currently Professor of Sociology and Head of the Department of Economic Sociology at the Higher School of Economics, Moscow.

Nataliya Tikhonova has published more than 120 works in Russia, the USA, Germany and the UK (*Social Stratification Factors during Transition to the Market Economy*, 1999; *The Middle Class in Contemporary Russia*, 1999, with M. Gorshkov and A. Chepurenko; *Arbeitslosigkeit in Russland: Dimensionen, Ursachen und Bekampfung*; 1998; *Russlands Sozialstruktur nach acht Jahren Reformen*, 1999). She is interested in the social consequences of economic change, particularly for social structure, and the positions, actions and values of different social groups, such as the unemployed, the poor, the middle classes and youth. She has a PhD in philosophy from Moscow State University (1981), and a higher doctorate from the Institute of Sociology, Russian Academy of Sciences (1999). She has been Deputy Director of the Russian Independent Institute for Social and National Problems since 1992.

Karen George studied at the School of Slavonic and East European Studies, University of London. She has a BA in Russian, and a postgraduate diploma in technical and specialised translation. For much of the 1980s she worked in the public sector as a senior welfare rights officer. She has been a part time lecturer in social policy at the University of Kent, and a member of the Institute of Linguists, since 1993.

Preface

Не до жиру, быть бы живу
Let's just try and get by...

This project was conceived in 1993 as a genuinely collaborative enterprise, to be shared jointly between UK and Russian colleagues. While the design and methods originated in the UK, the questionnaires, analysis and interpretation have been widely discussed between us. The study began in December 1994, with funding from the EU and DfID. Visits and workshops have taken place in either Russia or the UK at least once or twice a year since 1994. Fieldwork was carried out in 1996 and 1997, including a total of 600 interviews with policy actors and heads of households in three cities in Russia: St. Petersburg, Moscow and Voronezh. The Russian financial crash of August 1998 has exacerbated many of the findings we present here, although it is a measure of the extent to which the Russian economy has become demonetised that the World Bank (1999) reports less economic and social impact than had been feared.

The initial idea and methodological framework of the project was suggested by Nick Manning. The Russian team, headed by Ovsey Shkaratan and Nataliya Tikhonova took an active part in developing and improving the initial design in relation to current Russian social reality. The presentation of our findings in this book has been a genuinely collaborative piece of work, to which we have all contributed over many months of discussion. Not all of the points made in it are supported with equal weight by all of us, but the general findings and conclusions are. We have taken responsibility for the individual chapters as follows: NM for chapters 1-5, OIS for chapters 6-7, NET for chapters 8-9. However many individual contributions have been made across this division: NET to chapters 1, 4 and 10; OIS to chapters 4, 5 and 10. In addition other members of the team have made significant contributions, in particular Tatiana Sidorina, who was the author of Chapters 6 and 7 (the latter in collaboration with O. Shkaratan and L. Panova) and contributed to Chapter 4.

A note on money and measuring poverty

In the book, we have presented incomes in terms of 'old roubles' for consistency, although 'new roubles' (equivalent to one thousand old roubles) have been in use since 1998.

We took as a basis for the official Subsistence Minimum a figure of 400,000 roubles, which was better for our calculations, even though for March/April 1997 – i.e. when the second phase of the survey was carried out – it was 410,000 roubles according to the State Committee for Statistics data (Goskomstat, 1997, p.70). Our figure practically matched data on the subsistence minimum originating from the Centre for Macro-Economic Strategies of the Russian Academy of Sciences (*Argumenty I fakty*, vol.24, 1997, p.1) and statistical summaries from the Institute of Economic Problems of the Transition Period.

A typical example of the contentious nature of official statistical data is the government's approach to defining social indicators of poverty. Since the end of 1996, Goskomstat has been calculating the cost of an enlarged basket of consumer goods, containing 25 basic necessities. Moreover, this new basket of consumer goods, unlike the previous one, has official status, in that - in accordance with the law - it defines the Subsistence Minimum standard. The composition of the basket is based on the 'Methodological recommendations for calculating the Subsistence Minimum in the regions of the Russian Federation', established by the Ministry of Labour and Social Policy on 10th November 1992. According to specialist assessments:

> the new basket of consumer goods envisages a level of consumption of the goods in it, which is lower than World War II food rations... Nevertheless, the cost of this basket defines the Subsistence Minimum - or poverty line - in the regions and is used to calculate amounts of financial transfers from the Federal Budget (Russia-Europe Centre for Economic Policy, 1997, pp.243-4).

Section III in Chapter 1 examines the problem of understanding and measuring poverty in more detail.

A note on the choice of cities

The modernisation of Russian society and the transition to a market economy have given a new edge and meaning to problems of social development and employment in the different regions of Russia. Given perennial instability, economic and social crisis and deepening inequality between regions, the task of applying an analytic approach to these problems - without which appropriate regional policy, including employment policy, cannot be developed - has become increasingly acute.

Regional differences are generated by various factors. Some of these are the inevitable result of economic activity, including the free market and free competition. Others are tied in with a whole series of cultural and ethnic problems. It is especially significant, perhaps, that Russia is a country which might be seen as possessing a 'border civilisation', lying as it does between European and Asiatic civilisations, while at the same time having its own authenticity. In this respect, there is also an uneven degree of adherence to the traditional extensive model of economic and cultural development. As a result, some Russian regions are drawn more towards European culture and civilisation and are able to take on board the new value system that modernisation brings with it; while others stick to traditional extensive culture and reject (or at any rate have a problem coming to terms with) modernisation and its associated need for active use of new technologies and ways of working. In the event, some regions 'fit in' to the market more easily than others. In the 1990s, gaps between the regions began to grow rapidly: a process of stratification of Russian regions into qualitatively different types is taking place. This makes it necessary to develop specific and differentiated social policy in a way that would have been unthinkable under the Soviet authorities. This demonstrates one of the decisive differences between unified Soviet social policy and the post-Soviet version that is made up of different elements.

Under such conditions, we considered that it would not be sensible just to take small or medium-sized towns for this purpose, because our research design presupposed a whole range of groups in crisis in regional labour markets, as well as competent social policy actors who could speak as experts. Given all this, our choice was more or less made for us: the two Russian capitals - Moscow and St. Petersburg. For comparison we chose Voronezh - a city typical of a number of depressed regions, with an economic and employment structure not dissimilar from those of the two capitals. In Chapter 5 details about the cities are presented.

The difference between the cities - or the gulf between them, one could legitimately say - is illustrated by tax income to the consolidated State budget per head of population in 1996. The *per capita* bill for the Moscow taxpayer was 10.8 million roubles; in St. Petersburg the equivalent figure was 3.5 million roubles, and in Voronezh 1.6 million. We should point out that, using the same *per capita* taxation indicator, there are substantially poorer regions - e.g. Tambov province, at 1.3 million roubles, or Ivanovo province, at 1.2 million (Russia-Europe Centre for Economic Policy, 1997, pp.250-251). If we divide the regions of Russia into relatively better-off, relatively worse-off and those in a disastrous situation, our three cities would be in the first and second of these categories.

Acknowledgements

We would like to thank the many colleagues who have contributed to this project. The household and policy actor interviews in Moscow, and their initial analysis, were undertaken by Tatiana Sidorina, Nadia Davidova and Elena Pakhomova. In St. Petersburg this work was undertaken by Ludmilla Panova and Nina Rusinova. The Voronezh sample and analysis were undertaken by Nadia Davidova. Without the highly effective and professional commitment of this large team the data would not have been collected, analysed and summarised on schedule.

In preparing the final manuscript for the book, we would particularly like to acknowledge Lyudmilla Panova who contributed to Chapter 7 on St. Petersburg, and Nadia Davidova who provided substantial material towards the preparation of Chapter 3.

Karen George gave half her working time for the duration of the project, providing academic input on comparative social security and Russian society, and vital organisational and translation skills, all to exacting professional standards. Thanks are also due to Bob Walkden, Teresa Levitt and Nadya Davidova for invaluable work on draft translations and contributions to discussion of terminology.

We would like to thank those who gave critical feedback on the project at seminars. Veronika Kabalina commented on the draft of Chapter 7. In particular we are grateful to those contributing to the final workshop in 1999: Peter Abrahamson, Elena Avraamova, Ludmilla Khakhulina, Alastair McAuley, Lilyana Ovcharova, Sergey Smirnov, and John Veit-Wilson.

The project was originally developed in 1993, and submitted to INTAS for EU funding in 1994 (grant number INTAS 94-3725). This involved the active collaboration with several countries and research centres - Dr. Peter Abrahamson (Universities of Roskilde and, subsequently, Copenhagen) and Professor Francois-Xavier Merrien (Universities of Paris-Evry and, subsequently, Lausanne). In addition, substantial funding was obtained from the Overseas Development Administration (now the Department for International Development) (grant number R6387). Several smaller grants were also received from the British Academy and INTAS. International meetings were hosted by the Higher School of Economics (Moscow), the Russian Independent Institute for Social and National Problems (Moscow) and the University of Nottingham (UK). We would like to acknowledge all this support.

Part I

Background and Project Design

1 Russia in Trouble

Повадится беда - растворяй ворота
When misfortune appears, open wide the gates

It is ten years since State socialist societies embarked on an era of extraordinary change. At the beginning people's hopes were for personal freedom, democratic involvement, and greater prosperity. There are now 27 countries in this region, some of which have recovered and indeed exceeded their economic levels of ten years before, and some of which have had regular elections contested by stable political parties embedded in recognisable social groups. Five of them are set to join the European Union. However Russia is not one of these.

Russia has had a very troubled experience over the last ten years. After billions of dollars in aid, a myriad of economic and social advisors, the liberalisation of prices, the privatisation of much of its industry and housing stock, a new constitution, and several military adventures, the United Nations Development Programme announced on 29th July 1999 that 'A human crisis of monumental proportions is emerging in the former Soviet Union. The transition years have literally been lethal for many people. The hardest hit are the men of the region, who are living shorter, more unhealthy lives' (UNDP, 1999a). The shape of this crisis can be demonstrated through any number of social indicators. For example, Russia's level of inequality has jumped to twice its pre-transition level to become the highest in the region, with a gini coefficient of just 0.5. The birth rate has collapsed to the lowest in the region. Life expectancy amongst men has fallen to 58 years - this has mainly taken place amongst the middle aged and is a larger fall than for any other population group in any of the 27 countries. Indeed it is ten years lower than the life expectancy for men in China. As a result of the growing gap between the life expectancies of men and women across the region, there are a total of 9.7 million 'missing men', of which Russia accounts for the majority, at 5.9 million. Poverty has grown rapidly, from 4 to 32 per cent using the UN four dollars per day criteria. The shadow economy makes up between a quarter and third of GNP, all of which is lost as potential taxable activity, such that the state is chronically under-funded.

The experience of women has been genuinely contradictory during this extraordinary period. In many ways they have suffered more than men,

3

despite the pattern of changed life expectancy. Another branch of the UN, UNICEF, claimed in a report released on 22 September 1999 that 'The economic, social and political transition in the region has shattered the State monopoly on gender equality and exposed women to a wide-open environment where the conditions for equality are quite different, a territory rich with possibilities but not without risks. The transition process has cut into the employment and social welfare gains of women - a regression often linked to the sudden and significant shrinkage in the role of the State' (UNICEF, 1999, p.1). However women have also proved to be the key survivors for households over this period, adding to their traditional double burdens of paid and domestic work, a third burden of barter networking, and a fourth burden of grassroots activism (ibid., p.104).

In contrast to this unfolding picture of tragedy and heroism, largely unrecorded, has been the hothouse of policy advice and direction provided by international agencies and think tank advisors. At best benign, but at worst corrupt (Wedell, 1999), these have been elegantly denounced by Guy Standing as a 'Babble of Euphemisms' (Standing, 1999). He reviews a myriad of nostrums and policy reactions that have grown up to disguise the human experiences of ordinary people across the region, but especially in Russia: shock therapy, big bang, liberalisation, stabilisation, sequencing, State desertion, privatisation, restructuring, hard budgets, crowding out, social capital, administrative leave, wage arrears, rigidities, active labour market policies, dead-weight effects, substitution effects. All of these, he suggests, divert attention from the fact that the economy has become dis-embedded from society, and that this massive experiment has become a 'great transformation' in the sense that Karl Polyani described the earlier transformation of western societies after the 1930s. As was the case then, the economy needs re-embedding in society, through greater State action, but in a new way. 'One of the great ironies of the 1990s', he points out, 'may well turn out to be that with the collapse of State socialism there was a rush to introduce social policies based on Welfare State capitalism, precisely at the time when the latter was losing its capacities and legitimacy' (p.2).

It is the intention of this book to examine some of these issues for Russia in the late 1990s through an original set of policy and household interview data. The events of recent years in Russia have provided a 'pure experiment' unwittingly performed on tens of millions of Russians. Just less than ten years ago, there was a completely different social structure in Russia, a person's place in which - as in all stable social structures - was defined by social, and not psychological factors (such as workplace, parents' social origins and work status, educational achievement). It is to be expected that in another 10 to 15 years, there will again be a relatively stable social structure in Russia, in which both status and the economic position of the individual will depend primarily on social factors. For example, they may depend on educational and occupational status, which is connected with - among other things - the property status of parents: there is already a clear process by which people leaving various types of higher education achieve qualitatively different employment and, at the same time, the more élite higher education institutions - for all their pseudo-gratis status - are becoming increasingly closed to members of non-élite sections of society.

However, in Russia's new circumstances, those social strata who were very well looked after under the old regime (and did not possess a 'culture of poverty') have found themselves in the position of paupers. Moreover, these strata are huge, accounting for millions of people. For the most part, they used to work in the military-industrial complex, in whose scientific institutes alone there were millions of people, and where employees - who in most cases earn only around $100 a month - are currently going on long-term hunger strikes in order to receive their wages just for the previous year. In addition, there are millions of employees of State administrative bodies which are surplus to requirements in the new conditions. There are also numerous categories of budget-funded employees, such as teachers at institutes of further education, who used to belong to society's élite, but who now eke out a pitiful existence, especially in the provinces.

At the same time, however, large new social groups have come into being, also comprising millions of people, whose circumstances, in both status and property terms, enable them to be assigned to a new middle or even upper class. These are entrepreneurs, skilled managers and waged employees of structures such as banks, financial and credit institutions, insurance companies, consulting, auditing and marketing companies, and so on. These social strata have appeared literally 'from nowhere', as there was nothing like them in the society of the past. In reality, their members have been recruited from various types of research institute and design office, and even partially from the working class (in the case of small- and some medium-scale businessmen).

This sudden fracturing of the social structure has led to a social identity crisis, recorded in a number of studies, including those of Zaslavskaya (1995, 1999), Shkaratan (Shkaratan and Fontanel, 1998; Shkaratan and Tikhonova, 1996), Tikhonova (1999a, 1999b) and others (Gudkov, 1999; Denisovsky, Malkina and Nazimova, 1992; Doktorov,

1994; Yadov, 1993; Kozyreva, 1994). This crisis is certainly bound up with the issue of how far the actions of individuals are determined by particular social norms and roles, but it also involves the problem of describing poverty (setting a poverty line). Most western researchers base their ideas on their own experience of life, and unwittingly start from the notion that certain strata exist and are characterised by, among other things, distinctive standards of living and models of behaviour. Self-identification with these strata - social identity - also predisposes a person to certain behavioural reactions, even down to shopping preferences. If it is impossible to maintain these standards, the person will make a transition to a different stratum, in some cases entering the category of the poor.

For the population of Russia, apart from élite groups, the very premise that such strata exist is uncertain. Past phenomena such as mass migration from country to city or from European Russia to Siberia and the North, huge vertical mobility, and a situation where, in less than three generations, a group of people with higher education came into being where before there had been an almost universally illiterate rural population numbering millions, all combined to create very great instability in the social structure, with the result that the existence of such strata was very debatable. For ordinary Russians in the Soviet period, social homogeneity had in many respects become a reality.

Now, though, with a completely new social structure having replaced the old one, and with the market for goods having qualitatively changed - with a concomitant change in standards of consumption and potential for consumption - there are and can be no fixed ideas of what type of consumption or behaviour is normal for 'those around you'. This is firstly because there is no longer such a clear-cut group of people, and secondly because of the appearance of qualitatively new goods or potential ways of tackling one's problems. So *for the time being,* for a significant part of the Russian population, mechanisms for determining behaviour through identifying oneself with a group are largely inapplicable.

How have households survived in these rapidly changed circumstances, and what policies have been, or could be, adopted to facilitate the survival of individuals and their families in these circumstances? It is these questions that have stimulated the project on which this book is based. The research simultaneously addressed questions of policy and questions of individual and household actions. The data that has been collected, and the organisation of the book reflects this dual level of enquiry. The rest of this chapter is correspondingly divided into three sections: on policy, on household actors, and on poverty.

Section I - The Policy Context

Background to the Project

In Russia, prior to 1989, acknowledged social policy weaknesses included the under-funding of some services such as health, the over-subsidisation of others such as housing, and the bureaucratic stifling of incentive. Employment policy centred on the right to work. The immediate preoccupation in the wake of the 1989-1991 reform/revolution was the establishment of political pluralism and economic reform. Social policy issues (especially in terms of State largesse) were low on the agenda. Now however there is a renewed recognition that emergent capitalism needs to be mended by appropriate social policy, in the interests of the disadvantaged, and political stability.

The first steps included *ad hoc* measures appropriate to the period of transition: unemployment benefit and compensation for price rises. Most enterprises have now been privatised, yet the expected rise in unemployment has remained modest. Observers have repeatedly expected market constraints to lead to an increased rate of enterprise collapse, and unemployment. There is therefore a growing interest in the variety of social policy measures routinely used in capitalist democracies (see Chapter 3). Two key issues emerged in the Eastern European literature: how governments could create the popular acceptance of a principle of social policy appropriate to market inequalities, and the extent to which citizens could themselves actively cope with the new insecurities.

The early 1990s also witnessed the gradual separation of policy developments in St. Petersburg and Moscow, most clearly expressed in the local government reforms in the two cities, and the associated constellations of local power emerging. This made them a suitable focus for a comparative study of emerging social policy. Greater regional autonomy for many aspects of social policy suggested that it would also be essential to include a provincial city such as Voronezh (see Chapter 5 for a detailed discussion).

There is of course a long and rich tradition of social policy debate in western countries in which the specific issue of unemployment has stimulated work, especially at points of acute unemployment growth, the 1930s, early 1980s and now the 1990s. This work formed a background for comparisons about the experience of unemployment (Hill, 1973; Sinfield, 1981; Allen, et al., 1986; Gallie, et al., 1994), the causes of it (*Oxford Review of Economic Policy*, 1995, vol. 11, no. 1, *inter alia*), and the policy options pursued to deal with it (Therborn, 1986). Another flourishing literature surrounds the issue of poverty, which is so central to the Russian situation now that it is reviewed in more detail in Section III of this chapter.

In addition there are a number of more general areas in the Western European literature relevant to these concerns. In considering the pattern of Welfare State growth, quantitative analysis of factors associated with the expansion of welfare 'effort' in western societies, suggest that economic/ demographic and political/social (religious) forces have in turn been identified as crucial determinants. This debate has now moved towards an uneasy consensus: that both economic resources and political choices affect welfare state growth, but that the choice of countries, welfare indicators, and time series have an important bearing on the results (O'Connor and Brym, 1988). Such a differing mix of factors related to welfare systems, which appear to retain some relative stability or path dependence over time, has resulted in attempts to construct typologies of different extant welfare states (regimes). Ideologies, and the strategies/effects of State intervention have in turn been identified as crucial to the range of practicable alternatives available to governments. Dimensions such as levels of poverty and inequality, benefit commodification, State/market mix in service provision, labour market regulation, and universal/assistance mix in benefits, have been used (Abrahamson, 1999).

But, given the evident lack of stability in Russia, a perhaps more relevant literature has been the analysis of reactions to the West's economic, political, and welfare state crises of the 1970s. Initially this proposed a divergence between countries; now it is argued that there is a converging upper and lower limit to state welfare intervention in terms, respectively, of economic cost and political legitimation. This is a vital element in the debate over the likely consequences for 'social Europe' of the expansion of membership of the European Union to five Eastern European countries (Pascall and Manning, 2000). A key question is the extent to which citizenship, particularly including the social dimension described by Marshall, can be sustained in crisis circumstances (Manning, 1993). And even where resources and political support permit, political conflict underlying bureaucratic rationality, the crucial operation of 'policy networks' in different functional areas of government, and hence the variation in conditions affecting the implementation of particular policy, make the development of new structures and processes of social policy uncertain (Rhodes and Marsh, 1992).

Awareness of these issues led us to a design which attempted to contextualise quantitative data with detailed study of the historical, cultural and transnational influences on policy changes. We also explicitly compare alternative dimensions for summarising types of policy ideologies and strategies, and examine the divergence in policy implementation in St. Petersburg , Moscow and Voronezh, and thus examine the losers as well as the gainers from proposed changes. In addition policy development and household actions are examined in the context of emergent conflicts within Russian civil society, and popular and élite support for new policies.

To summarise, we have compared the restructuring of social policy in Moscow, St. Petersburg, and Voronezh focusing on the issues of (un)employment and poverty, by addressing the following questions.

Why have new policies emerged? What is the role of historical and cultural factors, or transnational agencies? Is it because there are new political actors (classes, church, parties, movements), or is it a result of economic and budgetary crises? If it is the latter, is there a self-contained social policy strategy, or an influence from other policies, such as a free labour market, or 'full cost' accounting?

What are the aims of the policies? Are they conceived as merely technical, or do they imply a change in prevailing relationships between citizens and State, or between State and market, or in the inequalities between groups such as classes/genders/nationalities? How do these aims relate to western welfare ideologies? What is the new basis for legitimate social justice?

How widespread is support for the aims? To what extent are they, or can they be, modified to gain popular legitimacy? What strategies do the public adopt in supporting/resisting policies? What is the attitude of major institutional political actors to the policies, and do they have the capacity to respond with alternatives? Is there a perceived limit to policy change, in terms of cost, or political legitimacy?

How successfully are policies implemented? What is the effect of conflicting aims between policies? What are the administrative resources available for effective policy action? Are new benefits targeted towards particular needs? Do recipients and non-recipients accept them? Who are the losers/gainers in the period of transition?

The study reported here involved a detailed examination of the origins of Russian social policies, and their aims, implementation, and effects up to 1999. While in the course of the research we gathered material on policies for health, housing, and education, our main policy tracer was change in the system of employment policy, and social security arrangements for the unemployed. More specifically we concentrated on employment policy and retraining, unemployment benefit, and measures to relieve family poverty (such as child benefit). We chose these both because this is where we expected the social costs to be concentrated, and also to facilitate our analysis of 'regime types' with dimensions commonly used in the literature.

The work involved: the collection in Moscow, St. Petersburg and Voronezh of official, political, media, academic and activist documentary evidence; the identification and reanalysis of existing institutional and social survey data on the unemployed, household income, wages, prices, and public opinion; in-depth interviews with ministers, politicians, senior officials, trade union leaders, industrial leaders and local officials concerned with policy; in-depth interviews with households about their work histories, household circumstances, resources, and attitudes towards employment policies. This sample was drawn from four groups: those in factories faced with closure; those on 'administrative leave'; the unemployed; and the recently redundant. All these interviews were repeated after an interval of one year, to gain a dynamic picture of policy debates and the circumstances of households. A detailed discussion of the methodology is presented in Chapter 4.

Labour Markets and Welfare States

The key policy context for this study is the interaction between the labour market and social policy. In Russia the labour market, industrial relations, and social policy are all operating in a largely changed environment since the early 1990s. These fields affect each other in many ways, not only in Russia, but in all industrial societies, and the inter-relationship between emerging social policy and changing employment circumstances is significant. Social policy, labour markets and industrial relations have close links. Empirically, labour markets depend on certain social policies, and social policies are made possible by certain aspects of the labour market. In the EU for example this has been made explicit through the close identification of social policy with employment policy. Conceptually, new typologies of European welfare states, generated through an examination of the situation of male workers, bear a great similarity to typologies of European industrial relations, even though the two fields are quite distinct academic enterprises.

These systems 'meet' at various levels: central and local government, within trade union work, and in the management of enterprises. But research at the level of the household, when looking at systems in transition as in Russia, can be the most revealing of realities 'on the ground'. This is particularly the case where rising unemployment helps to reveal changes in the labour market, industrial relations, and social policies attempting to ameliorate this situation.

In industrial societies there is a close relationship between social policy, the labour market, and the system of industrial relations. The defining moments of 20th century welfare innovation, such as the 1930's US New Deal, the 1940's UK Welfare State, and more recently the 1990's renovation of those systems in Clinton's 1996 welfare reforms, and the British Labour Party's 1997 welfare to work/minimum wage package, have gone hand in hand with assumptions about the labour market and industrial relations.

This was most explicit in the American case through the simultaneous enactment in 1935 of the Wagner Act alongside the Social Security Act. The Wagner Act attempted to regulate industrial relations by granting greater trade union rights and placing obligations on employers. This, it was hoped, would stabilise the economy and hence provide the means for funding pensions and unemployment benefits, and reduce the need for poverty relief.

At the founding of the British Welfare State a decade later, the report prepared by Beveridge also made it clear that the design adopted depended on a crucial assumption: that full employment would ensure the funds to pay for pensions, and minimise expenditure on unemployment benefit and poverty relief.

However full employment in the West has proved unattainable. Unemployment has been a plague for European governments for the last 20 years, both because it drives up the costs of social security, but also because of its potential to generate political instability, and a host of related social and health problems. Governments in Eastern Europe are now faced with the same problems. The creation of social needs and the social policies designed to meet them are crucially related to the operation of the labour market. Work not only provides the means to exist through meeting income needs (in Beveridge's time at the level of the 'family wage'), but on the whole it is good for our psychological and physical health.

In general, work has become an essential passport to other benefits - either through entitlement to social security benefits (typically pensions or unemployment benefit), or through work-related provision such as occupational pensions, subsidised housing, and health care. In both the US and Russia this so-called 'occupational welfare' has been very extensive. In the US, the majority of health care insurance is acquired through employer schemes - and this would have become effectively a universal scheme under the Clinton health reforms that were proposed, but defeated, in 1994. In addition the relatively generous US retirement pension arrangements are funded through payroll taxes, and distributed in relation to past earnings.

In Russia the extensive provision of welfare benefits through the enterprise is legendary (Shomina, 1993): health care, housing, food, holidays, education (including nurseries), were, and in part still are, widely provided, as well as entitlement to pensions. This non-money wage, the 'social wage', accounts for a very significant part of the enterprise's operating costs, and is a key element in work incentives and labour market behaviour in Russia. It probably amounted to about 25 per cent of the average industrial wage in the 1980s, but actually rose as a proportion to about 50 per cent in the 1990s partly because of the relative fall in money wages (Gerchikov, 1995, p.151). It appears that such provision is now slowly shrinking.

In general, while enterprise benefits can be understood as a wage cost arising through inter-employer competition for scarce labour, and this has certainly been a feature of the Russian labour market for most of the 20th century, at a national level welfare benefits can be understood as an important part of human capital investment. Social policy helps to provide both the daily reproduction of labour power through the domestic servicing of physical and psychological needs, and the longer term production of a healthy and literate workforce. Occupational and more general social welfare is thus of wider consequence than competition for scarce labour; employers also have a collective interest in social policy's efforts to sustain the workforce on which employers depend.

This interdependence is particular revealed for example in the way in which social policy in the EU is very closely defined in relation to employment issues. Thus in the EU the right to the free movement of labour and other employment rights, such as equal opportunities, the relatively high levels of expenditure on education, and on employment initiatives, and the relatively low levels of expenditure on health, housing or social security, highlight the close relationship of social and employment concerns. This was symbolised in the replacement in the final draft of the 1989 Social Protocol of the term 'citizens' by the term 'workers'.

These many points of connection between social policy and the labour market are easier to appreciate at times of economic change. Just as the key moments of early social policy innovation in the US and the UK, in the 1930s and 1940s, were intimately connected, both explicitly and more generally, with changes in economic policy and practice, we can see a similar process in Russia. Key turning points of social policy change there occurred with early industrialisation in the early 1930s, and industrial maturation in the late 1950s (Chapter 2). At the close of the 20th century all three countries are experiencing a new round of economic changes, and in all three there are related social policy innovations. In the case of Russia these have of course been monumental, and social policy changes have ensued on a similar scale (Chapter 3).

In addition to the empirical connections between these two fields, we can note a further and final connection. This is the parallel development of theory in two unrelated academic discourses - namely comparative social policy and comparative industrial relations. These are not traditions between which there has been any significant intercourse, which makes the theoretical parallels all the more remarkable. Generally we find that in the 1990s both have developed a set of typologies with which to understand the comparative changes in, respectively, social and employment policy in different countries. These typologies have tried to identify ideal typical features of groups of countries which appear to contain an internal logic in the way social and employment policies have developed: an 'American' type, a 'Scandinavian' type, and so on. These types have been a significant feature of both the international advice proffered to Russia by, for example, the World Bank, and of the internal debates in Russia about the way forward for new policies. And much of this advice integrates aspects of both employment policy and social policy.

Social policies in industrialised societies are typically theorised now as being embedded in an overall, internally consistent, national Welfare State system. It is important to try to identify what this is in order to fully appreciate the policy dynamics of any specific area, its limits and effects. Countries vary in their particular Welfare State model. Although early typologies of welfare policies were proposed in the 1970s, their theoretical specification and empirical demonstration were developed to a new level of sophistication in the field of comparative social policy by Esping-Andersen (1990). In a highly influential book, he laid down three types, or 'regimes' as he called them of 'welfare capitalism'. These were generated by considering the situation of male wage workers only, and while there has been substantial criticism of them for ignoring gender issues (Sainsbury, 1996), they nevertheless have dominated social policy debates in the 1990s. His argument was that in different countries social policies were organised around certain internally integrated features so that social policies of different types shared certain consistent assumptions and effects in terms for example of the nature of state intervention, the stratification of social groups, and most crucially the extent to which markets were replaced by bureaucratic distribution in a process of 'de-commodification'.

He suggested that there were three such types: neo-liberal (American), social democratic (Scandinavian), and corporatist (Franco-German). The neo-liberal type had a relatively low (and falling) level of de-commodification, a relatively high level of stratification in terms of income inequality, and state intervention typified by regulation of markets rather than the provision or finance of social welfare. By contrast the social democratic type had a high level of de-commodification, low level of stratification, and direct state provision or finance, as well as regulation. Corporatist types had a mixture of these features: heavily stratified by both income (especially in France) and social status, yet with considerable de-commodification, if only through the heavy regulation of non-profit providers, rather than direct state provision.

Although Esping-Andersen did not include the pre-transition societies of the Soviet era in his typology, it is not difficult to include them as a particular type: de-commodification through price subsidisation (especially of food and accommodation) was extensive, State regulation was widespread, and stratification limited. In addition the predominant role of enterprise welfare brought labour markets, industrial relations, and social policy into a particularly intimate relationship. This was qualitatively distinct from his model of a social democratic regime, and might have been described as State socialist. As we shall see, these interconnections have not dissolved as fast as we might imagine in the new world of privately owned Russian industry.

The relationship between industrial relations and social policy 'regime' in this comparative analysis becomes clearer if we look at traditional debates about the origins of Welfare States, and the explanations that we have for their more or less generous development. The crucial question is why Welfare State 'effort' - for example the per cent of GNP spent on social security - has grown to a relatively high level in some societies. Explanations typically include either the direct effect of economic growth (Wilensky, 1975), or the indirect effect of economic growth through the development of left wing political power, centered on trade union strength and its political representation in government (Castles and McKinlay, 1979).

The main conclusion from this body of work is the close shaping of Welfare State expansion by economic development and particularly the political effects of trade union development arising out of economic change. In short welfare 'regimes' can be grouped not only by their effects (de-commodification, etc.), but also by their origins in different economic and political developments.

A strikingly similar typology has emerged in the comparative industrial relations literature in recent years. There has not been such an influential single publication in this field to match the Esping-Andersen book, but a certain consensus has appeared. In contrast to the comparative social policy literature, the industrial relations models use less precisely quantified variables such as the strength of State intervention, the flexibility of regulation, the constitutional basis for industrial relations, and the extent of consultation in the system. A typology almost identical to that of Esping-Andersen is provided for example by Jesper Due, et al. (1991) who argue that there are three European types of industrial relations: the Roman-German (e.g. France), the Anglo-Irish (e.g. the UK), and the Nordic system (e.g. Denmark).

More typically these models focus on the strength and/or flexibility of the three parties conventionally involved in the regulation of industrial relations: the State, employers, and the unions. For example, Ferner and Hyman (1992) also develop a three-fold classification in which the British State is characterised as strong and inflexible, France as relatively weak, and Germany as again strong but also flexible. More completely, Baglioni and Crouch (1991) consider the other key sides, management and unions, sequentially to come up with two further typologies. In the first, collective bargaining practices are ranged between five different levels from strong to weak, with Sweden at the top, the UK in the middle, and France near the bottom. Turning finally to managerial 'styles in industrial relations' they argue for a three-fold typology, including constitutionally embedded collective bargaining obligations (Germany and Sweden), through voluntary consultation (many European countries), to laissez-faire systems typical of the US and now of the UK.

As we did for the classification of Welfare State regimes, we should again add the Soviet model to these European typologies. In the previous Soviet system of industrial relations, centrally integrated control by the Party-State apparatus of both employers and trade unions would have been characterised in these models as one of strong State intervention, limited flexibility, and little consultation. However with the dramatic changes of the 1990s, these relationships have moved away from this common model across Central and Eastern Europe, with the exception in many respects of Russia itself (Thirkell, Scase, and Vickerman, 1995).

To what extent can we make use of these models from comparative social policy and comparative industrial relations to illuminate contemporary changes in Russia? It is easy to see points of affinity between these typologies developed in the industrial relations and social policy literatures. They imply that there are likely to be resonances between industrial relations and labour market policies, and social, especially social security, policies. We might therefore expect to find certain consistencies between these spheres as they are developing in post-transition Russia, and we might further expect to find these resonances at both the level of the household, and in the interaction of local employment and social security policies.

How far the labour market has changed in Russia since the early 1990s is disputed. Within the literature there are three contrasting views of this situation, discussed in more detail in Chapter 3. First are those who do not expect there to be a massive shakeout, since the labour market is already making a successful adjustment to flexible restructuring: labour turnover is high, and wages have shifted rapidly. However this conceals a large segment of the labour market which is very stable, with a smaller segment turning over employment at a furious rate - the 'churning' of jobs. The main part of the workforce may thus be 'hoarded' by worker-controlled managements, which will eventually be forced to adjust, as inefficient firms are forced out of business. In a third view, excess employment is argued to exist for reasons of perverse tax incentives or its relatively low cost.

Just as it appears that the labour market may be unchanged, at least for some of the workforce, Russian industrial relations have also changed less than most other Eastern European societies. The high profile development of independent trade unions in relation to the mining industry where strikes have made the headlines is not at all typical of Russia. Independent trade unions have faded from the scene, and the traditional unions continue to hold sway, and on the whole to retain their wide membership (Gerchikov, 1995).

A major reason for this is the continued role of the old trade unions as purveyors of enterprise welfare goods and services. 'Occupational welfare' has changed far less than State social policy (Ashwin, 1997). This has been a major factor in the willingness of Russian workers to put up with being technically on leave - i.e. employed, but with no work or wages - since as noted earlier a substantial part of their income may continue to be supplied in the form of non-money goods and services.

However the labour market has changed, and with it in principle the old welfare system. The key changes are the appearance of unemployment, the pressure on budget funded services, and the sharp growth in regional inequalities, discussed in more detail in Chapter 3.

Section II - Individual Action and Social Theory

In devising a general plan for analysis of the issues we wanted to study, the structuralist approach, elaborated within the framework of the Weberian/ neo-Weberian tradition, contains a number of points of view which are important in principle, precisely because we are attempting to analyse social change in conditions of a transforming, transitional society. We have drawn on discussions of the relevance of the Weberian tradition to the Russian context outlined by Radayev and Shkaratan in *Social Stratification* (1996, pp.121-139). They emphasise that:

- This tradition places its main emphasis on systems of social action, and consequently, attention is centrally focused on typological characterisations of individual action;
- In seeking to understand the underlying economic causes of social mobility and stratification, the emphasis is not on property ownership, but on the market position of the group. Life chances in labour and consumer markets are shown to be stratifying markers, affecting even economic stratification;
- Life chances and prospects for social mobility are regarded as being subject not only to the objective economic characteristics of the group but also to the efforts of individuals themselves and their specific career possibilities;
- The analysis of status positions, defined by educational and occupational prestige, lifestyle, socio-cultural attitudes and behavioural norms, is related to market positions.

At the same time, however, the conventional set of stratifying features - the differentiating factors of social mobility that are used within the framework of the Weberian approach - seems to be inadequate and insufficiently reliable in the conditions of a transition-type society, where intensive processes of restructuring are in progress and affect all social structures. An alternative, the functionalist approach of Parsons (1953), and

Davies and Moore (1949), is inappropriate as a basis for our research because of one of its major deficiencies, for which it has already been subject to sustained criticism over several decades - its inability to explain effectively the processes of social mobility. Given that we were analysing precisely the processes of social dynamics and mobility, the flow of respondents from one group to another, and the possible formation of a stagnant 'bottom layer', and, moreover, that we had to do so in the conditions of rapid social change (when *a priori* the functions of the social groups that are forming cannot be clear, since even the type of society being formed is not yet clear itself) - then the functionalist approach, with its social roles, seemed to have very little application to the way in which social expectations and social roles in a transitional-type society are blurred.

Nevertheless, a whole range of Parsons' other ideas (about status as a reward not only for activity, but also for desirable qualities in the individual; about the fact that achievement values optimally ensure the potential to adapt to a dynamic social system; about the symbolic nature of consumption for designating the individual's place in the status system and in other systems) seem to us potentially useful for the analysis of the processes of transformation in the social structure of Russia (Parsons, 1953).

Finally, the analysis of social mobility processes in conditions of rapid change, led to a shift of focus in our work from social institutions and social systems to the concept of the actor. Without necessarily agreeing with Touraine (1997) that the move from the social system towards the actor is the main direction of development for international sociology, we are sure that this approach is promising, when applied to the conditions of a transforming society.

A natural consequence of this was that we began to look at the contributions of sociologists, both old and new, who have analysed issues of social mobility and stratification, and placed in the centre of our own research the person as actor and not as element (or cog) in a social system. The list of such scholars is very long, and includes people with sometimes very differing views. We give an exhaustive account, and here refer only to a few on whose ideas we drew directly for our work.

An early view from Warner (1949) stressed the role of subjective value characteristics in determining social status:

> [But] while significant and necessary, [the] economic factors are not sufficient to predict where a particular family or individual will be...

Something more than a large income is necessary for high social position. Money must be translated into socially approved behaviour and possessions, and they in turn must be translated into intimate participation with, and acceptance by, members of a superior class (p.21).

Warner attached great significance to socio-cultural aspects of behaviour, including models of consumption and use of leisure time, as well as educational aspirations, which are all very closely linked with a person's psychological motivation.

Another important influence on the formation of our approach was Townsend (1993), who examined the issue of how far people in the lowest strata have the potential 'to play the roles, participate in the relationships and follow the customary behaviour' considered acceptable in the societies to which they belong. In the Western European literature, there has been active debate on the issue of the so-called 'culture of poverty' or 'dependency culture', including elements of fatalism and passive reconciliation to circumstances. The watershed between scholars working on the issue lies precisely in the question of whether this culture is a cause or a consequence of poverty. However, in a range of research from the 1970s to the 1990s (see, for example, Ryan, 1971; Dean and Taylor-Gooby, 1991), this point of view has been challenged. It has become clear that although the various social strata really do demonstrate some differences as regards culture, these are not especially significant. In addition, it is difficult to determine the causal relationship between these differences and the social status of the individual: it is possible to record their presence, but not to show the primacy of one or the other. At the same time, specific results from research into the types of social contacts and social circles of unemployed people, their forms of social participation and their willingness to go as far as to deceive social security staff were also touched on in our research too, and this gave us the opportunity to compare the positions of the British and the Russian unemployed.

A second line of analysis critical of the concept of 'dependency culture' and the psychological causality of the social status of the individual is that dealing with the problem of self-identification. We have in mind the research of Tajfel (1981), Argyle (1990) and Harré (1993), and others, which has shown that, although people have a strong need to conceptualise themselves as members of a social group rather than simply in terms of specific, isolated, individual action, this belonging to a particular group is not so much a psychological trait inherent in individuals as a part of self-identification: it is situations themselves that determine how people will behave in one set of circumstances or another. Researchers have argued that individual action is, in the first instance, a result of 'social' and not 'personality' variables.

Of course two alternative approaches exist in contemporary sociology, of which one considers separate individuals either as elements of a social system (structure), whose actions are determined through their place in a system of socio-economic relations, or as elements of a cultural system within the framework of which they act under the influence of the norms and rules which have come to exist in the given culture (for example, 'a culture of poverty' or a 'dependency culture'). The other views them as active social subjects, 'rational actors', who bring into play all their numerous resources in pursuit of their own aims but take account of the rules determined by the limits of the specific situation within which they have to act (Giddens, 1984).

Is the situation for Russians and their responses a case of structure or action, system or actor, and to what extent should the subject under study be the cultural processes shaping behaviour, or the situational constraints and possibilities which a rational actor is in a position to utilise, or, indeed, some kind of personality characteristics capable of leading to certain models of individual action?

Two further authors also influenced our work - Bourdieu and Kohn. For analysing the issue of stratification, the most significant aspects of Bourdieu's (1993) thinking are his concept of the types of resources (different kinds of 'capital') which determine place in the social system, and the role of 'habitus' in the stratification process - which is very close, in our view, to the concept of mindset or mentality, as the latter is understood in the Russian sociological tradition. Bourdieu's distinction between 'economic capital in its various forms, cultural capital and symbolic capital, with all legitimately recognised types of capital able to play the role of the last' (p.141) - from which he sometimes also distinguishes social capital proper - has enabled him to examine the position of a subject in a social space as a derivative of these forms of capital. Moreover, as Bourdieu has emphasised, 'subjects are distributed in social space, firstly, according to their total volume of capital and, secondly, to conform with its structure, i.e. to the relationship between the different kinds of capital... within the overall volume' (ibid.). In our interviews, we attempted to identify household possession of these various forms of capital, and to ascertain its relationship to different strategies adopted by household members. A recent and related study that has applied Bourdieu's ideas, not to ordinary households, but to the formation of new élites in transition countries can be found in Eyal, Szelényi, and Townsley, *Making Capitalism without Capitalists*, 1998 (see especially Chapter 1, passim).

Kohn has analysed the value systems of different classes, primarily the distribution of individualistic/conformist orientations among members of different social groups with various status positions. Kohn and his colleagues have demonstrated a direct relationship between stratification position and values: 'Achievement orientations are a basic value for people of high social status who feel themselves to be competent members of a society that is well-disposed towards them ... Conformism, on the other hand, is typical of the lower social stratification positions, in which people see themselves as less competent members of a society that is indifferent or even hostile to them' (Kohn, 1990). In relation to issues of social mobility, Kohn has argued that people with a positive disposition towards life, who are not conformist in their ideas, have a greater chance of occupying a more advanced social position. Although he does not assert that this is the same as saying that the direction of social mobility is determined by the psychological characteristics of the personality, he has established that there is a correlation. Occupational status is linked with values and attitudes, and, moreover, this link is a reciprocal one. Stratification position, Kohn emphasises, both influences and depends on occupational achievement-orientation. This same orientation both forms and is formed by psychological characteristics. Moreover, as Kohn has noted, this 'relates not only to values, but also to such concepts as an active and purposeful outlook, frustration (failure), alienation and the ability to grasp and form ideas'. Some of these characteristics (achievement-orientation, an active and positive nature, a sense of frustration, confidence in one's ability to influence a situation) were studied in our research, using elements of Kohn's methods.

A final source of ideas, in interpreting the actors' actions, was Coleman's rational choice theory, which has subsequently been developed by a number of authors including Giddens (1973, 1982, 1984). This emphasises the significance of individuals' problem-solving strategies and of revealing how far they are effective. Taking the concept of rules and resources from this theory, we looked at the specific features of Russia, where exercising choice - as a rule, completely rational - can differ noticeably from European or American experience.

One further aspect of our approach should be noted. Because we were analysing a country where in no time at all (literally, against the yardstick of history) almost the whole population was marginalised, we were somewhat less interested in those characteristics of a stratification system which are connected with the activities of groups that are already fixed. We mean here defined standards of consumption, or the identification with a particular group (for Parsons, culture; for Weber, prestige). We were primarily interested in self-identification, in trying to understand the trend of the dynamics of social mobility through Russians' own estimations of themselves.

Section III - Poverty

Although not initially the primary focus of this project, the immiseration of Russia in the 1990s has become increasingly a key focus for this study as it developed at both policy and household levels, and for this reason poverty merits specific discussion in this final section.

Poverty, its nature and causes, have been a central focus for social science for more than two centuries. For much of this time the debate about absolute and relative definitions and measurement has been at the centre of discussions. Relative notions of poverty are not new. Adam Smith in *The Wealth of Nations* (1776) observed in connection with poverty that 'by necessities I understand not only the commodities which are indispensably necessary for the support of life, but whatever the custom of the country renders it indecent for creditable people, even of the lowest order, to be without'. Nevertheless the modern tradition of poverty studies, initiated by Rowntree (1901) in York in 1898, has in practice tended to take an absolute approach to poverty in trying to calculate the subsistence minimum needed by families for expertly defined basic necessities. And in practice most governments adopt this approach in setting subsistence *minima* for the calculation of benefit entitlements.

However over the course of the 20th century the weight of opinion has steadily shifted towards a consensus. Vic George (1973) summarised this argument as follows:

> It can be safely said, however, that all physical needs have a cultural element in them in the sense that their amount and quality are culturally determined. Clothing is a physical need for without clothing a person's health will suffer in this country. Clothing, however, has a cultural element in it in the sense that the clothes which the poor must wear should have some relationship to prevailing fashions. The same applies to food (p.44).

A similar position is taken by Piachaud in 1987: 'one thing does seem to have been clearly established: namely, that there must be a relative definition of poverty' (p.187).

We are all relativists now, it has been claimed, since it is impossible to extract the meaning of poverty, or particular manifestations of it from the social context in which it occurs: 'That poverty in economically advanced societies is to be defined relative to the standards of the society in question appears to be widely accepted' (Callen, et al., 1993).

This is not to deny that extreme poverty will damage people's health. Sen (1983) has argued this position, as have Doyal and Gough (1984) who suggest that there are irreducible 'basic individual needs' that have to be met for people to exist as persons in any sense: 'survival and personal identity are attributes which all persons need in order to be classified as persons at all' (p.14).

Nevertheless, for the industrial countries, the issue has become one of defining deprivation in a culturally relevant way. What does it mean to be deprived? The answer for Rowntree by 1936 was to include, in addition to the means of ensuring the maintenance of merely physical health, an allowance for newspapers, stamps, writing paper, radio, holidays, beer, tobacco and presents. And later for Townsend (1979), in a famous quote, people were in poverty 'when they lack the resources to obtain the type of diet, participate in the activities and have the living conditions and amenities which are customary, or at least widely encouraged, or approved, in the societies to which they belong' (p.31).

However a new issue has moved centre stage in discussions about poverty in the last ten years to rival the old debate on relativism: is poverty a matter of deprivation or income? With the rise of wage labour in the 19th century, and the decline of household and community production, almost all of the needs and wants that individuals and households have are satisfied through the market, or so it is widely assumed.

Governments have understandably as a consequence conflated poverty with income, on the assumption that below a certain income, individuals and households will be deprived of the goods and services that citizens should have. However this conflation is problematic on three counts. The definitions of income and deprivation are both contestable, and the relation between them is not straightforward.

Income, or resources to buy goods and services, might be thought to be easily determined. But as we know from considering weaknesses with the idea of negative income tax, there can be considerable short term fluctuations in income. At what time should real income be measured? A second problem is that money and other resources often flow into a household rather than direct to individuals. The payment of benefits for children through their mother acknowledged this; children nevertheless do not get the income personally. Similarly, wages to men may not find their way fully into the household economy.

A partial answer to these difficulties has been to ask the relevant population what they judge to be a minimum income needed, on the assumption that they will know what is required for people 'like them'. This so-called consensus approach to subsistence income definition, is now proposed by Townsend, Gordon, Bradshaw and Gosschalk (1998) in a new international poverty study, based on the UN World Summit on Social Development:

> Absolute poverty is a condition characterised by severe deprivation of basic human needs, including food, safe drinking water, sanitation facilities, health, shelter, education and information. It depends not only on income but also on access to services (UN, 1995, p.57).

> Overall poverty includes lack of income and productive resources to ensure sustainable livelihoods; hunger and malnutrition; ill health; limited or lack of access to education and other basic services; increased morbidity and mortality from illness; homelessness and inadequate housing; unsafe environments and social discrimination and exclusion. It is also characterised by lack of participation in decision-making and in civil, social and cultural life. It occurs in all countries: as mass poverty in many developing countries, pockets of poverty amid wealth in developed countries, loss of livelihoods as a result of economic recession, sudden poverty as a result of disaster or conflict, the poverty of low-wage workers, and the utter destitution of people who fall outside family support systems, social institutions and safety nets (UN, 1995, p.57).

These definitions have been condensed into short lists, for which respondents are asked to judge the income necessary to stay just out of absolute or overall poverty. However governments, including Russia, mostly use income definitions of poverty based on either budget definitions from food costs with suitable multipliers and adjustments for household structure, or below average incomes.

Deprivation, or lack of goods and services deemed customary, encouraged or approved, is as noted above culturally suffused. In post- or high-modern societies, characterised by cultural variety and difference, it can be difficult to know what 'customary' means, a point made with vigour by David Piachaud (1981) in criticising Townsend's definition, which was not rigorously derived from the population itself. Once again the current solution to this problem is a consensus approach, adopted by Mack and Lansley (1985) and now widely influential, in which the relevant population is asked what goods and services are deemed essential, the 'enforced lack of socially perceived necessities' (p.39) being the measure of deprivation.

Moreover the relation between income and deprivation is not as close as might be expected at first sight. An important issue is the price of goods and services that vary not just regionally, but in the 'micro-economy' of even small cities, where purchase in small quantities can considerably raise unit prices. This can include energy, food, transport and clothes. Moreover the mix of goods purchased may not be the most efficient as a result of partial information or opportunity, for example in terms of diet. What is customary is of course also the target of energetic advertisers, who have every incentive to persuade poorer people, as everyone, to want things they may not really need.

A final point raised forcefully by Stein Ringen (1988) is that those who are deprived may not lack income. They may either choose not to consume, or be constrained by other factors than lack of money (for example inability to access the money in the case of children or wives), or have high fixed costs, such as repayment obligations. Similarly, those who lack income may not be deprived, where for example the income is temporarily low, or there is access to other resources in kind - both common factors in rural or farming communities, and highly pertinent to Russia, as we shall see.

Halleröd (1995) has examined this issue with Swedish data, and there has been a systematic attempt to look at this by Callan et al. (1993) for Ireland. This is useful for thinking about Russia, since in all three countries industrialisation has come late, mainly in the 20th century, and the rural/farming community is therefore significant, both culturally and economically.

In the Callan (1993) study the deprivation indices were derived in the Mack and Lansley manner, by asking respondents what they regarded as essential. The 24 items were then factor analysed, and three types of indicators derived: those such as heat and food that are essential to everyday survival, those such as a fridge and a bath that relate to durables and housing, and a mixed residual category of items that might be more culturally variable such as presents or a hobby. When compared to typical subsidiary income measures of poverty, there was considerable similarity of the proportion of the population that experience at least two of the eight essential or basic deprivation items. 30 per cent of the population had incomes below 60 per cent of the mean, and 32 per cent of the population lacked two or more basic items.

However when looking at which households were in poverty, the overlap was relatively poor, and this was noticeably patterned in terms of the typical household characteristics that might be expected to account for poverty. *Only about half, or 16 per cent of the total, experienced both deprivation and low income*, and farmers were especially noticeable for constituting a quarter of the income poor, but only a little over 10 per cent of the income poor who were deprived.

The Swedish data also compared income poverty (defined using the Leyden or 'making ends meet' method) and deprivation items on a modified Mack and Lansley basis. The results of this survey found that, as in Ireland, the proportion in income poverty (21 per cent) and deprived (21 per cent) were the same, and that, again as in Ireland, *only a much smaller proportion (9 per cent) had both low incomes and were deprived.*

Russian Poverty Studies

In the Russian situation we would expect this mis-match to be worse for a number of reasons. With the hyperinflation of the early 1990s, the widespread delay in payment of wages and pensions, and the enforced leave experienced by a substantial minority of workers, households are using non-money strategies to survive.

Piirainen (1997) has identified three alternative strategies from a detailed qualitative study of families in St. Petersburg. Those who managed to set up or work for new enterprises were able to generate a relatively affluent lifestyle, epitomised above all by a very traditional western standard of men being able to support a non-waged partner at home. Others were surviving through wage labour, but with a declining living standard unless at least a second income came into the household via a wage or the possession of a pension by a member of the family. A third strategy was to withdraw from the labour market into a pre-industrial subsistence agricultural pattern, either already in the country, or through a return to the country, often via relatives still living there.

A great deal of mutual support through family and acquaintance networks has also been revealed in a number of surveys, and in detail in another qualitative study by Lonkila (1997). Echoing the picture of late Soviet life painted by Shlapentokh (1989), Lonkila showed vividly the application of Granovetter's (1973) observation that the 'strength of weak ties' was that they put people in touch with a wider network of exchange, support, and obligation outside of the market. This was noticeably more extensive than in Finland, and a key survival mechanism from the socialist era that has been also functional for the new situation in which households find themselves.

Rose's annual surveys in the region have identified the key non-monetary mechanism reported by households themselves as the growing of food. This ranks first, and slightly higher than waged income itself, as the key means of attaining resources for the household (Table 7, from Rose, 1996, p.24). Rose and McAllister (1996) have concluded from a series of surveys across the whole of Eastern Europe, including Russia, that 'money is not the measure of welfare in Russia'.

Where money income is available, it needs to be measured over longer than the normal period used in poverty surveys, and set against other resources in kind. This is neatly demonstrated by Ovcharova (1997). Goskomstat survey data suggests that around 35 per cent of households fall below the official Subsistence Minimum where their income is measured over one month, but that this rate falls to 20 per cent when measured over three months. Secondly she shows, like Rose, that between 40 and 50 per cent of food products in Russia are currently produced outside the market. Even 50 per cent of Muscovites have vegetable plots (Rose and Tikhomirov, 1993). This is the single most important addition to money income, and judged by households to be of similar importance to money. Taking this into account, Ovcharova finds that the one month income poverty rate drops from 35 to 27 per cent, and the apparently high rate for rural households of 60 per cent drops to the urban, and overall, level of around 27 per cent.

The pattern here echoes that of Ireland, especially the rural factor. Farmers in Ireland were the group most likely to demonstrate a gap between money poverty but absence of deprivation.

A final reason we would expect this mis-match to be more severe for Russia is that with the change in the status of households so quickly, and the continued provision of extensive enterprise support in the form of non-market goods and services, there will be for many households a possession of goods and services at a higher level than their income would be able to sustain over the long term.

Walker (1987) suggested that the arguments which have raged about poverty measurement could be resolved through a series of qualitative studies with smaller samples to elucidate what poverty actually means to households of different types, over time, and what strategies such households use to cope. However he acknowledges that this will seem expensive for the sample size. Some of this work has been done in the UK, but there is still a preference for the larger survey, possibly because for the data gathered, it is relatively cheap (a consideration repeated by Townsend, Gordon, Bradshaw and Gosschalk (1998, p.18)). Rose and McAllister (1996, p.88) have made a similar point with respect to unravelling the reality of poverty in Russia. Our project has thus adopted a contrasting design, with a modest sample size, but with a more in-depth focus, using repeat interviews after 12 months (discussed in detail in Chapter 4).

Russian research into the issue of poverty is also now being very widely conducted. VTSIOM is carrying out such work on a monitoring basis, researching differences in consumption behaviour of families at different income levels and comparing the strategies for improving their material circumstances that are available to different categories of families, and the effect of poverty on social participation. Research on the interrelationship of the issues of poverty and unemployment has been conducted by academics in Novosibirsk under the leadership of Chernina.

But the main pitfall for Russian researchers looking at the issue of poverty lies in the fact that no-one can unequivocally answer the question of what poverty (or 'poor') means, either in general, or in contemporary Russia in particular. Quantitative assessments of the number of poor people range from 20-25 per cent to 80-85 per cent of the country's whole population. It is acknowledged in the Russian literature that poverty can be understood both as a defined level of income (not only low cash income, but also the absence of other economic resources) and in relation to the possibility of maintaining standards which are perceived as 'normal' to a way of life (including forms of social participation). Applying each of these approaches gives a more or less different picture of poverty. Moreover, in each of these approaches, poverty can be characterised by its absolute extent - the number of people who have income lower than some kind of fixed minimum and/or have property or possibilities of social participation below a certain standard. But at the same time a question arises - if, according to these standards, most of the population is poor, then is it possible to regard the given standard as a standard of poverty, or are analysts simply trying to apply too high a standard to a poor country? So, poverty can also be examined through relative categories. In this case, the poor are usually seen as being those who have a level of welfare of roughly half the average according to all parameters in the population under survey (the region or the country), while the prosperous are those who have roughly twice the average level of welfare (for example Khakhulina and Tuchek, 1995).

What is more, even the use of what would seem to be a single criterion - the 'subsistence minimum' - can give more or less different results depending on what is understood by it. Thus, in conducting the VTSIOM research in March 1996, several criteria were used to define the subsistence minimum (Zubova, 1996). The first criterion was the level of current daily income corresponding to the official value of the Russian Federation's State Committee for Statistics/Ministry of Labour Subsistence Minimum (at that time - the point at which the first phase of our research was carried out - this was 366,000 roubles calculated per family member per month). The second criterion was a subjective assessment of the subsistence minimum by the public - 580,000 roubles calculated per family member per month; while the third was the threshold below which, according to public opinion, a person can be considered 'poor' (300,000 roubles, i.e. roughly about half the 'normal' subsistence minimum as assessed by the public). Data published by Zubova from this VTSIOM research show how an almost fourfold difference in assessments of poverty in Russia has arisen:

Table 1.1 **Describing the scale of poverty according to official data and to VTSIOM assessments**

Indicator	*Proportion of poor families (per cent)*
Official data	23
VTSIOM assessments:	
First criterion	62
Second criterion	81
Third criterion	52

Drawing on three years' data, Zubova notes that whatever poverty criterion has been applied groups of very poor families appear to be a constant feature, and raises the question of their chances of escaping from poverty, speculating that these chances are almost nil, and that permanent poverty may be forming. Ideally this issue requires longitudinal rather than cross-sectional data, in order to identify those households that have become trapped in poverty. The only survey known to have done this is the Russian Longitudinal Monitoring Survey that ran seven sample surveys in the form of a panel between 1992 and 1996, in which the same households were reinterviewed (as we have done in this project). Although using an income measure of poverty, which as we have seen is rather suspect for Russia, there was considerable movement in and out of poverty over this period. Lokshin and Popkin (1999, p.809) show that just over 50 per cent of Russian households' income fell below the official poverty line at least once, but that only 25 per cent were poor for more than one period, and less than 10 per cent were poor throughout all periods. This data compares quite well with our own, presented in detail in Chapter 8.

Similarly, Rimashevskaya (1997) distinguishes two forms of poverty: 'fixed' and 'floating'. The first is precisely the kind of poverty about which arguments are going on in other countries in terms of its relationship with a 'dependency culture'. The second, 'floating', form is related to the potential to 'jump out of' the state of poverty, to pass through it as a temporary stage in life. This form acquires a special meaning in relation to the emergence - alongside the traditionally poor (lone mothers and families with a lot of children, disabled people, aged single people) which existed in the USSR - of many millions of 'new poor'. Some of these remain in the category of the poor, while others can escape from this state.

In relation to this, we should note that the poor in Russia are made up of two completely different groups: the 'old' poor, i.e. those who also lived below the poverty line before the reforms (roughly 11-12 per cent of the population were in this group) and the 'new poor' (who form between a third and four-fifths of the population, depending on the poverty criteria used in measuring them). A significant proportion of the latter do not fall into socially weak but into socially strong sections of the population, and have become poor as a result of restructuring of the economy. Moreover, in the past, the 'old' poor had not become different by virtue of a particular process of social reproduction, activities in life, or access to social goods, but were primarily distinguished by particular features of their family status.

Rimashevskaya emphasises the role of adaptation to market conditions (reassessing the values and rules of interaction, and actively entering into market structures) as the most important precondition for escaping the circle of poverty, and suggests that perhaps 25 per cent of the population is not capable of adapting. The variation in the potential to adapt has led, as it were, to the formation of 'two Russias', dividing into social branches growing in different directions. They are sharply differentiated by behaviour, preferences and value orientations.

2 Soviet Social Policy

С грехом пополам
Half success, half failure

The Soviet Union was a large and diverse empire founded in 1917, which not only created a distinct pattern of social policy amongst the 15 republics that it contained, but imposed this pattern in large part on many other countries of Central Europe. Within this vast area, there was great cultural, linguistic, industrial, and natural variation. Even within the USSR, Russians comprised little more than 50 per cent of the population. The 'Eastern Block' has now separated into 27 separate states, and the USSR disappeared in 1991.

Social policy since 1917 has not been consistent or fixed. Changes in economic and ideological balance have been clearly reflected in changing social concerns, expenditure priorities and planning mechanisms. Nevertheless experiences were accumulated, and the approach to social issues became increasingly complex during the twentieth century. For us to understand the state of social policy immediately before the collapse of the USSR we need to briefly review developments over the course of the century. Social policy can be divided into six periods: utopian, urban, industrial, welfare, and stability/productivity (George and Manning, 1980). Distinct patterns of social politics are also associated with those periods.

Utopian, 1917-1921 The first brief period can be suitably described as one in which social issues were seen to be the result of social disorganisation brought about by the twin problems of war and capitalism. The solutions advocated were often utopian. Although this was a time of wide debate about the future of social policy, there was no particular difficulty in identifying the objective conditions which were problematic and there was general agreement on the values which were felt to be threatened. For example about 50 per cent of the population was illiterate, and Lenin argued that:

> an illiterate person stands outside; he must first be taught the ABC. Without this there can be no politics; without this there are only rumours, gossip, tales, prejudices, but no politics (quoted in Pinkevitch, 1929, p.375).

Similarly, epidemics were rife: cases of typhus rose from 22 per 10,000 in 1918, to 265 in 1919, and 394 in 1920. As Lenin put it, once again succinctly:

> either the lice will defeat socialism or socialism will defeat the lice (Lenin, 1965, p.185).

Mass campaigns were mobilised to deal with these threats, but initially the new government moved cautiously. Income support and medical care were only extended to wage earners, thus excluding the majority of the rural population. The most noticeable change was the forced redistribution of housing in urban areas from the rich to the poor, although even here the migration of many into the countryside had already reduced housing pressure.

With the advent of civil war from 1918, however, nationalisation was imposed on a wide scale, inflation resulted in the substitution of markets by barter relations, and income support and education were extended in principle to the whole population. Family policy was liberalised to sweep away all legal constraint over marital, parental and sexual relationships. Celebrated by the left as revolutionary gains, these utopian promises could not in fact be implemented.

Urban, 1921-1927 In the next period we begin to see the development of greater debate about the nature and existence of social issues, and therefore the kind of solutions which should be adopted. Bettleheim (1978) has graphically portrayed the struggles of this period in terms of the Party falling into the hands of the middle class, manifested in the prioritisation of urban over rural interests. Along with this process we begin to see the way in which sectional interests come to affect the perception of social issues. Having survived the immediate problems of war communism, the overriding concern was about the future direction and pace of economic development. Since the source of capital had to be the agricultural worker, the main social issue of the day became the recalcitrant farmer who was blamed for resisting collectivisation, eating too much food, and developing a taste for capitalistic agriculture.

This analysis of issues shows a clear shift from an assumption of value consensus, to a struggle over value conflict. Not surprisingly the imagery changes from a struggle with objective conditions (civil war) to a struggle to label problem groups (farmers). It was this change which paved the way for Stalin's 'Urals-Siberian method' for procuring grain. Problem groups justified the use of violence, since a more familiar method, namely education, was unlikely to produce the desired changes quickly enough. The conflicts about this policy in the Party at the time are well enough known, and illustrate graphically both the decay of consensus and the process adopted of re-establishing it, that is the isolation of opponents.

The main government programme was the New Economic Policy. This involved the de-nationalisation of small enterprises, and even allowed the operation of foreign firms in joint enterprises. Industrial and agricultural production increased, housing construction recovered, and social policy returned to a more realistic programme. The 1926 family code re-imposed parental and family responsibilities, health care was targeted on key industrial workers and children before agricultural workers, and progressive educational ideas came back under the control of the relatively conservative teaching profession. In all these areas, there was intense debate about the future which, in contrast to the immediate post-revolutionary years, was felt to be both more secure and open to more or less radical options.

Industrial, 1927-1953 During the next period which covers the years of Stalin's power, the main focus of concern was with industrialisation, both as a means of defending 'socialism in one country', and also necessary to re-build the country after the widespread destruction caused by WWII. This was the framework within which social issues were analysed and dealt with. Debate about the problematic nature of social conditions withered. For example, the inadequate production of housing for the rapidly growing and urbanising population resulted in a steady fall in average urban *per capita* housing space, to dip below four square metres by 1940. Yet this never came to be seen by the government as a problem.

In contrast the supply and discipline of labour was a perennial concern. Anything that appeared to get in the way of this objective was liable to be seen as deviant. Thus the rules which defined rights at work, social security entitlements, security of tenure, and sickness absence were all progressively tightened during the 1930s, so that their infraction came to be seen as an individual failing. As it turned out, the invasion by Germany and the subsequent destruction of people and property went some way towards justifying this policy, as Gorbachev and others subsequently suggested. But in this period up to the 1950s there was little room for the perceived luxury of discussing social problems.

Wage inequality, selection in education, and a tougher family code, especially the restriction on the right to abortion, were all adopted, but the most significant social policy was the abolition of unemployment benefit in 1930, followed in the 1937 constitution with the right to employment. This illustrates the mix of conservative and progressive elements in Stalin's Russia.

Welfare, 1953-1964   After Stalin's death, policy swung away from a pre-occupation with industrialisation towards a more general concern for the welfare of Soviet people. Whatever the limitations of Khrushchev's concrete achievements in the 1950s, he opened up debate in a remarkable manner which encouraged a whole range of issues to be thought about. The tone was set by his 1956 'secret speech' which raised Stalin's policies in their entirety as problematic. This change was not merely the whim of a new leader. The late 1950s and early 1960s were significant economically, and in parallel to the 1920s (and one should add to the 1980s) this gave rise to intense debate about the future direction policies should take; it also gave rise to new debate in the West about the real nature of Soviet society.

Between 1957 and 1964 Khrushchev sought to re-establish early ideals as his guide to policy, particularly through the 1959 20th Party programme, *The Road to Communism*, in which it was declared that 'the present generation of Soviet people shall live in communism'. This entailed the rebuilding of a vigorous Party after the decimation of the 1930s in order to overcome the interests of groups like industrial managers in existing patterns of investment and social policy. He used the media in an innovative way, both to raise issues for debate and to muster support for his ideas. However his success was limited. For example, housing was successfully promoted as a social issue in one respect, namely the development of mass production through pre-existing economic mechanisms. However control over the distribution of housing and the commensurate provision of environmental services necessitated a significant shift in power from industrial managers to local Soviets. This was never achieved, despite legal directives. The issue of poverty exhibited a similar pattern: a relatively open, survey based, analysis of poverty, combined with ineffective policy interventions to deal with it.

In the 1920s the opening up of debate indicated a lack of consensus over which social conditions were a problem, and therefore how they should be dealt with. One consequence was that perceptions changed from social issues as objective conditions to the identification of problem groups, in the competition to establish a particular viewpoint. Earlier this group had been the farmers. Now it was to be the new middle classes, made up by industrial managers, senior intellectuals, and Party careerists. This can be seen for example in Khrushchev's education reforms which prioritised workers at the expense of more privileged groups precisely in the most important site for the reproduction of inequalities in Soviet society. Even agricultural workers, excluded since 1921 from the social security system, were finally brought into the scheme in 1964.

This was a time of the politicisation of social issues. Khrushchev deliberately provoked debate, even crisis, as a means of melting political structures in the hopes that the resulting changes would crystallise out more in the pattern he wanted. As it turned out he took on more than he could control, and he himself became defined as the problem and was removed in 1964 by the very groups he criticised.

Stability and productivity, 1964-1983 The following 20 years, while exhibiting relative continuity in social policies, could not have been more of a contrast in the way social issues were perceived. Stability rather than change was paramount. There was a return to consensus about the problems facing Soviet society. 'Developed socialism' was to be built slowly and methodically. There were to be no great leaps forward (to communism), or in any other direction. Social issues thus became departures from a commitment to steady progress. Rather than a struggle to identify and label problem groups, perceptions shifted as in the 1930s and 1940s to the rooting out of deviant individuals. While this never attained the paranoid depths of the 1930s, the pursuit of dissidents and the misuse of psychiatry in the firm belief that dissent must be *de facto* a form of madness indicates the absence of legitimate debate. In a sense there were no 'social problems' in the 1970s. While of course social conditions changed (divorce rose, the population aged, the economy slowed, and life expectancy faltered), increasingly unreal assurances were given of 'business as usual'.

In terms of service delivery, there was indeed steady expansion of such basic indicators as teachers, doctors, nurses, flats, clothing, food, televisions, and employment for all. The quality of these services was low, but for millions of Russian workers this was a period of security and access to rising living standards; for the 50 per cent of the population which was not Russian, especially those living in Central Asia, this was an era of major improvement in living conditions, with the result that inequalities in inter-republic provision of such basics as income, housing and health care steadily declined. It is not surprising that many Russians outside the major cities now look back fondly on the 1970s and 1980s.

Problems of Social Policy, Pre-Perestroika

Under Brezhnev social policy exhibited the relative stability that was characteristic of most aspects of government from the late 1960s to the early 1980s. This was the achievement of 'developed socialism' (Evans, 1977) - a description adopted to signify the technological modernisation of Soviet economic life. The term however also acknowledged the absence of any of the fundamental changes in social relationships towards full communism that Khruschev, in the 1959 Party programme, had claimed would be achieved by 1980 (Gilison, 1975). Social policy in this era may be characterised as the pursuit of the gross expansion of 'intermediate' welfare indicators, such as the numbers of doctors or nurses, or the numbers of flats, or the numbers of teachers, or the early retirement age. The figures for these were proudly displayed as signs of the inexorable upward growth of 'developed socialism', although even these were subject to the restraint of the 'residual principle':

> The fall in the rate of growth and in economic efficiency has been especially painfully reflected in our inability to solve our social problems. Resources were allocated to the social sector according to the so-called 'residual principle', whereby capital investment was firstly directed towards industrial goals, while housing, the raising of living standards and other improvements in people's lives only received what remained (Aganbegyan, 1988, pp.15-16).

Thus 'final' welfare indicators, such as the meeting of social needs, or the quality of the goods and services provided, or the kind of social relationships that were produced or reproduced, were not so impressive. For example, the position of women as both workers in and consumers of welfare received relatively little analysis, and elicited relatively little concern within the Soviet Union. This was the result of a very weak women's movement, official equality for women, and the general lack of opportunity and resources for issue-based politics. Again, the conflicts of interest between different ethnic and national groups, so dominant in recent Soviet internal events, were assumed to be dissolving within a superordinate socialist society. Yet the mechanism for this, migration and russification, was deeply resented.

Kornai (1980) has suggested that this overshadowing of quality by quantity is a logical result of the Soviet model in which individual enterprises and organisations operate in a 'shortage' environment, thus enabling output to be distributed regardless of quality, and with 'soft' budgets as to the resources used. Indeed anyone who systematically questioned whether these gross production figures were sufficient indicators of the achievements of 'developed socialism' was likely to experience harassments of varying severity by agents of the State. There developed therefore a growing gap between everyday experience and the official version of the nature of social policies (Goldfarb, 1989). It is this general gap which underlies the specific problems that we can now identify in different social policy areas. We will briefly review one or two of the most significant problems in each area which built up in the years following the 1960s.

Social security is in all modern societies the most expensive social service, costing almost as much as all other services together. It is closely related to the labour market, either in the sense of the earning of entitlements, or in the sense of concerns about the general incentive to work. It is also relatively simple, in that it involves relatively little of the labour intensity or production activities of the other social services. It is consequently a relatively pure site for the expression of official preferences and *de facto* status differences within the population.

One of the great achievements claimed in the Soviet Union was that there was no unemployment, since work was a guaranteed right under Article 40 of the Constitution. Unemployment benefit disappeared in 1930 at a time of greatly tightened labour codes under Stalin's drive for industrialisation. This achievement was a mixed blessing for workers, however, since the employment that was guaranteed was often in unpopular parts of the country or in unpopular industries. Pensions were also closely shaped to labour requirements in that they were insufficient for many years, driving most pensioners out to work. However the Brezhnev years inherited from Khrushchev a dramatic improvement in the basic level of pensions (George and Manning, 1980), sufficient for the majority of pensioners to withdraw from the labour market for the first time, and at an earlier age than in most industrial countries. Nevertheless this severance of the link between labour conditions and pensions was not complete, for inequalities of working income were reproduced in pension rates. Moreover for most pensioners, with a 1986 *per capita* average of 89 roubles a month (and not index-linked), the basic level was insufficient to bring them much above the semi-official poverty line (70 roubles) established under Khruschev (Matthews, 1986).

This link between work history and social security in the Soviet Union illustrates the heavily 'insurance based' design of the system, which was essentially geared to entitlements carefully accumulated as a result of a good employment record. By contrast the 'social assistance' function, designed to provide income in response to a test of need, was unsystematically developed.

This helps to explain why the social security system was neglectful of a number of 'pure need' groups, such as poor children, the disabled, and the unemployed:

> Thirty years of almost uninterrupted growth in the standard of living of workers and collective farm workers, although at a very slow rate, have been accompanied by a scandalous backwardness in social allocations. The result is the appearance of a widespread layer of 'new poor' in the country. Tens of millions of people, including invalids, the disabled, widows, single mothers (they are still called 'deserted wives' in the Soviet Union), alcoholic down-and-outs, and youth on the fringes of society, are living well below the breadline (Mandel, 1989, p.12).

Health care seems at first blush to have been a great achievement of the Soviet era. It had more doctors, nurses, and hospital beds *per capita* than any other major industrial country (Mezentseva and Rimachevskaya, 1990). It had a rational structure of health facilities, which started with the allocation of doctors to local housing areas (where they could undertake quasi social work activities). Patients were registered at the local polyclinic where 'their' doctor was based, and probably also registered at the health station at their place of work - some of which, such as the railways, had highly regarded facilities. Specialist hospitals were regionally based.

However criticisms about Soviet health care steadily accumulated. Resources devoted to health care by comparison with international trends, even compared with the UK which was at a relatively low level, were extremely meagre in the Soviet Union: about 4 per cent of NMP (equivalent to about 2½ per cent of GNP calculated on a market basis), compared with 6 per cent of GNP in the UK, and 10 per cent of GNP in the USA (Davis, 1990). The consequence of this was that well known medical procedures were not available in the areas of technology, antibiotics, the control of cross-infections in health facilities, and the public health control of infectious diseases and other public health problems such as alcoholism. These criticisms were supported by the stagnation, and then degeneration, of both overall and infant mortality rates from the early 1970s onwards (Mezentseva and Rimachevskaya, 1990).

In a wider sense there were also deficiencies in health care arising through the effects of other policy priorities. The most infamous was the mis-use of psychiatric hospitals and treatment to both detain and to punish dissidents. This resulted in the expulsion of the USSR from the World Psychiatric Association in 1983 (Dossett-Davies, 1988b). A second example was the development of workplace health stations. These were typically presented as a generous extra dimension to Soviet health care in comparison with the West, such that Soviet workers' needs could be met more effectively. However an alternative interpretation is that the prior policy concern was about labour discipline and labour turnover/absenteeism (Navarro, 1977). Thus work absence on health grounds was sanctioned by medical personnel at the place of work; or at least good quality health care, in the context of an under-resourced general health service and a tight labour market, was a powerful form of occupational welfare with which to attract and retain labour.

Finally, social relations in such a labour intensive service as health care were questioned in terms of the experiences of women as patients, and the career structures which left women as predominant among nurses and junior doctors, while most senior positions were held by men (Navarro, 1977). The low status of women health workers was starkly illustrated by the fact that their wages had drifted down to about 70 per cent of the average by 1984 (Davis, 1989, p.435).

Notwithstanding these deficiencies, it must be acknowledged that the benefit of central control improved the provision of health care, and hence the morbidity and mortality rates of, for example, Soviet Central Asia were well below what would have otherwise been the case. By 1970 inequality in the distribution of resources had fallen steadily to the British level, and well below the American figure (the co-efficient of variation in the distribution of doctors in the 1970s for the USSR, UK, USA, respectively was 0.19, 0.15, 0.31 (George and Manning, 1980, p.117)).

Housing provision was a continuous source of dissatisfaction. For much of the century urban living space *per capita* was below the sanitary norm of nine square metres. This was a result of three factors. First the housing stock inherited after the October revolution was meagre. Second rapid industrialisation and urbanisation resulted, despite substantial housing production, in a steady decline in *per capita* living space from an already low level. Third the Second World War destroyed a further 15 per cent of housing stock, and it was only then that there was a sustained effort to remedy the situation, with an effective doubling of housing investment in the 1950s and 1960s (Andrusz, 1984).

This shortage of space had a number of consequences for domestic life. Young couples could rarely find their own flat in which to begin married life, and normally had to share with one set of parents. In addition a significant proportion of tenants were still in communal flats, sharing cooking and bathing facilities. This stressful situation stimulated divorce, and inhibited reproduction (Shlapentokh, 1989).

However the crude production of space was always going to be rapidly succeeded by further dissatisfactions. These included poor quality, resulting in damp, cold, and large repair costs. Associated infrastructure development, such as roads, sewerage, schools and shops were also poorly co-ordinated. Beyond these issues was the question of who owned and controlled the stock. There were four tenure types of housing stock: local Soviet; 'departmental' (owned by enterprises and organisations); co-operative; and private. The first two accounted for a large and growing proportion of the total stock: about 25 per cent was local Soviet stock, and a full 50 per cent was in the hands of enterprises. They supplied housing on two entirely different bases: the first according to need (family size, waiting time), and the second according to merit (the interests of the enterprise in rewarding its labour force). Over the years there were periodic attempts to transfer stock from enterprises to local Soviets on grounds of principle, but these failed simply because control over housing was too valuable a resource for enterprises in a situation of chronic labour shortage. Clearly with half the housing stock in a quasi 'tied cottage' tenure, labour market flexibility, let alone an individual sense of security and autonomy, suffered.

Education is of particular importance in all societies both as an investment in human capital, and as a site for the reproduction of social relations. It was regarded with pride in the Soviet Union. At the time of the October revolution, most people were illiterate. As noted in the first section this was seen by Lenin as a major barrier to mass political involvement, and great efforts were made to develop education. This necessarily involved adult education - a tradition that is still highly developed by Western European standards, and in principle was extended to all social groups.

As in the case of health care the size and scale of the education sector, including nurseries, was impressive. Again, while quality and sensitivity to individual needs frequently gave way to political education and russification, central control made possible the development of education in Soviet Central Asia to a level that would not otherwise have happened.

The main problem in education stemmed from the simple point that the main access to more desirable jobs and social status was the higher education system, yet the main work available was in blue-collar production. There was thus an inevitable conflict between the aspirations of the majority of pupils and the reality of working life for most of them, that is between human capital investment and social reproduction. Competition for the scarce resource of higher education was intense, and for a variety of family-based reasons a steep class gradient appeared in the opportunities available (Yanowitch, 1977).

One response, particularly embodied in the 1958 Khruschev reforms, was to expand the opportunities available in schools for university preparation, in order to maximise the chances for workers' children, while trying to retain a production-oriented curriculum. The effects of this policy, not unlike similar expansionary policies adopted in the 1960s in the UK and USA, was to secure the chances of all middle-class pupils, while making very few inroads into the inequality of access. The education system thus suffered a double failure: it allowed, at 60 per cent, too many pupils to enter the general academic school oriented towards university entrance, and hence wasted education investment for the majority, who never would proceed to higher education; moreover it failed to reduce class inequalities.

In conclusion to this section on the accumulated problems of social policy before the advent of perestroika, it appeared that Soviet welfare was, in Titmuss's (1963) terms, largely reminiscent of occupational welfare. Strictly speaking this is entirely compatible with the socialist principle of 'each according to their work', with social need being the guiding principle for distribution only under communism. Nevertheless, despite the Brezhnev re-timetabling of the 1959 'road to communism', via the period of developed socialism, it would be reasonable to expect the beginnings of pre-figurative communist distribution in the field of social policy if anywhere. But to make it more need-oriented would have been to break the links with the labour market, and ironically labour incentives were seen as a major priority, with social policy regarded as the key avenue for the improvement of the 'human factor' (Zaslavskaya, 1990, p.96).

Collapse of the Old Regime?

The origins of the desire in the Soviet Union for far reaching changes lay in three problems. First, and paramount, was the slow-down in economic growth during the 1970s. Second was the erosion of the popular legitimacy of the State. Third was the fear of a decay in family and community life. The specific expression of these problems however varied.

The slow-down in economic growth was partly the result of the inability of the Soviet economy to raise worker productivity, itself caused by the peculiar incentives for waste and poor quality of the 'shortage model' (Kornai, 1980), and the 'partial ignorance' (Ellman, 1989) that comes with highly centralised planning with poor data processing in a complex economy. While this was partly a technological weakness, there was also an absence of any politically acceptable means of intensifying work activities. The solution was the adoption of full cost accounting and limited marketisation in an attempt to de-centralise economic decision making and thus close the 'information gap'.

In the political area the erosion of the popular legitimacy of the State was evident in the disaffection revealed in the activities of dissidents of various persuasions - what Goldfarb (1989) characterised as the collapse of the 'totalitarian mind'. Towards the end of the Brezhnev era this was compounded by the growth of corruption throughout government. In order to win back the interest and trust of citizens, a new policy of openness about public affairs and new democratic mechanisms were constructed.

The third problem was the evidence of decay in family and community life. Both infant and adult mortality were rising, and such classic social problems as divorce, crime, drug mis-use, and particularly alcoholism, were growing to the point where they could no longer be ignored. This set of issues generated a reaction in terms of the remoralisation of social life, particularly expressed in the vigorous campaign against alcohol consumption instigated soon after Gorbachev was elected General Secretary.

While these general problems emerged from the 1970s onwards, and first began to shape policy noticeably with the leadership successions of Andropov and Chernenko, it is the election of Gorbachev that marked the beginning of a very different era. However if any date is needed for the appearance of the seedling which grew into perestroika, it can be taken as the presentation by Academician Tatyana Zaslavskaya (subsequently President of the Soviet Sociological Association, and elected Deputy) of the notorious 'Novosibirsk Manifesto' two years earlier, in April 1983, to a closed seminar of the economics departments of the CPSU Central Committee, the Academy of Sciences, and Gosplan (Zaslavskaya, 1984).

Existing officially in just 70 numbered copies, the report argued that the main obstacle to improved economic performance was the economic system itself. In this she was doing no more than many other liberals in asking for de-centralisation, and quasi-markets. But the real innovation in her report was in its social rather than economic analysis. In a nutshell she argued that economic and educational levels had risen to a point at which the social characteristics of workers superseded those required by strategic and technical mechanisms unchanged since the 1930s command economy. There were widespread frustrated aspirations which undermined motivation at work (Shlapentokh, 1989). Moreover she contended that sharply felt contradictory social interests had developed between different groups in Soviet society, which signalled the development of antagonistic social classes. Without an adequate understanding of these interests, and their support of or opposition to change, she argued little could be done to solve pressing social and economic problems.

Zaslavskaya and the head of her Novosibirsk Institute (Aganbegyan) came to Moscow as key advisers to Gorbachev in the mid 1980s - the 'mother and father' of perestroika. He advised on economics, and she set up the Soviet Centre for Public Opinion Research to try to identify those very social interests which would support or oppose perestroika. In the ensuing years change was frenetic. First was a period of *preparation* (March 1985-July 1986), during which Gorbachev launched the now well-known concepts of perestroika, glasnost, and uskorenie (acceleration). He also swiftly set about securing coalitions and allegiances at various levels of the bureaucracy, and launched one specific domestic change - the battle against alcohol. Second was a period of *struggle for political ascendancy* (July 1986-July 1987), in which democratic procedures, such as multiple electoral candidates, were promoted as the mechanism for loosening and overcoming entrenched resistance to economic change. Glasnost also began to show real results in the exposure of corruption, disinformation (for example over Chernobyl), and the existence of a wide variety of cultural interests at odds with the old Brezhnev line.

By this time, more than two years on, the inevitable upswelling of new or long dormant social and political forces began to appear, such that the next phase of *consolidation* (July 1987-June 1988) was increasingly threatened. Independent political clubs, demonstrations, new social movements, and popular fronts, were either formed or planned around issues of socialism, environmentalism, nationalism, democracy, and freedom of speech. Significantly, Yeltsin was sacked as Moscow Party chief. From the 19th Party Congress onwards (July 1988) came the *disintegration of the party*. The 19th Congress initiated the proposal for an elected Congress of People's Deputies, and an executive-style Presidency. In October 1988 the Baltic Popular Fronts were founded, in March 1989 People's Deputies were elected, and in May 1989 the first Congress of People's Deputies took place. This is important both because of the organisation of the Inter-Regional Group of Deputies (destined to become a social democratic opposition to the CPSU), and because social policy issues were widely debated (Rogovin, 1989).

The summer of 1989 witnessed widespread miners' strikes, and the highly symbolic staging of the Baltic human chain. From this point on we can add a fifth period, borrowed from Kagarlitsky (1990), who presciently identified the beginning of the *end of perestroika*. By 1990 the Party was in an insoluble dilemma:

> no legally guaranteed civil society, no democracy; no democracy, no meat or decent vegetables in the shops, no freedom from fear, no independence for nations, no freedom for Soviet citizens to travel (Keane, 1990, p.348).

The Party could proceed no further without opening itself up to real competition whether from a social democratic or conservative direction, yet to do so might mean losing the power to continue to direct the pace and direction of perestroika. This was why perestroika became bogged down, and lost its momentum. 1990 thus heralded both the final preparation of the social democratic alternative, in the shape of the Democratic Platform manifesto which appeared in April, and the growing power of the conservative opposition which successfully scuppered the Shatalin '500 day' plan for radical economic restructuring in September, and engineered the military suppression of Baltic autonomy at the turn of the year.

1991 witnessed a continuing struggle between conservative groups, centered partly in the military and partly in the Party, and the pressure for liberalisation coming from a mixture of republican nationalism, professional and managerial interests, and the West. Early in the year it seemed indeed as if perestroika was on the wane, yet the early summer witnessed real price reform, a reduction in travel restrictions, the election of Yeltsin to the Russian presidency, and every likelihood of substantial aid from the West. With this oscillation between progressive and conservative forces it is not difficult to see why the coup in August 1991 took place, nor that Gorbachev and Yeltsin saw it coming. There was thus a sixth phase, *the dissolution of the Union*, which began with the collapse of the coup, Gorbachev's resignation from the Communist Party, and the banning of its activities. The initial aim was for a united economic zone amongst the republics designed to replace the old command structures, but Gorbachev's desire for a new political union always looked unrealistic. During the autumn power began to ebb from Gorbachev as Yeltsin annexed more and more Union functions for Russia, culminating in the establishment of a new Commonwealth of Independent States, completely separated from the old Union. Clearly there was no further function for Gorbachev who in the end was denied the dignity of a formal, legal transfer of power, and he finally resigned late in December.

This marked the arrival of a seventh phase, *authoritarian populism* marked by the search for a positive alternative to communist ideology, and its political and economic structures. Yeltsin wasted no time in decreeing a relatively widespread price liberalisation in January 1992. Politically there was a retreat from democracy, for although Yeltsin was popularly elected, others in senior posts are appointed; and local government (in Moscow and St. Petersburg for example) moved from elected Soviets to appointed prefects.

New Crises of Social Policy

As we have seen in the discussion of the origins of perestroika, social policy in the form of the 'human factor' was seen by Tatyana Zaslavskaya to have a vital part to play in revitalising Soviet society. In common with other writers such as Ferge (1979), she distinguished *social policy*, as a mechanism for compensating for misfortunes resulting from the market or other social institutions, from *societal policy*. The latter refers to the use of social interventions to engineer change in the general social structure (Zaslavskaya, 1990, p.99). On the whole it was argued that perestroika needed to reintegrate social/societal policy as a central element in social development, rather than confining it to the distribution of 'residual' resources left after more important priorities had been satisfied.

For example, problems for societal policy included the gender and ethnic inequalities, which had been either unaffected by or exacerbated by the mass production of health or education workers. In these professions, as in western countries, women predominated particularly in the junior and middle levels, while men controlled the top positions. It seems no coincidence that the typical level of pay, even for middle ranking posts, had been around 30 per cent below average rates. Moreover as consumers of these services, women's specific needs were a low priority. For example the widespread use of multiple abortion as a form of contraception damaged women's health unnecessarily (Buckley, 1990, pp.196-98).

As far as ethnic inequalities was concerned, it is true to say that welfare provision in the Central Asian republics was higher than it would otherwise have been without Soviet influence. Nevertheless in terms of quality, there were notable problems. In health care there were high rates of infant mortality, infectious diseases, and poor hospital provision (Buckley, 1990, pp.195-96). In education the most vexed question was over the relative status of minority and Russian language teaching, since a disproportionate amount of published material, official documents, and even alphabet development was in Russian rather than native languages (Gitelman, 1990, pp.152-53).

In practice, after perestroika, social policy was characterised by a combination of pre-existing policy problems, new solutions, and new problems thrown up by the information and politicisation that glasnost had generated. Activity was more pronounced in some areas than others.

Soviet social policy commentators, such as Natalia Rimachevskaya of the Institute of Demography, observed that by 1991 there was a widespread sense of disorganisation and chaos such that policy prescriptions and their implementation were extremely uncertain in terms of their effects. Moreover, since there was a close connection between the labour market and social policy priorities, social policy was inevitably bound up with attempts at economic change. For example if, as many argued, economic restructuring would have to come from small and medium enterprises (SMEs), then a flexible labour market would have to be made possible throughout the economy. However there were likely to be obstacles to this.

The labour market   The first obstacle to a flexible labour market was the absence of true unemployment, the result of a right to employment enjoyed since the abolition of unemployment benefits by Stalin in 1930. This situation was changing, but there were attempts to cushion this effect, and if possible nullify it, by offering sufficient retraining schemes to enable every displaced worker to move jobs without extended spells of unemployment.

A second obstacle was the attitude to work activity itself. It was the experience of anyone who has stayed in the Soviet Union for any length of time that there was a low commitment to the quality of daily work. As the popular saying went 'we pretend to work, and they pretend to pay us!'. This was not just a matter of low pay, however, but also the time consuming nature of goods and service distribution. Many workers had to spend working time each day either shopping, or making arrangements through friends and contacts for the acquisition of everyday requirements (Shlapentokh, 1989). There was also the urgent problem of alcohol abuse in work time that leads to great loss of efficiency.

A third obstacle was the attitude to income distribution. Although Gorbachev (1987) had repeated his dislike of 'levelling tendencies', using the principle from Marx that under socialism 'from each according to his abilities to each according to his work', there was widespread support amongst workers for the principle of wage equality, such that differential effort should not be rewarded with differentials in pay. Survey evidence suggested that this attitude was deeply entrenched (Mason and Sydorenko, 1990).

A fourth obstacle was the attitude to general economic restructuring, particularly price reform. Cumulative all-union representative sample surveys carried out in 1989 and 1990 by the Soviet Centre for Public Opinion Research showed that there was little public support for the kind of radical restructuring of prices and ownership proposed in the Shatalin '500 day' plan. This included a rapid reduction in the existing subsidies for food, travel, and housing, and the general movement of prices to a level which more accurately signalled the real costs of production. It also planned for the widespread privatisation of enterprises, housing, and land. Negative reaction to Yeltsin's actual price reforms introduced in January 1992, confirmed this view.

There was growing hostility to such changes, with a large minority of citizens claiming that they would 'actively' resist them. The abandonment of this 'shock therapy' in favour of a more gradual programme of price reform and privatisation by Gorbachev was a more democratic decision than was apparent to western observers at the time. More specific surveys of particular factories in and around Moscow confirmed that there was a clear variation in attitude according to social class: managers supported change, but the shop floor did not (Toshchenko, 1987; Chichkanov, 1987). There was also sharp public criticism of the new co-operative ventures that were legalised, since they were felt to be exacerbating supply shortages through their superior purchasing power, and hence had become associated in the public mind with unjust privileges. These were in effect to become the nascent SMEs of the future.

A fifth obstacle was the absence of new sources of labour. The history of other societies in the midst of rapid industrial expansion, or restructuring, suggests that a good supply of new labour is essential. Traditionally there have been four sources: rural workers, migrants, women, and structural unemployment. None of these were available in the Soviet Union. Women were already economically active, and mass immigration was unlikely. While widespread unemployment was feared, there were significant efforts to protect workers. The only other source might have been the rural workers of the Central Asian republics; but growing regional autonomy, indeed the fission of the Union made this source very uncertain.

A sixth difficulty concerned the reproduction of labour both in terms of the urban birth rate and in terms of education and training. Here the conflict between the high rate of economic activity of women, designed to increase the short term labour supply, and the consequently diminished size of urban families threatened longer term reproduction (Chinn, 1977). Furthermore shortages of young workers were exacerbated by the difficulties of matching educational output to economic requirements, a problem whose solution (the 1984 education reform) had not worked.

It can be concluded that there was an unresolved tension between levels of social justice and attitudes towards work, and a flexible labour market, which hampered the introduction of SMEs on any large scale.

Social security Here important activities were improvements in pensions, and a commitment in the first Congress of Peoples' Deputies to monitor the standard of living of poorer groups, although it was still not easy for the government to discuss poverty openly. As far as pensioners were concerned, evidence about their economic difficulties resulted in the raising of minimum pensions to the level of the minimum wage (70 roubles per month) from January 1990. This was described as the 'small pension law' (Tsivilev and Rogogin, 1990, p.186) since it was supposed to be merely a stop-gap to a more comprehensive reform (necessary not least because of the appearance of significant inflation). As far as poverty was concerned, the relative improvement in published statistics in the late 1980s has enabled Ellman (1990) to calculate that in 1988, using a poverty line of 78 roubles per month (compared with a line of 75 roubles accepted by the Soviet Parliament), about 14 per cent of the population was in poverty.

Since the cornerstone of social security was the right to work, upon which other policies for income maintenance were based, the main problem looming on the horizon was the possibility of mass unemployment as the economy shed the estimated 30 per cent of labour that was economically unnecessary (Urban, 1987, p.3). However it is difficult to judge clearly what unemployment actually meant. For example, Adirim (1989) showed that 'joblessness' was in the region of 6 per cent, but that relative 'worklessness' in existing employment which resulted in incomplete wages might account for another 10 to 15 per cent, while a desire for a better job had been expressed by the majority of the population.

This process had already generated the new Employment Law drafted in the autumn of 1990, and formally adopted on 15 January 1991. This officially signalled the end of the right/duty to work by imposing a 1 per cent payroll levy to generate funds to finance unemployment benefit, retraining, public community work, and career guidance (Standing, 1991). 25 per cent of the funds were earmarked for a central all-union fund available for low-income high unemployment republics, the rest staying at republic level, although the events of August 1991 signalled the end of this inter-republic flow. As elsewhere, the usual problems of practical implementation existed here, most notably the scarcity of employment offices. In addition there were insufficient funds generated to pay for benefits set at or near the minimum wage for six months, or to support those who had exhausted their entitlements. The latter group exceeded 50 per cent of the unemployed, and in the absence of a national scheme of income support, poverty spread rapidly.

Housing Here there were few new problems, although homelessness and begging was, as in London, on the increase (Stetina, 1990). But the old ones of access, quality, and infrastructure remained. The main effort to tackle them was the commitment in the 1986 Party Programme (27th Congress of the CPSU) to provide all families with their own flat by the end of the century. Since an estimated 20 per cent lived in communal flats, this implied a massive increase in housing investment (Trehub, 1987, p.29). As noted earlier, half of the stock was enterprise-owned, and some enterprises echoed the Party promise, and also pledged to provide for all of their workers with separate flats. Rents, which even together with energy costs rarely absorbed more than 3 per cent of household income, had not yet been raised (as full cost accounting required) as a prelude to a more flexible housing market.

However, an indication of the changes planned for the housing market can be deduced from three important decrees issued in 1988 that gave carte blanche (and bank credit) for the expansion of private, and co-operative, housing construction (Andrusz, 1990). The final decree, in December 1988, granted the right for organisations and Soviets to sell their housing stock, as a result of which the Moscow Soviet in July 1990 decreed that all of its tenants (about 25 per cent of all households) had the right to buy their flats through a complicated formula which entitled families to a basic space allowance, over and above which the price rose steeply. For example in pre-independence Estonia, where flats were put on sale in late 1990, prices were set in the region of 150,000 roubles per flat. The Estonian Academy of sciences estimated that, with annual salaries at around 5,000 roubles, less than 100 local residents could raise such funds (Niit, 1997). In 1991, fearing an influx of North American money from returning expatriate Estonians for whom such a price was only $5,000, this market was suspended. The announcement in January 1992 of the end of the 'propiska' system of controlling the right to live in a city such as Moscow heightened this tension between public and private property, encouraging a new influx of hopeful city dwellers from the satellites and suburbs that had been held at arms length beyond the city limits.

Education The main effort here was directed towards raising the salaries of teachers by about 30 per cent, and continuing the slow process of implementing the 1984 school reform. While this was laid down a year before Gorbachev's elevation, he publicly committed himself to it. The basic difficulty here was that too many pupils wanted to get into higher education. They therefore resisted learning a useful production-related skill which they and the economy actually needed, although most of them would not have been able to realise their ambitions.

The 1984 reforms made a bold attempt to solve the first failure by planning for a reduction of the proportion of each cohort entering the general academic school from 60 per cent to 29 per cent. In addition, all children were to get experience of real work as part of their curriculum. As a political safety valve, the 60 per cent directed to go through vocational school were given the right to apply for higher education and take the relevant entrance exams (Zajda, 1984). This change looked very much like a move away from a comprehensive principle towards selective schools, in which the cream were identified early and the rest consigned to the factory. It had a negative effect on the class distribution of access to higher education, although it brought education more closely into line with the requirements of the labour market.

Public debate reported about this issue concentrated on three things. First, the availability of 'production-training' facilities was too limited. Second, the quality of vocational schools was too low for pupils to have any real chance of getting into higher education. Third, the vocational schools were seen as merely the place where weaker pupils were expected to go; they had little positive image. Indeed a report in December 1986 made an explicit comparison with the 1958 reforms, observing that then only 5 to 10 per cent of school graduates were placed in jobs that they were trained for.

The conflict of values between educational opportunity, and manpower planning, was very clear in this education debate. However since these reforms occurred with little real effect on the opportunities of more privileged children, they faced little opposition. The educational division between the upwardly mobile and the majority of workers, kept the conflicting aims (of educational opportunity and manpower planning) apart. The 'problem group' of those pupils who had inappropriately aspired to higher education, were being cooled out at an earlier point in the system, while the whole question of the reproduction of inequalities was avoided.

Health The main problem remained the under-funding of the health service. Substantial wage increases were granted in 1986 to bring medical staff pay up to average levels, and promises were made in the 12th five-year plan to inject substantial increases in funds for new technology and drugs. As elsewhere, these remain largely unfulfilled. However experiments in service restructuring were set up. For example in April 1988 the Leningrad health service was turned over to a strict internal market - well before the equivalent mechanism was even contemplated in the UK. Hospital budgets were set to zero, and polyclinics given the task of purchasing the services that they needed from hospitals, and paying a 'market price' through which hospitals were to earn their revenues. It did not work without major hiccups (Roberts, 1990), but there were some who saw the potential benefits in terms of greater efforts on all sides to think through the consequences of referrals.

However the main activity in the health field was not inside the health services, but rather an attempt to remedy the serious stagnation and decline in life expectancy and infant mortality that had developed in the late 1970s (Mezentseva and Rimachevskaya, 1990). This without doubt was the most serious health problem, notwithstanding other notable issues such as the Chernobyl nuclear disaster, AIDS, the disabled, children in care, and environmental pollution (Economist, 1990, pp.25-28; Dossett-Davies, 1988a; Steel, 1991; Pierson, 1988; Harwin, 1988; Perera, 1990). Indeed it was so troubling that the publication of the relevant statistics was suspended from 1972 to 1986 (Trehub, 1987, p.13). The main reason for this pattern - unique to the industrialised world - was felt to be alcohol abuse, although it was likely that environmental pollution was a poorly recognised contributor. In any event alcohol abuse was the easier problem to handle, and it was Gorbachev's immediate priority on being elected General Secretary. While of course alcohol consumption had been recognised as a problem before (there was an active temperance movement in the 1920s), Gorbachev identified himself strongly with this new and vigorous campaign. Less than two months after being elected, he launched the anti-alcohol campaign on 7 May 1985 with a decree and a flurry of media activity in the following two months.

There was a substantial improvement in the kinds of conditions which were provoking concern before 1985. However this was most closely linked to the simple reduction in the availability of alcohol. Anecdotal evidence such as letters to the press suggested the absence of a substantial change of public attitude. This was corroborated by indications that the public was actively seeking to undermine retail control in ways which would produce further problems in time. Homebrewing was booming: sugar sales mushroomed, and thefts of yeast doubled. This was matched by the spread of alcohol 'dens' in apartments, and the rise in poisonings occasioned by the increased use of alcohol-based perfumes and industrial alcohol.

Emerging Strategies for Welfare

The close link between occupation and welfare is thus one important model of Soviet welfare. This is very similar to the model of the 'organic labour state' outlined by Harding (1984). There are contradictory pressures between meeting needs, and hence severing this link, or motivating workers, and hence strengthening the link. But it is clear where Gorbachev's sympathies were. In *Perestroika* (1987), he says in a section entitled 'The social policy of restructuring' that:

> Intensification of social production suggests a new attitude to efficient employment and requires that the labour force must be regrouped. While working in this direction, we must thoroughly scrutinise how the principle of social justice is to be implemented... This is how the 27th Congress of the CPSU formulated the problem of social justice: under socialism, work is the foundation for social justice. Only work determines a citizen's real place in society, his social status. And this precludes any manifestation of equalising ... On this point we want to be perfectly clear: socialism has nothing to do with equalising. Socialism cannot ensure conditions of life and consumption in accordance with the principal 'From each according to his ability, to each according to his needs'. This will be under communism (p.100).

There was a desire to re-establish the material basis of incentives to work. For example there were numerous references to the desirability of 'economic-accountability' (this means fully-priced) services, for which money was to be earned in the more successful enterprises, and by the more senior staff. No wonder that management favoured perestroika, but workers did not; they had different interests in it.

Nevertheless the Soviet economy continued to decline. The shelving in 1990 of the Shatalin plan for rapid restructuring in favour of cautious price reform left inflation rising, production shrinking, exports down, and serious food shortages (Brasier, 1990); these figures were considerably worse for 1991, and the trend continued into 1992. Inevitably black marketeering was generated at points of acute shortage. Political legitimacy was shaken by the series of military interventions in the conservative build-up to the August coup, including the invasion of key Baltic institutions early in 1991, demonstrations of protest in Moscow, and executive permission for the military to patrol urban areas. There was a corresponding growth of social decay in terms of prostitution, crime, and alcoholism. To make sense of strategies for social policy that might have been possible, we can return to some theoretical explanations.

A traditional Marxist base-superstructure model of the kind adopted by Tatyana Zaslavskaya in her Novosibirsk manifesto (still a necessary code at the time it was written) would suggest that the traditional relations of production had become a hindrance to further growth. Modernisation/ convergence theory in a similar way might suggest that the technical logic of industrial development dictated a move to a more intensive stage of economic growth, often referred to now as post-Fordist. At the most general level, world systems theory would link these changes to the embeddedness of the Soviet Union in an increasingly international economic context, symbolised most obviously by its associate membership of the IMF.

However these models are particularly based on economic factors, whereas the problems outlined above include important political and social dimensions. An alternative might be to look to political theory about democracy, and sociological theory about the nature of social integration. From the former for example we could draw out the nature of individual rights and freedoms and the conditions for their realisation through democratic mechanisms, using these as a measure of the decay in political empowerment. For example the new administrative structure in Moscow city was in tension with the democratically elected Moscow Soviet: a system of prefect and sub-prefectures into which local citizens had very little input. From the latter we could set up models about the integration of individuals into society through family and school socialisation, through the meeting of life-cycle dependencies, and opportunities for satisfactory engagement in the activities of production and reproduction. Again these could then provide us with indicators of the decline in opportunities for social integration which might underlie the development of social problems.

One particular model which has received much attention recently attempts to make links across the range of these concerns, and could consequently serve as an organising model for identifying some strategy options - Marshall's theory of citizenship. This contained three elements. First was the legal constitution of citizens as of equal standing in relation to the law. Second was the access of all citizens to democratic apparatus for the exercise of political power over the State. Third was the provision of sufficient means for all people to engage in full social participation. The co-existence of these civil, political and social rights, it was argued, amounted to the conditions necessary for full citizenship. To Marshall they were both a historical description of the development of industrial societies, and the necessary pre-condition for their continued existence.

However Marshall was at pains to point out that these rights did not exist without tension. Ironically the development of citizenship rights had occurred alongside capitalism and its associated inequalities. In particular the limitation of political rights to the formal exercise of voting rights resulted in the juxtaposition of multiple inequalities in the economy and in family life, with political interventions that attempted to mitigate these inequalities through social and other policies. Moreover, he argued that the best condition for the successful development of industrial societies was to maintain a balance between the economy and social rights. Too much economic freedom would undermine the long term stability of the economy through the loss of political legitimacy and the breakdown of social reproduction. Too much political and social intervention on the other hand would stifle the dynamic growth of the economy, upon which everything else depended.

In sum Marshall argued that a balance between economic growth via capitalism, political empowerment through democracy, and social integration/ participation sustained through social policy was both historically and theoretically necessary for the sustained achievement of any one of these goals. Returning to the Soviet difficulties of 1991, we can see that the areas that Marshall discusses seem to be close to those of current concern: economic growth, democratic rights, and social integration. To the extent that simultaneous shortcomings were perceived to have developed in these areas, it seems reasonable to characterise the situation as amounting to a crisis in citizenship.

The resolution of this crisis would therefore be via the mechanism that established those rights in the first place, namely social struggle and social movements (Turner, 1986). For example there was a rapid growth in environmental and housing movements in the late 1980s, but by the early 1990s, disillusion and the pressure of daily survival had undermined their support (Manning, 1998). Our review of social policy shows little evidence of such mechanisms in the social field. Despite the repeated references to democratisation that Gorbachev made, and hence, one would expect, the definition of social issues in popular terms, specific social policy reforms were remarkable for their departure from public opinion. They were not being handled simply in response to popular grievances percolating up through the political system. Politicisation seems to have involved a campaign to change public opinion rather than to reflect it. The question therefore arises as to whose grievances were being addressed in this process? What were the emergent interests in Soviet society, and how were those interests presented as necessary in some sense for the nation/economy/socialism? It is clear from survey material that perestroika was regarded with scepticism by ordinary workers:

> While 20 per cent of the enterprise executives, their deputies and the chief specialists think that restructuring is proceeding rather successfully at their enterprises, not one shop superintendent is of this opinion (Ivanov, 1987).

> The greater part of managers are rather optimistic in assessing their own efforts and the level of their enterprises' successes in the first year of restructuring. The workers do not agree with them. In many cases they are inclined to think that management's words are often at variance with its deeds. That situation unquestionably bears the seeds of future conflicts (Toshchenko, 1987).

> 45 per cent of the enterprise directors and 35 per cent of the superintendents of large shops are firmly convinced that the new economic conditions have significant advantages, while only 16 per cent of the rank-and-file engineers, brigade leaders and workers are such determined optimists (Chichkanov, 1987).

Amongst Soviet writers, Tatyana Zaslavskaya had made the most extensive examination of the nature of social interests, not least in order to identify the sources of support for and opposition to perestroika. This survey evidence clearly supported her analysis (1990, p.186) of the place of social policy in perestroika, and the range of interests affecting its fate.

Much though one sympathises with the rhetoric of perestroika, and can understand the sense of excitement that it must have generated amongst the intelligentsia, and even agree that it could have led to greater economic growth, the social relations it sought to encourage were not progressive from the point of view of social need in the short term. On the contrary, the greater freedom for the intelligentsia to press its interests on the one hand, combined with the inevitable erosion of subsidised social provision on the other, would inevitably squeeze ordinary workers.

This is a different conclusion to that offered by Szelenyi and Manchin (1987), who suggested that the evidence from Hungary was that a resurgence of market relations in the context of a dominant State re-distributive system led to greater equality since it gave poor people an alternative source of power over the distributive system. But this depends on who has power in the first place, for those who are able to exercise influence in the administrative system, even if they are temporarily disadvantaged by a growth in the market, soon came to exercise it again.

3 Russian Social Policy

На бедного Макара и все шишки валятся
All the cones fall down on poor Makar

The environment within which social policy exists now has changed dramatically: the USSR has collapsed, there is a new constitution, Presidential, Federal and local elections have taken place, public administrative structures and budgetary arrangements have been in turmoil, industrial production has shrunk, prices and wages are free, and much domestic and industrial property has been privatised. Income support (pensions, and other benefits) have not kept pace with inflation, health and education are increasingly regionally and locally varied, and major enterprises are still in effect being subsidised through soft financial accounting arrangements. Unemployment continues to be relatively low, and living standards are growing steadily more unequal.

Reaction to the old system favoured reduced planning control in favour of markets, and reduced central control in favour of de-centralised and democratic administration. In theory this should correct the key technical failure of the old system which suffered from an overload of, and hence loss of, information as a result of central decision making (Ellman, 1989). It had been hoped that this would release self interest and political empowerment, which would invigorate a demoralised and passive population. These gains have been very unevenly developed, if at all. The changeover has brought with it some very sharp social costs. Widening incomes have left more women, children and old people in poverty, and undermined the security of public sector workers such as doctors and teachers. Classic social problems such as infectious disease, alcoholism, prostitution, and crime have grown, and consequently birth rates have dropped while death rates have climbed. Pressures on social services have escalated at the same time as inflation, tax evasion, and corruption have reduced the resources available to them, and administrative and legal capacities have shrunk.

The policy options here were stark (Gotting, 1994, pp.8-12). In the short run, a total absence of social support might have enabled the quickest re-structuring of the economy, but it would only have been possible with either the use of a Draconian suppression of social unrest (hardly possible any more in Russia), or where the economy was ready for 'take off'. The alternative was to take a slower path to economic change, and to target help as sharply as possible in the short term, with the longer term goal of a western mix of social insurance and private provision (Barr, 1994, pp.26-27). Russia opted for the latter, although benefits are still closely tied to enterprises and poorly targeted. However repeated declarations of social policy reforms, for example in 1993 prior to the new constitution, and in 1997 arising out of the 1996 Presidential election campaign ('The Social Reform Programme for 1996-2000'), and in 1998 '12 Main Tasks in the Area of Social and Economic Policy', are not being effectively implemented, particularly if a regional view is taken.

In legal and administrative terms the most significant development has been the new constitution proposed and adopted at the end of 1993. Social policy issues are covered in a variety of proposals, but there are also omissions. The constitution has to be read against a background of more detailed social policy proposals issued by Yeltsin in November 1993 before the December referendum. The constitution, many observers have noted, is heavily weighted towards the powers of the President. While Ministers take responsibility for managing various parts of the domestic policy programme, for example in Ministries for labour, social protection, or health, Presidential decrees continue to take the lead in policy initiatives.

On 3 November 1993, Yeltsin published his review of policy goals a month after the October confrontation. While it can be read partly as an election manifesto, the review appeared to form the basis of intended social policy plans:

> We are now working together to prepare a package of social decrees:
> • on a system of minimum social guarantees
> • on introducing allowances for those who are inadequately provided for
> • on measures to ensure that social protection for the population reaches the right people
> • on a minimum living standard
> • on a minimum wage
> • on a minimum pension
> • on charity and other measures
> (*Current Digest of Post-Soviet Press*, 1993, vol.45, no.44, p.4)

The then Council of Ministers prepared a number of measures during 1994 to deal with uprating various social benefits including family allowances, and to revise the contribution structures for the Pension Fund, the Social Insurance Fund, and the Employment Fund, and to prepare for the first time details of a mandatory medical insurance scheme. These proposals were the subject of some sharp disagreements between the State Duma and the President, notably in the summer of 1994 when the Duma agreed an increase of 50 per cent in the basic pension. In view of the pressure on the budget however the President decreed an increase of only 15 per cent. This resulted in some pensioners receiving a 15 per cent increase and others a 50 per cent increase, and the resignation of the Minister for Social Protection.

Such an administrative hiccup is an inevitable consequence of an unstable administrative system. It is the result of two main factors. First, many competent personnel are no longer in the civil service, either pushed out for close association with the old order, or pulled out to more lucrative jobs in the private sector (Lesage, 1993, pp.121-133). Second, there has been an element of policy making on the run, with a concomitant fluidity of administrative organisation. Part of this is the inevitable result of the political struggles since 1991 in Russia. Part of it however is also the result of the dominance of Yeltsin over government affairs, and the attempt to give administrative form to his changing policy agenda.

None of the proclaimed social goals is of course possible without the money to pay for it. The initial reaction, to print money or in effect to allow extended credit to central and local government and to enterprises, has enabled a rapid and cruel re-structuring of incomes through inflation. Pensioners and public sector workers for example have been unable to maintain their incomes, while others have been able to advance theirs. Thus both the beneficiaries and providers of welfare services have suffered during this phase. Monthly inflation has now slowed considerably: in 1994-1996 the official figure was around 4-5 per cent compared with 25 per cent in 1993 and 40 per cent in early 1992 (*Russian Economic Trends*, 1994, p.4); in January 1996 monthly inflation was the lowest since 1990 - 4.1 per cent (*Current Digest of the Post Soviet Press* (1997), vol. 49, no. 1, p.10), and despite the financial crisis late in 1998, monthly inflation remained at around 4 per cent throughout 1999 (UNDP, 1999, p. 151). Within the budget there were signs that social spending was rising. Ellman and Layard (1993, p.58) argued that the figures for early 1992 showed underfunding of social expenditure, for example only 3 per cent of GNP on education and 2 per cent on health, both of which were more than twice this rate in the OECD. By the middle of 1994, when the budget was accepted by the Duma on 24 June, these had risen to 4.5 per cent and 2.8 per cent respectively (*Russian Economic Trends*, 1994, p.12), and by 1998 to 3.6 and 3.8 per cent (UNDP, 1999, p. 151). However such figures assume that the funds earmarked in the budget are actually forthcoming. This is not the case. In particular, up to 1996 the great majority of budget debt has occurred in the social sector (*Russia-1997*, 1997, p.9), resulting in wage arrears for public sector workers and shortages of drugs, books and so on. The Institute for Economy in Transition has argued that the key feature of the status of social sector in 1996 was a substantial reduction of Federal budget financing. In 1996, State budget spending on health care, education and other social services constituted 65 per cent of the 1991 allocations (*Russian Economy in 1996*, 1997, pp.116-19).

These amounts are dwarfed by the costs of income support, which are now technically outside the State budget in four separate funds: employment, social insurance, pension, and medical insurance. Generated since 1991 by a 39 per cent payroll tax, in 1994 they amounted to 17 per cent of GDP, and ran a massive surplus of 4 per cent of GDP. The 'Social Reform Programme for 1996-2000' states quite realistically that in the medium term, a significant rise in the share of social spending in GDP should not be expected (ibid., p.122). As in many western countries this is the area that is most expensive, and is particularly sensitive to two factors: the rate of unemployment, and the level of pensions. Both these figures have been the subject of some debate. The official rate of unemployment as measured by registration with the Federal Employment Service is about 3 per cent (*Statistical Bulletin of Federal Employment Service*, 1997, p.7), but labour force surveys indicates that for 1997 it was really nearer 9 per cent with a further 6 per cent on involuntary leave and 5 per cent on short time (Chetvernina, 1997, pp.227-29; Standing, 1994, pp.35-50). By 1999 unemployment had grown to 14 per cent (UNDP, 1999, p. 95). Although this is much larger than the official figure, it is still quite low in view of the 50 per cent reduction of GDP over the period - a point taken up later. With unemployment benefit at around 10 per cent of the average wage, pensions take the lion's share of expenditure. The minimum has been indexed to about 20 per cent of the average wage, while the average pension is about a third of the average wage. Thus the pension rate drives the social budget.

Changes that took place in the Russian Government after the Presidential Elections in 1996 resulted in a new turn in Russian policy-making. The government suspended laws for the implementation of which there were no appropriations in the budget. This mainly applied to the social sphere. In the area of social benefits the Duma resolutely fixed the 'golden rule' that 'laws must be backed up by money', for both off-budget funds as well as for local budgets. At the Federal level it was argued that there should be an end to the policy of empty promises by a moratorium on the adoption of new legislative acts establishing such benefits. The new policy direction of the Russian government - abolishing entitlement benefits and gradually replacing them with a limited set of targeted, means-tested benefits - has become elevated to the key solution. In addition, responsibility for carrying out some of the functions of social policy (social assistance, education and health care) is being transferred to the local level. The government now argues that the most important thing to be done is to bring order to the system of social benefits and settle the question of who should get social assistance. The principle on which the traditional Russian system of social transfers had been constructed was based more on demographic categories and characteristics than on the actual level of material security. World Bank experts have pointed to the ineffective formal system of social protection. The reason for re-examining the concept is that Russia has more than 150 types of benefits and allowances, which are given to more than 100 million Russians. Groups with the highest incomes (upper deciles, 8-10) receive 42 per cent of social benefits expenditure, while those the lowest incomes (deciles, 1-3) only receive 27 per cent (Dmytriev, 1997). The poorest people who are really in need are not entitled to some kinds of State social support at all, such as transport and medicines.

It is felt that an uncomfortable choice has to be made: either don't pay anyone sufficiently, since there is not enough money for everyone, or drastically reduce the number of recipients. Russian policy-makers and some senior officials at the Federal level emphasise that the State should support only the poorest people. According to the opinion of one senior official from the Ministry of Labour and Social Development (the re-organised former Ministry for Social Protection), interviewed for this project, Russia does not have a social policy; what it has is an attempt to protect all strata of the population without the financial and legislative pre-requisites needed to do so.

At the beginning of 1998 Yeltsin stated in his Annual Message to the Federal Assembly that Russia needed a new 'upswing strategy', which pre-supposes steady economic growth and economic freedom reinforced by a purposeful state policy. When there is a shortage of budget money, he argued, the only way to change the social situation for the better is through targeted social assistance. In his 1993 declaration, he stated that the time had come to finally decide on a package of social laws. But in 1998 his comments indicate that the main policy goals seem different: 'if there isn't enough money to put some particular law into effect, the Deputies must be honest with the people and change that law' (*Current Digest of the Post Soviet Press,* 1998, vol.50, no.7, p.1).

In January of 1998 the Russian Government published '12 Main Tasks in the Area of Social and Economic Policy'. The President personally appointed the higher officials responsible for each point of the proposed programme. Among the main social goals are:

- ensuring the payment of pensions and wages on-time;
- urgent need to adopt a package of draft laws on targeted social support for the poorest strata of the population;
- reducing non-payments, linked to two factors: the unrealistic budget and the actions of natural monopolies; to solve that problem it is planned to conduct an inventory of the network of budget-financed organisations (first of all, state medicine and education);
- bringing legislative norms regulating labour relations into line with the realities of a market economy;
- construction of housing for servicemen and officers - money should directly go from the Ministry of Finance into the personal accounts of recipients.

(*Current Digest of the Post Soviet Press,* 1998, vol.50, no.4, p.1).

However the currency crisis in August 1998 has undermined the fragile economic stability that developed in 1997, and makes the implementation of this new social policy package highly problematic. Russia is faced with the complex task of finding a sensible compromise between the demands of economic growth and of social protection. Social needs exist which cannot be neglected if social stability is not to be threatened. Conceptually, reform of the social sphere has been fairly clearly formulated, but this does not yet mean real social reforms, and realisation of these as a whole will depend on the existence of political will and of effective co-operation between the authorities at different levels. The Russian Presidential election in 2000 and the higher legislative power of the Federal level will automatically shift the tackling of many social problems into the twenty first century.

Clearly ordinary citizens take a keen interest in these changes. What have been their reactions? It appears that while there is general approval for the new system of democratic government, there is less enthusiasm for the performance of the actual government since 1991. Rose (1993b, p.42) reports that much of this general approval seems to have been related to increased civil freedoms, but approval for actual government policies since 1992 was considerably poorer, with 32 per cent not approving at all, and an additional 45 per cent only partly approving (ibid., p.37). Much of this negative feeling relates to government provision of social benefits, and this judgement has grown stronger since 1991. In terms of adaptation to the new realities during the past 5 years of market reforms Bovt (1996, p.3) sees four Russias: Moscow, industrial cities, provincial cities and rural localities. Opinion varies across these since regional differences are growing fast, with Moscow considerably advantaged compared with the others, in descending order. Overall polls in 1996 show only 33 per cent of citizens feel that they have adapted to the new way of life, compared with 54 per cent in Moscow, and that 64 per cent of Russians want a regime with a 'strong hand' and State social support as it was in the former Soviet times (Institute of Sociological Analysis, 1997). At the beginning of 1997 the Russian Independent Institute for Social and National Problems reported that the population expressed extremely negative perceptions of 1996. The overwhelming majority of Russians (74 per cent) rated 1996 as a difficult, bad, even harsh year for themselves and their families. The greatest dissatisfaction in 1996 was caused by the delay in paying wages, salaries, pensions and social benefits. Unemployment and poverty were mentioned most frequently as the most acute problems (Gorshkov, 1997).

There is still solid public support for social protection in Russia, particularly for poorer families, and a strong sense of doubt that the government is effective enough in this area. Surveys in 1991 and 1993 reported by the survey organisation VTSIOM (*Information Monitoring Bulletin*, 1994, January, pp.24-25) show that there was a decline from 35 per cent to 26 per cent of people feeling that social rights are partly or fully observed in Russia, and a growth in the proportion who want free schools (41 per cent to 58 per cent), free health care (22 per cent to 46 per cent), and free housing (24 per cent to 32 per cent); this rate grows to nearly 90 per cent for rights to employment and a subsistence income (ibid., p.26). In 1997 VTSIOM monitoring indicated a further growth to 85-90 per cent in those who felt that 'the authorities and the various community organisations in the field of social protection' were doing either practically nothing or 'patently not enough' (*Information Monitoring Bulletin*, 1998, January, p.19). In view of these findings, the Institute for Economy in Transition argued that reducing the scope of free or subsidised services and revising the range of their recipients would be a radical and extremely unpopular measure in Russia (*Russian Economy in 1996*, 1997, p.122). The experience of reforms in the advanced market economies shows that market reforms in the social sphere can only be implemented successfully where the relevant government bodies work efficiently and effectively - hardly the case in contemporary Russia with its inefficient control over the use of allocated budgets.

Some Aspects of Regional Inequality

We have the made the point that regional inequalities, policies, and provision are becoming central to understanding Russian social policy. The former USSR was an allied state made up of 15 Soviet socialist republics. Although considered formally independent, in essence each was an inalienable part of the 'family of nations' - a great totalitarian empire, stretching thousands of kilometres from north to south and from east to west. Even after the collapse of the totalitarian regime and the disintegration of the Soviet Empire in the late 1980s and 1990s, Russia remains the largest European state, occupying a vast territorial area and demonstrating notable ethnic, cultural and social diversity. In the course of the period of transformation, the former Soviet republics have acquired real - rather than formal - independence, and are now sovereign States. As a result, the Russian population has fallen, although it still numbers hundreds of millions: 148,704,000, to be precise, according to State Committee for Statistics data for 1 January 1998. At present, there are 89 members of the Russian Federation, divided between 11 large economic/territorial zones: Moscow, St. Petersburg and the Kaliningrad enclave have a special status.

Yeltsin's task of achieving an 'upswing' in Russia is directly linked with the development of local self-government if it is going to promote reforms across the regions. The constitution retains policy for health, education, and social security at the Federal level (articles 39, 41, 43), leaving only housing to the various republics, territories, regions, and Federal cities (articles 130, 132). However the current government initiatives propose that local authorities should be in direct charge not only of housing, but other social areas. Since budgetary provision for these services has moved away from the Federal level, locally raised finance (taxes, charges, insurance, mortgages, charities, and so on) will assume increasing importance, with a consequent growth in regional inequity. The various regions of Russia are moving towards the market economy at different speeds, their economic resources are not equal in value and the political preferences of their local élites can be diametrically opposed: therefore, the Federal central government's intention to shift responsibility to the local level entails an increase in regional inequalities. Unlike education and health care, where local expenditure budgets are still relatively protected, social assistance (family benefits and benefits for poorer people) is suffering especially badly, because it has become completely dependent on the financial situation of the local budget. Further de-centralisation of social policy would require the creation of real, efficient mechanisms for Federal re-distribution of incomes from the more successful to the relatively poor regions. Yet this does not appear to be of major concern, and the Federal mechanisms for supporting regional social programmes remain extremely vague.

Different patterns of social and economic change have taken shape in the Russian regions as they adapt to the new conditions. Transition from the strictly centralised, equalising Soviet system has brought in its wake not only a significant regionalisation of the economy, but also an intensification of regional inequality, expressed through the widening gap between incomes, outgoings, wages and other indicators of the socio-economic position of people in different regions. Market relations have affected many aspects of everyday life: unemployment (mass unemployment in some regions), fierce competition (shading into criminal activities), and growing property and income differentiation. There are whole areas (the Kuzbass, the Maritime Area, the Komi Republic, Chechnya) where the social consequences of reform in Russia have been severe. This significantly affects people's material well-being, their living standards and their life chances.

Local differentiation of labour markets is growing, and this is inevitably leading to vital differences between regional levels of unemployment and between degrees of tension in these markets. By the end of 1997 the highest unemployment level was in the Northern Caucasus regions, situated in the zone of the Chechen conflict: in Ingushetia even up to 50 per cent. In some depressed republics (Kalmykia, Buryatia, Tyva) and territories of ethnic minorities in the North (national okrugs), indeed in about 20 per cent of Russian Federation Members, the level of unemployment in 1997 exceeded average figures by a factor of two. At the same time a third of the Russian regions are below average: Moscow, St. Petersburg, the giants of export trade in Western Siberia, and some highly-industrialised regions in the centre of European Russia. Rapid growth in actual unemployment can be traced in Eastern Siberia, the Russian Far East and North, in the regions of the coal industry (Kuzbass) and in the old industrialised towns of Central and Southern Russia experiencing appreciable industrial decline (for example, Ivanovo with a mono-industrial textile economy, or the regions with a high proportion of military sector in the structure of local economy) (see Table 3.1).

Turning to income and poverty, certain regions have found themselves in a very difficult situation. This is true, first and foremost, of the Northern Caucasus and the adjacent ethnically Russian regions of the South of Russia. Industrial and income decline have been precipitate. However the raw-material and export-oriented regions, and both capitals, have found themselves in a much better situation. As a result of market transformation the capital of Russia is now in a very special position. Here industrial decline has developed in parallel with service industry growth, and a phenomenal growth of people's average *per capita* income. Muscovites' nominal monetary incomes now are 3.5 times higher than the average Russian figures (see Table 3.2).

Table 3.1   Official unemployment (per cent) in economic regions (December 1997)

Moscow (special status)	3.7
St. Petersburg (special status)	9.0
North (6 regions)	13.9
Northwest (3 regions)	12.5
Central Russia (12 regions)	11.0
Volgo-Vyatka (5 regions)	12.3
Black Earth Area (5 regions)	9.4
Volga Region (8 regions)	12.8
Northern Caucasus (10 regions)	20.4
Ural (8 regions)	10.7
Western Siberia (9 regions)	12.7
Eastern Siberia (10 regions)	16.2
Far East (10 regions)	14.5
Kaliningrad Oblast (special status)	11.5
Russian Federation	11.2

Source: The Regions of Russia, collected statistics vol. 2, 1998.

Even if incomes are adjusted for the official subsistence level and local prices, Moscow is far ahead of the giants of the export trade of Western Siberia, let alone the other regions. Since the official Subsistence Minimum poverty line in 1997 was over 400,000 roubles, it is unlikely that there are many prosperous groups in many big territories of the Russian Federation. Ten depressed regions (mostly territories and republics with ethnic minorities) have experienced catastrophic deprivation with average *per capita* incomes below local minimum living standards.

Table 3.2   *Per capita* **monthly income, roubles and per cent regional subsistence levels (December 1997)**

	Roubles	*Per cent subsistence*
Moscow	3,576,000	662
St. Petersburg	1,019,000	219
North	1,029,000	191
Northwest	631,000	180
Central Russia	622,000	189
Volgo-Vyatka	539,000	153
Black Earth Area	611,000	204
Volga Region	614,000	184
Northern Caucasus	498,000	153
Ural	676,000	190
Western Siberia	1,478,000	263
Eastern Siberia	711,000	140
Far East	1,270,000	156
Kaliningrad Oblast	596,000	176
Russian Federation	1,002,000	224

Source: The Regions of Russia, collected statistics vol. 2, 1998.

However regional poverty is tied to regional prices, the abundance or scarcity of goods and the attempts by some local authorities to subsidise basic commodities. Income as a criterion of regional differentiation should be examined in the light of the cost of living, the structure of daily requirements, the standards of consumption, and the lifestyle inherited from the past (Davidova, 1998, pp.36-48). With these aspects in mind one can differentiate between 'expensive' and 'cheap' regions. In this case the cheap agrarian Black Earth Area has undoubted advantages over, for example, the Far East, where the costs of a standard food basket exceed those in cheap regions by four to five times. Besides, in European Russia food grown on personal plots is a significant part of people's aggregate income often ignored by statistics.

The Policy Response   Each of the Russian regions is trying to pull out of the crisis as best it can. A clear view of the social and political situation in different Russian regions is a vital pre-requisite to devising effective social policy. Social problems from this point of view are becoming magnified by growing variations between regional social policies, as differences between the separate regions of Russia intensify during the course of the reforms. Indeed Russia's stability depends on local capacities to heal painful economic and social issues. This, however, does not eliminate the need for a co-ordinated and efficient centralised regional policy.

The Russian North, Far East and Siberia cannot survive without Federal support. But discontent with this regional situation is successfully exploited by local authorities to cover up their orientation to narrow local interests, battles for resources and exploitation of local economic problems. They demand more from the Federal budget and try to shift responsibility onto the centre. Compradore foreign trade skilfully channelled, or even formed, by local élites, pursued against the background of the area's increased crime and corruption, has created an additional threat of crisis.

The local authorities of some other regions, which are not reform winners and where old nomenklatura have kept stronger power positions, are regulating prices to compensate for low incomes. The Ylianovsk model of conservative social support has, since the beginning of the reforms, been intentionally directed towards artificial price regulation, preserving the Soviet model of social assistance and inhibiting the course of market privatisation by a rigid administrative regulation of SME development. At an early stage of the reforms the population gained from this policy, but this cannot continue indefinitely in the new economic conditions. Price growth does not stop, while the standard of living depends, to a large extent, on other factors: the local economy, its structure and diversification, accessible sources of income, and so on. As a result, the population of the so-called 'red belt' (ruled mostly by the former communist élite, a very well-organised group in some regions since the early 1970s) described the 1995-1996 increased rate of price growth as one of the major issues of State importance, an issue rarely raised by the reform winners, in particular by Muscovites (RNIISNP, 1997).

Regional and local trends are becoming more and more important for the political and social practice of the Russian Federation. It has been emphasised at the Federal level since 1995 that regional social programmes should be based upon the principle of co-ordination of State, regional and local interests, because it is now clear that the interests of regions, and especially regional élites, could no longer be ignored (Dakhin, 1997, pp.148-53). The 'Programme of State Stimuli for the Economic Activity and Development' (1995-1998) which was adopted in 1995, takes into account the demographic situation in different Russian regions, the structure of local economies and the proportion of defence branch (MIC) in local production, the prognosis for employment/unemployment, some climate peculiarities, and so on. The programme gives priorities to supporting depressed regions, areas of military conflict, and especially the North and Far Eastern territories. It thus may be that the initial process of disintegration is very slowly changing towards some kind of new reintegration.

Employment and Enterprise Welfare

Turning now to specific areas of social policy, we will start with the most significant - employment. In Soviet times this was not merely the source of income for most households, as in all industrial societies, but also the major supplier of social services, especially housing, that are normally delivered in other countries through governments or markets. Many people continue to receive substantial enterprise benefits, and approve of this arrangement, but the process of Russian privatisation did not include adequate planning for the re-organisation of social provision, which had always been unprofitable. The vast majority of Russian enterprises are now technically in private hands. Enterprises have been encouraged to transfer their housing to municipal control and to sell their social facilities, mostly in sport, leisure and pre-school facilities, into private ownership. However employees would then lose the possibility to use the latter, since the new owners generally planned to turn social facilities into expensive private services. The main consequences of this process have been a reduction of social support for employees, a gradual change in the pattern of social protection, and a failure of local authorities, struggling with meagre budgets, to take on the additional enterprise social services.

In this fluid situation the enterprise operates as a multiplier of advantage; those enterprises doing well provide significantly higher levels of help and social benefits than do others. Rose (1992a, p.10) found in 1992 that more than 50 per cent of the urban population have at some time received help with medical care, child care, and holidays, and a third help with housing, food and other goods. A 1993 VTSIOM survey of the total population found that typically 20 per cent of the workforce felt that they could if necessary in the future count on enterprise help with housing, medical care, food, re-training, and leisure. Those that actually got help in 1993 varied, for medical care and food, from 19-20 per cent in the richer enterprises to 8-9 per cent in the poorer enterprises. In relation to discounted goods Gimpelson (1993, p.65) reports that at AZLK (a large car producer in Moscow) in 1992, the total value of consumer goods sold to workers at discount prices exceeded the annual wage fund. There is also a sharp gradient in favour of those on higher salaries within enterprises: VTSIOM found that 75 per cent of high paid workers received food or cheap goods, compared with 40 per cent of low paid workers, and housing or medical help was also at 35 per cent twice as likely to go to the higher paid. Although evidence from repeat surveys by VTSIOM throughout 1993 suggested that in all categories of employees there was a small but steady decline in enterprise support across the range of goods and services (VTSIOM, *Information Monitoring Bulletin*, 1994, p.46), a 1997 Ministry of Labour and Social Development Survey showed that 70 per cent of enterprises still provide free health care, with 48 per cent of employees stating that they have received it personally during last three years; corresponding figures for 'material support' are 55/33 per cent, for pre-school and leisure facilities 33/10 per cent, and for transport and food 50/25 per cent (Kovaleva, 1997, pp.26-32).

Employment is thus about more than money incomes, and hence labour market changes are crucial determinants of people's welfare. The response of the Russian labour market to the transformation shock has differed in many respects from that of other Eastern European countries. Notwithstanding an enormous decline in production, open unemployment is at a comparatively low level and by the sixth year of the market reforms had still not reached 10 per cent. Unemployment seems to be mitigated by the flexibility of the Russian labour market, reflected in high rates of job flow. In 1995 both Goskomstat and the Russian Economic Barometer reported a hiring rate of 19-21 per cent of average annual employment, and a separation rate of 27-28 per cent (Kapeliushnikov, 1997).

A study in 1992 of redundant workers by Gimpelson and Magun (1994, pp. 57-75) shows that more than 50 per cent were re-employed within three months, with over a quarter entering the non-State sector. This process accelerated in 1993, with about one third of medium-sized industrial firms expanding their employment throughout the year (*Russian Economic Trends*, 1994, p.90). In some areas, notably Moscow, this appears to have created a labour shortage in some sectors, particularly for skilled workers (Solovyev, 1994, p.167). In 1996 the number of unemployed grew at a lower rate than in the preceding three years (*Russian Economy in 1996*, 1997, p.62). Our own surveys reported in Chapter 9 confirm this general pattern. On the whole this pattern can be read as a favourable one for economic change - it appears to suggest a flexible labour market, with relatively modest unemployment.

However the meaning of this pattern is disputed, and highly regionally-varied. Within the literature there are three contrasting views of this situation. First are those who do not expect there to be a massive shakeout, since the labour market is already making a successful adjustment to flexible re-structuring. The evidence for this is of two types (OECD, 1996; Layard and Richter, 1994). In terms of the rate of labour turnover, the level is regarded as high at around 20 per cent, which would appear to suggest a rapid adjustment of workers to changed job opportunities. Secondly, there appears also to be a rapid adjustment of wages to market conditions.

Others dispute the significance of these figures. Labour turnover has always been high in Russia. 20 per cent is not particularly out of line with pre-transition rates. Moreover the figure conceals a large segment of the labour market which is very stable, with a smaller segment turning over employment at a furious rate - the 'churning' of jobs. The main part of the workforce may thus be very stable, amounting for some commentators to the 'hoarding' of labour by worker-controlled managements (Commander, 1995). This situation, it is argued, cannot continue but will eventually be forced to adjust, as inefficient firms are forced out of business.

In another view, the inflexibility of the labour market is also proposed, but excess employment here is argued to exist for different reasons: it is hidden for a mixture of perfectly rational administrative reasons, which will (and should) soon give way to mass unemployment. Roxborough and Schapiro (1996) for example cite the effects of the wages tax as a strong incentive to retain workers on low or no wages (e.g. through compulsory 'leave') to keep down the average wages on which the tax is calculated. Since this tax was recently overhauled, there is now an opportunity to test the effects of this interpretation. A variant of this view concerns the explanation as to what the rationality is for the retention of labour - it is kept because the patterns of enterprise work (including the provision of social welfare services) would require too much investment of time and effort to change: 'enterprises retain labour because they need it and it costs them little to keep it' (Clarke, 1996, p.52). In this view there is no particular prescription to shed labour, unless the investment necessary to create alternative activities were forthcoming.

A major reason for this is the continued, and even developed, role of the old trade unions as purveyors of enterprise welfare goods and services. 'Occupational welfare' has changed far less than State social policy (Ashwin, 1997). This has been a major factor in the willingness of Russian workers to put up with being technically on leave - i.e. employed, but with no work or wages - since as noted earlier a substantial part of their income continues to be supplied in the form of non-money goods and services.

Household Survival Beyond Employment: Income, Social Security Benefits, and Poverty

In industrial societies people generally gain the resources necessary for everyday consumption through either wage labour, family and friends, or State benefits. In post-1991 Russia, all three mechanisms continue, but others, such as growing food are also important. The reason for this has been the very sharp growth in income inequality in Russia. The ratio between incomes of the wealthiest and the poorest 10 per cent was 15.1 in 1994 (*Russia in figures*, 1997), and as noted earlier, the inter-regional income gap is also large. According to the Moscow City Committee for Statistics, the Gini co-efficient for the city is at the 0.55-0.60 level. In other words, in terms of income polarisation Moscow is ahead of Brazil. However across the whole country since 1995 there has been a halt to the growing re-distribution of incomes in favour of the higher-income groups; the income ratio of the wealthiest and the poorest 10 per cent had narrowed somewhat to 13 in 1996, and the Gini co-efficient moved down from 0.38 to 0.37.

Beyond primary employment in the labour market, many people have a mixture of secondary work, friends, family, and unwaged work to maintain their incomes. Shlapentokh (1989) and Lonkila (1997) have shown the importance of these connections under the old regime. Since 1991 they have become if anything more important - at least during the years of acute adjustment of the labour market and consumer prices. Rose (1993a, p.25) distinguishes three types of economic activity: official (employment, or pensions); uncivil (secondary work for money, or exploiting connections); social (non-monetary work, or exchange). He argues that those relying on the first type only are *vulnerable*, on the first and second are *enterprising*, and on the first and third are *defensive*; the rest are *marginal*. In his 1992 survey he found a distinctive pattern for Russia compared with other Eastern European countries in that a higher proportion were *vulnerable* (a third) and a lower proportion were *marginal* (10 per cent) (Rose, 1992b, p.21). Even so, more than a quarter of the Russian sample of working age people declared that their main job was not the most important for their standard of living. About the same proportion declared that growing food was their second main source; indeed overall more than half of the sample grew food, and more than a third reported that they grew most or some of their food during the previous year. Other important activities included exchanging help for house repairs, and giving or receiving connections for essential services, particularly medical care and medicines (over half the sample). Our own data for 1996 and 1997 confirms this general pattern.

The third main source of income is of course the State. Here the most important activities have been related to pensions, family allowances, and unemployment, and a commitment in the first Congress of Peoples' Deputies to monitor the standard of living of poorer groups. The reform of pensions came in 1991 (Barr, 1992, ch.2) when the pension fund was created, financed by a payroll tax of 28 per cent from employers and 1 per cent from employees, relieving the State budget from responsibility, and since 1991 this fund has been generating a large surplus (4 per cent GDP in 1994). The fund is subject to the control of the Ministry of Social Protection which co-ordinates policy, and calculates benefits and entitlements. Pensioners are entitled to a minimum, enhanced by the number of years' work, and previous earnings, although there is as yet no retirement test to qualify. In principle the benefit rate should be calculated automatically, but rapid inflation has politicised the rate. Current proposals by the new Ministry for Labour and Social Development are for a western-style 'funded' system (such as occupational pensions) based on genuine insurance principles, with a clear relation between lifetime payment and benefit. However this is not easy to achieve. For example the British and American government schemes still work on a pay-as-you-go basis, with each generation in effect being taxed to pay for the previous generation. A fully-funded scheme for Russia would involve the transfer of a massive amount of resources into pension funds, which would have to be built up over many years, in addition to paying for current unfunded pensioners.

Family allowances have almost by default become a significant element in the Federal policy for poorer people, since children have become increasingly represented amongst the poor. A new system has been in operation since January 1994 (*Russian Economic Trends*, 1994, p.48). All children under 18 months are entitled to an allowance of 150 per cent of the minimum wage (up from 60 per cent, and now totalling about 15 per cent of the average wage); up to six years of age the rate is 105 per cent (up from 45 per cent), and thereafter 90 per cent of the minimum wage. This is quite high by international standards. It is enhanced for families in the North. The Pension Fund disburses the money, but the funding comes from the State budget. Clearly this benefit is dependent on the political fortunes of the minimum wage level, which has not been stable: between May 1992 and May 1993 this benefit in real terms declined to one-third of its previous value, but the 1994 change reinstated it. With inflation now settling down these wild swings in benefit rates have ceased.

The cornerstone of social security under the old system was the right to work upon which other policies for income maintenance were based. Therefore the main problem looming on the horizon is the possibility of mass unemployment (even if as yet it has not materialised). Fear of this problem generated the Employment Law drafted in the autumn of 1990, and formally adopted on 15 January 1991. This officially signalled the end of the right/duty to work by imposing a 1 per cent payroll levy to generate funds to finance unemployment benefit, re-training, public community work, and career guidance (Standing, 1991). However unemployment benefit has not been as big a cost to the government as was expected in the years from 1991. This is partly because few claimed it, but were voluntarily moving between jobs; it was also probably because the rate of benefit was so low. For the first three months it was 100 per cent continuation of wages, then 75 per cent from the employment service for the next three months, 60 per cent for the next three months and 45 per cent for the next three months. The minimum is equal to the minimum wage (i.e. 10 per cent of average wages). Since this is calculated on the basis of the previous year's wages, and is not indexed, with the high inflation rates of 1992 and 1993 most recipients were in effect on the minimum. However with inflation coming under relative control, and unemployment rising steadily, if not dramatically, the cost of this benefit are escalating. Conditions of receipt include work-seeking, and the acceptance of at least the second appropriate job offer. Benefits are paid from the 1991 Employment Fund. Proposals for a flat rate benefit (to simplify administration), and means tested unemployment assistance (for those whose benefits are exhausted) continue to be discussed.

Beneath this discussion about incomes is the question of poverty. In June 1994, using a Ministry of Labour basket of essential foodstuffs for the poverty line, *Russian Economic Trends* calculated that 14 per cent of the population were in poverty - the same as in the mid-1980s (Ellman, 1990, pp.147-48). However, calculated on this basis, it had peaked at 36 per cent at the beginning of 1993. Rising average incomes, combined with a slow-down in inflation (which when high particularly affects those on benefits which are only periodically uprated) appear to have resulted in this improvement in 1994, although the new 1994 rates of family allowances must also have helped. Since the minimum pension is currently around

20 per cent of the average wage or half the Ministry of Labour Subsistence Minimum poverty line, and the average pension is around 31 per cent of the average wage or 80 per cent of the subsistence level, the pension rate might be expected to determine the poverty rate. However, average pensions have closely matched the average wage since the mid-1980s, suggesting that the image of impoverished Russian pensioners should be replaced by impoverished children, particularly since it has been and still is quite common for pensioners to also take on paid work.

Goskomstat official data in 1996 suggested that average *per capita* monthly incomes of 22.6 per cent of households were below the Ministry of Labour subsistent minimum. In 1997 this figure decreased to 20.9 per cent (Goskomstadt, 1997, p.69). The Centre of Complex Social research has identified three levels of absolute poverty: destitution, indigence and need. In 1995 about 12 per cent of the Russian population were destitute, with incomes lower than the cost of the Subsistence Minimum set of foodstuffs; up to 20 per cent were indigent; and a further 30 per cent were needy (Koval, 1996). Our own project data, processed using a multi-dimensional methodological approach based around Townsend's model of poverty, estimated that 8 per cent of our respondents from labour market 'crisis' groups in 1997 were indigent or destitute, 15 per cent suffered from acute poverty and 24 per cent were in need (see Chapter 8).

Surveys in 1992 and 1993 by the Russian Longitudinal Monitoring Survey and Goskomstat respectively, reported by *Russian Economic Trends* (1994, p.47), show that the composition of the poor was significantly tilted towards children: for both 1992 and 1993 the proportion of children in poverty (at around 40 per cent) was about twice that of men over 60. The reduction in poverty, reported as halving between January and February 1994, was related to the new higher rates of family allowances from January, however this does not mean that children have featured less centrally in Russian poverty in recent years. We have found in our own project that in 1997 the primary cause of poverty, and especially profound poverty, was the respondents' family circumstances: one-parent families with children under 18; families with many children; families of the disabled. Among families with one parent or many children, the number of those who found themselves in very poor material circumstances exceeded the average by a ratio of three. Since the rate of pregnancy amongst young unmarried women is growing rapidly (in contrast to the overall birth rate which has fallen sharply in the 1990s), family and child poverty is likely to get worse (UNICEF, 1999). 1997 VTSIOM survey data suggest that this is not for want of public concern. Russians consider that as a first priority social support should be provided for single mothers and single old people (35 per cent), families with children (32 per cent), disabled and poor (29 per cent), and pensioners (24 per cent). In the eyes of ordinary Russians, migrants, refugees, unemployed, and veterans need State social support far less (7-14 per cent) (Khakhulina, 1997, pp.39-45).

In Russia today levels of property, housing and material security are very disparate. Bessonova and Krapchan (1994) distinguish nine types of household, of which only two (those at the highest and the lowest levels) show a marked relationship between type of property, housing and incomes. It is precisely this general absence of any significant relationship between a person's housing and - to some extent - property situation and their income that leads Russians to connect poverty only with income level: in the opinion of 70 per cent of Russians, poor housing conditions or poor medical services are not evidence of poverty, if the family's income is sufficient. Thus in Russia the standard set of property markers of a secure (but not wealthy) life are as follows: 'a dacha, a car and a flat' (Zubova and Khakhulina, 1991).

Poverty Themes

Survival Mozhina and Popov's (1994) longitudinal research into families in four Russian cities showed that people's approach to maintaining their material circumstances is displayed, first and foremost, by families providing for themselves through work on their allotment or dacha land and through more active work at home (piecework, sewing, repairs). The second most significant way of adapting to the economic situation was to take on extra, unregistered work, while the third was to look for a new job. Regardless of the level of welfare, the first thing everyone economises on is clothes and footwear, either through cheaper goods, or none at all. Further headings under which people made savings differed sharply. In second place, the poor economise on food, while everyone else cuts back on leisure and entertainment spending. In the third place, for the average this was food, but for the well-off it was day-to-day household expenditure. Overall, the research showed that, where the family has some resources, they try to economise on food last, after every other significant area of expenditure in the family budget.

Krasil'nikova (1996) also provides evidence of this. In the lowest decile, only one per cent replied 'never' to the question about how often they had to economise on foodstuffs, while in the highest decile there were 24 per cent. Those in this decile who economised did so on completely different things from the poor, and the same applied to the averagely well-off. Thus, 14 per cent in the lowest decile never had to economise on meat products; 41 per cent in the highest never did, and here some people's economies related to various meat products and others to delicatessen meat products. Similarly, we took data on the structure of household economies in various income groups into account when developing our research questionnaire.

Identity   Rukavishnikov (1994), Gudkov (1996) and many others have shown that the generally accepted criteria of differentiation by property status have still not entered the social consciousness. Therefore, responses to questions about 'boundaries between wealth and poverty', like responses to questions about the respondents' levels of material welfare, are not only linked to their real material circumstances, but also to their ideas of the income level which would allow them to fully satisfy their families' needs at current prices, and to their ideas about wealth in general. People who had the same level of income frequently placed themselves in different categories. This self-assessment depended on place of residence (city, medium-sized town or village) and on age (the younger the respondents were, the higher their income demands, in order that they could place themselves in a particular group).

Gudkov argues that most people give a low assessment of their own material circumstances because of a sharp change in the level of aspirations and their reference system, and this is connected with the fact that a previously closed society has found itself facing new standards of living and new models of social achievement, and, correspondingly, new criteria for self-assessment - criteria which only a relatively small part of society can meet. Views about what is 'normal' life - and which embody a certain level of demand - are a concentrated expression of this. Only three per cent of respondents maintained that they themselves were living normally, and 28 per cent that they had a normal life ten years ago. But 22 per cent thought that 'to live normally' meant to live as the well-off strata abroad do, while another 37 per cent thought that it meant to live as the well-off strata in Russia do.

Russian citizens predominantly view the 'subsistence minimum' as the level of income which should provide a socially acceptable standard of living. Most Russians considered the marker of poverty to be 'lack of means to live like most other people', and only about a fifth of respondents perceive poverty as 'lack of means for the most essential (items)' (Zubova, and Khakhulina, 1991). In other words, in Russia there are practically no differences between the standards of consumption which groups with different levels of income would try to achieve: even respondents from the poorest families were not differentiated by modest aspirations. As Chernina (1994) has noted, Russians have an intuitive definition of poverty which is very similar to Townsend's concept.

Employment The standard of living falls sharply in the families of unemployed people, and in families where there are small children this fall as a rule takes them below the poverty line. Osadchaya (1997) provides evidence of a sharp deterioration in the social well-being of unemployed people, of a growing sense of anxiety, and of a reduction in tolerance and in satisfaction with life for these families. According to her data, after losing their jobs, half the families experienced problems in family relations and in bringing up children.

Evidence on the response of unemployed people to their labour market situation is mixed. Popov, Sazonov and Reznikova (1993) found that only 7 per cent of their unemployed respondents declared that it would suit them to draw unemployment benefit for as long as possible, while the vast majority (80 per cent) wanted to get into work as quickly as possible. However our own data, discussed in detail in Chapter 9, suggests that 36 per cent of those who took part in the survey reported that they were neither pleased with nor distressed by the change in their usual way of life, while 15 per cent said they were pleased to have more free time. Only 28 per cent (45 per cent of men and 22 per cent of women) indicated that they were spending most of their time seeking work; in parallel, 53 per cent were occupied in the home (64 per cent of women and 23 per cent of men). In other words, although a significant section of the unemployed would like to work in principle, and even feel to some extent oppressed by their situation, that section is not actively trying to get work and, on the whole, has accepted a new way of life.

Other researchers have also recorded the way in which unemployed people tend to highlight the positive aspects of their position. In research conducted by Gordienko and his colleagues (1996), only 47 per cent of the unemployed thought that there was nothing good about unemployment, while 52 per cent found various positive things in it. Among these were a great deal of free time (23 per cent saw something positive in this), unemployment benefit (17 per cent), the possibility of devoting more attention to family and children (13 per cent of women and three per cent of men). Other significant pluses of unemployment were the potential to look at oneself in a new way, a feeling of freedom and new possibilities, and a chance to rest - with the last more typical of women. Since there is a general social perception that unemployment does not lead to a lowering of social status, but rather is an undeserved temporary unpleasantness, there is sympathy towards the sufferer, and thus it is not surprising that most of the unemployed themselves also perceive their own status with a degree of composure.

In her Novosibirsk research projects, Chernina (1994, 1996) tried to answer the question of whether the poor were starting to split off from the general mass of the population into a social stratum with particular behavioural and cultural traits. However she found that household economic activity is a common feature in all categories. On average, 46 per cent indicated its overriding importance, although in prosperous families the figure was only 39 per cent; furthermore, she noted a growth trend in levels of activity in the household economy in recent years. She also noted that the chief way of handling a crisis situation was orientated towards mobilising personal resources. Strategies that are 'defensive' in nature (such as the sale of property) figured in only 10 per cent of responses; and the proportion of passive behaviour, such as receipt of outside help, was extremely small (2 per cent) - although the number of respondents who declared that they could not cope with their problems themselves and needed outside help was almost ten times higher.

In analysing the interdependence of poverty and unemployment, Chernina recorded that the poor unemployed experienced multivariate deprivation and psychological stress, and that 'interesting work' and 'stable living conditions' were highly significant values for them by comparison with other unemployed people. Some of Chernina's results allowed us to hypothesise that the poverty which has appeared as a result of job losses has contributed to painful changes in people's circles of social contacts. Given that we are not talking about all the unemployed - only those who, as a consequence of losing their job, have joined the ranks of the poor - these results do not contradict other research data, which show that most unemployed people maintain the same circle of social contacts.

Overall, the results she obtained led Chernina to conclude that a culture of poverty may be beginning to form, apparently manifesting itself through:

> firstly, the poor's tendencies to limit consumption to a range of poor quality goods, products and services; secondly, their economies on all expenditure, starting with food; thirdly, their denying themselves certain types of consumption behaviour (health maintenance, educational improvement,

tourism, etc.); fourthly... their marginalisation through loneliness or loss of individual social contacts (1994, p.60).

This prospect - the development of a Russian underclass - is the subject of our next project, in which we are extending our study of the dynamic formation of the poorest strata into the poorest regions of the Northern Caucasus, particularly Vladikavkaz, 100 miles east of Grozny, capital city of Chechnia.

Health, Illness and Health Care

Here, the main policy problem is the under funding of the health service, which has been at relatively low levels for many years. Substantial wage increases were granted in 1986 to bring medical staff pay up to average levels, and promises were made in the 12th 5-year plan to inject substantial increases in funds for new technology, drugs, and so on. These remained largely unfulfilled. In June 1994 the average wage in the health care sector was 75 per cent of the average industrial wage (*Current Digest of the Post Soviet Press*, 1994, vol.46, no.33, p.22). The budget for 1994 does seem to have increased the intended allocation to 2.8 per cent of GNP, up from 2 per cent two years before, and by 1998 this had reached 3.8 per cent (UNDP, 1999, p. 151). However the main source of new money comes from the Federal Medical Insurance Fund set up in 1993, itself derived from a 3.6 per cent payroll tax although only about three-quarters of this money was spent on health care in 1993, the rest being kept as surplus (Akopyan, 1994, p.7).

Interestingly 3.2 of the 3.6 per cent will go to the regional level, where social budgets are increasingly being controlled. As with the other insurance funds, there is a great deal of uncertainty as to who really controls these huge sums of money, since they are not clearly separated from each other or from direct state interference. In 1995 an attempt was made to revise the operating model of mandatory medical insurance. A draft law reflected the interests of health care system administrators and under it market regulation was to be replaced by State regulation whereby territorial funds were to report to the executive local authorities. Non-State insurance companies were to be excluded from the range of medical insurance interests. The Institute for Economy in Transition on the other hand considered that such a law would undermine incentives to maintain and improve the quality of health care services. It argued that problems should be solved by rejecting the principles of State medical insurance as the basis of health care organisation in a market economy (*Russian Economy in 1996*, 1997, p.119).

Other sources of new money will in the future be private. There has always been a flow of private money to physicians in the form of tips or bribes to gain access to services, and in more recent years the shortage of medicines resulted in a growing illicit market. Budget caps on hospitals which have now been imposed, combined with an explosion in the price of pharmaceuticals (many of which were in the past imported from Central Europe), have forced health carers to charge for services. In his 1992-3 surveys Rose reported that half of the population had to use connections to get goods and services difficult to find, the majority of which were medicines and doctors (Rose, 1992a, p.16). An estimated 10-15 per cent of the population have been receiving health care from their place of work (Preker and Feachem, 1994, p.309), but as we saw earlier these services are, albeit slowly, on the decline. Should this decline accelerate, it may leave an already stretched health service with a substantial additional burden.

1996 witnessed a number of changes and debates about alternatives for the future of health care: the combination of the Ministry of Health and the Medical Industry into a single Health Ministry, and the State Duma debates over draft amendments to the Law 'On Medical Insurance' to reflect the regulation of three special-interest groups: medical administration, medical funds, and medical insurance companies, including the private sector (*Russian Economy in 1996*, 1997, pp.120-23). However to date the Russian Government and the Health Ministry haven't yet agreed a common model for health care. There are a number of proposals which have been discussed in Russia since the adoption of the package of medical laws in 1993 by the RF Supreme Soviet, but none of these intentions have been finalised: extending medical insurance along Western European lines; the commitment of the former Ministry of Health to retain the main health facilities; de-centralisation to the regions; public ownership, and also the opposite suggestion made by the Russian President in 1994, to privatise medical facilities (*Social Security*, 1/4/1994; Akopyan, 1994, p.8). The main problems of health care reform in Russia - the sensible use of available money, the inadequate co-ordination of different financial bodies operating in health care, and the lack of efficient mechanisms of public control over medical insurance funds at different levels, stay unsolved.

The poor health record, to which the 1980s anti-alcohol campaign discussed in Chapter 2 was a reaction, has continued to get worse (and

Yeltsin's public behaviour cannot have helped). For example by 1992 average alcohol consumption had reached the same level as in 1984 before the campaign. At the same time the increase (from 62 to 65) in life expectancy for men that resulted from the campaign declined to 62 again. By 1994 this had dropped still further to 59 years, and by 1997 to 58 years, directly as a result of alcohol consumption (Nemtsov and Shkolnikov, 1994, p.13). Price liberalisation has resulted in the comparative decline in the price of vodka compared with food for example. In addition new sources of ill-health have appeared. Diphtheria, cholera, measles and general intestinal infections have spread across Russia in higher and higher numbers since 1991. For example diphtheria cases have doubled annually since 1990, when 30 people died in a year, to January 1994, when 50 people died in a month, the main reason being a less than 50 per cent coverage of immunisation (Eratova, 1994, p.24).

One of the main reasons blamed for many of these illnesses is the pollution of drinking water. An official report by the Ministry for Environmental Protection in August 1994 admits that for almost half of the population, drinking water standards are below official limits (Shapetkina, 1994, p.17). In 1993, 2,992 died as a result of poor quality drinking water, and many more were ill. In the absence of money to invest in cleaning up supplies, the population is urged to boil any water to be drunk (Yermakova, 1994, pp.17-18). In a recent survey as part of a project on environmental movements, it was found that 80 per cent of the population in Moscow do in fact boil drinking water, compared to 50 per cent in Estonia, and 3 per cent in Hungary (Manning, 1998). The second main reason for illness is pollution in the atmosphere. The Moscow Chief Medical Administration Report for 1993 records that respiratory diseases are the most common, both amongst adults and children, and that there was an increase of over 20 per cent for children between 1992 and 1993 (*Current Digest of the Post Soviet Press*, 1994, vol. 46, no. 33, p. 20).

Paediatricians note the universal physical and mental decline of children. Many indicators of children's physical health have worsened appreciably. School reform has resulted in a stratified system for Russian children, and many of them end up not only without a school education but also without school meals and medical services. The Chairman of the Russian Union of Paediatricians, Baranov, states that today only about half of the younger generation in the Russian Federation meets the standard for mental development. In general, today's teenager can be compared, in terms of physical development, to young people of their age group in the 1950s (*Current Digest of the Post Soviet Press*, 1998, vol.50, no.12, p.10).

Overall this increase in illness, and continued underfunding of health care, on top of the general disruption to people's lives caused by the economic and political changes since 1991, has had an inevitable effect on birth and death rates. In Moscow birthrates almost halved from 12 per 1,000 people in 1989 to 7 per 1,000 in 1993. Mortality rates have increased in the same period from 12 to 17 per 1,000. In addition about three million abortions are performed in Russia every year. Two out of three pregnancies end in abortions, which is the second highest figure in Europe (behind Romania). One-child families continue to predominate. In combination, these rates have thus moved from balance to severe imbalance, with an inevitable decline in the population. Outside Moscow, in 49 regions (about two-thirds of the total country) in 1993 there was a decline in the population, compared with a decline in 41 regions in 1992 and in 33 regions in 1991 (Russian Federation State Statistical Committee, 1997, p.10). Although demographers say that in 1995 the population stopped declining, the statistics are still alarming. In 1991-1995 the overall birthrate dropped by 23.2 per cent and the overall death rate increased by 31.6 per cent (Konstantinova, 1998, p.15). The total population is expected to shrink from 149 million in 1992 to 140 million in 2015 (Vishnevsky, 1998); by 1997 it had declined to 147.5 million (Goskomstat, 1997, p.3). Zaslavzkaya (1997, p.171) has estimated that the total social and demographic costs of the reforms amount to 650 million years of human life. Even if the peak of demographic crisis, which hit Russia very hard in 1992-1994, has passed Russia probably will not emerge from the overall demographic crisis for several more decades.

Housing

Although almost free, housing was a traditional source of dissatisfaction under the old regime, with long queues, small flats, and a monotonous reliance on high rise architecture. New problems in recent years include homelessness and begging, as housing has become a major sector of the privatisation field. At first the rate of privatisation was slow. With few buyers interested in the very high prices, and the unattractive prospects of taking on maintenance and other charges, there was little point in householders becoming owners, unless they were leaving the city, or had other reasons to want to move anyway. In 1992 and 1993 activity rose, partly as a result of government encouragement, and the setting of apparent deadlines for completing the transaction. However since the deadlines were never put into practice, what started in 1992-3 with some vigour stalled in 1994 at a quarter of the 1993 rate. Nevertheless, by 1997 half of all flats were in private ownership (*Russian Economic Trends*, 1994, p.84; Dmytriev, 1997).

With the introduction of a new system of charges for maintenance costs in January 1994, charges are projected to grow from 15 per cent of overheads in 1994 to 100 per cent in 1998 (Rubtsov 1994). Since 1993, maintenance expenditure in an average household budget has doubled: from 10 per cent in 1993 up to 20 per cent in 1997 (*Russian economy in the first six months of 1997*, 1997, p.86). However VTSIOM monitoring data shows that 50 per cent of Russians considered maintenance charges as too high a burden for household income. Only a third of respondents in 1997 stated with confidence that maintenance costs never constituted a serious difficulty for family budgets (*Information Monitoring Bulletin*, November 1997, p.44). Many commentators have therefore argued that now is not the time for radical housing reform. For example throughout 1997 the Vice-Premier of the Russian Government, Nemtsov, repeatedly declared the urgent necessity to revise the current system of housing maintenance costs projected to rise imminently to 100 per cent. The argument was that the State should take into account the financial situation of households where many working members have been unpaid for a long time due to wages debts. Conducting such housing reform requires gradual development with proper social adjustment, otherwise it is achievable only by means of force which would drive up social costs beyond any beneficial economic effect (Khakhulina, 1997).

In any society the high costs of new building and the amount of value locked up in existing property makes the issue of housing finance highly significant. In Russia this issue is being tackled in a rather haphazard manner. Initially, free privatisation to existing tenants, while confirming the existing privileges of favoured occupants, changed the flow of finance very little, and rents, energy and maintenance charges remained nominal. In principle reforming the system of charges should raise revenue that can be re-cycled to invest in the improvement of buildings, although it may in reality end up as a means of reducing Federal expenditure from other budgets. Two Presidential decrees (in December 1993 and June 1994) have also tackled the financing of housing by authorising mortgage lending on the value of a property, housing savings accounts, and local government construction funds for low-income housing. However as is the case in other areas of social policy, the exact mechanisms for actually implementing these decrees are not fully in place, for example the means for an institutional lender to repossess a property in the case of default by the borrower - i.e. eviction. The Ministry of Finance has suggested that enterprises may be able to provide guarantees for their employees, but as and when such enterprise support is run down, or cannot be provided by insolvent institutions, there will continue to be a gap in this part of the financial circle. Recent VTSIOM data show that in 1997 about 20 per cent of enterprises continued to provide their existing employees with free housing, but only 5 per cent of respondents had received this kind of social support for the first time during the previous two years (*Information Monitoring Bulletin*, September-October 1997, pp.30-31).

As far as construction is concerned, there has been a virtual collapse of State housing starts, with a small boom (from a very low start) of private single family houses. Figures for St. Petersburg show a fall of 90 per cent for 1993 over 1989 in State housing construction, but there are 10,000 private houses under construction (Baranov, 1994, p.159). There is undoubtedly a long way to go in terms of total space, public or private (*Current Digest of the Post Soviet Press*, 1997, vol. 49, no. 1, p.10).

Two further consequences of the state of Russian housing may be observed. One is the perennial difficulty of matching labour market flexibility and housing market flexibility. We have seen that there is growing evidence of flexibility in the labour market, with approximately 20 per cent of the labour force changing jobs in the last year. Clearly many of these workers can find new jobs in the same city, and with public transport still cheap and effective, this would not require relocation. However any attempt to move workers around the country, as production needs change, is severely hampered by the lack of anything approaching a normal housing market (Layard and Richter, 1994, p.88).

The second consequence is the growth in homelessness. As in Western Europe, estimates for the level of this problem are very difficult to agree on, partly due to the invisibility of the problem, and partly due to disagreements over the definition. An estimate of 30-50,000 homeless has been given for 1994 in St. Petersburg (Orebro Workshop, 1994, p.34). For Moscow, a similar figure of between 30,000 and 100,000 is reported by Andrusz (1994, p.15), 10 per cent of whom are estimated to be the victims of housing transaction crime (ibid., p.22).

Overall, housing is a big issue both in terms of its political significance as a continuing source of dissatisfaction, and as site for potentially large flows of finance. As is the case for State industrial enterprises, privatisation has in most instances been a paper exercise. However it is happening, and a market is emerging, which will no doubt grow in size and effect in the future.

4 Project Methodology

Скоро сказка сказывается, не скоро дело делается
The tale is soon told, but the job is not soon done

As in the Soviet period, official sources, including State statistical sources, offer extremely limited data on social activity. They cover information on numbers of unemployed people, on living standards, and on the proportion of the population below the poverty line. At the same time these data have attracted valid criticism: they are open to dispute, and often correspond little to internationally accepted statistical indicators. But their main deficiency is that they cannot be used to reconstruct the actual life circumstances of most of the population, especially people affected by the labour market crisis, who not only fall outside the field of statistical calculations, but also escape the observation of sociological services and centres for the study of public opinion, which carry out representative surveys.

For example, the Russia-Europe Centre for Economic Policy gives the following comparison of data on rates of poverty in Russia:

> According to official data, in the first quarter of 1997, 21 per cent of the Russian population were living below the poverty line. This is evidence of the maintenance of a trend which has already been active for a long time, towards a reduction in poverty rates, in so far as this indicator is lower than the corresponding indicator for the first quarter of 1996 and almost equal to the average for 1996. However, data obtained from other sources show the situation in a different light. According to calculations made on the basis of the 'Russian Longitudinal Monitoring Survey', the extent of poverty is growing. From the poverty survey conducted by these authors, it turns out that the proportion of families below the poverty line has been gradually increasing - from 13 per cent in November 1993 to 29 per cent in October 1995 and 36 per cent in October 1996 (Russia-Europe Centre for Economic Policy, 1997, p.89).

The contentious nature of official statistical data is also displayed in an example which is typical of the official approach to defining social indicators of poverty. Since the end of 1996, Goskomstat has been calculating the cost of an enlarged basket of consumer goods, containing 25 basic necessities. Moreover, this new basket of consumer goods, unlike the previous one, has official status, in that - in accordance with the law - it defines the Subsistence Minimum standard. The composition of the basket is based on the 'Methodological recommendations for calculating the Subsistence Minimum in the regions of the Russian Federation', established by the Ministry of Labour and Social Policy on 10 November 1992. According to specialist assessments:

> the new basket of consumer goods envisages a level of consumption of the goods in it, which is lower than World War II food rations. Especially striking are the standards for consumption of meat and meat products: the 25 products in the basket of consumer goods include 8.4 kg of meat. Nevertheless, the cost of this basket defines the Subsistence Minimum - or poverty line - in the regions and is used to calculate amounts of financial transfers from the Federal Budget (Russia-Europe Centre for Economic Policy, 1997, pp.243-4).

People in Russia today are paying the price for such 'scientifically-based' calculations, and for action taken on the basis of them. Birman notes that the well-known 'Gini coefficient' is widely used to characterise social differentiation in Russia. But how can the relevant calculations be trusted, when:

> in the 'household budgets' indicator, there are no data on the incomes and outgoings of the very rich and the very poor; nor is it any better to calculate figures according to the same 1989 coefficient for different countries, since they have largely differing structures of consumption (Birman, 1997, p.7).

We have tried to find a reliable and valid means of overcoming the problems posed. We took into account the specific nature of the research 'field' - the field of social policy, encompassing the issue of how to organise the lives of socially vulnerable groups who need social support and protection. We selected two methods of information gathering: interviews with social policy actors and with people affected by the labour market crisis. The latter included those who were on compulsory unpaid leave or on short-time working at the instigation of their management, those under notice of redundancy, the registered unemployed and those who had found work again after a period of registered unemployment.

The method we adopted to locate these groups was to analyse segments of the labour market where we found that they were clearly discernible. This, of course, is not the only possible method, but it was important in a country which for decades had not recognised unemployment and its secondary phenomena, such as, for example, compulsory unpaid leave.

Typical VTSIOM data shows that, over recent years, unemployment itself has moved into the first rank of problems which worry Russians. In January 1997, 61 per cent of respondents assessed it as being the most acute problem facing Russian society; in January 1998, the figure was 66.1 per cent, but had risen as high as 74 per cent in small towns, Siberia and the Far East. By comparison, as recently as 1995, this problem had ranked far below crime, absence of law and order, the economic crisis and the impoverishment of the population. In addition, the problem of unemployment is increasingly being seen in the context of growing stratification into rich and poor (43 per cent in 1997 saw this as important; 48 per cent in 1998). Against the background of the gradual impoverishment of the mass of people, awareness of social class is becoming more widespread (Golov, 1998, p.4; *Information Monitoring Bulletin*, 1996, p.84).

Household level interviews

Let us begin with a description of the interviews with people affected by the labour market crisis. The interviews were carried out at household level, because we were trying to make sense of a social situation where macro-level and meso-level problems (for example, the structural reorganisation of industry, the crisis taking place in a number of sectors, or the different paces and methods of reform in different regions) were superimposed on micro-level problems (household structure, state of health). The use of a short questionnaire, a representative survey, quantitative methods of analysis or any combination of these did not fit our research focus. We were convinced of this by secondary analysis of our 1994 survey on employment problems (Shkaratan and Tikhonova, 1996). We therefore preferred a method employing partially pre-coded interviews, which enabled the existence of problems and relationships of one kind or another to be established. Although this would not permit a reliable evaluation of the scale and extent of the various positions recorded, in our case - where it was important to understand the essence of the various phenomena and the causation underlying them, rather than their extent - this drawback could be ignored.

The specific reasons for using partially pre-coded interviews in our research actually lay in the following. Such interviews are usually carried out on small samples and using open questions. Our research objectives involved not only comparing and analysing the interaction between macro- and micro-level factors, but also comparing the situations in different regions on the one hand, and in respondent groups with differing employment statuses on the other. This meant an increased number of questions and a broader-based sample. Given that the research covered three regions and four groups of people in each region (i.e. 12 relatively independent objects for research), the sample for each of them, even using in-depth interviews, could not be smaller than 15-20 people.

The total number of respondents, therefore, had to be over 200. We should add that our groups could (and did) include people experiencing the most severe socio-economic deprivation; and experience in other sociological research has shown that this contingent often has difficulty in expressing itself, especially in response to open questions.

In drawing up the questionnaire, therefore, the specific nature of our research objects was taken into account as far as possible, and the majority of the questions were of a closed and semi-closed type, although, in fact, this did not rule out the addition of any opinions not considered when the schedule of questions and response variables was being drawn up. We took into account that respondents usually try to draw their answers from the list of those offered and rarely get the chance to express opinions outside the bounds of the variables already formulated. Therefore, in all cases where it was essential to understand and investigate the structured nature of respondents' views and of personal opinions, we used open questions in both phases of the survey. After content analysis, most of them were coded.

The use of a large number of closed questions in the interviews naturally meant that the questions themselves had to be of high quality. Almost all the closed questions were therefore taken from interview questionnaires that had already been used during other studies and had worked well, both in the way they encompassed all possible respondent positions, and as regards the importance of the results obtained. These included questions from the western social researchers such as Townsend and Rose, and Russian social researchers such as Chernina and Magun, and from monitoring surveys carried out by RIISNP and VTSIOM. Besides the quality of the closed questions used, this approach to creating research instruments ensured comparability of the results obtained from the survey of unemployed people in Russia with data from in-depth interviews with unemployed people in Europe, on the one hand, and of data for members of the groups affected by labour market crisis with data for other Russians, on the other hand.

This allowed a quite large body of data (480 interviews with 274 people, taking into account substitutions and the two stages of the research) to be used to capture certain phenomena and trends, which it would not have been possible to record using statistical methods, quantitative representative research methods or the classical in-depth interview method with really small samples.

Social policy actor interviews

Our survey of social policy actors played a significant part in the research, and information on the composition of the sample is given below. These people - using the criterion of how well-informed they were expected to be - were chosen as experts on the problems that we were interested in. We wanted to know how knowledgeable these policy actors were, and hence to explore whether declared policies were actually being implemented. This would enable us to compare official policy pronouncements in three respects: with what we understood from other sources to be actually in operation; with the likely impact on households; and with the understanding and support expressed by local policy actors. Like people affected by the labour market crisis, they were surveyed twice: in the spring of 1996 and 1997.

Generally, the expert survey method presupposes that people are selected not only on the basis of their formal professional status (a rule which we observed), but also as a result of testing their knowledge and on the basis of attestations from colleagues: we were able to achieve this because of the high rank of a significant number of the respondents and the specific nature of personal relations within the nomenklatura/bureaucratic milieu. However, the representativeness of a group of experts should be assessed not so much statistically as in terms of quality indicators, as well as of the nature and quality of argument in the respondents' freely expressed opinions: here too, it became possible to recognise, with some reservations, that our social policy actor respondents were experts.

Unfortunately, the method we employed to obtain information did not always provide us with reliable results, since the accuracy of the data obtained was limited both by the respondents' own practical experience and by their professional and - most especially - their personal/corporate interests. It is also almost impossible to avoid the 'traps' inherent in this type of interviewing method, which are described in the literature. In the first place, the sampling of actors on the basis of formal characteristics such as professional status narrowed our range of competent informants; in the second place, the same principle brought non-competent people into the sample; and in the third place, the questions put often fell into the researchers' areas of interest, but were not within the competence of the respondents.

Our case particularly bore out these well-known drawbacks of surveys of expert actors. This is because all Russian officials, businessmen, managers and trade union leaders were and still are neophytes in the world of the market, and neophytes in the new institutional structures which have existed for only six or seven years. To improve the reliability of our results, we increased the size of the sample by comparison with the customary number, we conducted repeat interviews with the same people after a year, and we took into account in our second survey (in 1997) the results of our parallel survey of members of the groups in labour market crisis who were 'under our respondents' wing'.

In drawing up the interview questions, we attempted to reflect the objectives of the research to the greatest possible extent, by emphasising above all the importance of the specialists' personal opinion in the questions. Conducting the survey in two phases helped to reveal the essence of the respondents' positions, and later to assess the level of congruity of their opinions on the most important points. Although most of the questions were repeated in the second survey, some others were then asked for the first time. The inclusion of new questions in the second survey enabled us not only to uncover changes in the processes which both we and the social policy actors had reflected in 1996, but also to detect processes and phenomena which had either not been accounted for at that time, or were not happening a year previously. It was also interesting to find out how the actors' attitudes to current events and their assessments had changed, and what changes there had been in the degree to which they were informed about, interested in and involved in tackling social problems.

In conducting the interviews, we used the customary method of developing a survey of experts:

- an indication of the crux of the issue being researched and of our motives for approaching the person in question as a specialist;
- information demonstrating the competence of the social policy actor: area of work, time spent working in this area, skills and qualifications;
- fuller information on the order (and the content) of the proposed questions;
- putting the questions as formulated on each issue, inviting either free expression and comment and then asking their permission to point out things that have been omitted, vulnerable aspects or dubious items in the argument, or else inviting them to put their case for formulating the question differently;

- additional remarks, comments and suggestions.
                    (Gordon and Chertikhina, 1983; Sheregi, 1996, pp.63-67).

It could be said that the survey of social policy actors we carried out, despite all its particular features just mentioned, is closest in nature to a 'focused' interview (Merton, Fiske and Kendall, 1992).

If we were to draw a preliminary conclusion, it would be that the interviews we gathered justified our fairly sceptical attitude to official documents, and gave us a franker evaluation of the situation around social issues, reflecting the positions of actual or potential subjects of social policy in Russia. The respondents selected, who were social policy and employment policy actors, represented social groups from the Russian élite and from middle-ranking officials whose type of activities brings them closest to an understanding of these very important issues.

Household Research Methodology

General Description of Sample

The research was longitudinal in nature (the respondents, heads of households, were interviewed twice, with a 12-13 month interval). This enabled extra information to be obtained on a number of issues that arose during the first stage, and also helped to trace both the effectiveness of and reasons for choosing various family (household) survival strategies, and the respondents' labour market behaviour. The first survey took place in March/April 1996. The pre-coded interview method was used to survey 240 people (100 in Moscow, 80 in St. Petersburg and 60 in Voronezh).

The respondents were divided into four groups: 1) *unemployed* people officially registered with the Employment Service; 2) employees in *insecure employment* (on compulsory unpaid or part-paid leave, or on short-time working); 3) people under formal *notice of redundancy*; 4) people who had *found work after a period of registered unemployment*. Numerically, in the first stage of the research, these groups were distributed as follows: group 1 - 70; group 2 - 58; group 3 - 57; group 4 - 55.

Analysis of the results of stage one of the survey (in 1996) demonstrated the necessity to employ a more detailed respondent classification. Therefore, in stage two of the survey, a further three groups were added to the first four:

- unemployed people not registered with the Employment Service (in some cases, removed from the register because of the length of their period of unemployment) - the '*de facto* unemployed';
- normally employed people with no experience of unemployment in the past ('normally employed' people were, for the most part, members of the group under notice of redundancy at stage one of the research, who had managed to find work straight away, without any period of unemployment);
- self-employed people.

At stage two, the respondents were distributed numerically among the groups as follows: registered unemployed - 47; in insecure employment - 26; under notice of redundancy - 3; found work after a period of unemployment - 104; *de facto* unemployed - 30; normally employed with no history of registered unemployment - 25; self-employed - 4.

At stage one, random sampling was used to select the registered unemployed group from Employment Service records, controlled to ensure that the respondents' socio-demographic characteristics matched statistical data on the composition of the unemployed. Each person received an explanation of the purpose of the research we were undertaking; they were told that it had to be a two-stage process, regardless of whether the person was still on the unemployment register in a year's time. Interviewing started after the respondent's agreement to continued co-operation had been obtained; respondents were required to give their names and addresses, and this information was subsequently checked by ES staff.

The addresses of employees under notice of redundancy, and also of people who had returned to work after unemployment, were provided by ES staff. A sample population was compiled from the full list offered. The interviewers then got in touch with the respondents by telephone or home visit and, on receipt of agreement to co-operate, the respondents were interviewed in their own homes. In rare cases (in particular, in Voronezh) there were visits to enterprises which were implementing mass redundancies, but the proportion of respondents drawn into the group of those under notice of redundancy in Voronezh by this means was less than a third.

The second survey was carried out in April/May 1997. For various reasons, 37 people in total were substituted at stage two, i.e. 15.4 per cent of the sample as a whole. There were 17 per cent substitutions in Moscow, 15 per cent in St. Petersburg and 13 per cent in Voronezh. The distribution of substitutions, by stage one respondent group, was as follows: registered unemployed - 11; under notice of redundancy - 5; group in insecure employment - 13; people who had found work after a period of registered unemployment - 8.

In making substitutions, attention was paid to the gender, age and labour market circumstances of the respondent at the time of stage one of the survey, which helped to minimise displacement within the sample along these parameters. The gender composition of the sample was the same at both stages: 41 per cent men (99) and 59 per cent women (141). This distribution took into account particular features of the gender composition of groups affected by the labour market crisis in the cities being studied, especially the high percentage of women among the unemployed (between two-thirds and three-quarters of all the registered unemployed in the cities being studied).

Russian unemployment has a number of specific features by comparison with, for example, unemployment in European countries. Two-thirds of our respondents were specialists with specialised secondary or higher education, with almost half having higher education. Some 70 per cent of all the respondents at both stages of the survey were people who were at their peak in terms of their qualities as members of the labour force (between 25 and 50), with one in three aged between 25 and 40. In terms of occupational status, during stage one of the survey, almost half of them had previously held - or were still in - skilled white-collar or management posts. Thus, in terms of formal occupational characteristics, these people belonged to the best section of Russia's working population.

In view of the fact that we were also researching issues of poverty and survival strategies, we also paid considerable attention to the respondents' household composition. There were very noticeable differences between numbers in households in the three cities. Thus, among the unemployed in Moscow, half (14) were living alone or in two-person households, while in Voronezh there were only four such people. On the other hand, large households (five or more members) were more common among the unemployed in Voronezh - eight such households, as against five in Moscow. In St. Petersburg, the corresponding figures were nine small households and eight large. On the whole, though, 2- or 3-person households predominated in Moscow and St. Petersburg, and 4-person households in Voronezh.

Voronezh also had the highest percentage of families with dependants. While in St. Petersburg 74 out of 80 families had no dependants, and 46 out of 100 in Moscow were in this position, only one-third of the Voronezh respondents had no dependants. However, when the number of working people was taken into account, the family dependency ratio in Voronezh differed little from that in Moscow or St. Petersburg.

A Social Portrait of the Moscow Respondents

The main features of the stage one *unemployed* respondents in Moscow were: their age - two-thirds of them were over 40, and one in five was over 50; 53 per cent had higher education; the predominance of women, who made up two-thirds of respondents; the very low percentage of blue-collar workers (17 per cent) and the high proportion of managers (23 per cent), with the majority of these managers being fairly senior in rank, at least department or workshop level (17 per cent). These features are typical of the Moscow unemployed generally, which meant that we could view our survey sample as reasonably representative of Moscow conditions.

It should also be noted that the unemployed were more marginalised than the other Muscovites. There were quite a lot of first-generation migrants among them - 27 per cent had begun their working life somewhere other than Moscow; most of them had received their higher education while working (of the 53 per cent who had higher education at the time of the survey, only 17 per cent had had it when they first commenced work). In other words, these were 'self-made' people, and were no doubt proud of this, which made their altered circumstances particularly hard for them to bear.

Another particular feature of the Moscow unemployed was the much larger percentage of single people in comparison with a representative survey of Muscovites (47 per cent as against 31 per cent), and the significant proportion who had never been married (30 per cent). The families of most respondents were very small in number, with two or three members (37 per cent and 30 per cent respectively), and only 17 per cent had two or more children, who were for the most part already grown-up. So, we can see that the unemployed people surveyed in Moscow in 1996 were mainly women who were no longer young, with marginal status, who had made a fair career for themselves in the pre-reform era through their own efforts. They were mainly either single or members of households consisting of two adults.

The respondents were fairly evenly distributed between sectors, with a slight prevalence of those from the defence industry; they had been made redundant mainly from large state or privatised enterprises (67 per cent had been released from enterprises with over 200 employees).

As regards occupational self-identification, two-thirds of the unemployed identified themselves as engaged in intellectual work (specialists or 'white-collar workers' - the boundary between these concepts in contemporary Russia is not especially distinct). At the same time, only one person classed himself as a highly-skilled white-collar worker, while the extremely numerous managers in this group largely failed to identify themselves as 'administrative'. Two of them named their usual occupation as 'housekeeping', which suggests that some of the unemployed have lost their internal orientation towards productive activity.

In view of the fact that four of the 30 unemployed had not been in work for two or more years, with two out of work for ten years or more, this loss of occupational self-identification is unsurprising. Taken overall, however, the period of unemployment for the majority of respondents (15 in number) was between three and nine months, i.e. it coincided with the period during which the unemployed receive 50-75 per cent of their salary from their last place of work. Seven people had been unemployed for less than three months and the remaining four from nine months to two years.

Muscovites *under notice of redundancy* at stage one of the survey differed substantially from the unemployed according to a number of parameters. In the first place, they were considerably younger: 32 per cent of them were under 30, and only 41 per cent over 40. The predominance of women among them was even more marked (73 per cent). The percentages of single people (41 per cent) and of people who had never been married were also high. For the rest, the average household size was noticeably larger than that of the unemployed - 40 per cent had families with four or more members, and only 18 per cent had families with fewer than three members. 64 per cent had children, and 23 per cent had two or more. There were substantially fewer first-generation migrants among them - 13 per cent. Most of those under notice of redundancy had the same level of education as at the start of their working lives. Only about a third of them had higher education, while most of them had secondary or specialised secondary education (23 per cent and 32 per cent respectively).

Thus, this group was less marginalised than the first group, but on the other hand it was less well-educated and had a higher family dependency ratio. In occupational terms, it was also quite distinct. Those under notice of redundancy were much less evenly distributed between sectors than the unemployed. The most significant section of this group worked in trade and catering (23 per cent). A further nine per cent worked in municipal housing and public utilities. Thus, a total of 32 per cent of this group was employed in the currently flourishing service sector; only 27 per cent were working in the crisis-ridden industrial sector.

Among those under notice of redundancy, there were substantially fewer who worked in state and joint-stock enterprises, and more who worked in private and joint-venture enterprises. There was a correspondingly smaller percentage being released from large enterprises, and more from enterprises with fewer than 50 employees. There are no statistics available especially for Moscow on those under notice of redundancy, but certain circumstantial data indicate that this sectoral structure is currently fairly typical for redundancies, and is connected with restructuring of the city's economy.

The age and gender composition and the family status of members of the group *in insecure employment* differed perceptibly from those of the other groups. They were for the most part men (68 per cent) aged between 30 and 40. 28 per cent of the respondents of this group were under 30, and the remainder were over 40. Like those under notice of redundancy, they were almost all Muscovites going back several generations. Practically all respondents lived within a family, and 32 per cent of them were in families with four or more members. There were dependants, including small children, in 36 per cent of the respondents' families.

The educational level of this group was the highest of all four groups studied. 56 per cent were employees with higher education, and only 16 per cent did not have specialised education. 40 per cent of the insecurely employed were manual workers, and 32 per cent worked in occupations categorised as highly-skilled manual work. 48 per cent worked in occupations involving skilled or highly-skilled white-collar work. The occupational self-identification of this group within these parameters was appropriate. The only exception was self-identification as a manager. According to the responses on occupational self-identification, 12 per cent of respondents held management posts. But in coding the occupations, we could not find a single person among these respondents who might have been classed as a manager.

The distribution of the respondents in this group across different sectors was also quite distinctive. Most of them were employed in heavy industry (48 per cent) or the defence industry (8 per cent). At the same time, this group had a broader representation of education and science than the other groups (16 per cent). Given this sectoral composition, it is hardly surprising that 64 per cent of the respondents worked at enterprises with over 200 employees, with 36 per cent working at enterprises with over 1,000 employees; only 8 per cent came from enterprises employing fewer than 50 people. The majority of these were State or joint-stock (privatised) enterprises. As we can see, the members of this group were mainly fairly young men engaged in skilled manual or white-collar work in industry and science, with high social status on the pre-reform prestige scale. Because of the importance of work to them (for various reasons), they had stayed on at their enterprise regardless of its current financial position.

People who had found work following a period of registered unemployment were, like the unemployed group, relatively old - 62 per cent of its members were over 40. In contrast to the unemployed, however, the group which had found work was mostly made up of men. This group contained the highest percentage of married people - 62 per cent, and also of people with no other working family members - 52.2 per cent (the equivalent figure for the unemployed was 36.7 per cent).

This was a fairly well-educated group (43.6 per cent of its members had higher education), although, like the unemployed, they had mostly reached this level of education after starting work. The occupational status of the group differed distinctly from that of the other groups. Throughout the ten years preceding their period of unemployment, roughly a third of the group had worked in highly-skilled manual work, and only 13 per cent in white-collar work requiring higher education. Occupational self-identification matched these figures. In terms of sectoral composition, members of this group had mainly found their new jobs in State or joint-stock trade and catering enterprises and in municipal housing and public utilities, all with relatively few employees. One-third worked at enterprises with fewer than 50 employees and the same proportion at enterprises with over 200, which is fewer than in any other group. Thus, in Moscow, people found work after a period of unemployment chiefly in those sectors which had seen the greatest outflow of redundant staff.

A Social Portrait of the St. Petersburg Respondents

Of the officially registered *unemployed* in St. Petersburg at the time of the 1996 survey, 32 per cent were managers or specialists with higher or specialised secondary education, 24 per cent were white-collar technical and service personnel, and 24 per cent were skilled blue-collar workers. In terms of their last place of work, the respondents in this group were evenly distributed over a wide range of different sectors.

A distinctive feature of the St. Petersburg group of *insecurely employed* people was the highest representation (in comparison with the other survey groups) of highly-educated people (73 per cent) - members of the technical and cultural intelligentsia, working primarily in the defence industry and science. Among these respondents, 55 per cent were managers or specialists with higher or specialised secondary education, 18 per cent were white-collar technical and service personnel, and 23 per cent were skilled blue-collar workers. The reason for this composition was that, although people in insecure employment are mostly to be found in industry, most of those actually on compulsory leave are engineering and technical personnel in enterprises or scientific staff in industry-dedicated institutes that form part of scientific and production groups.

The largest section (47 per cent) of the group of people *under notice of redundancy* consisted of skilled blue-collar workers employed at large enterprises owned either by the State or in joint-stock form, in civilian heavy industry.

Like the group of people on compulsory leave, the group of *people who had found work* after a period of unemployment also featured a high proportion of people with higher education (56 per cent). However, the status of posts held by those who had returned to work was, on average, substantially lower than the posts retained by people on compulsory leave. We recorded a relatively small proportion of people who, at the time of the survey, were holding down posts requiring higher or specialised secondary education. At the same time, there was a distinct larger number of people employed in the service sector.

More than half (58 per cent) of the total number of unemployed respondents had been released from State enterprises. About a quarter of unemployed respondents said that their last place of work had been a joint-stock company, while a sixth had been with a private company. Among those on compulsory leave, there was a significantly larger proportion who were currently employed at enterprises with a joint-stock form of ownership (45 per cent). In the group of people under notice of redundancy, there was a still higher proportion of people working at joint-stock companies (60 per cent).

The majority of the registered unemployed had been released from middle-sized enterprises, 36 per cent from large enterprises and 12 per cent from small enterprises with fewer than 50 employees. Those on compulsory leave worked mainly for large enterprises and organisations (64 per cent). Middle-sized enterprises accounted for 32 per cent of the respondents in this group, and 4 per cent were at small enterprises. A similar pattern of distribution applied to the size of the workforces at enterprises where our respondents were under notice of redundancy.

The status of a person who had got into circumstances where their employment was under threat was apparently linked to the size of the enterprise worked at. Among the registered unemployed, the proportion who had previously worked at enterprises employing fewer than 200 people was almost double the equivalent figure for the group under notice of redundancy, and ten times the figure for those on compulsory leave. At the same time, in comparison with the registered unemployed, a significantly greater proportion of the hidden unemployed was employed at major enterprises (over 1,000 employees).

Of the registered unemployed, 36 per cent had lost their job because of staff reductions or closure of the enterprise, while for a further 48 per cent of respondents the official reason for leaving was voluntary. About one-third had been on compulsory leave prior to redundancy. As for those who were on compulsory leave at the time of the survey, their circumstances could be described without fear of contradiction as chronic or long-term. More than 85 per cent of the respondents in this group said that this was not the first time they had been obliged to take unpaid or part-paid leave because of a shortage of work at their enterprise or organisation.

A Social Portrait of the Voronezh Respondents

Of the 15 registered *unemployed* in Voronezh, one-third were men and two-thirds women. Seven respondents were aged 30-40, five were aged 40-50 and three were under 30. The educational level of the unemployed was fairly high. At the time of the survey, 27 per cent of the respondents had completed secondary education, 20 per cent had specialised secondary education, and more than half the respondents (53 per cent) were specialists with partial or complete higher education.

40 per cent of the unemployed (and this was specific to this particular group) were former defence industry employees. 13 per cent of respondents said that their last job had been at a heavy industrial enterprise and a further 13 per cent named 'other manufacturing industries' - most of them meant the military-industrial complex. Outside manufacturing industry, 13 per cent of respondents were employed in education and science, seven per cent in transport, seven per cent in municipal housing and public utilities and seven per cent in other sectors.

A particular feature of registered unemployment in Voronezh was that industrial giants, whether in the defence sector or producing largely uncompetitive products for civilian consumption, were suffering most in the transition to a market economy, and they formed one of the main sources of redundant labour. 73 per cent of the unemployed had previously worked at enterprises where there were more than 200 employees, and 53 per cent at enterprises with over 1,000 employees. The vast majority (73 per cent) had worked in their old job for more than seven years, and 20 per cent had been there for over 15 years.

One-third of respondents had been in blue-collar occupations at their last workplace; the rest were white-collar workers - either non-specialists or people with specialised secondary or higher education. From the point of view of occupational self-identification, 13 per cent of respondents considered management to be their usual occupation (20 per cent had actually been managers), 13 per cent gave their usual occupation as skilled manual work (20 per cent had in fact worked as such), and 27 per cent thought of themselves as skilled white-collar workers, whereas, in reality, only seven per cent had worked in posts requiring specialised secondary education. None of the respondents gave their usual occupation as that of unskilled manual worker.

We should add that unemployment had overtaken employees who had a long working life behind them, with long experience of working in the particular occupation which they considered to be their usual one, and this meant that it was not easy for them to adapt readily to their sharply altered status. 73 per cent of the registered unemployed had a working life of 15 to 20 years behind them. Many had managed to raise their level of education during the course of their career. 60 per cent of them had completed secondary education when they began work, but by the time of the survey, 73 per cent of respondents were specialists with specialised secondary or higher education; there was no respondent at all who still had no secondary education at all by this point. For most of the respondents, the period of unemployment was fairly lengthy. Only one-third had been unemployed for less than six months; 40 per cent had been unemployed for up to a year and a quarter of the respondents had been unemployed for more than a year.

There were substantially more women and young people in the group of people *under notice of redundancy* than in the other groups. The proportion of respondents aged under 30 was 36 per cent (people in insecure employment - six per cent; unemployed - 20 per cent). Only one in five respondents fell into the 40-50 age category, and none of them was any older than 50.

The vast majority of respondents (85.7 per cent) were specialists with higher (50.0 per cent) or specialised secondary (35.7 per cent) education, but they were mostly employed as non-specialist white-collar workers in posts not requiring a high level of skill. Particular features of the occupational and sectoral structure of the group being released indicated, firstly, that the labour market in Voronezh was moving low-skilled labour into the developing - and promising - non-manufacturing sector, and secondly, that the outflow of fairly highly-skilled specialists from the military-industrial complex was continuing. There was a startling difference in the sectoral membership of people in this group by comparison with the registered unemployed group, where two-thirds of respondents were ex-employees of manufacturing industry. 64.3 per cent of the respondents under notice of redundancy were being made redundant from the private sector (only 27 per cent of the whole Voronezh sample worked in this sector), from which a noticeable outflow of staff into registered unemployment began in 1996.

Over half of those under notice of redundancy were employees at medium-sized or small enterprises, where the number of employees did not exceed 200. One in five of them worked at a small company employing fewer than 50 people. This was another way in which those under notice of redundancy differed from the rest of the Voronezh sample, the great majority of whom had worked at large civilian or defence enterprises.

In contrast with the registered unemployed, respondents under notice of redundancy had considerable experience of labour mobility, and they had quite frequently experienced a recent drop in social and skills status in a new job. In addition, 14 per cent of them said that they had previously experienced breaks between jobs (five per cent for the Voronezh sample as a whole), and a further 14 per cent had had experience of registered unemployment in the past (five per cent for the Voronezh sample as a whole).

One major feature of the *insecurely employed* group was the predominance of men, which made the group stand out from the other Voronezh respondents. Perhaps this was why, in this group, the largest number of respondents (18 per cent) from any group in the sample stated openly that they had other paid work besides their main job. Looking at age structure, we find that the group in insecure employment was the most 'elderly': more than half the respondents were aged over 40 (which was true of only one-third of the other Voronezh respondents). Besides this, we found two respondents in this group who were coming up to pensionable age, something we did not observe in any other group. The age structure of the group in insecure employment offers a partial explanation as to why people stay on at their old job despite, essentially, having joined the hidden unemployed: people in the older age bracket do not have much chance of obtaining new and 'successful' jobs on the contemporary labour market.

A high level of education was typical of Voronezh respondents, and the respondents in this group were no exception: 59 per cent of them had complete or incomplete higher education. A little over half the respondents had begun their working lives with diplomas from higher or specialised secondary education institutions, but by the time of the survey the proportion of such people in the group had risen to 82 per cent. The group in insecure employment also featured a comparatively high skills level. With representatives of both skilled and highly-skilled manual labour, the proportion of specialists was high (77 per cent). At the same time, the proportion of non-specialist white-collar workers was very small. It would seem that they are the first to be released in a situation of insecure employment, while enterprises seek to preserve the high skills potential of narrow specialists in both white-collar and manual work, in the hope that there will be demand for their abilities again in future. It is no coincidence that the number of respondents in this group who had worked in their usual occupation for more than ten years was very high, at 69 per cent. The same applied to only 27 per cent of the unemployed, 29 per cent of those who had found work and 36 per cent of those under notice of redundancy.

Another feature of this group was that they were virtually all employed by industrial giants with over 1,000 employees (77 per cent, as against 47 per cent for the sample as a whole). 65 per cent were employed in the defence sector, in the radio electronics industry, which has been almost destroyed by the market economy, or the engineering industry, which is in long-term crisis.

Thus, the category of insecure employees in Voronezh presents us with a fairly skilled, educated and experienced section of the workforce, who surpass all the other respondent groups in terms of continuously holding the same job, total length of working life and accuracy in occupational self-identification. Two-thirds of the respondents in the group of *people who had found work* after a period of unemployment were women. The gender distribution of those who had found work corresponded exactly with the gender structure of the unemployed. Those who had returned to work, however, were somewhat younger than the registered unemployed. The respondents in this group were a little behind the rest of the sample in terms of their educational level. Only one-third of respondents had higher education. Those who had found work were predominantly (43 per cent) specialists with a technical secondary-level education. Those Voronezh citizens who had successfully overcome a period of unemployment had less experience of working in the occupation they thought of as their usual one than the other respondents. Even before losing their last job, a fifth of the group were already working in an occupation other than their usual one, so respondents who had returned to work viewed with equanimity any current discrepancy between the employment they actually held and their idea of their usual occupation.

In renewing their interrupted labour participation, many of our respondents had consented to work in posts that reduced their social status and did not match their level of skills or education. The Voronezh labour market was able to put them to work essentially as non-specialist white-collar workers, as well as offering a wide range of vacancies for manual labourers, without any great skill requirements.

The skills potential of these respondents was not being fully utilised at their new place of work, although half of them did find work within their field (29 per cent of the respondents in this group were working in their usual occupation and another 21 per cent were doing a type of work that was familiar to them and fell within their own idea of their usual occupation but did not make full use of their knowledge and skills). A further one in five of the respondents, though obliged to change occupation, was managing in the new job and was completely happy with it. Only 29 per cent of this group were decidedly dissatisfied with the job they had obtained, since the difficult material circumstances of the household and the absence of any other breadwinners had forced them to take on unskilled manual labour or to try their hand at a type of work with which they were unfamiliar. These were the people who said that, at the time of the survey, they had not abandoned active attempts to find acceptable work. Taking the group of those who had found work as a whole, however, over 70 per cent of respondents had successfully overcome a period of unemployment and, despite all drawbacks, the work they had obtained suited them.

A Comparative Analysis of Moscow, St. Petersburg and Voronezh (1996/7)

As we have seen, in 1996, in the group of registered *unemployed* in all three cities, women made up the majority, and their level of education was higher than for the sample as a whole. Respondents everywhere were distributed fairly evenly between sectors, with a slight prevalence of the military-industrial complex, heavy industry and engineering; the enterprises from which they had been released were primarily large, with some medium-sized ones (over 200 employees). In Moscow the percentage of blue-collar workers in the registered unemployed group was very small (17 per cent), whereas in St. Petersburg the percentage of skilled blue-collar workers was quite high (40 per cent). Age and some other characteristics of the registered unemployed group also differed across the three cities, especially the percentage of single people and the family dependency ratio to those in employment.

In the group *under notice of redundancy*, women were in the majority in all three cities; the age composition was slightly younger than the average for the sample, and the skills level was below average. In Moscow and St. Petersburg the level of education was lower in this group than in others, while in Voronezh it was high, although these people were working in posts not requiring special skills. In Moscow and Voronezh people were mostly being released from the service sector, whereas in St. Petersburg there were many skilled industrial workers among those under notice of redundancy. The households in this group were, on average, larger than those of the unemployed.

The group *in insecure employment* had the most common features in all three cities, and demonstrated a fairly distinct social type. These were middle-aged and older people, mostly with families but with children already grown up, with a high level of education and with the occupational status of highly-skilled and skilled workers (with a relatively high proportion of skilled blue-collar workers), and with long service at their enterprises. For the most part, they worked in the heavy or defence industries, as well as in education and science at large enterprises. These were, therefore, skilled specialists with a high social status on the pre-reform prestige scale. Because of their age and the significance that work held for them, they had stayed on at the enterprise or institution despite its difficult financial position.

Finally, in all the cities, *people who had found work* after a period of registered unemployment took up new jobs with partial loss of social status, and with either a change of occupation or a transfer to less skilled work. In all the cities, they found work primarily in the non-manufacturing sector - trade, catering or municipal housing and public utilities. In Moscow and St. Petersburg, these were in the same age groups as the unemployed, whereas in Voronezh they were relatively young people. The composition of those who had found work also differed between the cities in terms of gender, household composition and education. This made us pay particular attention at stage two to the motives and reasons for some people finding work while others remained long-term unemployed.

How did the main characteristics of the groups examined change over the year? Almost not at all - and some typical group features, which were apparent at stage one, became even more marked. As in 1996, the majority of the registered *unemployed* in 1997 were women, but the proportion of them had become even larger, rising from three-fifths to two-thirds of the group. Meanwhile, among the *de facto* unemployed, the numbers of men and women were practically equal, so that - taken as a whole - the picture was similar to that of a year previously. In terms of age, at both stages, three-quarters of the group were concentrated in the 41-60 age range, and even the proportions distributed by age within this group stayed the same. In this group, there was also a substantially greater concentration of managers (their numbers had remained the same as in 1996, although the group itself was 1½ times smaller) and unskilled labourers (there had been four and now there were three) than for the sample as a whole. There was an even clearer trend for the ranks of the unemployed, and especially the long-term unemployed, to be swollen by respondents from small enterprises engaged in trade or catering, rather than from large State or joint-stock industrial enterprises.

In the group *in insecure employment*, there was a substantial rise in the proportion of men, with something of a shift towards older age groups. The number of people over 50 remained virtually unchanged, but the number of people in insecure employment in the other age groups more than halved. The number of blue-collar workers had fallen, and the level of education had seen a steep rise. The number employed in the manufacturing industry had diminished, and, correspondingly, the proportion of education and science personnel had risen. This group had thus acquired its final form, moving towards the classically pure type. Its members were primarily specialists and redundant middle- and lower-grade managers employed in education and science (40 per cent) or the defence industry (16 per cent), at large or medium-sized State enterprises.

As previously, among *people who had found work*, gender and age did not play a particular part; but, in 1997, the proportion of women who had found work in the total composition of the group was even higher than in 1996. The proportions distributed by age within this group had stayed the same overall and most were still concentrated in the 41-50 band, a fact which was governed by the corresponding age composition of the unemployed. We have already said that when returning to work, our respondents were to some extent compelled to take jobs which did not match their skills level. As a result, there was a slight fall in the number of white-collar workers and a rise in skilled and unskilled blue-collar workers. These processes were most characteristic of Voronezh, with its narrow labour market. If we look at occupational status shifts over the year in the four groups studied throughout the research, however, we see that most respondents who returned to work nevertheless stayed within the same occupation or type of post, albeit perhaps experiencing a loss of status in relation to that group. Of course, it is far from easy to talk about 'loss' in this sense when we are considering the contemporary situation in Russia, where an occupational status system has not yet had time to settle down.

Specialists and skilled blue-collar workers found it easier to find new jobs following receipt of redundancy notices: they made up a relatively large part of the group of people working normally without any period of unemployment. The situation was comparatively less rosy for white-collar workers and unskilled blue-collar workers, who represented a higher proportion of those who had found work after unemployment. On the whole, however, the structure of employment of those now working was fairly similar to the occupational structure of the sample - based on respondents' self-identification - with the exception of Voronezh. Those who found work without any period of unemployment mostly went into the defence industry, education and the construction industry, while those who first experienced a period of unemployment went on to jobs in trade, education, municipal housing and public utilities.

In 1997, most of those who had found work were employed at joint-stock companies (58 out of 129 people, i.e. almost twice the proportion of the group in 1996), followed by State enterprises (39 people, i.e. less than one-third of this group - although, in 1996, half of those who had found work had gone to State enterprises), with almost the same number employed in private enterprises (37 people, i.e. one in three, whereas in 1996 the figure had been about one in five).

The Questionnaire and How it was Analysed

The research was longitudinal in nature and the method involved designing a partially pre-coded interview of between 1½ and 3 hours in duration. The same people were surveyed in both stages of the research. The form of the interview questionnaire altered slightly between stages one and two of the project. At stage one it comprised 247 questions, and at stage two, 215. Of these, 125 questions were taken from the 1996 version, in order to record changes that had happened to the respondents during the year, while 90 questions were new and were introduced to address new objectives that had arisen during the course of the research (the relationship between poverty and unemployment, the issue of resources and their role in determining survival and employment strategies, deprivation and forms of social participation).

Preparation of the interview results for processing entailed coding the open questions - after content analysis - and creating scales. In processing the results of the open questions, particular attention was paid to those which represented the career and life of the respondent: questions about occupation and about family. In working out scales relating to income levels in each of the cities, we took into account the Subsistence Minimum based on official figures in the given city at the time of the survey. Questions about desired occupation, ownership of consumer goods, reasons for refusal of benefit payments, reasons for rejecting jobs offered by the Employment Service, as well as some others, were processed using only content analysis. It was pointless to apply scales in these cases because responses were not reducible to any common denominator.

Answers to the questions associated with the socio-occupational status of the respondents were processed out using a method developed by one of the present authors, Ovsei Shkaratan. In this method, there are three scales which can be used to code occupations, one of which - the permanent social groupings scale (PSG-14) - we used to measure our respondents' socio-occupational status (Shkaratan and Tikhonova, 1996, pp.149-53).

The research results were processed, using SPSS, with sub-samples identified for each city separately, and - within each city - further sub-samples identified for each of the four crisis groups at stage one and for eight groups identified on various principles (seven in terms of employment status at the time of the survey, and one identified during mathematical processing of the sample, relating to the presence of more than three unemployed people in the respondent's immediate circle) at stage two. To establish the degree of relationship between variables and their joint subordination at stage two of the research, the CHAID program was also used.

Using CHAID, with subsequent verification in SPSS, an analysis was made of the causal relationships between the resources available to the respondents, on the one hand, and the dynamics of change in their material circumstances and their unemployment/employment status - as well as their survival strategies and their employment optimisation strategies - on the other.

Types of Resources

In analysing the comparative significance of various resources in the respondents' choice of a certain behaviour strategy, as well as for analysis of the different types of resources available to respondents from differing groups and cities, we used the resource classifications proposed by Bourdieu and Shkaratan. In line with these classifications, there were questions in the questionnaire enabling the concept of resources to be put into practice. The following resources were represented, in Bourdieu's terms:

- social resources (questions on circles of permanent social contact, visits to clubs, religious groupings, etc.; possibilities of having visitors and visiting other people or spending free time outside the home; possibilities of approaching those around one for help in the event of a deterioration in one's circumstances; support being received from them, including financial support, at the time of the survey; references to lack of required connections to find a job, etc.);
- economic resources (questions on whether the respondent owned any residential property, a *dacha*, a piece of land, a garage, household articles, businesses, shares in a business or other securities; and also questions as to whether respondents had obtained various types of social assistance or services from the enterprise or from State or municipal bodies, from community or charity organisations, or from friends or relations; whether the respondents had acquired various types of possessions over the intervening year; what sources of income there were in the respondent's household, what income each member of the household had and the average *per capita* income in the household; and other questions giving a picture of the property resources position of the respondent);
- cultural resources (questions about level of education, about training/ retraining courses during the period of employment/unemployment crisis, about reading newspapers and magazines, visits to theatres, concerts or cinema, etc.);
- symbolic resources (questions about the period of employment at the enterprise, which was extremely important in the stratification system of pre-reform Russia; about restrictions on the possibilities of finding a job because of being unemployed or as a result of one's appearance; about willingness to accept lower social status; about potential to support a certain lifestyle and social contacts, etc.).

Apart from these types of resource, we also added one which we called the 'personality' resource, which was in essence very close to what Bourdieu called 'habitus' (aspects of thinking, values, subjective social mood, etc.). This resource was operationalised with the aid of questions such as those about the respondent's values; conformism/ non-conformism; sense of how possible or impossible it was to exert any influence on what was happening, including what was happening in one's own life; about the prevalence of attitudes of dependency/expectations of paternalism in resolving problems and the problems of other needy people, the unemployed, the disabled and other socially vulnerable groups; about the willingness of the respondent to take various active steps, including political protest, to protect their own interests; about the respondents' possible reactions to news of receipt of a large inheritance or complete loss of all sources of income; about the feelings experienced on being obliged to ask someone for help; about labour motivations and values; about active/passive forms of job-seeking; about what is most unpleasant for the respondent about being out of work; and others (Bourdieu, 1993, pp.53-87).

In addition, when we developed the questionnaire, 'psycho-physiological' resources were viewed as separate types of resources - gender, age, ability to work and health. Within this, the method used to reveal the respondent's state of health was one adopted in the course of research on unemployed people in the UK during the late 1980s, represented by the 28-item scale of the General Health Questionnaire (GHQ), alongside a number of additional questions related to the respondent's own assessment of his or her health.

This operationalisation of the resources available to respondents enabled a comparison to be made during the research between Bourdieu's conception of resources and the resource-potential approach proposed by Shkaratan for analysis of the behaviour of separate individuals. This conception assumes that among the resources possessed by individuals there are some which are linked directly to the personality of the respondent, resources linked to the human environment and the respondent's previous life experience (and connections), and resources linked to household composition and circumstances. By *respondent-related resources*, Shkaratan meant the following characteristics:

- psycho-physiological potential - gender, age, health and ability to work;
- skills potential - educational level; post held and social status at main (most recent) place of work; total length of working life to date, length of service at most recent place of work, length of service in most recent post; occupation; sector; type of enterprise (State, municipal, joint-

stock, private, etc.) at most recent place of work; size of most recent place of work; managerial experience; entrepreneurial experience;

- personality potential - aspects of work-related motivation; when drafting the questionnaire, we included questions which might enable us to measure values, expectations of paternalism, particular aspects of the person's social and emotional state, feelings of security or insecurity in social matters, of aggression, of despair, of social disadvantage, and so on;
- potential for active mobilisation and enlargement of one's own resources - the respondent's claims on various resources; willingness to change the conditions and content of one's own work activities; willingness to make real sacrifices entailed in various kinds of social and economic activity; occupational mobility and willingness to change jobs; existence of secondary employment (nature of this employment, its relationship to the respondent's usual occupation, and its role in income formation) (Shkaratan, 1985).

By *resources connected with past environment*, we mean whether or not respondents have family, friends and work contacts who might help them to solve their present problems. By *resources connected with the household* we mean: various kinds and levels of income in respondents' households; *per capita* income; housing and other property; consumer durables; the opportunity to choose various household survival strategies not directly involving an increase in income in money terms; the opportunity to use various forms of social infrastructure (housing, education, medical insurance, health care facilities, holiday homes, etc.); the use of various means of social assistance, including Unemployment Benefit, and the part they play in family life.

As we can see, in order to operationalise the various types of resource, Shkaratan's and Bourdieu's, a body of questions with a significant degree of overlap was required. Exceptions were psycho-physiological potential (gender, age, ability to work and health) and potential for active mobilisation of one's own resources and work motivations (as an element of personality potential), which were present in Shkaratan's system but not in Bourdieu's.

Poverty

The next difficult issue we had to tackle was that of putting the concept of 'poverty' into operation. We had to do this in a country which has had difficulty in acknowledging - even to itself - the very existence of this problem, and where official statistics are still a long way from using generally-accepted approaches to setting a poverty line. In view of the persistent uncertainty surrounding the concept of 'poverty', the first thing we did was to attempt to put various possible interpretations of poverty into operation, and to see which of them 'worked best' in the respondents' real life situations.

We examined the following possible interpretations of poverty: 1) an absolute concept of poverty (a budgetary approach), which is based on establishing a minimum list of basic requirements (a Subsistence Minimum) and the measure of resources needed to ensure these requirements; 2) a subjective approach (the social consensus approach), based on the proposition that people themselves are the best judges of what poverty is; 3) a relative concept of poverty, in which a certain proportion of the average or median income for a given society is used to define the poverty line; 4) a behavioural approach, which assesses the nature of the deprivations people experience and the existence of possibilities for them to participate in the life of the society to which they belong.

Therefore, when we analysed the questionnaire, 27 questions were specified in order to enable manifestations of poverty in its various interpretations to be traced - as a set income level (questions on *per capita* income and proportion of income going on food, which were then compared both with the measure of Subsistence *Minima* defined by various State and non-State bodies in Russia and with statistical data on average incomes in Russia at that time); as not just low monetary income but also the absence of other economic resources, including various types of assistance, fixed and moveable assets, etc.; and as the accessibility of accepted forms of behaviour - primarily certain forms of social participation (a block of questions associated with a certain way of life, including questions on accessibility and quality of food, on the potential to acquire household articles, to buy newspapers, magazines or theatre tickets, the potential to sustain valued social contacts, changes in attitudes from friends and neighbours on entry into crisis groups, etc.). In addition, in view of the present breakdown in Russians' self-identification and of the absence from the public mind of clear ideas of what constitutes poverty, our analysis also involved a further block of questions, in which the respondents gave their own assessments of their level of welfare (material circumstances generally, in relation to others, in relation to what they had been a year previously and to expectations for a year hence) and their own assessment of their life as a whole.

This specific block of questions, pulling in all possible interpretations of 'poverty', was then processed as follows. The block was first analysed for correlations with questions from the entire data mass obtained from the survey, until all statistically significant relationships had been exhaustively investigated. This revealed that a number of questions from this specific block were closely interrelated, while others were of a random, peripheral nature. As a result, 11 questions were identified, which more frequently appeared among the correlations obtained, and formed a core differentiating all the respondents according to their level of welfare. In particular, these included questions that enabled factor analysis to be used to identify particular thresholds between indigence, poverty, being badly-off, being averagely well-off and being relatively prosperous. These material statuses found a corresponding reflection in the indices established.

At this stage of the analysis, a group was also revealed, independently of the original objectives of our study, of respondents who had more than three unemployed people in their immediate circle. The questions about the presence and number of unemployed people in the immediate circle unexpectedly demonstrated statistically significant relationships with a number of questions in the material welfare block.

Thus identified, the most active 'core' of questions was then analysed for correlations with, firstly, all the questions which characterise different types of resource as possible factors in the situation in which the respondents found themselves, and then with all the questions about the survival strategies they used as a consequence of this situation. Established relationships at the first level of significance according to CHAID were successively excluded from the process. This analysis was continued to the level where any statistically significant relationships were present. As a result, 38 questions were identified as recurring at least twice in the 11 identified 'trees' of dependent variables, including ten questions which recurred 6-8 times and enabled causal relationships to be traced between way of life, level of welfare and survival strategies employed. These questions were further analysed in respect of the eight groups studied in 1997 and the four 1996 groups, using the paired correlations method to gain a deeper understanding of the nature of their interrelationships. The same method was also used to improve our understanding of results obtained from some questions not present on the list of statistically significant questions. The total volume of paired correlations examined was over 1,000 cells.

A similar method of multi-stage analysis, revealing a 'core' of significant indicators and then processing this to establish causal relationships, was also used in analysing the respondents' employment situation. Apart from this, in considering individual questions from the block on welfare, extensive use was also made of the possibilities offered by the CHAID and SPSS programmes.

Use of this multi-stage data processing method to establish the causal relationships between the variables studied enabled us to obtain adequately reliable mathematical confirmation of the resources, lack of which is crucial. in driving people into poverty or unemployment; of whom Russians really regard as poor, of who actually is poor and what makes them feel that they are poor; of what differences there were on these issues between the groups and cities studied, and so on (Tikhonova, 1998).

The Welfare Index

The basis for this index may be said to fall within the framework of Townsend's concept, where poverty is interpreted as a defined set of deprivations and 'level of welfare' is generally interpreted as reflecting the limitations imposed by a family's material circumstances on their structure of consumption and way of life. In order to draw up the Index, we initially specified 27 questions, enabling us to establish what level of welfare the respondents belonged to (consuming meat, delicatessen meat or fish products, fruit or sweets; buying newspapers and magazines, clothes, footwear, domestic and audio equipment; going to restaurants, the theatre or cinema; visiting or receiving visitors; tourist travel; using paid medical or educational services, and a number of others).

These questions, pulling in all aspects of levels of material welfare, were then analysed for correlations with other questions in that block. This revealed that a number of questions from that specific block were closely interrelated, while others were of a random, peripheral nature. As a result, 17 questions were identified as occurring more frequently than others among the pictures of correlations obtained, and these formed a distinctive 'core', capable of differentiating all the respondents according to their level of welfare. These 17 questions were those covering the possibilities of:

- trips outside the city for the whole family;
- using fee-paying educational, medical or health and leisure facilities or a non-State pension fund, or purchasing or building some kind of property (a house, dacha or garage) over the last three years;
- purchasing meat/fish delicacies;
- visits to the cinema, theatre or concerts;
- acquiring domestic equipment of various kinds;
- buying brand new clothes/shoes for oneself or other family members;
- purchasing newspapers and/or magazines;
- inviting family/friends to visit you at home to celebrate birthdays, public holidays, etc.;
- buying fresh meat;
- visits to restaurants/cafes;
- buying fruits/juices;
- buying chocolates/sweets;
- acquiring clothes/shoes for children;
- fee-paying lessons for children;
- acquiring any consumer durables, other than domestic appliances (video/audio equipment, furniture, etc.);
- visiting family/friends to celebrate birthdays, public holidays, etc.;
- going out socially for the evening or at the weekend in the fortnight before the survey.

Other questions were 'peripheral' indicators (for example, consumption of fine wines or tobacco products, which many respondents saw as unnecessary).

Of the 17 questions, some were significant as 'thresholds' between the ways of life of different strata only in the higher property/ income strata. These were questions about the possibility of trips outside the city for the whole family, purchasing meat/fish delicacies, acquiring domestic equipment or other consumer durables (video/audio equipment, furniture, and so on), visits to restaurants/cafes, using fee-paying educational, medical or health and leisure facilities or a non-State pension fund, or purchasing or building some kind of property (a house, dacha or garage) over the last three years. However other questions were significant for lower strata. These were questions about the possibility of using one's own funds to obtain fee-paying medical facilities over the last three years (the system of free medicine in Russia has practically collapsed, and people are prepared to deny themselves even essentials in order to obtain medical services; therefore, in Russia today, not being able to spend money on medical treatment is evidence of being not just badly-off, but really poor), about the general possibility of buying brand new clothes and shoes for oneself or other members of the family, purchasing newspapers and/or magazines, inviting family/friends to visit you at home or visiting them to celebrate birthdays, public holidays, and so on, buying fresh meat, and acquiring clothes/shoes for children.

A third group of questions were of importance for several strata, but the frequency of performance of a certain action within them differed. These were questions about frequency of visits to the cinema, theatre or concerts, buying brand new clothes/shoes for oneself or other family members, purchasing newspapers and/or magazines, inviting family/friends to visit you at home to celebrate birthdays, or public holidays, buying fresh meat, fruits/juices and chocolates/sweets, and also about the possibility of fee-paying lessons for children and of going out socially for the evening or at the weekend in the fortnight before the survey.

Questions which were significant for certain groups of respondents - for example, those with dependent children - stood rather on their own. At the same time, these 'special' questions showed a very high heuristic significance, since these respondents were less likely to skimp on their children, and questions about whether paid sessions at children's clubs or new clothes for children could be afforded were very clear 'threshold' questions for this section of respondents.

The 'threshold' values of material welfare, reflected in the 17 questions and identified using the methodology described above, were used to draw up a Welfare Index, where values 1 to 6 corresponded to attribution to different property and income strata. Index value 1 was for the indigent, 2 for the poor, 3 for the badly-off, 4 for the averagely well-off, 5 for the well-off and 6 for the prosperous. The Index was calculated from tables where positive responses to 'threshold' questions were deployed along the horizontal, and the numbers of respondents who had provided these responses were deployed vertically. An index value was thus calculated 'manually', for each person individually, on the basis of the number and nature of positive responses to the various questions. For example, a respondent who had indicated, in their responses to the 17 questions examined, that they had access to only one of the specified items of consumption, services or forms of leisure pursuit which involve additional expenditure - even though they felt they needed it - would fall into the indigent group; someone with two or three items in this position, into the 'poor'; and so on. We should emphasise that such foodstuffs as bread, potatoes, pasta, vegetable oil, grains, etc., which form the staple diet of the poorest sections of Russian society, were not included in our questionnaire.

Subsequently, in order to check the results obtained, the Index was also recalculated to take into account quantitative and subjective assessments of the level of welfare. By quantitative, we mean the level of *per capita* income in the respondent's family, and by subjective - their own assessment of their material circumstances. The reason why these indicators needed to be taken into account as control factors was because there were respondents who said that they economised on literally everything, even though they had an income of over a million roubles. Clearly, in such cases, respondents were not objective enough in their responses to specific questions about level of welfare. In addition, some of them displayed an irrational structure of consumption: for example, they might actually deny themselves anything like a normal diet, but had acquired some sort of audio or video equipment (these deviations were particularly typical of the extreme age groups).

Recalculating the Welfare Index to take into account these two other approaches involved several amendments, but they were very insignificant and affected only the four poorest groups out of the six identified. As a result, the number of averagely well-off respondents varied by two per cent, the badly-off by one per cent and the poor and the indigent by three per cent, since, in each case, several people moved from one group to another.

The Adaptation Index

The 'potential for real adaptation' (PRA) was constructed on the basis of responses to a number of questions which related to the actual labour market situation and to the alternatives which that situation offers people affected by the employment crisis. These questions included attitudes to equality of opportunity or equality of income, which reflect a willingness to accept social inequality - without which working in the non-State sector can prove very problematic; agreement with the proposition that leaders must be obeyed; state of health; importance for getting work of a willingness to work in a disciplined manner, or having contacts; willingness to work in a job with inconvenient hours; willingness to work at a distance from home; willingness to work in a situation where you do not get on with workmates, or with management; agreeing to accept poor working conditions, uninteresting work, or a reduction in social status when taking a new job.

In calculating the PRA index, the responses to each question were grouped in a binary system, where one response was taken as indicating the existence of potential to adapt and was counted as 'yes', while another response was taken as a sign of inability to adapt and was counted as 'no'. The sum of the positive responses made up the PRA index, which, correspondingly, could fluctuate between 0 and 12. For ease of use, this gradation was consolidated; to begin with, it was proposed to break down the responses obtained into three levels in the following proportions: up to and including 4 'yes' responses - low level of adaptability; 4-8 'yes' responses - average adaptability; and 8-12 'yes' responses - high level of adaptability. The indicators arrived at in totalling the stage one data, however, were so low that another scale had to be introduced. In certain groups (among the Voronezh respondents), there was not a single person with a PRA index of over 5 points. In the great majority of groups, a figure of 6-7 points was very good and fairly rare. A figure of 9 out of the 12 possible points was typical of literally only a few isolated individuals in the total sample, and was the highest we found.

In the light of this, 6 or more points were taken as an indicator of a 'high' PRA level. In defining the limits of the 'average' band, it was decided that more people across the sample as a whole should fall within it than into each of the high or low groups, in order to reflect its 'average' nature. So its limits were set at from 3 to 5 points on the scale. 'Low' PRA corresponded to points from 0 (there were ten people with this indicator across the whole stage one sample: one in Moscow, three in St. Petersburg and six in Voronezh) to 2. It is possible that, if a representative survey sample of the whole population of these cities had formed the background to the research, then the breakdown into bands would have been different, but no such sample was available and we could work only with the data we had obtained. Thus the overall gradation according to this index was a high PRA (6 to 12 positive responses), an average PRA (3 to 5 positive responses) and a low PRA (0 to 2 positive responses).

Other Indices

In describing the methodologies employed, we should also point out that the 'paired values' formula suggested and used by Lapin in his nationwide research into the values of Russians in 1990 was taken as a basis for defining our respondents' value systems. However, his method was modified somewhat. Previous research conducted by the present authors had revealed that, of the 44 value judgements proposed by Lapin, many have no bearing at all on the respondents' actual behaviour or their assessments in answering other questions, and consequently they may be seen in many respects as declared values but not internalised ones (Tikhonova, 1995, pp.96-119; Tikhonova, 1996a, pp.45-61). This knowledge led us to select 16 basic values which reveal the distinctive outline of the respondents' overall value systems, and have real bearing on their behaviour in life. Ten key values out of these 16 were included in the text of the pre-coded interview in stage one, and six were covered in stage two of the research.

In addition, in the questions that were linked to the respondents' socio-psychological status, use was made of individual elements of the methodology which had been used by western and Russian authors mentioned earlier.

Comparison with data from representative Russian research was made using data obtained during monitoring studies carried out by the Russian Independent Institute of Social and Nationalities Problems (RIISNP) in Moscow during 1992-1997. At one time or another, this research had involved the populations of 12 typical Russian regions, plus the city of Moscow. In each case, the sample was over 1,000 people and gave a fairly complete picture of all social groups in the populations of large cities and among rural dwellers. Sampling of respondents used a quota sampling method, with the main criteria being the representativeness of the socio-demographic composition and the representation on equal terms of all types of Russian region. The advantage of this research, by comparison with others, was that one of the present authors had participated in it, and so many of the questions used during the interviewing of our crisis groups could be repeated.

Social Policy Actors Research Methodology

Research Instruments Used in the Survey

Interviews were conducted using a questionnaire which we prepared on the basis that it could be used in discussion with a member of any group of social policy actors. This methodology was chosen as the one best corresponding to our aims of obtaining information on the respondents' subjective perception of the issues in question, and on their leanings, motives for action and opinions. Following the research schedule, the survey was carried out in two stages: spring/summer 1996, and spring/summer 1997. The interview questionnaire was tested at the pilot stage of the research in Moscow and St. Petersburg in February 1996.

The 1996 questionnaire drawn up to meet the objectives of our research comprised 48 questions. The questionnaire used a method of conceptual grouping of questions, in which the respondent is gradually drawn into the research topic and the questions are relatively evenly spread over different blocks. There were four such blocks in the 1996 questionnaire:

- The 'Unemployment at a local level' block (eight questions): these questions were aimed at assessing unemployment in the survey cities, its causes and future development, identification of the causes of unemployment, and tackling the problems of finding people employment. We felt it was right to begin the interview by dealing directly with problems of unemployment in the city, on the basis that this would give a general but detailed examination of the situation on the regional labour market and of social issues as a whole;
- The 'Employment policy' block (16 questions) was intended to help identify groups of subjects of employment policy and reveal their involvement in the issue of finding people employment; to clarify the potential influence of actors of employment policy, the degree of their actual influence; and to demarcate spheres of competence and responsibility for the implementation of employment policy as between Federal and regional authorities. It also attempted to clarify the state of Federal and regional labour market legislation and employment policy funding; the directions in which policy is aimed; the nature and effectiveness of private and State services for finding employment; and employment regulation mechanisms under labour market conditions;
- The 'Employment against the background of social policy' block (11 questions) was largely devoted to strategic issues of social policy generally, at both Federal and regional levels. In these questions, we particularly addressed the relative roles of regional and Federal bodies in implementing social policy, issues of legislation, prospects for the social partnership, potential use of foreign experience, and funding mechanisms for social policy;
- The 'Socio-demographic profile of the Interviewee' block (13 questions) enabled us to obtain some objective information about the respondents: to determine their current social status, level of education and political convictions, and to trace the stages of their

careers, on which we could base assumptions about their potential to adapt to new socio-economic conditions and how they have done so.

If we break down the content of these blocks, the questionnaire covered the following range of questions:

- Causes of unemployment. The possibility of mass unemployment;
- Losses of staff potential. Possibilities of preserving jobs;
- Hidden unemployment. Danger of structural unemployment;
- Vulnerable and unprotected groups. Potential to support them;
- Ways of retraining certain sections of the population, and prospects for this;
- Interdependence between social policy and employment policy;
- Extent of co-ordination between Federal national social policy and local social policy;
- The relationship of overall local social policy and employment policy (town halls, company directors, employment service, trade unions);
- The quality of social legislation and the direction in which it needs to develop;
- The institution of the social partnership: evaluation of its efficacy and prospects;
- Nature of respondents' activities in social policy matters and in employment regulation;
- City departments of labour and employment and their territorial employment services: programmes, effectiveness; interaction with directors/entrepreneurs;
- Mutual assessment of the activities of other subjects of social policy;
- Subjects of social policy;
- Social policy programmes of political parties and movements, and respondents' assessments of these;
- Social policy actors' assessment of the possibility of applying western social policy models to Russian conditions;
- Situation with regard to provision of resources for Employment Services. The creation, activities and prospects of Employment Fund.

The questionnaire was compiled so that comparison of assessments obtained in the different topic blocks would enable hidden meanings to be revealed. Thus, analysis of the combined data from Blocks One and Two enabled us to determine the qualitative dynamics of development of unemployment and the reasons for this process unfolding in that way. Comparing Blocks One and Two also enabled us to define the tasks facing potential social policy and employment policy actors, how well-informed they were, and their potential to develop the mechanisms needed to tackle social problems. Comparison of responses from Blocks One, Two and Three gave us a more precise understanding of the impact of economic and social reforms in tackling social policy and employment problems, and enabled us to determine prospects for the development of social policy, the degree of interest that regional élites have in tackling these problems and whether these problems can, in principle, be solved at this stage.

This procedure was the key to our obtaining additional data on our research themes - the hidden aspects of the employment situation which are not revealed using formal statistical procedures; it also enabled us to gain an understanding of such serious issues in the reproduction of human potential in Russia as the prospect of mass structural unemployment, the loss of the country's staff potential, the need to strengthen and reinforce specialist institutions in the field of employment and to reorganise social policy generally, and so on.

During January to March 1997, amendments were made to the interview questionnaire to take into account the results of stage one of the research. The main amendments concerned the structure of the questionnaire. The emphasis on overall social policy was reinforced, whereas in 1996 more attention had been given to employment policy. A number of questions were added, relating to macro-economic issues which have an impact on social policy: the relationship between State and market, funding social policies, etc. Special attention (involving the introduction of new questions) was paid to the issue of 'horizontal and vertical' relationships and their effect on the behaviour of social policy actors nationally, in the regions and in the cities. Questions were introduced that aimed to elucidate the problems of poverty - nationally and locally - and the extent of awareness of anti-poverty programmes among our respondents. We agreed the desirability of replacing a number of theoretical questions by 'pictures from real life', and examples taken from real social policy, discussion of which would enable the respondent to be 'set talking', resulting in more definite information. (The results of stage one showed that by no means all the respondents were adequately informed or had a wide-ranging understanding of social issues.)

The questionnaire for the 1997 social policy actors' interviews comprised 48 open questions, with 29 questions remaining unaltered from the 1996 version. The new version of the interview questionnaire had three blocks of questions:

- 'Unemployment at a local level. Employment policy' (19 questions). As in 1996, the questions in this block were aimed at assessing unemployment, its causes and prospects for development, identifying the objects of unemployment and tackling the problems of finding people work. Some questions were transferred to Block Two ('Social Policy'), thus giving them a wider resonance: those which aimed to explain the degree of involvement of members of the various expert groups/employment policy actors in the issue of finding people work, to reveal their potential influence, the degree of their actual influence and the demarcation of spheres of competence and responsibility for the implementation of employment policy as between Federal and regional authorities, as well as possibilities for funding these activities.

  The majority of the questions directed the respondent's attention to the changes which had taken place in the area of employment during the period between the surveys; a question was introduced asking what the respondent would describe as key issues in the area of employment today; questions were added which related to the mentality and specific national features of the unemployed in Russia, and so on. There were two particular questions to elucidate the positions of employers, as well as three questions about the industrial policy of the Federal and city governments, which have an indirect bearing on how problems of employment and finding people work are tackled;

- 'Social Policy' (16 questions). This block also incorporated a number of new questions. These were primarily associated with evaluating the effectiveness of social policy and of changes in it, and with establishing a 'Social State' in Russia; there were also questions about the problems of poverty and impoverishment of the Russian people, and issues of social protection for deprived people. There were a number of questions specifically aimed at elucidating the attitude of respondents to the redistribution of the spheres of influence of Federal and regional authorities in social matters, the direct participation of respondents in dealing with and discussing social issues, their specific actions on social issues, the potential of and prospects for the social partnership, and so on;

- 'Information on respondents', remained virtually as before, in the form of customary 'biographical details'. Some extra questions were introduced, covering the respondent's political attitudes, any political bias, and membership of any political party or movement.

The questionnaire for stage two of the research thus contained a wider range of questions (with some of the previous questions removed), covering:

- changes in social policy and, in particular, in employment policy at both Federal and regional levels;
- respondents' evaluation of government social programmes;
- evaluation of activities of the subjects of social policy (local authorities, company directors, trade unions, the Employment Service, etc.) during the period of our research;
- evaluation of influence of specific features of the Russian mentality in a situation where the level of unemployment is rising;
- changes in approaches to tackling social issues on the part of different political parties and movements;
- identification and evaluation of the part played by social and economic relationships in tackling social problems.

Selection of Respondents; Analysis of How the Interviews Were Conducted

When selecting social policy actors to take part in the research, we started from the basis that respondents must:

- have a high skills level, with considerable life experience and work experience, and have at their disposal the necessary information about current social and labour market processes;
- have direct access to Russia's labour resources, and be actively involved in employment regulation processes;
- have a direct relationship with high-level State, Party, ideological and legislative structures capable of influencing the formation of social policy.

Five respondent groups were created:

- ministers and officials at the top level of power (ministers, deputy ministers, chairs of committees and heads of departments at Federal and regional levels, heads of associations of industrialists, etc.);

- middle-ranking officials (local officials dealing with employment policy - staff of prefectures of administrative regions, heads of city and district employment services, etc.);
- politicians;
- trade union leaders;
- employers (directors of industrial enterprises, deputy directors in charge of personnel matters, heads of private companies).

The main socio-demographic characteristics of the respondents are summarised in Tables 4.1-4.3.

In 1997, some changes were made to the composition of the respondent sample. In particular, there was a reduction in the number of officials working for the Employment Service in Moscow; and the average age of the respondents went down in all the cities (see Table 2). There were no major changes to the other demographic parameters for the respondents. The composition of the sample also underwent minor changes for a number of reasons outside the researchers' control: these were mainly because one respondent or another had left the job altogether or had been posted away for a long time. The result of this was that, at the second stage of the research, 34 per cent of the composition of the sample was new in Moscow, 15 per cent in St. Petersburg and 26 per cent in Voronezh.

Table 4.1   Level of education as stated by respondent

	Moscow		*St. Petersburg*		*Voronezh*		*Total*	
	'96	'97	'96	'97	'96	'97	'96	'97
1. full 2nd	0	1	0	0	0	0	0	1
2. special 2nd	2	1	0	0	0	0	2	1
3. higher	24	23	21	21	11	10	56	54
4. degree	9	10	4	4	4	5	17	19

Table 4.2   Age as given by respondent

	Moscow		St. Petersburg		Voronezh		Total	
	'96	'97	'96	'97	'96	'97	'96	'97
1. under 30	2	2	0	1	0	0	2	3
2. 30-40	5	8	1	1	1	2	7	11
3. 41-50	12	14	10	12	7	6	29	32
4. 51-60	12	9	14	10	6	6	32	25
5. over 60	4	2	0	1	1	1	5	4

Table 4.3   Gender as stated by respondent

	Moscow		St. Petersburg		Voronezh		Total	
	'96	'97	'96	'97	'96	'97	'96	'97
1. male	25	24	18	21	10	10	53	55
2. female	10	11	7	4	5	5	22	20

The methodology assumed a free and non-pre-coded discussion between the interviewer and the respondent, who had been informed in advance of the themes to be discussed.

The interviewers, while observing the obligation to discuss the framework questions, did not adhere strictly to the interview schedule, which turned the conversations into something like confidential discussions. However, in some cases, the interviewer was unable to achieve real openness in the conversations. This was most manifest in the questions about the respondents' social contacts. The respondents showed excessive caution in replying to these questions. It could be said that this fact bears witness to the peculiar nature of the socio-cultural environment, which had grown up in élite groups in Russian society in Soviet times, and which will, it seems, not be readily overturned.

We were struck by the way in which, in cases where a good rapport was established with the interviewee, information which was qualitatively new was recorded during the interview. This was one positive outcome of the fact that, in most cases, the same respondents were interviewed twice, which disposed the respondent to be more open at the second meeting.

Conducting the interviews in a free form enabled interviewees to express their views on the issues that were most important to them, not only (and not so much) on the issues which were *a priori* important to the researchers. This helped to weaken the so-called 'interviewer effect' and its influence on the content aspect of the information obtained.

One result of conducting interviews in a free form was that emotionally-coloured information was obtained, on whatever was uppermost in the respondent's mind. Another result of using a free interview form was a build-up of excessive and contradictory information, which made analysis very difficult. Consequently, it was necessary to do more during the interviews than just obtain information on an item of interest: some assessment of the reliability of the information had to be made, with some kind of suggestion as to the angle of spin on it and some kind of explanation as to why the respondent was providing particular information, whether it was of personal significance, and so on. The information obtained from a focused interview enables a particular respondent typology to be defined, with these types being the bearers of certain socio-cultural characteristics; it also helps in understanding key figures, and to reveal specific perceptions in one or another group of respondents. In most cases, the respondents were happy with the proposed discussion style: for many, it was a chance to be heard, to share pressing and painful problems with an interested and understanding listener. The average duration of the interviews was 1½ hours. Interviews were tape-recorded and the texts were then transcribed and coded before being subjected to partial computer processing (Kabalina, 1997). It should be noted that there were a number of differences between the sampling of respondents and the way the interviews were conducted in the different cities involved in the research.

Aspects of Sampling and Interviewing in the Different Cities

Moscow

In selecting the respondents in Moscow, we tried to consider and adhere to the principle of representing possible types of subject of social policy. Moscow offered fairly broad potential for the creation of respondent groups because Moscow is the location of ministries and departments at Federal and regional level, as well as of political bodies such as the State Duma and the Moscow Duma; Moscow is also the home of the 'Moscow city government', which has a good deal of authority in dealing with local city issues; and the leading trade union bodies are concentrated in Moscow - the Federation of Independent Trade Unions, the Moscow Trade Union

Federation and the leadership of SOTSPROF. In selecting the Moscow social policy actors, we set out to interview directors of enterprises who were actively engaged in dealing with production control problems, and this turned out to have substantial bearing on the content and nature of the interviews.

In Moscow, as has already been mentioned, 35 actors were interviewed on questions of social and employment policy:

Group One - high-ranking officials - Russian permanent secretaries, heads of departments of Federal and Moscow ministries, Chairs of committees for labour and employment, social protection, etc.

Group Two - middle-ranking officials dealing directly with the issue of employment, i.e. staff of the Moscow Government's Committee for Labour and Employment, including heads of directorates for job creation and preservation, of statistical and analytical directorates, of directorates for the social partnership, of directorates for legal and legislative issues and of directorates involved in organising the Employment Fund; local Employment Service managers; heads of directorates and departments in administrative districts (prefectures) of Moscow; and so on. It should be noted that, since the interview questions required the respondents to be fairly well-informed about the state of social protection and employment in the regions studied, we restricted the number of representatives of local employment services (in stage one of the research there were five, and in stage two, two). Their judgements reflected the positions taken by the representatives of the Moscow Government's Committee for Labour and Employment: therefore we placed them in this respondent group.

Group Three - politicians. We interviewed representatives of opposition parties: MPs from the Moscow Duma, heads of the Moscow section of the DVR movement [Russia's Democratic Choice] (Chairman - Egor Gaidar), heads of the Moscow section of the 'Yabloko' movement (Chairman - Grigorii Yavlinskii), representatives of the Moscow section of the LDPR [Liberal Democratic Party of Russia] (Vladimir Zhirinovskii's Party), and also representatives of the Communist Party of the Russian Federation (who kindly made programme documents available to us).

Group Four - trade union leaders. In this category, we interviewed leaders of traditional (old) trade unions - the FNPR (both Federal and Moscow organisations) - and also of a number of 'new' trade unions, in particular SOTSPROF.

Group Five - directors and entrepreneurs, represented by heads of companies in various branches of industry. The enterprises differed both in terms of their area of specialisation, and in the form of ownership they were under: State, joint-stock or private. Special emphasis was placed on enterprises in the military-industrial complex, where employment problems are most acute at present.

In 1997, we were able to repeat our interviews with the most important of the respondents in terms of status and awareness of the issues. Some of the changes made to the composition of the sample are mentioned above.

The first stage of the survey coincided with the election campaign for the President of Russia and the Mayor of Moscow, which had a detrimental effect on our work, because the respondents representing the political and administrative élite of Russia were taking an active part in pre-election activities and it was difficult to arrange meetings with them. We ascribe certain other difficulties, which we encountered in conducting the first stage interviews, to respondents not having the required level of information or knowledge in the field of social policy.

Stage two of the research, however, revealed some positive changes in the respondents' level of information. We assume that this was the result of the three election campaigns that had taken place in Russia in 1996: for the President of Russia, for the State Duma and for the Mayor of Moscow. It should also be noted that, in 1997, the respondents were more agreeable to giving an interview and were also more open in detailing their personal stance.

Most of the Moscow respondents were reasonably happy to take part in the interviews. In stage one of the research, the discussions that were fullest (most exhaustive) in terms of the information contained in them were those with the heads of Moscow district employment directorates and branches. The meetings with these people usually took place in a warm and friendly atmosphere, and tended to last 2-3 hours. The main reason for this was that the respondents in this group have 'hot' information and, more than any others, think of themselves as knowledgeable in the subject. The responses to the questions at times spilled over into real discussions, touching on contiguous issues in addition to the main topic. Genuine interest was shown both in the issues our research was tackling, and in seeing our results, which the respondents felt would undoubtedly be of great benefit to their work.

However, on analysing the interview material, we noticed that most of the discussions with Employment Service officials tended to gravitate inevitably towards the issues of finding people jobs, unemployment, retraining, payment of benefits, etc. In stage two, therefore, some adjustments were made to the list of respondents: the groups of higher-ranking officials, politicians and trade union leaders were enlarged, these being actors whose work involved their tackling or discussing overall social policy issues. In stage two of the research, it was precisely the interviews with these respondents that were the most interesting in terms of content.

At both stages, serious interest in the research was also shown by officials (managers and heads of directorates and departments of the Labour and Employment Committee of the Moscow City Government).

The least informative discussions were those held with prefecture staff, who were extremely reluctant to enter into conversation. The discussions failed to provide any precise information on the role and place of these State institutions in addressing social protection and employment crisis issues, and this certainly reflected the low level of interest (not to say indifference) shown by these officials towards social issues. The respondents themselves explained their unwillingness to talk about social policy issues by saying that these problems were not the most severe or distressing at present: there was an Employment Service to deal with all social matters. Our attempts to go beyond the work of the Employment Service and to discuss the economic and political causes of Russia's social crisis elicited no response from the heads of prefectures. Generally then, although the sphere of their professional activities presupposes a broad spectrum of potential and actual authority (up to and including offering sites to small businesses, opening up new job possibilities, and organising public works schemes), local authority officials may be seen as no more than *de jure* social policy actors.

The position adopted by company directors on employment policy was extremely interesting. This was the category of respondents who were above all capable of having - and indeed in practice do exert - an influence on the state of things where the hiring and firing of staff is concerned. At the same time, some of the Moscow respondents representing the 'employers' group clearly felt that the undertaking they had made to talk about social issues was an onerous one. The negative impression that this made forced us to assume that these director-level representatives of a number of Moscow enterprises were not involved in putting social policy into effect, even in the direct area of finding people work, which one might expect to be of direct concern to directors of enterprises, given the fact that they constantly encounter staff problems.

We associate this situation first and foremost with the presence in this Moscow group (especially at stage one of the research) of managing directors of major Moscow enterprises (the 'Yak' Aviation Corporation, the

'Cosmos' Sewn Goods Group, the 'Kalinin' Engineering Works). These are enterprises which have found their feet in the developing Russian market economy. They are not faced with the problem of high staff turnover; wages are paid on time; and pay rates match the fairly high Moscow Subsistence Minimum. The directors who took part in the interviews attempted primarily to discuss prospects for production development, as they very much associated the issues of employment and the social welfare of employees of the enterprise with this factor.

In our view, the problems - of content - which arose in discussions with the Moscow directors at stage one of the research were at least partly linked to the fact that the majority of them were 'red directors', who had come up through the school of paternalistic enterprise management. Some of them had managed to readjust and find a way of coping with today's difficult economic situation, but nonetheless, they had not yet turned from 'the fathers of the enterprise' into manager-directors. Even at enterprises now working successfully, modern personnel services had not yet been set up, and there were no programmes aimed at retaining core skills at the enterprise and organising its potential for innovation. Social issues were being addressed in a far from directed way, but rather in an oblique fashion, as a consequence of decisions concerning economic issues. In our opinion, this also went a long way towards determining the nature and content of the discussions held with Moscow enterprise directors.

The politicians we interviewed were consciously selected from among representatives of opposition parties. This decision was taken as a result of the following logic. Interviewing representatives of the ruling party, 'Nash dom - Rossiya', seemed pointless because a stance of unconditional support for the Federal Government's actions on social and labour issues was *a priori* not of interest to us. We familiarised ourselves with the fairly widely available published programme of the *Yabloko* block, and its position seemed to us to differ very little from the programme being implemented today by the authorities. As regards the LDPR [Liberal Democrats] and the KPRF [Communist Party], the line taken by these parties is tied up with Russia remaining a superpower, in which the military-industrial complex must not be allowed to break up. The measures put forward by these parties fall under the general heading of this position. However, we thought that the views of these parties should also be heard and taken into consideration as an alternative policy variant.

Our survey revealed a rather curious picture of the ideas circulating today among professionals working on employment problems and social policy in Moscow. The mood that has become established among our respondents could be described not even as indifference to current processes, but rather as a general feeling of security and of the remote significance and non-urgency of these processes: they were felt to be unfolding in their own way somewhere or other, and hence affected some stratum of the population - but that this was a disease which was taking such an imperceptible, non-hazardous course that there really, honestly, was no point in worrying about where it would end.

Of course, district departments and offices of the Employment Service, which work directly with groups of citizens affected by the crisis, are more concerned about the situation in Moscow. But their concerns are reminiscent of the fussing of a 'kindly old auntie': look at these poor unfortunate (unemployed) people, they need to be helped, given benefit, found work, retrained, perhaps loans should be arranged to set up a small private business to create jobs for half a dozen of these victims. Yes, the queues stretch out of Moscow job centres from early in the morning. Yes, the Employment Service management is concerned about the queues getting longer. But this is all part of the scenario described above.

The attitude of many members of the other groups of social policy actors was such that many of them were more than indifferent. This was particularly true of representatives of local administrations and of most entrepreneurs and military-industrial complex directors, as well as of the leaders of political parties. The 'red directors' from the military-industrial complex were of the view that employment problems and lack of social protection are imaginary - they are prepared to find a job for anyone. But at the same time they can only pay a derisory, little more than symbolic, salary of $40-100 a month.

St. Petersburg

Interviews were held with 25 respondents. The sample was formed in three stages. The main criterion used in forming the group of politicians was whether they were members of the legislative assembly of St. Petersburg. The group of directors included the heads of major enterprises in the city and (primarily) deputy directors who dealt with personnel matters. The trade union leaders included chairmen of sector-wide occupational unions in St. Petersburg. The survey also included officials involved in preparing and taking decisions at the city level and in sub-city administrative units. Most of the social policy actors selected were people who were fairly well-known in the power structure.

The search for respondents was a rather complex procedure, because of a number of circumstances. April/May 1996 happened to be a time when a considerable proportion of social policy actors, particularly among politicians and high-ranking officials, were embroiled in a pre-election battle to choose a City Governor. This involvement in an election campaign - and the resulting lack of time - was specifically why refusals were received from the Chair of the St. Petersburg Employment Committee, the Chair of the Economics and Finance Commission of the City Government and the heads of two St. Petersburg district administrations. Also unavailable were representatives of the City Government's Committee for Social Affairs. The reason given for this refusal was the need to obtain permission from the Chair of the Committee, who could not be contacted, first because of the election campaign, and later because a new City Government was being formed and a hand-over of power was taking place. There were some changes in the composition of the sample in 1997.

Among the St. Petersburg respondents, it was the directors of major industrial enterprises who were the most difficult to contact; the reason for this, according to the members of the St. Petersburg research team, was the directors' constant and very demanding work schedule. Nevertheless, this was the most numerous respondent group, and in most cases the industrialists showed an active interest in discussing the city's employment and social protection problems.

Among the director-level social policy actors represented, the majority were deputy directors working on personnel matters. Their responses dealt to a large extent with issues of hiring and firing, cutting workforce numbers and retaining skills potential. In contrast to the Moscow respondents, they had no vision of a general solution to the problem, but they gave more information on specific employment policy methods. In this sense, the responses of the Muscovites were broader - they were thinking about how to change the system as a whole, how to save production, how to adapt to the market, and in the final analysis, this interrelates with employment issues.

In most cases, the opinions of the interviewees in St. Petersburg were quite strongly emotionally-coloured. The necessity for the changes that were taking place was not questioned, but in almost every case there was serious criticism of the methods used to implement social and economic policy and employment policy.

Virtually all the respondents stated their views frankly. In the event of an insufficient grasp of an issue, or a reluctance to speak on a particular subject (about their political convictions, for example), there was no awkwardness, since the possibility of such situations arising had been discussed in the preliminary conversation at the beginning of the interview. There was one fairly frequently recurring situation that should be mentioned, where a respondent, having given a brief response to a question put to him, talked in greater detail on issues directly relating to professional activities. Judging by the literature, this is a fairly typical picture.

Our own views of the reputation of each of the social policy actors were checked in discussions with preceding interviewees. However, requests for help in making contact with another social policy actor often ended in failure.

Analysis of the interview texts reveals a certain degree of contradiction between judgements expressed. A negative evaluation of current social policy was frequently encountered: one extreme expression of this view was the utterance 'We have no social policy at all'. Responses to more specific questions, however, reveal that this was more an emotional reaction, showing dissatisfaction with the unco-ordinated nature of social support measures and with the vagueness of the conceptual approach to shaping such policy.

The duration of the interviews was between ½ hour and 1½ hours. There were two reasons for such a large variation in the length of discussions: some of the respondents were very busy with their immediate work obligations, and - although less commonly - there were people who had a vulnerable grasp of particular matters (the social partnership, for example, or individual aspects of the work of the Employment Service).

Voronezh

In 1996, 15 respondents were interviewed. In 1997, 11 of the respondents were re-interviewed, with four (26 per cent) being substituted; these were local authority representatives who had lost their posts during the elections for a new Governor and second-convocation Provincial Duma in 1997.

In view of the absence from the Voronezh interviews of a group of social policy actors equivalent to ministers or permanent secretaries in rank, a 'scientific élite' group was identified, in line with the initial aims of the research. This group comprised two experts who had a high level of awareness of and competence in our research issues, and who also carried some weight in decision-making at a local level. During the interview and its subsequent analysis, the personal stance and allegiance to the 'party of power' of the Deputy Director of the Administration for Social Affairs enabled us to assign this respondent to the 'political leaders' group.

Right from the first interviews, we noticed that the nature of the discussions in Voronezh was largely determined by the specific features of this region: market processes developing slowly, many respondents with pro-Soviet leanings, looking to the past rather than the future.

The election of the Voronezh Provincial Governor in 1997 strengthened pro-Communist feelings among the political and economic élite of Voronezh. The current Governor is the one-time Secretary of the Provincial Committee of the Communist Party. The Provincial and City authorities were placed at loggerheads. Social issues are being tackled according to emphases determined by the battle for spheres of influence and for the electorate. Priority is being given to pension matters (the majority of voters are pensioners): job creation and employment problems are hardly being addressed at all. The official unemployment level in the city remained almost unchanged through the year; but this does not reflect the real situation. Most industrial enterprises are standing idle, and many workers are on long-term unpaid leave. Those who are still working receive their wages months in arrears. Despite this situation, there are still no special programmes in Voronezh to address employment problems, there is no regional legislation dealing with employment, etc. These were among the factors that dictated the nature of the interviews with representatives of Voronezh power structures.

Voronezh company directors were quite willing to be contacted at both stages of the research. The decisive factor in this, however, was less a desire to help tackle social problems and employment problems in particular, and more of an urge to reach a wider audience, to be heard, to make a statement about the serious problems faced by their enterprise: and most of all, about their Employment Fund liabilities. Many directors of industrial enterprises (even those directors who had managed to keep production going) are unwilling to pay into the Employment Fund, on the basis that this in itself encourages people to be dependent. The directors did not feel that they were actors in social protection and employment policy, which they considered to be compensatory in nature.

Content analysis of the interviews showed that the stances adopted by the respondents in relation to socio-economic priorities did not vary significantly. Certain discrepancies in the responses were associated primarily with particular aspects of the professional and social status of the social policy actors. The average interview duration in Voronezh was 1½ hours.

Analysing the Primary Data

The preparation of the interview results and the way they were processed was different at different stages of the research. After primary analysis of the interview texts (pilot stage), we were convinced that certain relationships genuinely could be observed between the respondents' replies and the group to which they had been assigned at the beginning of the study: there was a homogeneity and similarity of stance between respondents in a single group in relation to the central theme of the research - employment policy in the context of social policy. Even as a first approximation, the actual distribution of the responses matched the nominal distribution of the respondents.

On obtaining the first results from processing interviews on the main themes of the questionnaire, we discovered that responses to the open questions in the interview deviated from the subject matter of the research. On the other hand, they were able to explain a lot, as they disclosed - in a way that we had not expected - the real problems faced by the respondent, and their real interests in social and employment policy. As a result of the interviews, we obtained a considerable body of information on the questions that we were interested in. However, a special way of processing the interview materials was needed to reveal emphases in the responses to questions, and to reveal the respondents' degree of commitment to tackling one or another issue, either in employment policy or in social policy generally.

Primary processing at the first stage of the research (1996) consisted of searching for and recording blocks of content in the interview text, taking as a basis key questions which reflect the specific nature of the area of social policy. These content blocks are subsequently grouped, analysed and compared. Certain discussion questions were constructed in a form that enabled coding using defined algorithms, and we produced two-dimensional frequency tables using the degree of involvement of the respondents in employment policy as one of the 'markers'.

The basis for selection of key questions for computer processing involved such factors as awareness of and involvement in the formation of a labour market in Russia, participation in tackling employment problems, and an understanding of key issues in Russia's socio-economic situation. A total of 12 questions was selected.

This processing could be described as secondary, since the questions selected on this principle had to be constructed as closed questions, suggesting variables from typical responses based on actual material from interviews already conducted. As the second distribution 'marker', we looked at the characteristics of the respondents themselves. According to our research objectives, this aim of the analysis covered: defining the social policy actors' level of activity and how far they can be seen as key figures in employment policy. The tables we created gave us additional information on the degree to which the subjects of employment policy are involved in tackling labour market issues and in the formation of a labour market in Russia's strained social and economic situation.

After primary processing of the interview texts, the response to each question was re-cast in a compressed form, or - to put it another way - the essence of the response was isolated and a precise formulation was recorded. This procedure was carried out for all the questions on the questionnaire. The next stage of the work consisted of comparing the responses from individual respondents: the judgement of each respondent was compared with the response of both the preceding and the following respondent, and so on. This gave us response variables for each of the interview questions, and their distribution was calculated as a percentage of the total number of responses, which enabled us to perform further additional analysis of the data.

The questionnaire also included questions containing 'interviewer's prompts'. These questions may, in principle, be viewed as 'closed', and this allowed us to present the social policy actors' alternative approaches in a formalised and systematic way. This work was carried out with assistance from staff at the Institute of Human Population Issues of the Russian Academy of Sciences.

At stage two of the research (1997) the entire body of interviews (from research stages one and two) was processed together. For this purpose, coding sheets were drawn up to match the subject matter of the questionnaire (two coding sheets for 1996 and 1997); each coding sheet included around 40-45 questions, enabling the survey materials to be formalised after interviews had been conducted in all the cities studied. In order to standardise the processing procedure, each question on the coding sheet gave five response variables, and the coding sheet also included socio-demographic information on the respondent.

A coding table was drawn up for each interview: so there was a total of 150 coding tables from the results of the two stages of the research. However, the difference between the composition of the two (1996 and 1997) questionnaires required us to create an additional (third) coding sheet in order to reflect the content of the resultant integrated questionnaire. This enabled us to compare and contrast, directly and fully, the responses in the two stages of the survey, and also met our objective of ensuring a successive approach to analysing the responses to the basic question group (25 questions common to 1996 and 1997); a matrix of the social policy actors' responses was drawn up to compare the two research years.

After processing the formalised responses using SPSS, we obtained a broad mass of information about the position of the social policy actors on the questions that we were concerned with. Taken together, this amounted to some 500 tables distributed across respondent groups and across survey cities (both summary and differentiated tables). Using the basic question group, we drew up histograms illustrating the results obtained and allowing us to represent visually the distributions of responses by city and by respondent group, as well as to represent the dynamics of the interviewees' views. The data obtained enabled us to identify changes, trace trends and establish points of emphasis.

Our research showed that the respondents we enlisted to take part in these focused interviews (directors of industrial enterprises, ministry officials, politicians, trade union leaders, etc.) - the presumed actors of the new social policy in Russia - were in reality only formal, or nominal, subjects of this policy. Undoubtedly, in terms of their social status, their rank at work and their professional allegiance, the members of the professional groups we chose genuinely fell within the conception of a social policy with multiple subjects. However, at the moment, they are still only potential subjects. Most of our respondents were sufficiently well-informed about specific issues (connected with their professional interests); however, they often had a very ill-defined image of the social situation in Russia and the aims and objectives of current social policy, and its relationship to economic policy. In Russia, in practice, no social partnership institutions are working, trade union activities are ineffective, the social programmes of the leading political parties and movements are unknown not only to the public but also to the very people who are being put forward as social policy actors. It should be noted that social problems as a whole do not represent any kind of serious interest for them: they see the essential priority as being to tackle first economic problems, and then specific work-related, political and industrial objectives. They have no intrinsic commitment to the creation or implementation of effective social policy, or to addressing social problems effectively. In the course of the survey, we formed the firm impression that our respondents practically never thought about most issues of contemporary social life, and that - in particular - they did not think of themselves as being people with the potential to carry out actions essential in tackling these issues.

5 Moscow, St. Petersburg and Voronezh

Молочные реки, кисельные берега
Flowing with milk and honey...

The modernisation of Russian society and the transition to a market economy have given a new edge and meaning to problems of social development and employment in the different regions of the Russian Federation. Given perennial instability, economic and social crisis and deepening inequality between regions, the task of applying an analytic approach to these problems - without which appropriate regional policy, including employment policy, cannot be developed - has become increasingly acute.

Regional differences are generated by various factors. Some of these are the inevitable result of economic activity, including the free market and free competition. Others are tied in with a whole series of cultural and ethnic problems. It is especially significant, perhaps, that Russia is a country which might be seen as possessing a 'border civilisation', lying as it does between European and Asiatic civilisations, while at the same time having its own authenticity. In this respect, there is also an uneven degree of adherence to the traditional extensive model of economic and cultural development. As a result, some Russian regions are drawn more towards European culture and civilisation and are able to take on board the new value system that modernisation brings with it; while others stick to traditional extensive culture and reject (or at any rate have a problem coming to terms with) modernisation and its associated need for active mastery of new technologies and ways of working. In the event, some regions 'fit in' to the market more easily than others. In the 1990s, gaps between the regions began to grow rapidly: a process of stratification of Russian regions into qualitatively different types is taking place. This makes it obvious that there is both the need and the potential to carry out specifically social policy that would have been unthinkable under the Soviet authorities. This demonstrates one of the decisive differences between unified Soviet social policy and the post-Soviet version that is made up of different elements.

Under such conditions, sampling our research subjects meant to a large extent also choosing the angle from which we would look at the position of the populace, the individual social groups and the nature of current social policy. It is well-known that, in purely numerical terms, there is a predominance of depressed regions in Russia - regions where the populace and the local authorities were unprepared for life in market economy conditions. But also there are regions where development is furthest on - those which could be regarded as a model of the immediate future for the whole (or almost the whole) country.

We considered that it would not be sensible to take small- or medium-sized towns for this purpose, as for example Goldthorpe and Lockwood and their colleagues (1969) did in the 1960s when they chose Luton as their subject town, because our research design presupposed analysis of the whole range of groups in crisis in regional labour markets, as well as the existence of a 'harmonious grouping' of social policy actors who could speak as experts. In addition, we were interested to study how social and employment patterns and policies might be changing for the future. Given all this, our choice was more or less made for us: the two Russian capitals - Moscow and St. Petersburg. For comparison we chose Voronezh - a city typical of a number of depressed regions where social and economic change was less marked, but with an economic and employment structure not dissimilar from those of the two capitals.

The difference between the cities - or the gulf between them, one could legitimately say - is illustrated by tax income to the consolidated State budget per head of population in 1996. The *per capita* bill for the Moscow taxpayer was 10.8 million roubles; in St. Petersburg the equivalent figure was 3.5 million roubles, and in Voronezh 1.6 million. We should point out that, using the same *per capita* taxation indicator, there are substantially poorer regions - e.g. Tambov province, at 1.3 million roubles, or Ivanovo province, at 1.2 million (Russia-European Centre for Economic Policy, 1997, pp.250-251). If we divide the regions of Russia into relatively better-off, relatively worse-off and those in a disastrous situation, our three cities would be in the first and second of these categories. Let us now examine the individual features and characteristics of the cities selected for our research.

Moscow was, and is, the capital of an enormous Eurasian country, reflecting all the idiosyncrasies of this part of the world, both its gravitation towards European culture and ways of life and its rejection of Europe, striving to protect, at whatever cost, its own privileged character. St. Petersburg was, and remains, the only major city in Russia with a predominantly European lifestyle. Hence the centuries-old contrast, drawn in both academic and creative literature, between the two capitals: Moscow and St. Petersburg; and the two types of citizen found in them: the Muscovite and the St. Petersburger; and the two lifestyles: the Moscow lifestyle and the St. Petersburg lifestyle. In Moscow, the city-dwellers themselves, along with bus and tram drivers when naming stops, will always say 'Such-and-such store', 'Such-and-such market', whereas in St. Petersburg it will be 'Such-and-such factory', 'Such-and-such museum'.

Moscow was, and has remained (and this is currently being further strengthened in the economic life of the capital), a gigantic centre for trading and financial capital; while St. Petersburg was, and still is, the centre for industrial capital. The feature that is common to these two cities is the highest level of development in science and education in Russia, and this in turn means that a high proportion of the population of these cities is engaged in these spheres of activity. There is a considerable historical difference in the way the populations of the two cities were formed. Although Moscow, of course, drew in migrants from all over the country, the dominant influx was from regions to the south of Moscow. St. Petersburg, on the other hand, mainly took people migrating from northern provinces of Russia. The difference is that in the northern provinces, serfdom was virtually unknown - people traditionally lived by crafts and simple enterprises - whereas Moscow filled up with one-time agricultural peasants, the children and grandchildren of serfs.

Moscow and St. Petersburg are of particular interest for comparative research into regional development and for an appraisal of alternative national conceptions of social policy. At the beginning of the 1990s, a gradual divergence of policy between St. Petersburg and Moscow could be observed, the most obvious manifestation of which was the local government reforms in these two capital cities, which resulted in a certain degree of confrontation, both among local city authorities and between them and the Federal level of government.

The Situation in Moscow

In terms of its range of employment, Moscow is one of the most varied regions in the country: the non-State, 'alternative' economy is developing more rapidly in Moscow than in the vast majority of other regions. On the one hand, a high proportion of Russia's richest people and highly-paid employees is concentrated in Moscow; on the other hand, the percentage of pensioners living on tiny pensions and of other categories of citizens unable to work is exceptionally high.

Like the rest of Russia, Moscow has seen a sharp fall in industrial output. Taking 1990 as a base, the fall in output in 1995 was 50 per cent for Russia as a whole, but for Moscow it was 59 per cent. In 1996, industrial output fell by a further 8 per cent in the country as a whole, but in Moscow the figure was 30 per cent. Nevertheless, the capital still accounts for 5.7 per cent of the total national volume of production. The financial circumstances of Moscow enterprises are substantially better than in other regions: the proportion of loss-making enterprises out of the total was 43 per cent for Russia as a whole, but only 29 per cent in Moscow.

Serious re-structuring of Moscow's economy took place during the period 1992-1997. Industry lost its previous importance for the city's economy. Import-export operations have been developing successfully, and retail trade, the financial sphere and insurance are also growing. In other words, there has been a squeeze in the secondary sector of the economy (manufacturing industry), with a rise in the tertiary sector (the service sector); but the squeeze in science and scientific services, as well as design organisations and the like, has led to a contraction in that fourth sector - which was the sole guarantee of Russia's transition to a post-industrial, information economy.

For Russia as a whole, the nature of the labour market is still determined by the development of industrial production; but the unique feature of Moscow's labour market is the rapidly growing contribution of the non-production sector, construction capital, financial institutions and banks. These industries are seeing a continual increase in employment and a demand for employees. By 1995, the non-production sector accounted for 38 per cent of employment, as against 27 per cent in Russia as a whole. A special role is played in the capital by small businesses, which in November 1997 employed over one million people.

The level of registered unemployment in Moscow is the lowest in Russia (0.8 per cent), as against 9.4 per cent for Russia as a whole at the end of 1996 (according to data from research conducted using the ILO definition). Unemployment in Moscow is structural in nature, with a high demand for labour at enterprises and organisations offering pay lower than the Subsistence Minimum, or for unskilled labour to work in dangerous or severe conditions. The blue- to white-collar ratio among advertised vacancies is roughly 3:1, while the reverse situation pertains in the social composition of the unemployed. The proportion of unemployed people with higher education is more than twice the mean Russian maximum.

Just as in Soviet times, the outer zones of the Moscow conurbation serve as dormitory suburbs for the capital. The city traditionally contains jobs for the entire conurbation. Some three million residents of the Moscow suburbs travel to work in the capital every day. There are also many foreign workers in Moscow who will accept pay and conditions of work unacceptable to Muscovite job-seekers. In the first half of 1996 alone, 56,600 foreign citizens were invited by various companies to work in Moscow. According to official statistics, the largest number of foreigners works in industries like building (over 34,000) and transport and communications (10,500). Most numerous among these are Ukrainians. The real number of foreign workers, especially seasonal building labour and decorators, is several times greater (Russo-European Centre for Economic Policy, 1997, pp.236, 242, 247-248).

Moscow is home to 70 per cent of the country's financial assets, and the majority of financial transactions take place in the city: this has required the formation of a corresponding segment of the labour market. About 1,200 credit organisations and their branches, over 1,000 insurance companies and many auditing and legal firms are located in Moscow. The city also houses the headquarters of major financial and industrial groups - above all, of the oil and gas monopolies like LUKoil, YuKOS, Gazprom and others. All these pay taxes in Moscow. At the same time, half of the Moscow city budget is made up of contributions from small businesses (9,000 billion roubles - $1.5 billion - from local tax receipts alone). In addition, Moscow has managed to make itself attractive to foreign investors. In October 1997, there were 85,000 foreign firms operating in the city, a large number of foreign traders were located there, while international tourism is increasing fast; more than 57 per cent of the accumulated foreign capital which has come into Russia is attributable to Moscow (*Finansovye Izvestiya,* 13/11/1997; *Izvestiya,* 24/10/1997; *Moskovskii komsomolets,* 13/11/1997).

Both public opinion and expert assessments have it that Moscow has been the biggest gainer from the economic changes which have taken place. The *per capita* GDP indicator shows the situation in the capital to be three times better than in Russia as a whole. A high proportion of incomes in Moscow come from entrepreneurial activity, especially minor retail operations involving foreign trade. Muscovites constitute only 6.5 per cent of the country's population, but their share of total personal income is over 20 per cent (although it has to be remembered that the State Committee for Statistics' method of calculating personal incomes is not perfect). In 1995, residents of the capital received a little under 10 per cent of total Russian wages and salaries, and about 7 per cent of the total amount of pensions. However, some 30 per cent of all other income was attributable to them, that is income from entrepreneurial activity, property and transactions in the shadow economy. If we look at registered average monthly pay levels, in September 1997 the picture was as follows: the fuel industry - 3.5 million roubles (with a current exchange rate then of around 6,000 roubles to $1); the electricity generating industry - 2.3 million roubles; the food industry - 1.7 million roubles; the defence industry - 0.69 million roubles; communications - 0.56 million roubles; and, with pay at under one million roubles, a similar miserable standard of existence for employees in education and science, health care and the arts (Russo-European Centre for Economic Policy, 1997, pp.238-239; *Moskovskii komsomolets*, 18/11/1997).

In the press, Moscow is likened to the successful Russian model of 'municipal capitalism'. In 1995, the city authorities held an estimated 14 per cent of the authorised capital of joint-stock companies set up out of city property. Moscow City Government representatives sit on the boards of directors of all joint-stock companies in which the city has a shareholding (*Kapital*, 9/11/1995 pp.1-2). At the same time, analysts are also noting some consequences of the handover of the capital's economy to the municipal authorities which are not necessarily favourable at all. By far the greater part of its property is under the control of the city administration. By raising rents and shortening the duration of rental contracts, the money accruing from capitalisation of these fixed assets and land can be concentrated in the hands of the city administration, thus helping to finance their ambitious construction and other projects. In strategic terms, though, this policy is detrimental, since it is hindering the formation of a competitive market in property. Another process taking place is the handover of property to the city by large enterprises (for example, the ZIL and Moskvich vehicle plants), with their output being forced upon consumers who are in one way or another dependent on the city authorities. Handover of property to the municipal authorities has given rise to an extremely high level of debt at most major enterprises. The result of this has been that the city authorities have been able to take packages of shares in such enterprises into the local budget (Ulyukayev, 1997).

Nevertheless, Moscow has become the only city in Russia with strong growth in its economy, housing and office construction on a scale never seen before, and modernisation of the urban infrastructure. Its place in the country's economy is expanding fast. Even back in 1995, the capital contributed 13.1 per cent of national GDP. In the first half of 1997,

Moscow contributed 40 per cent of Russia's consolidated budget (*Izvestiya*, 24/10/1997).

It is hard to assess what contribution has been made by objective factors to the prosperity experienced in the capital, and to what extent it has been a result of the handover of property to the municipal authorities described above, with its associated economic and social policy, which in many ways differs from that of the Federal level of government. Whether Moscow's Mayor Yuri Luzhkov acknowledges it or not, the policy conducted by him and his government is clearly Keynesian in character; whereas, since autumn 1991, the Federal government (with some vacillations) has been following a neo-liberal monetarist course that has had absolutely no perceptible support from the people of Russia. The Mayor of Moscow, on the other hand, in good old Soviet style, can rely on the unanimous support of his citizens. The business journal *Den'gi* [Money] published an article by the author of a commentary on Keynes' book 'The General Theory of Employment, Interest and Money'. He writes that Luzhkov 'is almost literally following Keynes' recommendations'. Following Keynes, Moscow's Mayor is saying that the only way out of the crisis is to ensure that all resources are engaged through an increase in overall demand for them.

In a self-regulating economy, escape from crisis and provision of full employment are not possible. So, according to Keynes, the State must actively involve itself in the economy. The State must improve the attractiveness of direct capital investment in comparison with other ways of utilising money; it must use the State budget to finance investment projects of all kinds; it must make direct State purchases of goods and services, and, especially, organise public works schemes and so on. And that is precisely what the Moscow city government is doing - actively stimulating employment among Muscovites and putting major new investment projects into effect. It may even be that the potential to act in this way at the Moscow regional level is actually linked to the fact that the brake it puts on money in circulation is of benefit to the Federal government, i.e. the traditional course taken by neo-classical monetarists (Kalashnov, 1997, p.24).

The policy being conducted by the Moscow government pre-supposes a decisive rejection of developing or organising the economy purely on the basis of market self-regulation - 'the invisible hand of the market'. The policy variant acknowledged as being most effective is a regulating market operating under administrative bureaucratic control. The main slogan used in expressing Luzhkov's populist 'supreme mission' is 'Efficient economy

+ Universal prosperity'. It is no coincidence that, in December 1997, at the Second Congress of the Union of Public Bodies, entitled 'A Russian Movement for New Socialism', the Mayor of Moscow expressed his belief in social democratic principles (*Ekspert*, vol.48, 15/12/1997, p.5).

The Situation in St. Petersburg

A different situation has arisen in St. Petersburg. For much of the transition period since August 1991, St. Petersburg has been run by very active supporters of the Federal course of creating a self-organising market economy, headed by the city's Mayor, one of Russia's best-known democratic activists, Professor Anatoli Sobchak. How, then, did the development of the country's second great city look as a result of this policy, contrasting in so many ways with Moscow policy?

Of the major cities of the former USSR, St. Petersburg was the only one which, under Soviet power, had lost many of those prerequisites for development and functions that had guided its fate and its place in Russian life prior to 1917. The city had thus not only ceased to be the official capital of the country, but was no longer its 'window on Europe' either. Industry had grown out of all proportion, placing extreme loads on the vulnerable northern natural environment (latitude 60°N). In terms of the proportion of its population working in industry, St. Petersburg was in second place, after Nizhnii Novgorod, in all Russia. St. Petersburg was not just Russia's leading industrial centre, with a high percentage of high-tech industries: it was the *de facto* capital of the military-industrial complex. The city was home to major scientific and production complexes with a military industry orientation, each employing tens of thousands of people.

During the 1970s and 1980s, the present author and his colleagues tried on more than one occasion to suggest a redistribution of urban development functions with more emphasis on such industries as science and art and international tourism, with the aim of gradually transforming St. Petersburg from a super-industrial to a post-industrial centre, with a developed services sector and information-based industries. These suggestions, however, met with a hostile reception from the city's Communist Party leadership. As Grigori Romanov, then First Secretary of the Leningrad Communist Party Association and Member of the Politbureau of the Central Committee of the CPSU, explained: 'They pin medals on our chests for the achievements of our defence plants, not for opening theatres'.

It seemed that St. Petersburg could hardly have been less prepared to make the transition to a market economy and private enterprise. So when, in the late 1980s, serious attempts began to be made to set about converting military industry to civilian production, many experts assumed that St. Petersburg was facing a looming tragedy, with mass unemployment and mass emigration. Among the in-built restrictions to economic development were:

- the out-of-date structure of parts of the economy, which was oriented towards shipbuilding, manufacture of military hardware, production of machinery for power generation;
- the low proportion of economically active people in the population, with a corresponding high proportion of pensioners;
- the existence of an enormous historical centre, which is not particularly well-suited for residential use, but requires constant investment in rebuilding and restoration;
- poor environmental factors.

However, despite all the difficulties of the transition to a new economic and political system, the city has done more than just survive, it has won a sound position for itself in the Russian and world markets. The crucial factor would appear to have been the massive cultural capital built up by the city. St. Petersburg was far more ready than other cities to embrace occupational and social mobility and modern management methods. For the first time in recent decades, the manufacturing industry has lost its leading role (31.5 per cent of employees worked in the manufacturing industry in 1991; by 1996, the figure had fallen to 15.3 per cent, and the forecast for 2000 is 8.6 per cent). If we take industrial manufacturing output in 1991 as 100 per cent, in 1996 it was 39.5 per cent. A continuing decline is being observed in metallurgy, engineering and the light and chemical industries. The current St. Petersburg city administration is forced to admit that a considerable proportion of the manufacturing industry is not being accepted by the market, and is providing no income.

There are however a few islands of success: the electricity generating industry, where a rise of almost 50 per cent is expected by 2000; and the food industry. The management consultancy company Al't, one of the best of its kind in Russia, carried out a survey of specialists from brokering firms and banks, Federal and municipal officials and journalists, from which they found that St. Petersburg is where the greatest number of successful industrial enterprises is concentrated - 89 of them. These included factories producing nuclear-powered ships and marine diesels, turbine blades and women's clothing, beer and bread. Sales have been on the increase at all these enterprises in the last few years; wage payments are generally not delayed, and managers are able to adjust output rapidly to produce new and needed goods, manage company finances skilfully and maintain a clear view of the way forward for production development. In contrast to the old Soviet way of thinking, the state is seen as a customer, not as the person calling the tune (*Izvestiya*, 16/7/1996, 14/11/1996; *Moskovskie novostii*, vol.43, 27/10/1996).

Despite all that has been said about its obsolete structure and the severe burden placed on the delicate northern environment by giant enterprises, the city's industry thus still has significant potential, and retains a promising future in many areas. St. Petersburg's industry is mainly made up of high-tech types of manufacture with a high science content, to a large extent oriented towards the military-industrial complex. This fact does, it is true, make it very difficult to restructure the city's economy, which in turn prevents a rapid expansion of labour market capacity; but on the other hand it gives confidence in the future, as adaptation to the 'rules of the game' in a market economy proceeds.

Small business is rapidly increasing in the northern capital, as in Moscow. Some 600,000 St. Petersburgers were engaged in this sector in 1997 - almost double the number working at large industrial plants. The proportions of employees working in small businesses were 5.1 per cent in 1991, 25.7 per cent in 1996, and 36.4 per cent in 2000. Forecasts for the year 2000 show more than four employees in SMEs for every one factory worker. In 1996, small businesses accounted for 17 per cent of receipts paid into the local treasury (more than half those the city received from all large industrial plants).

A distinguishing feature of St. Petersburg banks is the way they work closely with the real sector of the economy. Thus, in terms of long-term credits made available in 1995 as part of the overall structure of credit investments by banks, St. Petersburg was second in Russia, with only Samara ahead of it; and in terms of rate of absolute increase it lay first. St. Petersburg banks contrast favourably with their Moscow counterparts in their willingness to go beyond speculative activities and promote the investment process.

Business activity in St. Petersburg is assisted by liberal tendencies in the tax policy being implemented by the City government. Despite low taxes, budget income is rising more quickly than in Moscow (2.5 per cent compared to 2.4 per cent); there is a smaller percentage of loss-making enterprises, among other things (Voloshina, 1996). In early 1997, the City Duma passed the St. Petersburg City Government's Taxation Act, which established a three-year moratorium (the period for which the Act is in force) on rises in any regional taxes, a move without precedent in Russia.

Not surprisingly, therefore, foreign investors are showing an increasing interest in St. Petersburg. The end of 1995 saw the opening of the JSC Coca Cola St. Petersburg Bottlers Plant, the result of a $25 million investment. Cellular telephone systems are developing rapidly, with two American companies investing in this area - Motorola ($12.5 million) and North West GSM ($20 million). Some very large St. Petersburg enterprises, which could have been a focus for social conflict were it not for foreign investment, are being reconstructed. The American company Caterpillar and Kirovski Zavod AO [Kirov Works Joint-Stock Company] have set up a joint venture with authorised capital of $5 million; and Kraft Foods International Inc. has invested $11 million in the city's confectionery industry. New investment projects are on a much larger scale. The American pharmaceutical company ICM, for example, has acquired a 75 per cent shareholding in Oktyabr AO, and intends to invest $180 million over the next few years in the construction of a new factory and three research centres. The Swedish company Baltic Beverage Holding has acquired 43.5 per cent of the shares in Baltika AO, with an undertaking to invest 150 million Swedish crowns in production development, with the result that this company's beer had become Russia's market leader by the summer of 1997 (Kudrin, 1997, p.426).

With the disintegration of the USSR, Russia's new borders have also had a crucial bearing on the new situation regarding links between Russia and the West, with St. Petersburg once again becoming a direct 'window' onto Europe and the geopolitical significance of areas adjoining the city rising substantially. In view of the difficulties that have arisen in relations with contiguous states (the Baltic countries and Poland), we see this trend as optimal for links with Western Europe. Intermediary trading, market infrastructure and transport communications are already providing a significant part of the northern capital's profits, if not their main component. What this is, in essence, is a 'commission' received by the city in various ways from other regions because of its advantageous geographical situation, its reformist reputation and the high skills level of St. Petersburg specialists. This mission as intermediary will, in all likelihood, continue to strengthen as time passes. By the turn of the century, forecasts predict, the city on the Neva will be handling up to one-third of the foreign trade turnover of all Russia.

The main features of the city's labour market depend on the high level of skills that the population has built up over several generations. About 10 per cent of the workforce are in science and scientific services, and over 12 per cent are in education. Strong expansion in the financial and credit sphere and the development of the small business sector have together opened up promising avenues for solving employment problems among the city's population. People who have lost work at older enterprises in the city have in many cases found new jobs in the commercial structures which have sprung up during the years of economic transformation.

Registered unemployment in St. Petersburg ran at around 2.2 per cent during the period 1995 to 1997. This is a relatively low level, for although it is approximately double that of Moscow, it is also approximately half the level for Russia generally. The percentage of people with insecure employment (working less than a full working week or on compulsory leave without pay or with only partial pay at the employer's initiative) is a little higher than in Moscow (3.5 per cent). Female unemployment is high, in fact double that for men, but still the percentage of women among the Moscow unemployed is about 10 per cent higher than in St. Petersburg. The youth unemployment level is lower in St. Petersburg than in Russia generally. The number of unemployed blue-collar workers is a little higher than that of white-collar workers and specialists, although the trend is for the numbers of the former to diminish, relatively speaking, while the numbers of the latter are increasing relatively. Besides this, there are more unemployed for each white-collar or specialist vacancy than there are blue-collar unemployed for vacancies in skilled blue-collar occupations.

Among the industries advertising vacancies are manufacturing industry, construction, transport and communications, i.e. those industries where the fall in output has been greater than average for the city. Their announcements of vacancies indicate that a redistribution of the workforce is taking place as part of the re-structuring process, with flows of employees to industries that are in better shape and offer relatively good pay. Predictably, people in search of work constitute 30 per cent of people with a total *per capita* income below the Subsistence Minimum. As part of this process of labour flows, the number of employees no longer working in their normal occupation is also on the rise; but nonetheless about half of them are quite happy with their new circumstances and have no intention of changing them. Despite continued tension in the labour market, related to the search for better-paid work, indices for full-time and part-time employment in St. Petersburg stabilised during the first quarter of 1997.

Standard-of-living indicators show that St. Petersburg is in a much worse position than Moscow. At the end of 1996, 34 per cent of the St. Petersburg population had a *per capita* income below the Subsistence Minimum (312,000 roubles), and the income of 10 per cent of St. Petersburgers was below 200,000 roubles per family member (Ivanova, Nikonova and Mozgovaya, 1997, pp.7-11).

Thus, despite the very difficult circumstances in which St. Petersburg has found itself and remains, the city has managed to survive by becoming increasingly actively involved in the market economy, bringing its economic structure up-to-date, attracting investment and addressing the problem of employment.

Turning to regional politics, in the spring of 1996, the residents of St. Petersburg elected a new head of the city administration. During the pre-election campaign, various slogans were put forward by the candidates. While the first Mayor of St. Petersburg in post-Soviet times, Anatoli Sobchak, promised that theatres, museums and banks would prosper, his main opponent, Vladimir Yakovlev, promised the voters that he would reject the priorities of his predecessor and divert support from tourism and culture towards the city's manufacturing industry. However, these were merely vote-winning words. The reality of the actual changes boils down to a perceptible swing towards the policy line pursued by the Moscow city authorities. The new city authorities have started intervening decisively in the economic circumstances of the city, beginning with tackling the major objectives of developing the manufacturing industry and going right through to intervention in the provision of consumer goods. In 1997, the city authorities managed to bring down bread prices by eliminating the chain of intermediary firms and organising direct grain purchases. They also returned to a unified customer service system for many other types of product, in each case doing away with superfluous links in the producer-to-consumer chain.

In 1997, the city authorities succeeded in arresting the decline in the city's manufacturing industry and achieving a slight rise in output (2 per cent). The authorities stepped up their search for investors and set several large investment projects in train, in which new enterprises were to be built and the railway station and airport were to undergo reconstruction. The largest of these was the 'Major Sea Port' construction project. St. Petersburg's sea port is currently handling only 12 million tonnes of cargo, with most income from the transfer of Russian goods going to the

Baltic states. The port reconstruction will allow the city to handle up to 100 million tonnes of cargo a year, with virtually all the income from transport operations thus concentrated in the city - and inside Russia.

The Situation in Voronezh

The third city in the survey, Voronezh, is the Russian backwoods, notoriously remote from where social policy is devised. It is an ancient Russian city which retains intact the network of the Soviet Communist nomenklatura.

The nature of the local sub-culture led to the creation and reproduction of the rural peasant-type, as opposed to the industrial, worker. This had a bearing on the quality of labour and the quality of industrial products, manufactured in ever-increasing volumes by the new industrial giants.

In its ambitious plans, the Bolshevik leadership of Russia never had time for people's individual interests and idiosyncrasies. As those leaders loved to say, it was never a problem for 'a man to change his skin'. Nowadays, though, when another of their favourite sayings - 'we shall not count the cost' - has lost its meaning, and when the market has begun to assess product quality and production cost, it is the common people who are having to pay the price for the cynicism and recklessness of those leaders and their talentless successors still in positions of power in the provinces. It is now clear that functionally illiterate employees - from directors down to ordinary fitters and machine operators - are of no use to anyone.

Let us move on from this general picture to statistics. The population of Voronezh is around 900,000. The city is an important transport crossroads for the European part of Russia. The manufacturing industry is made up of enterprises from 10 basic sectors. About 30 per cent of industrial output is in engineering and metals processing, 21 per cent is in the form of electricity generated (developing, like engineering, primarily at military and industrial complex enterprises), while over 20 per cent is attributable to the food industry, 17 per cent to the chemical and petrochemical industries, with other industries taking about 10 per cent. In terms of industrial production output, Voronezh is in 37th place among Russian Federation members. At the same time, the location of Voronezh in the Central Black-Soil region, a region with developed and efficient agriculture, coupled with the fact that three-quarters of the territory of Voronezh Province is taken up by *chernozem* black-earth soil, which is of global importance in agrarian and food production terms and which has unique potential for the development of agrarian industry, certainly means that the food industry plays a large part in Voronezh's industrial output structure; but it also means that many of Voronezh's inhabitants maintain close links with agriculture in the Province.

The defence industry, which makes up 78 per cent of Voronezh's industry, earned the city a reasonable living at one time. Now it has been abandoned, and this is the reason why a large part of Voronezh's population is poor. The local economy is currently based largely on manufacturing machinery (mainly at plants that have been converted from military to civilian production), and this is in crisis; and also on the agro-industrial complex, with its steadily falling production levels. Consequently, the majority of the most important economic indicators show a crisis in Voronezh that is deeper than for Russia as a whole. Inflation in Voronezh Province in 1996 was about 30 per cent, as against 21.8 per cent for Russia as a whole; the decline in investment was 28 per cent as against 21.5 per cent; and GDP, again for 1996, fell by 10 per cent or 11 per cent compared to five per cent or six per cent for Russia generally (Sokolov, 1997, p.16).

The particular character of the regional economy (with its high proportion of military-industrial complex enterprises) and of the political sympathies of the leadership and residents of the region means that the proportion of state and municipal ownership remains high. According to a State Property Commission report for 1996, Voronezh Province was among those regions where the course of privatisation had been 'inhibited', with fewer than 30 enterprises being privatised during the year.

Small businesses are also relatively underdeveloped here, accounting for around 12 per cent of the total volume of production in the region. The creation and expansion of SMEs in Voronezh is hampered by administrative barriers, regulations and procedures devised by the local authorities. Thus, differentiated stamp duty rates for the registration of enterprises in St. Petersburg are only half what they are in Voronezh. The Voronezh authorities place all kinds of obstacles in the way of fixed assets being brought into economic circulation, preferring to let fixed assets and equipment out on short-term leases (Aborieva and Remizov, 1997, pp.44-48).

Besides this, Voronezh possesses a number of features which exert some influence on social and employment policy as practised in the city. The most important feature of these is that it is one of a group of conservative agrarian/industrial areas where the population supports the

Communist *nomenklatura*. In conjunction with economic decline and the lack of any light at the end of the tunnel of economic depression, this has lead to a slowing of reforms, which are proceeding extremely slowly in Voronezh, and are consequently particularly painful for the populace. To some degree it may be said that the region is socially, politically and economically isolated - above all, from the influence of Federal centres of power.

At the same time, the Central Black-Soil Region is one of Russia's traditional key centres of science and culture. Voronezh takes third place in Russia, after Moscow and St. Petersburg, for its number of higher education institutions, and it also has several national research centres. Science is currently experiencing a massive fall in labour demand, and is one of the areas that has suffered the most through employment cutbacks.

In the Voronezh region, indices for economic activity among the populace - based on the proportions of our respondents involved in entrepreneurial activities or regularly receiving 'earnings on the side' - are among the lowest, and if we compare the situation for secondary employment in Voronezh with that in Moscow, the discrepancy between the figures can be by as much as two or three times. In the spring of 1997, the level of registered unemployment in Voronezh was four per cent. Over 60 per cent of the unemployed are women. In contrast to Moscow and St. Petersburg, the percentage of young unemployed is high (about a third of all those without work), whereas the percentage of persons of pre-pension age is small.

Long-term unemployment is widespread. In the first quarter of 1997, one in six of the registered unemployed had been out of work for over a year, and only a third had been unemployed for less than four months.

Comparative Data for the Three Cities

Placing Moscow, St. Petersburg and Voronezh and their particular development trends in the context of other Russian regions is much facilitated by the excellent research carried out from 1992-1995 by the Expert Institute (Russia) and Birmingham University's Centre for Russian and Eastern European Studies (UK). The authors of this research identified specific features and differences in the socio-economic situation of the Russian regions, including each region's level of development, its specialisation and the structure of its economy, the influence of its geographical situation on its economy, the policy of authorities at all levels in relation to the region, entrepreneurial activity among the populace, support or lack of it for reforms, and changes in migration flows (*Voprosy ekonomiki*, 1996, pp.42-77).

They divided the regions by level and rates of growth of nominal incomes into high, medium and low. Moscow was placed in the category with high incomes and high rates of income growth; St. Petersburg was assigned to the group of regions with a high level of incomes but medium rates of income growth; and Voronezh was one of the regions with low incomes and low income growth rates.

Table 5.1   Typology of regions by nominal incomes for 1990-1995

Incomes	*Rates of growth*		
	High	Medium	Low
High	Moscow	St. Petersburg	-
Medium	-	-	-
Low	-	-	Voronezh

Comparison of Russia's regions in terms of the ratio of monetary incomes to the Subsistence Minimum for 1993-1995 showed that Moscow and St. Petersburg are among the regions with high purchasing power, while Voronezh and Voronezh Province enjoy medium purchasing power.

Table 5.2   Typology of regions by industrial output for 1992-1995 (IFOPP - index of physical volume of industrial output)

Decline in Output	*1995 as % 1991*	*Regions*
Deep	Less than 35	-
More than average	35-40	Moscow, Voronezh
Average	40-50	-
Less than average	55-63	St. Petersburg

Using the indicator of depth of decline in industrial output, the authors identified four types of region: severe decline, more-than-average, average and less-than-average decline in industrial production. This classification placed Moscow in the group of regions with a decline greater than the average, while St. Petersburg, despite all the problems with its huge military-industrial complex, was assigned to the group with an average level of decline. One explanation for this is the dominance of productive capitalism in the city.

Applying these typologies to our selection of research subjects, we can conclude that two of our cities are differing advanced centres of market reforms, with growing adaptation to the new situation (Moscow and St. Petersburg), while the third city (Voronezh) may be defined as a centre of slower development with a conservative leadership and population.

Part II

Social Policy: Actors and Debates

6 Social Policy Actors

Без друзей да без связи - как доктор без мази
*Being without friends and connections is like being a
doctor without ointment*

The profound transformation processes which have taken a grip on Russian society in the 1990s compel a new approach to a lot of social problems. The country has turned away from the pre-determined programmes that have been so typical of Russian society as it has 'jerked forward' at various stages in its history and in severe crisis situations: but this immediately poses the problem of how to maintain continuous feedback between those in charge of reforms and the objects of reform. This is particularly the case for social problems which form the most vulnerable part of contemporary State regulatory activity. For it is in this area that the State exercises real control over the quality of changes being made and determines the forward trajectory of reform. The State in Russia today is losing its monopoly over social policy, and this implies the appearance of new actors in the field of social policy. Starting from these ideas, we were able to plan a research strategy for this part of the overall project to look at social policy in Russia 'through the eyes of its actors'.

Our initial plan was to study new 'subjects' of social policy. In part the respondents we included in the survey could be described as 'experts'. They play a real part in both the economic and the social processes which inevitably influence the formation of social policy. However, their activities (as previous research has shown) still lie far from the real work of forming social policy, while their evaluations are actually more typically representative of their social milieu, measuring the results of social policy against their own inner feelings and experiences, rather than professionally; not as subjects but rather as objects (or consumers) of policy in operation. Therefore, we concluded that the most appropriate term to use would be the concept of 'social policy actor' (Touraine, 1993, pp.6-19).

The sample was drawn up with reference above all to the respondents' presumed participation both in the formation of social policy (in particular, employment policy) and in tackling specific problems in their cities. We formed five groups of respondents, to include specialists whose professional allegiance brought them into unavoidable contact with tackling or discussing social problems. We assumed that these would be directors of industrial enterprises, officials from ministries, committees and departments dealing with labour and social matters, representatives of local government bodies, trade union leaders and political figures (representatives of the leading political parties and movements) - who are gradually coming to form a body of social policy actors.

Our key research objectives were:

- to obtain from our respondents, who were included in the sample as 'experts', an evaluation of social policy in post-Soviet Russia, as it is currently being conducted by Federal and regional authorities; to clarify their opinions about the real policy of the authorities in their regions and its specific features, and about the situation which has evolved in the social sphere as a whole and especially in the sphere of employment; finally, to clarify which ways of tackling social problems they believe to be most effective;
- to assess the level of competence of our survey sample, and how informed they were; to establish how far their opinions of and attitudes towards the social changes now taking place depend on their social status, their social environment and their proximity to centres of decision-making, as opposed to their knowledge of involvement in tackling specific problems;
- to establish whether there are particular features which differentiate respondents from Moscow, St Petersburg and Voronezh;
- to compare the results of the two stages of the research, in 1996 and 1997, in order to trace changes in the respondents' views.

The Field of Social Policy

The content of the results of our series of in-depth interviews, carried out in the three cities under study in 1996 and 1997, was analysed in several stages. The preliminary stage of analysis was the specific 'deconstruction' of the interview texts themselves, applying elements of post-coding, and dividing them into blocks according to content. We proceeded from the view that the subject of our research was 'the field of social policy'. Our 'de-construction' of the texts gave us a certain set of fragments (themes or topics) that constitute the empirical space of 'the field of social policy'. This space includes the whole set of themes (or topics) of social policy which are current for a given social formation and at a given period of time. The bases of the theory of social space used here are discussed by

Champagne (1996, pp.208-228), Kachanov and Shmatko (1996, pp.61-71), and Kachanov (1992, pp.61-81).

In attempting to order the set we had obtained, we had to construct its topology - a structurally unified system of sub-sets which were linked to a defined thematic unity and represented the object of our study. Since the elements of each sub-set do not give exhaustive coverage of the whole of the relevant segment of the 'field of social policy', we should qualify them as open sets.

However, we did not try to describe one fragment or another of the 'field of social policy' exhaustively - in practice this is impossible, since we are dealing with an evolving (and therefore unstable) social phenomenon in an evolving (and therefore unstable) socio-economic and socio-political situation (Kachanov and Shmatko, 1996). So we have, in a sense, only an image of the space, which can be used as a research instrument to enable us to construct the empirical space of the object of our research. Of course, the empirical space of the field of social policy is significantly broader than that of the spectrum of themes (or topics) which were obtained from processing and post-coding our interview texts. Nevertheless, we tried to form a 'grid' of issues that would enable us to assess both the situation in this area and the positions of the experts taking part in the research.

Thus, our content analysis of the survey's results represents one interpretation of the accounts given by those who took part. It enabled us to look at the respondents' accounts as reflecting the views of typical representatives of regional élites and middle-ranking officials. These accounts contain qualitative assessments of the state of social problems, which can help to create a fuller picture of the position of broad sections of the Russian population.

The questions put to the respondents may be divided into two major groups: the first relates to evaluating the current situation in social protection and employment policy, and the second group to means of improving policy in these areas. We did not ask about the reasons behind the actual position in social issues, nor did we include a group of 'forecasting' questions, covering the future of the social sphere. All our respondents are practitioners, so their thinking has been formed under the influence of a need to make concrete evaluations of problems that arise (as a rule, locally), and to take concrete action aimed at resolving them. They typically offered neither a conceptual approach nor made any kind of in-depth analysis.

Social Policy as Social Protection and Support

The General Social Policy Background

In 1996, the main question intended to elicit responses giving a generalised assessment of social policy was: 'How would you define the nature of social policy as it is currently being conducted?'. In the first instance, this implied State policy, and this was correspondingly reflected in the responses.

In our interviews, we were less interested in the respondents' assessments of the content of social policy than in those factors, such as how actively a policy was being implemented, which primarily enable us to diagnose whether the policy exists as such and what influence it has on the life of society. In 1996, only seven actors in all, out of 75, assessed social policy as 'active' or 'fairly active'. The main bulk of respondents (40 out of 75) assessed social policy as 'fairly passive'. This response was given by six out of the seven high-ranking officials. Insofar as the latter are either active decision-makers or people who are participating directly in taking decisions, it is possible to draw the conclusion that a group of respondents competent in the area considers social issues as peripheral in the overall process of State administration. The stance of middle-ranking officials also confirms this conclusion: the majority of them (18 out of 26) defined current policy as 'passive' or 'fairly passive'.

Our Moscow respondents took an especially critical stance, almost unanimously assessing social policy as 'passive' (politicians - three out of the four; company directors - six out of the nine); while company directors across all three cities felt that State policy in the social sphere was 'passive' (eight out of 18) or 'fairly passive' (also eight out of 18).

Another 1996 question, about the effectiveness of current government social policy, provoked a principally negative reaction from all groups of respondents in all three cities:

> It seems to me that the government still hasn't defined where it is with social policy. Their declared aim is the right one, but there's nothing backing it up. What can anyone say to the company's staff to justify any social policy, when we haven't been able to pay their wages since January? And we are owed nearly 26 billion roubles from last year: just to provide our workers with some

kind of Subsistence Minimum wage, we are taking out a fourth line of credit. (Director of an industrial enterprise, Voronezh).

We don't have social policy as such in Russia, if by 'policy' you mean the totality of some kind of goal-oriented activities, something purposeful. You could say that there are some kind of separate measures being taken in the area of social protection. But, it probably isn't true to say that they are in any way effective for most Russians. (Executive Director of Centre for Analysis of Humanitarian and Political Issues, St. Petersburg).

In 1997, the same question acted as an indicator of growing scepticism in attitudes towards current social policy. In answering it, 60 out of 75 respondents replied 'no' or 'not really', with the majority (40, or 53 per cent) giving a definite 'no': in 1996, a greater proportion (51 per cent) had settled on 'not really':

It is astonishing that social policy has remained at its 80s level. That's already the Stone Age - reforms in other spheres have gone much further forward. It's impossible to go on as if we were in 1988. The whole pension system and health care system are the same as then. A process of active reform in social matters is vital. (Member of Moscow City Duma, representative of the DVR movement [Russia's Democratic Choice]).

Current social policy in Russia is directed towards impoverishing the population. What we are experiencing is genocide - low pensions and a beggarly Subsistence Minimum. It's an impoverishment policy.
(Representative of the Liberal Democratic Party of Russia group in the State Duma).

In 1997, similar or analogous questions were put to respondents in the aim of revealing a dynamic of change in the actors' assessments of social policy evolution in Russia. Whereas in 1996 the main emphasis in the central question assessing general State activity in the social sphere was on the nature of current social policy (its active or passive nature) and considered its overall effectiveness, in 1997 respondents were asked: 'Has social policy in Russia taken the form of goal-oriented State activity around social issues?'.

The majority of respondents recognised that social policy in Russia was unformed (55 out of 75).

At the moment there's no social policy in anything. You can write what you like in the constitution, but there's no social policy in Russia. It's as if the State has resigned, vacated, lumped it all onto others. (Consultant to the Liberal Democratic Party of Russia group in the State Duma).

Instead of social reform, we're now being offered cuts in State expenditure on social protection for Russians. In circumstances where funds are short, this approach is a clear manifestation of the 'finger in the dyke' policy that the Government has been carrying on in recent years. (Representative of the 'Yabloko' group in the State Duma).

In 1997, responses moved towards a critical evaluation of social policy. The following are fairly typical opinions from the 1997 interviews:

Any mention of public service reform arouses apprehension rather than hope. You can see it wherever you turn: education in collapse, health care at rock bottom, a catastrophic demographic policy... (Member of Social Forecasting Research Group, Provincial Employment Centre, Voronezh).

I don't think social policy has taken shape in Russia. There isn't any, because there are no visible, significant changes in the position of the public or of enterprises. It's easy to see that the majority of State enterprises don't have any orders nor, especially, any new jobs. Finding people jobs is very difficult: even if there are vacancies, then they are for either very low-paid or low-skilled jobs. (State official, St. Petersburg).

Analogous results were obtained in response to the question - 'Is Russia a Social State?'. This is a position affirmed in the 1993 Constitution of the Russian Federation. However, out of 75 respondents, 56 did not agree that it was the case. In no group of experts (either overall, in each city or in any group within each city) did we find a majority of adherents to the point of view that Russia is a Social State:

I think that this all remains on the level of rhetoric, because you can only talk about a Social State when people are guaranteed secure rights by means of laws passed by government. The State should guarantee that laws are enforced. In Russia, things are developing in precisely the opposite direction. It's a mockery. Take, for instance, the Veterans' Law (covering people invalided out of work, as well as war veterans and so on). The most vital subsidy for them would be to grant the 50 per cent reduction in payments for housing and municipal services. People have been fighting for that since 1994, talking and talking, but there still hasn't been a penny of funding forthcoming. (Member of the Moscow Government Committee for Social Protection).

Turning to the question of the main aims and objectives of current social policy, in 1996, 21 out of the 56 respondents who answered this question took the view that social policy was directed towards ensuring stability in society. The second largest group (16 people) inclined towards the opinion that social policy was being conducted in the interests of the élite. And, finally, ten people considered that social policy was directed towards helping the deprived:

The point of present social policy is to keep people quiet, to guard against social stratification, in case society splinters in the face of severe impoverishment. It's a policy of appeasement. That also gives rise to calls to 'concentrate on business' - which is interesting if you go back to the period 1989-90. Those who were called conservatives used the same words - we shouldn't be holding meetings but getting on with business. Policy is created by those in power. These people are highly professional in managing their own affairs. They've clearly defined their own goal - it's better to live like a Western billionaire in a semi-destitute country, maybe more like Latin America, and somehow appease other people and keep them quiet. And there's another thing. The rising Russian bourgeoisie has shown that it has the kind of pretensions that put Western expectations in the shade. I've had occasion to associate with some very well-to-do people who have come here from the West. For them, a salary of $20,000 dollars is not at all bad. But they can't buy the kind of things that some Russians do, and they were stunned by the building work going on in the city suburbs. Even the hereditary gentry in Russia used to live more modestly than the new rich do. (Representative of the Russian Communist Party, Voronezh).

In 1996, all the high-ranking Moscow officials (three out of three) saw the main objective of social policy as being to ensure social stability. Middle-ranking Moscow officials pointed out that social policy is directed first and foremost towards ensuring social stability (four people), but also towards securing the interests of the élite (two people) and helping the economically-active section of the population (two people). This suggests that the State leadership has a low level of interest in tackling social protection issues. If there is any notion of what social policy should be, then first and foremost it is to pursue the goal of keeping society calm ('social stability'), ensured in considerable measure by hand-outs to the lower classes ('help to the deprived').

By contrast, of 13 company directors who answered this question, six thought that social policy was being conducted in the interests of the élite, three considered its objective to be helping the deprived, while only two directors agreed that social policy was pursuing the aim of ensuring stability in society. Moscow company directors particularly stressed social policy's defence of the interests of the élite. Some trade union leaders (three in Moscow and one in St. Petersburg) agreed that social policy was being conducted solely in the interests of the élite. So, from the point of view of the 1996 respondents, the main conclusion was that social policy - though weakly expressed - is directed towards ensuring social stability, particularly to ensuring and defending the interests of the élite:

> The government and organs of state administration defend the interests of the ruling élite, major financial groupings, entrepreneurial structures, the biggest Russian corporations. And on that level, their policy corresponds completely and appropriately to the expectations which the élites and financial circles that support the present government have of it. The fact that they are adequately meeting this aim is confirmed by reciprocal support from the biggest Russian bankers and largest entrepreneurial structures for the current President at the time of his last election campaign. The government, from its side, has also responded appropriately: the government has thanked those bankers and major entrepreneurs who put the biggest investment into that campaign - by making relevant staff appointments, passing enforceable statutory instruments, etc.
>
> The second aim that I can define is the preservation of macro-economic stability and preventing inflation - in other words, by means of not admitting any sharp increase in the expenditure section of the budget. But this aim is closely linked to the first. Thirdly, I would single out maintaining stability in Russian society: despite having other priorities, the authorities still strive to avert the most severe conflicts, those that could spill over into wider society, could become a trigger for social upheaval. What you might call a knee jerk reaction is taking place. If the miners strike, Chubais flies to see the miners, if teachers in a particular region lie down on the railway lines, then the head of that region's administration rushes to meet them. (Executive Director of Centre for Analysis of Humanitarian and Political Issues, St. Petersburg).

In answering the same question in 1997, 28 out of 75 respondents named as the most important objective of social policy 'ensuring social stability'. This was proportionally fewer than in 1996, when 24 out of the 56 people who responded expressed that opinion. In 1997, 21 considered the main objective of social policy to be ensuring the interests of the élite, a figure which exceeded the 1996 one. In all the survey cities, politicians - who, as a group, devote attention to strategic social policy issues, because of their professional orientation - inclined towards the idea that social policy is being conducted in the interests of the élite. Like politicians, the majority of directors (62 per cent in Moscow, 50 per cent in St. Petersburg and 100 per cent in Voronezh) considered the main objective of contemporary social policy to be ensuring the interests of the élite. Alternative responses were mentioned by only a small number of respondents.

Improving Social Policy in Russia

The next group of questions concerned ways of improving social policy. To the question of whether it is worthwhile directing the conduct of government social policy towards the preservation of free services, the majority of our respondents in 1996 replied 'yes' or 'by and large, yes' (42 out of 73). However, the distribution of responses across groups of respondents and cities gives a more heterogeneous picture. Thus, Moscow company directors either did not give a firm opinion (three people out of ten) or took a negative stance ('no' or 'not really' - four people); only three of them said 'yes' or 'by and large, yes' - in other words, supported provision of free services. It was fully understandable that trade union leaders either did not give a firm opinion or else spoke out in favour of free services. The overwhelming majority of officials at all levels and in all cities spoke out in favour of free services. In the politicians group, it was the Muscovites who most actively supported the preservation of free services.

However in 1997 by contrast, in response to the question: 'Should the proportion of State expenditure going into the social sphere be increased?', half replied 'no' or 'probably not'. Such a distribution of responses was typical for practically all the cities and all the groups of respondents. Recognition that it was not worthwhile increasing expenditure in the social sphere was closely linked to acknowledging social policy's lack of effectiveness. To the majority of actors the social sphere represents a bottomless pit into which 'it would be senseless to pour so much water - to increase expenditure - with no expectation of getting anything out'.

Nevertheless in 1997 the overwhelming majority of respondents (50 out of 75, or 65 per cent) replied positively to the question about needing to preserve free services. Only an insignificant minority (eight respondents) replied 'no' or 'not really'. Supporters of the value of preserving free services were found in all groups of respondents (with the exception of St. Petersburg politicians) and in all cities:

Many people talk about the corrupting effect of free goods. But in Russia, the general majority of people are very poor. Many simply cannot afford to pay for medical treatment, education, etc. Of course, there should also be fee-paying services, but the level of provision has to be taken into account. (Adviser to the Liberal Democratic Party of Russia group in the State Duma).

Free services are essential for those who cannot pay themselves... It's becoming terrible: every day there are broadcasts on the television and radio saying that people are going to hospitals and finding they can only get treated if they pay. In relation to free education, I would put it as follows: let fee-paying education develop as an alternative. There is sharp stratification in Russian society, into rich and poor. We should help the middle class - so there should be both fee-paying and free education. Someone who has money can send their children to study at the Sorbonne, but the majority of people's children go to comprehensive school, and the teachers there are on strike now. What can they give children now, if they are just fed up with their work: they get meagre pay, their families and friends have nothing to eat, so how can they teach? Vacancies in schools nowadays are, as a rule, not filled for ages. Young people are either looking for work in private schools or over-committing themselves to the point that, by the end of the working day, they are 'dropping on their feet' from tiredness. (Head of Administration of the City Employment Service. Moscow).

It should be noted that there was a distinct contradiction between the distribution of responses to the last two questions: a system of free social services is meaningless without vigorous State support. Current funding for free services, even in major cities, is completely unsatisfactory: objectively, therefore, to preserve and support free social services would require increased State expenditure in the social sphere. The first question concerned general (or strategic) problems of State policy, while the question on preserving free social services is a question about tackling a specific social policy issue: even given this, there was a clear contradiction between the respondents' opinions.

It is curious that, in 1997, the number of responses supporting free social services had increased; thus, among Moscow company directors, the proportion of supporters of free social services rose from 30 per cent to 40 per cent. It is possible that this change was connected with the fact that the process of social polarisation in Russian society had become much more evident by 1997. Even given the fact that their orientation had shifted towards limiting budget-funded social expenditure, our actors could not fail to take into account the facts of post-Soviet reality, where millions of citizens who are not capable of work, members of disadvantaged groups within the population, are not in a position to provide for themselves or their families even at a minimum needs level.

In the course of the interviews, respondents were asked a question relating to the nature of social assistance: should social assistance be targeted or universal? In 1996, 36 people out of 71 inclined towards targeted social assistance. But in addition, it should be noted that a significant proportion supported universal social assistance (19 people, i.e. a quarter). Discussions with interviewees showed that the stances of many actors on this issue have still not taken shape, and they are still 'struggling' to reconcile the idea of targeted social protection with the need of many millions of Russians for universal social assistance:

> As far as social assistance to various sections of the population (the old, children, and others) is concerned, then here the main thing is: does the country in general take on responsibility for this assistance? If there is agreement that the country decides to ensure - for example, to support the birth rate, then it is not important whom it helps: a millionaire or a beggar, the main thing is that it helps. That is the strategy - ensuring the birth rate. But from another angle, some differentiation is necessary, if there is not enough money for everyone. Then targeting is necessary. (Director of an aviation industry enterprise, Moscow).

In Moscow, targeted social assistance was defended by most company directors, high-ranking officials and middle-ranking officials. Trade union leaders and politicians in equal measure recognised the need for both targeted and universal assistance. Unlike Moscow, in St. Petersburg, high- and middle-ranking officials distributed their preferences equally between targeted and universal policy. Politicians and company directors were twice as likely to favour targeted social policy, while trade union leaders were in favour of universal. In Voronezh, all the respondents, except some of the middle-ranking officials, supported the line of retaining universal social assistance:

> In our State, there can be no effective targeted assistance. The public and the authorities are not disciplined enough for it. Social support should be based on the principle that everyone gives to the State and the State gives to everyone. (Director of an industrial enterprise, Voronezh).

In 1997, too, the majority of respondents (54 people out of 74 who answered) considered that social assistance should be targeted, while only

15 inclined towards universal social assistance. However, by comparison with 1996, this marked a significant increase in the number of supporters of targeted assistance:

> It is impossible to find any solution to social problems without going over to targeted social assistance and introducing a Subsistence Minimum as the established social standard for setting the minimum wage, minimum pensions and benefits. It's no good spreading the porridge in a thin layer over the whole plate - the result will just be that those who have very high incomes will get the same as those who, for objective reasons, cannot provide themselves with a Subsistence Minimum. So child benefit should be paid not depending on the child's age but depending on the *per capita* income of the child's family. If that income is lower than the Subsistence Minimum in the region where the family lives, the community should help it to raise the child. (Representative of the 'Yabloko' group in the State Duma).

> A rich State can allow itself any form of social support to the public at large. For example, in Sweden, the king's children get the same benefit as the children of someone who's unemployed. In principle, that is correct - every child has the right to material support from the State. There, the way it turns out is that first you give everyone their fixed amount, and then you look at who needs additional help. We can't allow ourselves that luxury; we can't help everyone to the same extent. We are giving billionaires child benefit. Why do they get this money, when they spend more than that on cigarettes in a day? What's the sense in it? (Member of the Social Affairs Commission of the St. Petersburg Legislative Assembly).

Thus, while in 1996 - although there was a general majority in favour of targeted social assistance - many respondents, especially in Voronezh, spoke out in favour of universal social support, by 1997 practically all groups of actors were convinced of the necessity for targeted social assistance - and targeted only on those sections of the population suffering as a result of economic crisis. On the one hand, this appears to suggest a growing understanding of the economic situation and social policy methods in a market environment; on the other hand, the pace and scale of the move towards the principle of targeting suggests also that this is a consequence of the influence of ruling groups, transmitted both through social networks and through the mass media.

This inclination towards targeting on the part of the leading actors of social policy may be explained not by their being convinced that this is the optimal solution to social problems, but by the fact that the notion of targeting offers them the possibility of divesting themselves of responsibility for the fate of whole sections of society. Liberal residualist social policy pre-supposes the existence of a resource base in the household. At the same time, over the course of decades, social policy in the USSR was directed towards concentrating social protection and support in the hands of the State, not of citizens themselves. Additionally, Russians' savings have been wiped out by inflation, while the State has refused to recognise this as an internal debt. Only a few people enjoy the prerogative of being able to build up new savings in conditions of insuperable economic crisis. Therefore, unfortunately, such sizeable groups of people need social guarantees and State social protection that doubt is cast on the possibility of going over entirely to strictly targeted social support.

Preserving Russia's Human Resources

One of the key questions in the second phase of interviewing (1997), which highlights the difficulties of current social policy was: 'Do you think that the deteriorating health of Russians has become one of today's most severe social problems?'. Responses to this question were unequivocal: 56 out of 65 replied 'yes' or 'probably, yes':

> Russia's gene pool is deteriorating, the nation is becoming degraded. I think that the authorities should develop a special programme; academics, doctors, sociologists, psychologists and other specialists, including our Employment Service, should take part in creating it. But not on the same basis as now - we shift responsibility to the regions, and then let them get on with it. It should be a goal-oriented programme, where everything will be laid down in clear, precise detail. If we don't get a programme like this in the next five years, then we will not be able to restore Russia's gene pool. Despite a general ignorance, a kind of coarseness, Russia has always been noted for very high moral standards, but now - not without the help of the mass media - a great deal is being destroyed. Alcoholism is leading not only to the destruction of Russia's potential and to deteriorating health, but also to an increase in disability. Russia could gradually be reduced to a country in its death throes. (Official of the Voronezh Provincial Employment Centre).

A deteriorating state of health is a complex indicator which shows the extremely unsatisfactory state of many and various spheres of social life: health care, income levels of the population, provision of jobs, and the general psychological climate in society - practically all aspects of social reality are connected with a population's state of health. We note that in those countries where social protection problems have been tackled effectively, indicators of the state of health and life expectancy of populations are also among the best.

In their responses to the 1997 question: 'Can current social protection measures halt the processes of impoverishment, social stratification, falling living standards and deteriorating health among Russians?', the majority of our respondents (45 out of 71) declared that it is not possible for current social protection measures to restrain the growing impoverishment of the population:

> In Moscow, something in the order of 40 per cent of the population is below the poverty line. Social protection measures cannot hold back the process of impoverishment, they are not saving us from poverty. The distinction is that a poor person lacks both property and a certain level of income. (Head of the Moscow Labour and Employment Committee).

Here again, we come up against a similar contradiction: the social policy actors speak against increasing State expenditure on social needs and for stronger targeting of social assistance; but they simultaneously acknowledge the inadequacy of existing social protection measures and the need for large-scale public assistance.

The main point lies in the fact that those taking part in the survey represent the interests and attitudes of their milieu. In fact, they are not willing to promote any adjustment to the stance of members of the prevailing economic and political groups, or to the latter's strategic interests, an approach which would pre-suppose better co-operation between the main groups in society and the achievement of relatively stable compromises between differing interests. Our respondents are more than familiar with the post-Soviet reality of the existence of a quasi-market economy and the merging of the State with financial oligarchies, with monopoly pricing - a reality which makes itself known at every step. It comes into contradiction with their market aspirations and illusions: the mythology that Russia is already living by the laws of a market economy also demands, obviously, an orientation towards social policy which corresponds to pro-market economic guidelines.

This contradiction in the actors' position demonstrates their orientation towards the interests of the upper echelons of society. This is also obliquely confirmed by the distribution of responses to the question asked in 1996: 'What exerts the greatest influence on current social policy?'. The majority of respondents then expressed a preference for economic factors, overshadowing the influence of political forces, the competence of the country's leadership and other non-economic factors.

The Politics of Social Policy

Which of the parties (or political movements), if it came to power, could best of all tackle social problems? In 1996, out of seven high-ranking officials, only one spoke out (in favour of the Communist Party of the Russian Federation), while the rest did not express a preference for any political party. The bulk of middle-ranking officials, trade union leaders, and company directors also did not express a preference for anyone. Out of 13 politicians, only three did not express a firm opinion; Yabloko and the Communist Party received four votes each, and the DVR and the Liberal Democratic Party of Russia [LDPR], one each. Overall, the strongest positions were those of the Communist Party - 12 votes, then Yabloko – eight votes and the DVR - six votes, with the LDPR receiving only one vote.

In Moscow, the position of the Communists was almost the same as that of Yavlinsky's Yabloko (five votes as against four). If we also take into account one vote for the DVR, we can draw the conclusion that, in the view of Moscow social policy actors (middle-ranking officials, politicians and company directors), Communists and Democrats have equal chances of resolving social problems. In St. Petersburg, Yabloko and the DVR together even surpassed the Communist Party (seven votes as against five). In Voronezh, the DVR and Yabloko each received one vote, and the Communists two. However, it should be noted that both overall and in any one of the cities studied support for the Communist Party exceeds that for any other political force taken separately:

> Why do we need a Communist opposition? So that we remember we should help the poor, the sick and the old. (Director of an industrial enterprise, Voronezh).

The sum total of support gained by the democratic parties ensured a fragile equality between Communists and Democrats. It is noticeable that a very large proportion of social policy actors would not express a firm opinion, not preferring any one political party. On the one hand, this is an indicator of their deep social pessimism, and on the other it also means there are certain 'reserved preferences' which may be revealed over time.

In 1997, the respondents' opinions on the potential of existing political parties (or movements) to influence the resolution of social problems still remained pessimistic. To a question about which of the political parties (or movements) could best tackle social problems, out of the 66 respondents, 48 (73 per cent) replied 'none of them'. By comparison with 1996, the level of negative attitudes in evaluating the potential of political parties had risen. In 1996, the response 'none of them' was given by 62 per cent of respondents:

> Unfortunately, nowadays in Russia there is no alternative political force: I can't see one now, and I don't even see one taking shape anywhere. Maybe if mass disorder were to break out in Russia, that would push someone towards some kind of alternative. The people are tired. The élite strata of Russian society are afraid to engage with these issues, since they understand the unjust origin of their own wealth, though they have sometimes indulged in rhetoric about 'universal' equality and everyone having started 'on an equal footing'. We don't even have a law protecting property rights, and while we don't, all our financial assets will leak out of Russia to the West, instead of developing the prosperity of our own nation. If you create normal conditions, money will start to return. (Director of an industrial enterprise, Voronezh).

Explaining who really forms social policy and imbues it with specific content - central government or the regions - is of principal importance in analysing social policy problems. In 1996, the majority of respondents (43 out of 72, or 60 per cent) attributed services to the regions and only nine to the Federation. In Moscow, out of the 35 respondents, 18 recognised the social policy achievements of the regions:

> Our Moscow programmes are not in any part Federal programmes. And although nowadays they are always declaring their good intentions, unfortunately, the Federal authorities have forgotten what a capital city is, and they exert no practical influence on legislating for Federal programmes that they themselves have ratified before. For example, we would now need 2.7 trillion roubles of budgetary receipts - that is, from the Federal budget - in order to implement those programmes at city level; but, up to today, not a single kopeck has been received for this. (Trade union leader, Moscow).

Only four people - one each from the high-ranking officials, the middle-ranking officials, the politicians and the company directors - considered the achievements of social policy to be the result of central government activity. A large number of people did not express a firm opinion, which suggests that the very nature of this problem is ambiguous. It is possible that some influence is also exerted by the fact that, in Moscow, social problems are not critical: in many respects, the situation there can be described as a happy one, especially by comparison with the provinces. Relative success dulls their perception of the overall situation. In St. Petersburg and Voronezh, the percentage of those who did not express a firm opinion was significantly lower. In both these cities, the overwhelming majority of actors in all groups recognised that the achievements of social policy were the result of the regions' own activity (St. Petersburg - 70 per cent; Voronezh - 64 per cent).

It is interesting that, in answer to a question about how the powers to tackle social problems should be distributed between central government and the regions, respondents were split evenly. Only in the group of high-ranking officials was there a small majority (three to two) in favour of regional powers. In St. Petersburg and Voronezh, respondents mainly spoke out in favour of Federation powers. This reflects the way the regions feel burdened by the weight of responsibility for tackling social problems, which central government has to all intents and purposes foisted on them, having first removed from them any powers for decision-making or seeking additional resources.

In 1997, in response to the questions: 'What do you think about the competence of Federal and local authorities and about the effectiveness of their current social policies? Whose social protection activities or initiatives are more evident to the public?', there was a shift in favour of the regions:

A huge social ministry has been created, though it's difficult to make out what it has been doing up to now. This conglomerate has grown so much that we don't even know where or whom to apply to. We receive documents that contradict one another. By and large, the whole weight of social problems falls on local bodies. (Official of the Voronezh Provincial Employment Centre).

If, all across Russia, no wages are being paid, but you and I are getting some kind of pittance, then it's likely that this is not due to the efforts of the Federal authorities, but of the city authorities... Social protection programmes exist at both city and district levels. But the problem is that local social policy doesn't come out of budget funding: it comes out of money that we earn ourselves. And of course, there isn't enough; that's the problem - the fact that there's no money. (Deputy Prefect of one of Moscow's Administrative Districts).

Programmes adopted at a Federal level are in practice not being implemented within the Federation's member areas. The Federation's member areas can put forward demands for Federal programmes to be implemented at their level, and the Federal budget, to ensure funding of specific programmes, is obliged to provide for allocations to carry it out. But no money is forthcoming from there. There are 'Disabled Children' and 'Orphaned Children' programmes, both of which were ratified by the St. Petersburg Government and provided for by funding from both the Federal and local budgets - with a lot more, moreover, coming from the Federal one. What have we got? We have got implementation of neither programme. The only way we have been lucky is that this year's St. Petersburg City budget has seen the introduction of a budget head called 'The St. Petersburg Programme', with - secondly - a sub-head called 'The Orphan Programme' and - thirdly - under that sub-head, a funding allocation of 29 billion from our budget. (Member of the St. Petersburg City Legislative Assembly's Social Affairs Commission).

So, to all appearances, the respondents were starting to realise the hopelessness of expecting effective help from central government, and this was expressed through the way in which preferences were redistributed in favour of the regions. In 1997, 44 actors out of 70 spoke out in favour of the regions. We note that six respondents out of the 12 who supported the centre were Muscovites, and it should be taken into account that the effect of Federal decision-making is more perceptible in Moscow, and that it is not always even possible to differentiate whose ruling (the Federal or the City authorities) has been implemented. Added to this, as we have said before, the social situation in the capital is also objectively somewhat happier.

A fundamental issue in determining the behaviour of both public and authorities in a country with powerful traditions of paternalism, established over centuries, is the problem of how individuals identify themselves as actors on the labour market and in civic relations. Responses in 1996 to the question, 'Who is responsible for people's welfare: the State or the individual?' were for State responsibility in the majority (40 out of 74). Only eight people stated that the need to strive for one's own welfare is the concern of the person or their family. Overall, in all groups of respondents, preference was given to the State:

There is some kind of limit, some kind of threshold of potential for people to solve their own problems independently. And below that threshold, the State must create a system - lay down some rules of the game - that will give people the possibility of finding work. (Member of Social Forecasting staff, Provincial Employment Centre, Voronezh).

In this regard, the 1997 responses were very significant. The question had been amended to: 'Do you think Russia's 'Social State' should take on the responsibility of maintaining people's welfare, or should this largely be the concern of the individual and of the family?'. In 1997, out of 75 respondents, 24 replied 'no, the State should not take on this responsibility' or 'it probably shouldn't'. The proportion of those supporting the responsibility of the person for their own fate was much higher than in 1996. Such a sharp change in the respondents' positions suggests the growth of a sceptical attitude to the potential of the State in Russian society:

> Starvation and impoverishment don't arouse any kind of response from the State - it's a case of 'everyone has the right to choose how much they want to eat'. In the Soviet period, a starving person in the street would be akin to a catastrophe - they would have sent a commission of enquiry from Moscow. Unfortunately, what we have got is not 'freedom to', but 'freedom from'. On the one hand, we are free from obligations - from the obligations of civil society; but on the other hand, we are also free from the protection of the State. It has also freed itself from us, and only does what it considers necessary. This freedom does not imply any mutual obligations from one to another. (Representative of the Communist Party, adviser to Voronezh Municipal Council).

Employment Policy

The Nature of Employment Policy

In 1996, the central question which was intended to evaluate employment policy as it was then being conducted in Russia was: 'How would you characterise current employment policy? Can it be seen as active?'. The majority of respondents (48 out of 75) assessed employment policy as 'passive' or 'fairly passive', while 33 assessed it as 'active' or 'fairly active'. Overall, in each of the groups of respondents, the majority assessed employment policy as passive. However, this is more than anything an expression of opinion relating to the results of employment policy and not to its nature or intended directions. Breaking the data down by city also confirms this. In Moscow, a contradiction can be observed between the opinions of high-ranking officials (three people in all), who assessed employment policy as 'passive' or 'fairly passive', and that of middle-ranking officials (eight people - 'active' or 'fairly active' and three people - 'fairly passive'). We see the explanation for this as lying in the fact that, in our 1996 survey, the middle-ranking officials were mainly from the Employment Service, and, in their responses to this question, they were talking, first and foremost, about the results of their own work. This would suggest that, naturally, Employment Service staff themselves felt they had to evaluate their own work fairly positively, if only out of corporate solidarity, and this may explain the result obtained.

However, we must recognise it is true that a lot is being done in the capital to tackle employment problems. The Labour and Employment Committee and its administration are working actively; new forms of employment promotion are being introduced; there are no delays in paying benefits in Moscow; new jobs are opening up; there is financial support to industrial enterprises, and so on. Employment Service officials give the impression of being people who are enthusiastic about their work and interested in the results of their undertakings; they speak with pride of the achievements and promising outlook of employment policy in Moscow. So, we believed that their assessments of employment policy were sincere, if somewhat excessive. Other Moscow respondents noted deficiencies in current policy, the abundance of unresolved problems, financial difficulties, the undeveloped nature of labour legislation, and so on.

As far as high-ranking officials are concerned, their judgements were related mostly to national, strategic employment policy issues, not to the 'parochial' details of the situation of crisis groups in Moscow. This was the approach taken by the Head of the Moscow City Labour and Employment Committee, who holds the rank of Permanent Secretary in the Moscow administration - a very influential social policy actor. In answering the question, he assessed the situation on a national scale, comparing his own department's (the Committee's) activities with the activities of similar structures in developed countries where employment policy is, in reality, established in form and active in nature:

> If we are talking about Federal employment policy, it has lost practically any direction it had which was linked with restructuring the economy and creating new jobs, or with changes in production specialisms. That is because, although a year ago there were some resources for that approach, now - with such poor tax collection - there are not even the resources to pay benefits. (Head of the Moscow Labour and Employment Committee).

Attention should be drawn to the opinion of Moscow politicians, who consistently assessed employment policy as 'passive' (three people) and 'fairly passive' (one person). This response must be seen as connected with their need to examine current State policy in a critical light, especially on the threshold of an election campaign.

In St. Petersburg, the distribution of responses to this question was similar to that in Moscow; although here it was true that middle-ranking officials confirmed the opinion of high-ranking officials (four 'fairly passive' and one 'passive'). The responses of middle-ranking officials in Voronezh were similar:

> Policy has been officially proclaimed as giving priority to active measures (getting people into work and retraining). But in reality the Employment Service can do hardly anything. (Official of the Voronezh Provincial Employment Centre).

The opinions expressed by politicians, trade union leaders and company directors in St Petersburg and Voronezh were approximately equally balanced. Thus, differential analysis of the respondents' replies by city enables us to draw the conclusion that there is some ambiguity in assessments of employment policy. The most independent groups of actors (trade union leaders and company directors), while inclining to some thoughts on predominantly passive tendencies in the conduct of employment policy, also regarded it as fairly active.

In 1997, the proportion of sceptical opinions on the active (or passive) nature of current employment policy had increased: 42 respondents out of 71 (60 per cent) considered it 'passive' or 'fairly passive':

> As far as the actual direction of present policy is concerned, then I would not say that it is active in nature; on the contrary, the situation in Russia, in this region, is so difficult that we are even seeing some kind of curtailment in both Federal and regional policy. It is becoming more passive. Instructions have come from the Federal Employment Service for us to spend our limited financial resources only on paying benefits and, to a minimal extent, on vocational training - well, there you are, those are all the expenditure items. In other words, there are not enough resources to carry on an active policy. (Official of the Voronezh Provincial Employment Centre).

However, in discussion of policy as conducted in the regions, opinions diverged significantly. So, in 1997, many actors noted substantial progress in relation to employment policy in Moscow over the previous year:

> Current employment policy in Moscow is completely active, primarily because it is starting to exercise a prophylactic function, beginning to reveal the state of enterprises in advance of their problems. When will cuts be made, how many workers are they proposing to axe? With the arrival of new management in the Department of Employment, this policy has started to be put into practice. So that is already one active policy which is very important. Then, in addition, new programmes and new developments are appearing (you know, vacancy fairs, model employment centres), i.e. there are thoughts and visions as to what should be done. (Member of Moscow City Duma).

By contrast in St. Petersburg, the proportion of sceptical opinions was very high. 16 out of 25 actors called employment policy 'passive' or 'fairly passive':

> Russia lacks any active employment policy. Some Employment Service centres are actually engaged in matching the unemployed to jobs, but even so this approach is just a formality, because the pay for jobs that are being offered to 30- or 40-year-olds isn't really what it should be - they are still offering salaries of 150,000 to 200,000 roubles a month. There is no sense in taking a job like that. But some Employment Centres don't even have that. They are not doing any active work. (Head of a personnel department, St. Petersburg).

Similarly in Voronezh 11 out of 15 assessed employment policy in the city as 'passive or 'fairly passive':

> The financial and economic position in Russia today pushes the Employment Services towards a passive, rather than an active, policy. (Official of the Voronezh Provincial Employment Centre).

When interpreting these data, it should be remembered that the first stage of the survey was carried out in May and June 1996, when social policy overall - and employment policy in particular - was pressed into a more active mode because of the election campaign for the Presidency of the Russian Federation. Therefore, the 1997 responses from the actors may be more instructive. Here it is very important to draw attention to the divergence between the opinions of respondents in Moscow and in other cities in the survey. The unanimity of respondents in St. Petersburg and Voronezh in assessing employment policy as passive confirms the generally accepted fact that employment problems continue to be much more acute in these cities than in the capital, and have to be tackled with fewer resources.

Preserving Skills (or Staff)

A widely debated concern in the 1990s has been whether the talents of a skilled and educated workforce are being lost. However this concern was not echoed by our respondents. In response to the question: 'In tackling employment problems (redundancy, recruitment, retraining, etc.), should the need to preserve the skills of employees be taken into account?', in 1996, out of 18 company directors, nine replied 'no' or 'not really' and eight - 'yes or 'probably'. Similarly, half the middle-ranking officials saw no need to preserve skills potential. On the other hand trade union leaders, politicians and high-ranking officials spoke out in favour of preserving skills.

Moscow respondents demonstrated the highest level of indifference to the problem of preserving skills. It should be noted that, while it is true that the responses of enterprise directors are to a great extent conditioned by the absence of real economic possibilities, the officials justified their responses by referring to the excessive surplus of many types of specialist workers and to their low occupational training levels. In St. Petersburg, negative attitudes towards preserving skills were found only in the group of middle-ranking officials. In Voronezh, all groups of social policy actors spoke out in favour of preserving skills.

In 1997, the distribution of responses to this question on skills remained practically unchanged. As before, half the company directors (eight out of 16) did not see that there was any possibility of preserving their enterprise's skills; and only five inclined towards preservation. In 1997 too, the majority of company directors and entrepreneurs in Moscow expressed the same negative opinions, adducing what they saw as weighty arguments:

> I trained at the Bauman Engineering Institute in Moscow and was supposed to build housing and bases for space scientists - that was my specialisation. In the upshot, I now build service stations, houses, flats, never mind what: but I worked for 20 years in a research institute, building accelerators. That kind of change is very widespread now. Do you see? If a person has education - and

by that, I mean above all the ability to think and to work intelligently with the written word - then the person won't be done for. If you exclude personal interests, likings and attachments, then I - for instance - am indifferent as to what I do for work. There's still experience, but experience is something you build up. (Managing Director of a construction firm, Moscow).

In St. Petersburg, in general terms, the situation repeated the one in Moscow. In Voronezh in 1997, most of those who replied expressed doubts about needing to preserve skills:

> During a certain period in Russia's history, we invested little in technology and a lot in training staff, because we were trying to solve technological problems at the expense of developing high skills. In theory, we bound ourselves hand and foot to the human factor. Today, market transformations are bringing demands for vocational training of workers: what is needed is a steady flow of skills potential, and particular employers are asking for them. Preserving the old skills makes no sense. We've just been marking time for ten years. And without a constant process of renewal, skills die out. (Deputy Director of Engineering, industrial enterprise, St. Petersburg).

Policy Actors in the Field of Employment

A special block of questions in the interview was devoted to evaluating the activities of policy actors themselves. All the respondents were asked about the role and potential of local authorities, company directors, the trade unions and the employment services in tackling the problems of the Russian labour market.

In contemporary Russia, the role of company directors is acquiring increasing significance in tackling the problem of finding people work, since - as has already been noted - out of all the groups of actors, only company directors are direct employers. So, among those questions directed at revealing the respondents' assessments of which institutions are able to tackle employment problems effectively, the most important was the question: 'How would you assess the role of company directors in tackling employment problems? Is it an active one?'. In 1996, 32 people out of 74 inclined to the response 'yes' or 'fairly active', 18 did not express a firm opinion, and 24 respondents replied 'no' or 'not really'. However, those most ready to recognise their active role were company directors themselves (18 out of 19). Politicians considered that company directors were not really active (four 'not really', two 'fairly active' and six who did not express a firm opinion). High-ranking officials and trade union leaders -

by a small majority of one - were inclined to the opinion that company directors are active in tackling employment problems. In 1997, respondents gave a fairly high evaluation of the role of company directors in conducting employment policy. Out of 66 respondents, 37 replied 'yes' or 'fairly active'.

Notwithstanding the company directors' first-hand connections with attempts to resolve employment problems they may have a great desire to view their personal participation in finding work for a significant number of employees as meaning that they are active in tackling employment problems (although, in fact, it is a slightly different thing - a particular form of activity directed towards job creation, re-skilling). And, at the same time, corporate solidarity may play a significant role in conditioning the responses of those who are company directors themselves.

The distribution of responses to the question about whether trade unions are active in tackling employment problems provides a striking contrast. In 1996, half the respondents (38 out of 74) assessed the role of the trade unions as 'passive' or 'rather passive', while almost a third (22 people) noted that the role of the trade unions was 'active' or 'fairly active'. A significant section (14) did not express a firm opinion. Out of all those taking part in the survey, company directors and middle-ranking officials are most familiar with the work of the trade unions. The overwhelming majority of company directors (15 out of 19) did not consider the trade unions to be real participants in tackling these problems, and the larger proportion of middle-ranking officials (16 out of 25) shared this opinion. In 1997, responses to this question were virtually the same as the 1996 results:

> Trade union organisation today is a mere formality. Everything has been left at the door of the employer. There is no way for the worker to influence me. Employees have no-one to defend their interests. We have had no conflicts with the unions, because we haven't looked for any. Unions today remain undeveloped. (Director of an industrial enterprise, Voronezh).

On the issue of whether local authorities have been active in tackling employment problems, in 1996 company directors, trade union leaders and politicians were generally negative. By 1997 even greater scepticism had arisen in relation to the effectiveness of regional authority policy. In Moscow, St. Petersburg and Voronezh, practically all the company directors evaluated their activities negatively. In Moscow, the trade union leaders were also inclined to make a negative evaluation. Even middle-ranking officials in St. Petersburg and Voronezh, who, objectively, must be said to have an interest in assessing the role of the local authorities positively, described their efforts in tackling employment problems critically in 1997.

The Employment Service has to tackle the problem of unemployment on a day-to-day basis. In 1996, out of 75 respondents, 34 gave a positive evaluation of the work of the Employment Service, 28 were inclined to the opposite view, and 13 people did not express a firm opinion. Out of 19 company directors, 13 held negative views on the activities of the job placement professionals. Trade union bosses, on the other hand, responded entirely differently on the subject: six out of ten gave replies well-disposed towards Employment Service activities. Out of 13 politicians, six gave a negative evaluation. The overwhelming majority of officials at all levels considered the Employment Service to be active and effective. These opinions were practically identical in all three cities and were repeated in the course of the 1997 interviews:

> The Employment Service was devised by bureaucrats, to give themselves something to do. We came to them a good two years ago, when they had just appeared on the scene. We wanted to make an agreement inviting people to work here - and up to now, we've not had even one single worker from them. (Director of an engineering works, Moscow).

> I must have sent them a thousand requests for cutters or for seamstresses. They haven't sent me anyone worthwhile - in fact, they've sent me nothing but drunks. Everything there is badly organised. They need some kind of progress-chasing service, with complete information. Somewhere where I can take on workers. Thousands of people who want to find work apply to the ES, and they don't send me anyone. I can't even find a cleaner. (Director of a sewn goods group, Moscow).

One consequence of attitudes towards the State Employment Service is the behaviour of employers when filling vacancies. In 1996, in answer to the question as to whether employers are willing to make use of ES services, out of 75 respondents, 24 (32 per cent) replied positively and 37 (36 per cent) negatively. In 1997, the proportion of negative responses rose to 61 per cent:

> We ourselves know our potential employees: there aren't that many of them. We know all the aviation engineers. It's a tight circle, a fraternity - we don't need an employment service. If we have the money to pay wages, we can

always find staff ourselves - and staff offering any specialised skills. (Director of an aviation works, Moscow).

One of the important questions looking at how to resolve employment problems was: 'What is the role of Federal government bodies in tackling employment problems? What impact do their activities have on the situation in the city (or in general)?' In 1996, in the three survey cities, a significant section (48 out of 75, 64 per cent) replied that they had 'significant' or 'fairly significant' impact. In all the groups of social policy actors, with the exception of politicians, the majority were inclined to acknowledge the important role of Federal bodies.

It is curious that, in Moscow itself, opinion giving a high assessment of the role of the Federal capital in tackling employment problems was not so distinctly expressed. In St. Petersburg, the importance of the role of Federal government bodies was evaluated more highly: only St. Petersburg politicians doubted the importance of this role. In the other groups, the predominant opinion, by a large majority, was for the importance of the Federal capital. In Voronezh, out of 15 respondents in the survey, only one (a politician) failed to give a positive evaluation of the Federation. Overall the distribution of responses both across groups and across the cities came down to an acknowledgement of the Federal authorities' important role.

In 1997, this theme was strongly reversed in answers to a question about the expediency of redistributing powers between Federal and regional authorities. The majority of respondents inclined to the opinion that preference should be given to the regions (53 out of 66):

In a critical situation, it's necessary to extend the powers of the regions - and our situation really is critical. It's thought we have a low level of unemployment, that we are maintaining it at 2.6 per cent; but in fact it is really 16 per cent, if you take into account those who are not working but don't come to us, as well as the 'effectively unemployed' who are counted as being on leave. (Official of the Voronezh Provincial Employment Centre).

The regions should undoubtedly have firm rules for setting local budgets, so that they have a firm knowledge of what conditions they can count on when establishing various regional programmes. (Member of Social Forecasting Research Group, Provincial Employment Centre, Voronezh).

Turning to the question of 'who - in the first instance - should help a person to tackle work problems?' in 1996, out of 67 respondents, 28 considered that the person should help themselves, while 22 thought that the State should help. The rest thought that the enterprise or friends should help. Company directors, trade union leaders and high-ranking officials appeared to have already relinquished any illusions of paternalism suggesting that people should help themselves. Middle-ranking officials, along with the majority of politicians, however retained the view that this problem was the concern of the State.

In Moscow, 42 per cent were inclined to consider work problems to be the business of workers themselves. This tendency was even more marked in St. Petersburg, where 56 per cent of respondents thought that work problems were a person's own concern. With the exception of politicians, all the groups of social policy actors taking part in the survey saw the solution to work problems as lying with the active nature of the person themselves. But then, in Voronezh, only one out of nine respondents indicated that seeking work was the problem of the person themselves, while seven saw it as the problem of the State, and one thought that the enterprise should help. Responses to this question in Voronezh, specifically, reflect the frank need of provincial Russia for help from the State. Their responses also reflected the fact that State aid has been reduced in recent times - and that further reductions are inevitable. The Russian 'backwoods' are not able to become fully self-sufficient, and the respondents' answers tell us this.

A final question focussed on employment legislation. The responses revealed general dissatisfaction with the state of legislation. Out of 74 respondents, 52 expressed dissatisfaction, 14 did not know how to answer this question, and only eight gave a positive evaluation. Not one group of respondents had a majority with a positive attitude to the legislation, although some were equally balanced between positive and negative.

An Integrated Evaluation of the Actors' Opinions

Preliminary Remarks

We should now highlight the main features revealed during analysis of the interview texts. First and foremost, it should be remarked that the respondents lacked any conceptual approach to either social problems or the economic situation overall. We could go so far as to say that the actors' belief system on these issues did not display any real coherence. Even where we offered an integrated view of the issues we frequently observed contradictory responses to different questions.

For example contradictions frequently arose between responses to questions of a general nature, relating to the main components of social policy and employment, and discussions of specific questions which assessed the real state of affairs and concrete possible ways of tackling social problems. The respondents' range of basic ideas about social action and State social policy was limited, and as a rule it boiled down to the set of ideological clichés that currently dominate ruling circles.

On the basis of the results of our interviews, we formed a very firm impression that a real perception of what is happening in Russian society is present in the thinking of our respondents only at a subtle, lower level; they are aware of it intuitively, and therefore their assessments of it are superficial. But such assessments of Russian society in the 1990s, although not always 'mature' or well-thought through, revealed the essence of what is happening.

Thus, our conversations to a great extent confirmed the hypothesis, put forward at the start of the research, that State social policy is drifting towards the neo-liberal model. Having analysed the results of the interviews, we came to the conclusion that an overt tendency towards radically liberal views distinguished those respondents who had not long moved out of the Soviet nomenklatura. The general attitude in these conversations was: 'a person should mainly rely on their own strengths, and not expect help from elsewhere', 'assistance should be targeted', 'employment policy should be active', 'new jobs should be opened up, not limited by paying out benefits'.

The position of those who are employers is even further from paternalism: directors nowadays are interested, first and foremost, in profit and in the success of the enterprise, and they believe it is preferable to preserve the specific workforce. Thus between 1996 and 1997 the interviewees showed a shift towards neo-liberalism under pressure from the country's general economic situation - in this, they are representative of the contemporary Russian élite, and of social groups that are close to it. The need to subscribe to the ideology of the market is correspondingly transforming our respondents' mentality. For example, to the question: 'Who is most likely to help a person find work, whom can they most rely on?', the majority replied : 'The individual themselves, their relatives or friends, but not the State'. In other words, according to the results of our interviews, the conclusion can be drawn that, in fact, no system (in the sense of a real institution) exists in Russia at the moment which can guarantee to find the individual a job that is able to provide a family with the Subsistence Minimum. It has become clear that the system run by the State Employment Service is far from offering a solution to this problem, while private agencies place employees only in a narrow segment of the labour market (basically in commercial firms): a person must rely primarily on their own forces. In this respect Russian citizens share the experiences of workers of many other countries (Granovetter, 1995).

Moreover, the respondents practically avoided the question as to whether State expenditure on social matters should be increased, although it might have been presumed that, following in the socialist tradition, it is precisely from the State that they would expect solutions to social problems. Although this might appear to be an aspect of a neo-liberal strategy in conducting social policy, it is more than likely that people have simply stopped expecting help; they think that if even the State cannot manage the economy - let alone social matters - then a person should count only on themselves - and indeed, this is the real state of affairs. Among the actors, the opinion that resources need to be invested in the economy, to support enterprises that remain 'afloat' ('well, people can come "later", they'll fend for themselves: they'll pay for medical treatment, education and leisure') is very widespread. It probably also testifies not to the fact that new actors in social policy in Russia consciously support neo-liberal tendencies, but to their pessimistic assessment of the economic situation and, correspondingly, of social matters. And this again raises doubts as to whether the forced implementation of a neo-liberal model of market transformation in Russia is really defensible.

Analysis of the survey materials provided the basis for a further judgement about particular features of the social policy actors' accounts. This was that we could trace, in the responses of representatives of all the groups and cities, a distinct attempt to shift the possible solution of any problems that arise onto 'external factors'. 'External factors' means primarily the State - but not only the State. In some cases 'external factor' meant the objective situation as it had developed (external circumstances), and in others, other influences on social policy. This suggests a continuation of social passivity, exactly as was previously typical for members of the various élites in Soviet society.

Responses to the same questions in 1996 and 1997 coincided on many points, and this was significant. The second half of 1996 and the first half of 1997 were a period of political instability in Russia, provoked by a bitter power struggle between political and financial groupings, by their opposing the Communists during the presidential elections, and later by the

President's prolonged illness. Political instability was aggravated by a deep crisis in social relations, caused first and foremost by long-term non-payment of pensions and wages (which are pitifully low anyway). These non-payments affected major groups of employees (staff of enterprises, doctors, teachers, armed forces personnel, other staff in the budget-funded sector), and this has actually brought the country to the brink of explosive social unrest. In this situation, it is very important to discover what is happening in the minds of emerging social policy actors, how their perception of the social situation is changing, and how their opinions and assessments have changed direction over a year full of anxieties and great internal tension.

Dynamic changes in the political sphere would normally be expected to bring in their wake serious transformations in the views of our respondents, in their approaches to assessing social problems and in methods of tackling them. However, analysis of our interview materials revealed hardly any such changes. In this sense, a certain stability and a degree of repetition in the responses at both stages of the research (1996 and 1997) obviously gives us a basis for assuming that the underlying processes of social and employment policy are moving sluggishly - if at all - and are not directly related to current political events - even to the most striking of these.

This conclusion is also confirmed by the high degree of uniformity of response to questions which lie outside these groups of actors' own remit. So, they were practically all unanimous in their responses to the central questions of the interview, which asked for general assessments of social policy and employment policy. Practically all the respondents recognised both that social policy is passive, and that no integrated system of measures has been developed which could turn social or employment policy into a considered and systematically achievable programme of action. The vast majority of our experts deny that the State has the potential to exert any constructive influence on social and employment policy. Moreover, they apply this view equally to both the executive and the legislative authorities. In many ways, the distribution of these responses also gives us a basis to assume that their sceptical attitude to the role of the State not only - and not so much - signals the actual weakness of the contemporary State, but also evidence of many of the particular features of the respondents' accounts that we have noted above.

In talking about the contemporary Russian State, our respondents were unwilling to draw any comparison with the State as it was in the Soviet period, presumably because of their previous social experience. However, the responses to certain specific questions tell us that the role of the post-Soviet State in the social sphere is far from insignificant. So, most of our interviewees considered that the proportion of State expenditure that goes on social matters need not be increased. However, despite all their criticisms, they nevertheless felt that the leading role in tackling social policy and employment issues in future should still be taken by the State. This view was also evident in their fairly high evaluation of the actions of regional authorities, which also represent the State in tackling social problems. In their replies, many respondents revealed an inclination to reinstate the old Soviet social protection mechanisms for the general public. The majority of them were inclined towards granting free social services and towards preserving universal employment. Significantly, these actors of social policy also demonstrated their lack of knowledge of alternative methods for tackling social problems. So, in relation to hiring and firing workers, they had a weak conception of the State Employment Services' legal and organisational potential, while many were simply ignorant of the work of private recruitment agencies.

Overall, the nature of the responses offers a basis on which to draw a very important conclusion about reasons for the lack of effectiveness of social and employment policies. The fact is that all the groups who took part in the survey presented themselves as if they were the main components in a mechanism that is the very one implementing social policy. Yet their responses showed that passivity in their thinking - which stood out as a particular feature of all the groups of respondents - also carried through into the nature of their real social policy activities. True, they were knowledgeable about the state of affairs: however, it was extremely rare for them to tell us anything new or unexpected in the course of the interviews. In answering questions about any active input into tackling these problems and, above all, about the nature of their own activities, the actors demonstrated that members of all the groups of respondents were distinctly ineffective as social policy actors. The 'predictive' questions about the role of other groups of actors in tackling employment problems were especially significant in this regard: practically all the groups of respondents gave negative evaluations of the others.

Thus, the outcome of our research has been to show that one of the fundamental reasons for the ineffectiveness of social policy is the inability of leading groups of social policy actors to tackle successfully the *new* problems which they encounter as a result of the changing dynamic in political and socio-economic circumstances. We are, in fact, dealing with social policy neophytes who merely have the prospect of becoming real subjects of social policy, and who can only very conditionally be referred to as 'actors' or 'experts' in this area. In reality, the main issues are the problems of development in a country where social policy is in a critical position and the fact that a body of professionals who can initiate and implement it has not been formed yet. In these circumstances, what is the mindset of those who are now 'running the show'?

Regional Characteristics of Social Policy Actors

Our results confirmed our expectation that the opinions of the various groups of actors would be linked both to their professional allegiance and to specific features of the city where they lived and worked. So, we noticed that the Moscow respondents as a whole seemed more competent and independent in their judgements. We would suggest that this was to a large extent determined by the specific features of a capital city - proximity to the central organs of power, where the most important decisions on social matters are taken; a higher level of information; and greater involvement in tackling not only the difficult social problems of a gigantic megalopolis but also Federal problems.

All innovations, including social ones, are first 'run in' in the capital. Market relations are also 'harsher' in Moscow; and, naturally, these circumstances had an impact on the respondents' answers. The majority of the Moscow respondents were inclined to reject universalist principles of social policy, to rely less on State aid, and to see potential for tackling social problems in the activities of alternative social policies and of the individual.

The responses of the St. Petersburg respondents were on the whole 'softer' than the Moscow experts' opinions. This may be a result of the fact that many social and employment policy problems in St. Petersburg are being resolved fairly successfully. It is possible that the particular features of 'the crisis social formation' are not perceived so acutely in St. Petersburg, insofar as the city is still managing to preserve a solid industrial base. It is important to note that, on the whole - and more so than in Moscow - the St. Petersburg respondents were important central government officials, directors of powerful industrial groups, the leaders of the Federation of Independent Trade Unions, the Trade Union Federation of St. Petersburg and Leningrad Province and SOTSPROF, as well as politicians - in fact, probably the middle class of Russia's new society. Thus, the perceptions of the St. Petersburg actors are closer to the perception of the forming middle class. The St. Petersburg actors are mainly concerned about specific (production) issues and their own private social and welfare problems. At the same time, they also revealed the highest level of knowledge (by comparison with respondents from Moscow and Voronezh), commenting actively on the aims and objectives of social policy, the role of the State in social policy formation, and how far Western models are applicable to Russian reality. About 50 per cent of the St. Petersburg respondents were in favour of a social democratic means of development.

At the same time, the St. Petersburg respondents (to a greater extent than those from Moscow) linked their hopes of resolving social problems to the activities of the regional authorities. There was a greater degree of sympathy here towards universal social policy of the type formed during the Soviet period, a fact that is clearly connected both with a degree of provincialism in the St. Petersburg actors and with certain objective features of the city's economy, as well as with the particular social status of our respondents - in other words, with particular features of social relations, whose pace of development lags behind that of Moscow. The opinions of the St. Petersburg respondents most probably reflect a picture typical of large Russian cities, as well as the perceptions of members of the Russian middle class.

The responses of the Voronezh respondents in a sense form the opposite pole to those of the Moscow respondents. This results from a number of objective circumstances. Voronezh is in the Russian backwoods, so market transformations and innovations are notoriously 'late' in arriving there. The city's economy, although it has suffered serious collapse, has remained in essence Soviet. Naturally, this has also had an effect on social affairs, and that in turn gives rise to the Voronezh respondents' pessimism in assessing social and employment policy.

Not one respondent in Voronezh could formulate their desired type of policy. The fact that Voronezh is one of the regions left behind in the new pace of economic development puts its stamp on both the nature of social policy being conducted in the city and the way in which the survey respondents perceived these measures. Social policy in the city can be evaluated as an attempt to return to a degree of social levelling. A certain section of the Voronezh experts vests its hopes in a return to the previous system. Neither in Moscow nor St. Petersburg did we encounter this way of dealing with the issue. Not one of the Moscow respondents, in expressing their general perceptions of the current crisis in Russia, even mentioned the possibility of restoring the socialist system.

We should also note another important characteristic of opinions in Voronezh - that they were not very constructive. They supported a universalist-type of social policy, but did not see any force which would be able to revive the socio-economic advantages of the Soviet period. The reasons for this may be explained as follows: the weak economy of a relatively small city (by comparison with Moscow and St. Petersburg) is unable to cope with a build-up of social problems. The absence of help from central government and the limited level of the actors' information (a particular characteristic of the information space of the Russian provinces) give rise to the fact that strategic thinking in this city is not really adequate to cope with the realities of the socio-economic processes now unfolding in Russia. The Voronezh respondents' thinking is still directed 'back' to the Soviet era, and this is demonstrated in their distinct inability to take decisions about real problems and in their greater social passivity when compared with the Moscow or St. Petersburg respondents.

The Main Categories of Social Policy Actors

Before moving on to discuss the particular characteristics of each group of social policy actors, as revealed in our analysis of their interview responses, we would like to mention the following aspect. Five groups of respondents took part in the survey. However, the textual analysis that we made of the interviews drew our attention to the employers grouping (company directors and entrepreneurs), in that it showed contrasts between the members of this group and the other survey participants.

In the former USSR, over a period of decades, directors of industrial enterprises became involved in tackling socio-economic objectives. Russia has been living under private enterprise for only a few years in all, but directors today have quite different rights and independence from before. So now, in a period of social and economic reform in Russia, the rule-bound 'Soviet' director is becoming an actor in social policy - a partner of the State, equal before the law, in tackling social issues relating to imminent changes in enterprises and on the Russian labour market. In these circumstances, how do directors judge the unemployment situation in their cities? What sort of possibilities for tackling employment problems do the members of the director class have? How does the contemporary body of directors picture itself? Are directors able to interpret the processes which are taking place in enterprises, and do they link what is happening with employment problems? How does the contemporary director assess the state of social affairs, and does he or she link prospects for developing the enterprise with the resolution of social problems? How far are directors included in the system of social partnership?

We surveyed directors and senior members of the administrations of large State and privatising enterprises (aviation and engineering enterprises, ship repair plants and factories), as well as a number of private firms (construction, motor transport maintenance services, personal services).

As our meetings with members of the directors' group showed, the fact that their hopes for State assistance were close to nil actually made them more active in their work as real employers, influencing the state of affairs in the area of hiring and firing staff, and supporting a sufficiently skilled staff group. It is time to challenge the negative presentation of Russian company directors that is widespread in the economic press. A body of 'new directors' has already been formed, people with a clear view of the rules of the game in a market economy and of their own role as employers, who conduct a fairly strict policy of co-ordinating the volume and structure of labour resources with the overall state of the enterprise and with the state and dynamics of the market. (In the majority of the enterprises and organisations we looked at, organisational restructuring and staff cuts were being implemented.)

This sub-group of directors assesses the loss to Russian industry of skilled staff as a tragedy. However, at the present time, they do not see any real possibilities for solving social problems - in particular, for preserving skills potential or the social aspects of enterprise activities. They are concerned about the issues of setting up and developing production, and raising profits; and, first and foremost, they want to talk about just that - the situation and the prospects of their own enterprise. This creates the impression of a certain aloofness in their approach to tackling social problems. However, it is precisely with the future of production development that the contemporary director's prospects for tackling employment problems and finding jobs for workers are linked.

In continuing our description of these social policy actors, we should note that the directors' group was distinguished by its 'harsher' assessments of all that is happening in Russian economics and social affairs. In contrast, the distribution of replies across the other groups of respondents on many issues coincided. It was still hard for members of these respondent groups to overcome the influence of ideas formed during the Soviet period (to a greater extent than the company directors). In this sense, the 'harshness' of the directors' responses was a result of their involvement in the 'harsh realities' of market transformation. Unlike officials, who lead - relatively speaking - 'a quiet life', and even trade union leaders (despite their declarations of active involvement, our respondents were in fact bureaucrats at the top of the unions), directors are not inclined to give ambivalent, approximate (or vague) responses, and they are not scared either of the 'wrath' of bosses higher up or of the opinion of the electorate.

So, the content of responses from the company directors' group stood out from that of the other interviewees. Company directors as a whole demonstrated a certain yielding fixation, an evolution in their belief systems that was undoubtedly a result of their closer involvement in the newly-forming system of economic relations. So it could be said that company directors were in a sense 'more ruthless' than other groups of experts. Most of them were inclined to see their employees as a raw material essential to the successful operation of their enterprise. Unlike directors in the Soviet period, on whom concern for the workers was imposed as an obligation and who in reality fulfilled the social function of 'father of the enterprise', company directors in the post-Soviet period are attempting to shed everything they don't need - anything that might prevent them from fulfilling their direct obligations. It is not by chance that this group was also distinguished for its greater scepticism in relation to issues of the State's potential for tackling social policy and employment problems effectively.

Company directors tend to be very pragmatic. Their criticism is directed primarily towards the removal of any obstacles which hinder their operating independently, and their responses are those of people who are totally self-reliant in their approach to any problems they come up against in life, taking the view that other people should be the same. They are fairly indifferent to politics, but because they are very involved in the system of market relations, they demonstrate pro-market attitudes on a number of issues.

Most of the information on the other groups of actors has been presented elsewhere in this chapter: therefore, we will merely give a general summing-up here. Analysis of their responses showed that officials, to a greater extent than other respondents, were inclined to give fairly high assessments of the potential of both Federal and regional authorities. They expressed any negative opinions with caution, especially on issues relating to structures of authority and to their own work. In discussion of anything connected with the possibility of solving social problems, officials displayed restrained optimism, particularly at the regional level. It was difficult to judge what model of social policy (liberal residualist or dirigiste) these people favoured: the members of this group had amorphous political ideas. For the majority of officials (as for the directors), the crisis in the social sphere is the consequence of crisis in the economy, deriving from the general economic situation. Members of this group do not consider issues related to preserving and developing skills, the nation's health, and so on, to be Russia's most severe and painful problems at present.

The survey of the officials group was prepared with special care, since it was assumed that this is the group which is to a large extent successor to the power élite of the former USSR, familiar with mechanisms and possibilities for tackling social problems. In preparing the survey, we attempted to form our sample so that it included officials at various levels of authority. As a result, we were able to divide them into a group of senior officials and a group of officials at a middle level. We succeeded in obtaining the greatest degree of representativeness in Moscow: among the Moscow respondents were officials of the Russian Federation's Ministry of Economics and Ministry of Labour and Social Development (deputy permanent secretaries, heads and deputy heads of departments, heads of the main relevant sections), chairs and deputy chairs of the Moscow government's Committee for Labour and Employment and Committee for Social Protection, section heads of the Moscow Duma, heads of various administrative districts (prefectures) of Moscow - i.e. of local authorities - and managers of district directorates and departments of the city's Employment Service.

The result justified our expectations that these respondents would be experts in social policy only to a small extent. It revealed that members of this group, in answering questions that lay outside their own narrow professional interests, demonstrated the absence of a conceptual approach and inadequate level of information, striving to shift the conversation onto the plane of specific situations. Even representatives of the higher central government institutions in contemporary Russia are removed from the real state of affairs in the social sphere, and are inadequately informed. This is also the case with middle-ranking officials, who were represented in our research by staff of the Employment Services, local government bodies, and so on.

These respondents were fairly willing to tell us about their professional activities, and the general impression gained from our conversations was favourable to them. We were presented with programmes, reports and forward plans for the work of the relevant organisations - the Labour and Employment Committees, the Social Protection Committees, the Ministry departments and the Administrative Districts (prefectures). After the majority of interviews, we were left with a positive feeling that the respondent was personally involved in their work and far from indifferent. However, in most cases, this applied just to the sphere of the actor's own activities.

As far as an integrated understanding of the totality of social problems was concerned, the ability and desire either to analyse the general situation in Russia and in the city concerned or to evaluate current policy as a whole were both practically absent from our discussions. This could also be said of the respondents' practical involvement in tackling social problems. To the question: 'Which social issues have you taken a direct part in trying to tackle?', practically none of the officials gave a concrete answer. When we looked at issues not directly connected with the professional sphere of the specific expert/official, we encountered difficulties because of the real absence of any serious work for collecting and disseminating relevant information within the given ministry, which meant that the respondents' own professional knowledge, personal involvement and general ideas formed the basis of their judgements. It should be noted that it was precisely among officials that dependence on the tradition, dating from Soviet times, of 'fear of one's superiors' and a tendency to avoid conversation on the subject of social connections were most strongly revealed. Obviously, just as in the period of the former USSR, officials continue to function as one of the most time-serving and pragmatic social groups.

Beyond those marked out by this characteristic, practically all the respondents expounded their views openly. The trade union leaders who took part in the survey demonstrated a very critical attitude towards what is happening on the social front and towards current social policy. This was true in the first instance when they answered questions which required them to evaluate the activities of structures of authority and of company directors (especially questions relating to employment policy). The responses of members of this group display both their obvious feeling that they see themselves as defending workers' interests, and their overt preference for preserving a universalist system of social protection.

The responses of the politicians who took part in the survey displayed their political biases. As a rule, politicians took a very critical attitude to the authorities, primarily to central government. However, this critical approach arises out of their particular interests. Politicians are not always competent or informed about specific social policy issues, and are often out of touch with real social problems. We formed the impression that respondents in this group as a whole lacked a serious attitude to tackling social and employment problems. It was as if their statements in defence of workers' interests, in favour of raising living standards and providing jobs were based on populist motives. On this level, it is difficult to determine their inclination towards a particular model of social relations.

We should emphasise certain other particular features revealed in the respondents' answers: vertical relationships have an obvious effect on the responses of 'middle-ranking officials'. Members of this group are overtly oriented towards the opinions of those at the top, and over-estimate their own potential influence on the real situation. Vertical relationships are also very noticeable in the trade union leaders' group, where dependency on their 'paymasters' - the broad mass of workers - was obvious in their evaluation of the situation.

All we have said above leads to the fairly unexpected conclusion that, when considering the totality of measures directed at solving social and employment problems, the central component which would enable a serious advance to be made in tackling these problems is not the issue of funding, nor of changing the administrative apparatus, nor the adoption of legislation, nor the creation of new organisations, but in fact a set of measures which would accelerate the process of formation - in many ways, obviously, from scratch - of a 'corps' of social policy actors, a process which would draw the most capable of the main currently active 'executors' of social policy into the new 'rules of the game' - rules which are generating changes in Russia's system of political, economic and social relations.

Social Policy in the Context of Social Network Formation

In reality, on the social side of things in Russia, formal bases are now being proposed that will enable the emergence of new subjects or new actors in the 'field of social policy' - potential partners or competitors for the former monopoly subject of social policy: the State. In many respects, this situation is being defined by the laws of the market coming into play, as well as by the emergence in Russia of a new social stratum of 'visible' owners, capable of engaging in activities opposed to State policy in the social sphere. However, social policy with multiple subjects will be a development for the future.

In approaching our survey of several groups from within the Russian political, administrative and industrial élite, we assumed that we would find potential or already active social policy actors, but the results did not confirm these expectations. At both stages of the survey, we gained the impression that our respondents were very far from dealing with real social issues, except where these were ones they were directly concerned with in their own work. What can we expect of current members of local authorities' action on social issues, if all the prefects of Moscow districts who took part in the survey gave the concerted response that social issues - and in particular the issue of unemployment - 'occupy a very low position on the list of severe problems in need of urgent attention'?

The following explanations of this situation are possible:

- either those who took part in the survey were not actually frank with us (for whatever reasons);
- or they are a long way from getting really involved in tackling social issues: social problems still continue to be perceived as something secondary;
- or members of the professional groups concerned have still not engaged with social policy: they do not see this 'field' as their own, and so they still have only the weakest notion of how to get their bearings on a whole range of social issues.

In fact, all three variants are probable enough. In reality, even during those interviews that went best, some questions gave rise to a certain amount of tension - when, for example, subjects such as social connections, industry contacts, external support or relations with structures of authority were unavoidably touched on. While our interest lay first and foremost in explaining possible ways of tackling social issues, it was also important to us whether a given social policy actor - an enterprise manager, an entrepreneur, a trade union leader - could tackle social issues in conjunction with other social partners: in other words, whether real social networks exist in contemporary Russia and are promoting more effective approaches to social issues. Respondents displayed greater caution in answering these questions. We saw this as being specific to the socio-cultural environment which has formed in recent years around the élite groups of post-Soviet society (in the major Russian cities, at least) as a result of the quasi-market economic processes typical of 1990s Russia (often 'paternalistic' or 'Mafia-style', as they are defined in the literature).

Although the current post-socialist system strives to demonstrate how it differs from the previous system, essential elements of the economic relations which characterised the 'socialist', pre-reform economy remain unchanged, as do interpersonal and behavioural relations. In spite of all the economic innovations, people continue to be guided by accustomed, pre-reform stereotypes based on certain social notions. An 'ideology of hopelessness' is flourishing in Russia, and this, as Dondurei writes in his article, 'Who gains from hopelessness?':

> makes it impossible to discuss different models for modernising the public economy, its dead ends, achievements and problems... no-one is doing anything to help the Russian people focus on and adapt psychologically to a true market ideology... or to cultivate public awareness of values that would help people not to be afraid of the market... no-one is telling us about the joys and pains of being in business on your own account... no-one is doing anything to rehabilitate unequal property ownership or to propagandise equal opportunities; propaganda institutions are not doing anything to discredit mediocre state ownership, to show how helpless and hopeless it can be... (Dondurei, 1997, pp.11-14).

Given the tenor of this, the responses of our 'experts' - members of the post-Soviet economic and governing élite - were significant. They fully reflected the duality within the developing economic system: the interdependence of hidden and open structures that are intrinsic to it. Despite all their openness and dedication to new market priorities, those taking part in the survey displayed a particular type of 'social solidarity', one which has formed in recent years within the framework of the kind of economic relations growing up in Russia. In his article 'Key arguments on a swindling economy', Nevler calls this type of solidarity 'paternalist' or 'Mafia-style', explaining that:

> this is a system where everyone knows what happens and how, everyone shields one other through collective avoidance of individual responsibility, and where there is no-one who can be forced to act as a buffer between the open and hidden parts of the economic structure... We have lived too long in the belief that people are silent because they are afraid of the KGB. The events of the last ten years show that this system of collective avoidance of individual responsibility consolidates society more strongly than any ideology. So, from a social point of view, 'Westernisation' in Russia can be defined as the parallel disappearance of the threat of political denunciation and the growth of the threat of economic denunciation. (Nevler, 1997, pp.24-26).

The issue of social connections and their influence on tackling social issues directly affects the general context of the research we carried out. So, in drafting the questionnaire, we included a range of questions about the respondents' social connections and professional contacts, and the influence of these on their approaches to issues in the social sphere.

However, even at the first stage of the research in 1996 we found that our respondents, as it were, 'closed up' when answering these questions. The interviewer was interested only in who was most helpful at work: friends, Ministry colleagues, colleagues in professional associations, local authorities, trade unions, the Tri-partite Commission; in how far connections have been made in the respondent's professional milieu, how effective these are, whether they determine the success of action taken. In most cases, these questions were left unanswered. The most widely-expressed opinion was: 'Practically none of the old connections are left; it's good if connections do start up, but, in practice, you have to do everything yourself'.

At the second stage of the research in 1997 having almost lost confidence in the possibility of obtaining any information on the existence of social networks and their influence on social issues, we made several changes in the questionnaire, bringing in a number of new questions. In particular, we tried to elucidate what has replaced the network of Party control and leadership that was so effective and enduring in all areas of the Soviet State:

> if we view the Party apparatus of the Soviet period as professionally involved in settling problems, getting through bottlenecks, regulating the centrally planned system and dealing with failures of co-ordination, then it is obvious that it must also have functioned to maintain the informal connections which 'oiled the wheels' of the whole system of state planning and distribution. (Ledeneva, 1997, p.101).

During the interviews, our 'experts' willingly answered on this theme from the past. Moreover, displaying a critical attitude towards the former Party leadership (perhaps as a concession to current thinking) did not prevent them from acknowledging its positive, unifying role. However, as in the first phase, this conversation did not go any further: respondents preferred to be 'frank' only within certain limits.

The conclusion which first suggested itself was that fully-formed social networks or structures of social connections are absent from contemporary Russia, having been destroyed during the transition period. However, a look at the survey participants' socio-demographic characteristics revealed that most respondents were middle-aged and elderly people (for example, in 1997, there were 32 respondents aged

40-50, 25 aged 50-60 and four people over 60); and, on average, the overwhelming majority had occupied a senior management post for about ten years (enterprise directors, Ministry staff, leaders of top trade union organisations, members of local administrative bodies, etc.). In a situation like this, the formation of a system of social connections is inevitable. Of course, we should take into account the fact that fundamental changes in all aspects of life in Russia cannot but have affected the system of social relations:

> The processes of political and economic liberalisation that started in 1985 have led to radical changes in Russia: not only were the Party and State system of institutions and the regional administrative bodies destroyed, but everyday practices also came under attack, including co-operation within groups of individuals, relations between friends and personal connections at work. The political and economic reforms of the 1990s and the so-called 'shock treatment', topped off with de-centralisation of planning, elimination of State pricing and privatisation of public property, is also leading to still deeper social changes. (Ledeneva, 1997, p.95).

Many connections have broken down, and in many respects the nature of relations has also changed. The 1990s' reforms, directed towards introducing a market economy and privatising public property, have led in turn to a serious re-assessment of existing connections. The phenomenon of 'getting things done by pulling strings', formerly so widespread in the USSR, has in many ways lost the substance of what it usually meant in Soviet life:

> Now, the very fact of knowing people does not play such a big role (as in the Soviet period) - even if you know people, it is certain that everyone else knows exactly how much this or that service costs, as well as how much of that cost does not reach the pocket of the person actually performing the service... Nevertheless the old guard of the nomenklatura - Party apparatchiks, directors of enterprises and leaders of regional, city and district administrations - has held onto its positions. Old connections and the collective avoidance of individual responsibility have developed into so-called corporate interests. It is no secret that many banks, enterprises and consultancy firms have been founded by 'the old guard'. They have access to vital information about the market, about proposals from foreign partners for investment schemes and about regional statistics, not to speak of moral and material support. (Ledeneva, 1997, p.99).

Returning to our research, it should also be taken into account that the 'snowball' method was used in sampling our 'experts': we asked the respondents themselves for help in selecting subsequent survey participants (although, naturally, we did not rely solely on this information). As a result, the core of each respondent group (in Moscow, for example) consisted of people who knew each other well, or at least had heard of one another. In this sense, the group of Moscow respondents, with certain allowances, could be seen as an example of a kind of social network, united by professional and personal contacts, which included the directors of aviation, engineering and textile enterprises, members of the Moscow Duma (in particular, one of the politicians had recently belonged to the management of a large aviation group in Moscow), officials of the Moscow City Labour and Employment Committee, and heads of prefectures of Moscow districts. However, this kind of 'tracking' did not do away with the problem of elucidating these connections and their influence on the formation of social policy and tackling social issues; gaining access to each respondent (social policy actor) in turn was far from easy, even on the level of just obtaining information.

Moreover, the nature of existing and newly-created social networks and of their potential influence on social policy as it is now being conducted was far from obvious. It is not clear whether we should transfer to Russia what we know about social networks in the West, and try to extrapolate trends in the formation of social networks within the milieu of western actors in order to understand social processes in Russia. Here, it seems to us, we ought to take into account the specific nature of Russian culture, national tradition and particular features of the Russian modes of social action.

It should be acknowledged that the Russian political élite and business élite are a particular social phenomenon. Members of the Russian élite are rather less Europeans and rather more 'Asians with European faces'. Although this is only an image, it conveys the idea that - for all Russia's external adherence to European standards - Russians lack the basic structure of European rationalist habits: there is no parallel correspondence to European behavioural and motivational traditions, principles or culture. In Western Europe, and later in America, traditions of social relationships, professional associations and political networks have arisen, with the decisive role in many cases being played by family relations, relationships formed while still at élite educational institutions, and so on. In Russia, by contrast, these traditions either are only just starting to form or are largely absent.

What was needed in America to create a situation in which whole complex structures of social relationships formed successfully and created the essential conditions for successful implementation of democratic social policy? Why was America able to repeat the European experience? Why do democratic social networks really 'work' there and not in Russia (European Russia)? What is preventing analogous social formations from taking shape in Russia?

It is essential to take into account that a post-industrial information society has fully developed in America. This is a special type of capitalist economy, with special social relations and social policy: a high standard of living, a modest standard of social protection and Welfare State-type social policy. Further, America is a country based on western Christianity and western individualism, where freedom for each person does not mean freedom for all.

In Russia, we are dealing with a completely different model of economic development. What has been put into practice in Russia is the model of a country of 'a revolution in military technology' (to use Lapin's terminology), which in many ways explains the situation. As has already been noted, in the USSR, social connections were based on so-called 'pull', while membership of the Party-nomenklatura system lay at the basis of developed social networks. We should also take into account that, in practice, real 'freedom of conscience and freedom of religion' were absent for many years, with Russia's traditional attachment to Orthodox religion being destroyed over several decades. Today the situation is changing; but no-one can forecast how long the newly-forming Russian society will take to move from 'time-serving' and 'shady' interactions to a genuinely democratic system of social connections and relations.

Burtin has provided a distinct and graphic description of what is happening with the ruling élite. He notes that, however paradoxical it may seem, a situation is arising in Russia today where it is as if the ruling élite is guaranteeing the population *against* social protection, against any kind of official support from the state:

> The phenomenon of a permanent shift in the social order, made by the ruling stratum in Russia over the last decade, has long been in need of sensible interpretation and of political and moral assessment. Communist Party apparatchiks, having rejected the idea of Communism, continue to form the dominant stratum in an ideologically opposed, pseudo-capitalist world. So let us not mince words: this means that Russia is living under the power of werewolves - consummately unscrupulous and unprincipled double-dealers.

Such power, even if it is being reproduced through democratic procedures, is notoriously untrustworthy and... this applies even more so to the property of those who now own Russian life. (Burtin, 1997, p.171).

7 Russian Debates on Social and Employment Policy

Старая песня на новый лад
An old song to a new tune

Over the decades of Soviet power in Russia, the State monopolised social policy, and this was inevitably reflected in the nature of the social policy put into practice and in its results. The State not only organised social policy, but also acted as guarantor, responsible for many vital aspects of life - the life of the society and the life of the ordinary person.

In the Soviet period, the various aspects of social policy developed disproportionately, and this has become obvious to Russians in recent years as the experience of other countries has become better-known. For example, employment policy was mainly concentrated on the right to work, while health care was funded at an unjustifiably low level. At the same time, until the 1960s - and to a greater extent than other socialist countries apart from East Germany - the Soviet State took almost complete responsibility for providing the public with housing.

On the verge of a period of transition, it was felt that there was a distinct need to reinterpret the nature of social policy and to establish social policy actors within conditions of pluralist forms of ownership, as well as to institute research and analysis which would enable a better understanding of the social situation, of the behaviour of both clients and producers of current social policy and, consequently, also of their reactions to any given activities in that sphere.

In this chapter, we have attempted to analyse the situation that really pertains in tackling social and employment problems in Russia during the reform era; to review approaches to the formation of State policy in this area; to compare the evaluations and opinions of leading Russian economists and sociologists on the social consequences of economic reform in Russia and the prospects for social reform proper. In preparing this chapter, we have drawn on material from academic publications, statistical digests and the press, as well as the results of our survey of social policy actors.

Section I - Debates on Social Policy

Liberal Reforms and the Role of the State

In 1990, on the threshold of radical economic reform and transformation of the political system, the Russian government, in setting about these radical reforms, was faced with the problem of choosing a paradigm that included social policy in its economic strategy. The notion of reform had originally arisen from a need to make the economy function more efficiently. But, at the same time, social aspects were seen as an element of the general economic strategy. Within the new system, the criteria for determining efficiency stressed economic factors, while social issues were viewed as being among the limitations on economic efficiency. Despite many declarations about 'a socially oriented economy', 'a Social State', and so on, developing the social sphere was not listed as one of the clear goals of the reforms (whether in the short- or the medium-term). In fact, only one aspect was taken into consideration - the possibility of acute social crises.

In many respects, such an approach to selecting a socio-economic development strategy was often justified by the presence of a certain reserve of durability in the social system. Thus, Kosmarsky and Maleva (1996) analysed the reasons why attempts to solve social problems could be postponed during the early 1990s:

- Russian society was subject to weak property and income stratification and, consequently, enjoyed relative social homogeneity, which in turn led to a more or less even distribution of the burden of reform on society;
- ordinary Russians had at their disposal some financial and material resources accrued under shortage economy conditions and, at the moment when the reforms started, they had not yet spent these;
- a similar reserve also existed in the different branches of social provision, giving a momentum that allowed these to function relatively successfully for some time, even without receiving new resources;
- high expectations of the reforms and an idealistic mood were widespread in society (pp.4-5).

Moreover, given that a liberal model of transition to the market was being established as the ideological basis of the economic reforms being carried out in Russia, a strictly liberal approach could also be taken to social provision - resulting in significant damage being inflicted in this area. A significant number of restrictions on the behaviour of economic subjects, including the general population, were removed. Presented as a compensatory measure, in reality this meant that one should no longer expect help from the state and should pursue one's own possibilities for generating income within the new system of institutions. This made it possible to come down in favour of the second of the two policy variants that related to the general public - either to earmark additional resources or to introduce new rules of the economic game.

At the same time, it was proposed to combine the liberal approach, gradually freeing the State from its role in orchestrating economic and social processes, with the use of those reserves created by the former system. However, in essence this also meant that no national programme was developed, in which social policy would be treated as a more or less autonomous - and a genuinely social - issue.

The practical implementation of economic reforms and political transformation in the early years demonstrated that social policy can often be called on to provide the means of tackling a large number of the most diverse objectives. In circumstances of political instability and conflict, amid growing economic difficulties and the severe social costs of the current transformation, social policy has been barely able to restrain tension. So, it has naturally taken on the character of an urgent - and not always appropriate - reaction to the most acute problems.

In the academic literature, the prevailing opinion is that, although a social protection system based on monetary compensation mechanisms has been preserved, the predominant feature of Russian social policy in the transition period is emergency measures relating to various strata of the population. The social policy of this period has been characterised in the literature as urgent measures policy (Offe, 1993). Analysis from Yavlinsky's EPICentre gave a similar evaluation of social policy during the first years of reform:

> we should not view central social policy today as something unified, with its own institutions, mechanisms for implementation, resources, defined logic and aims... rather, it is a spontaneous and contradictory system of self-preservation (Yavlinsky, 1993).

As the results of our interviews in Moscow, St. Petersburg and Voronezh show, the social policy actors who took part in the survey had a critical attitude towards the State's current social policy. The majority of respondents stressed the compensatory nature of the actions undertaken. The most common response was: 'Social policy in Russia is unformed' (see Chapter 6).

Some Peculiarities of Social Policy in Russia

As a direct consequence of the nation's general conception of social policy and its subsequent embodiment in the State budget, there was an unprecedented growth in State expenditure on social needs, as a proportion of GDP, in 1992-4. Over these three years significant growth took place in social expenditures, as percentages of GDP, mainly from the resources of extra-budgetary funds and territorial budgets. This growth affected practically all the main categories of social expenditure, including expenditure on arts and culture, education, health care, pension provision, social insurance, and payment of social security benefits, as well as unemployment benefit (Table 7.1).

At the same time, however, the absence of a clear-cut programme or policy to address social problems was manifest everywhere: the most inefficient element in the use of resources in the social insurance system was subsidies to enterprises for their outlay on sanatoria and health resort services for staff; in the pension provision system, the chief inefficiency lay in encouraging the practice of early retirement for workers in a number of industries; in the area of social security benefits, the problem was that of failing to target payments. In the health care system, one example of the disproportionate expenditure of resources was the unjustified emphasis on forms of hospital treatment, to the detriment of the development of primary medical services; in education, the main problem was that in higher and secondary vocational education, the system of budget funding strengthened the supply structure of educational services, rather than responded to the new structure of demand for labour. In particular, in the higher education system, there was a clear oversupply of preparation of staff for engineering, technical and medical occupations. However in 1995 the State, burdened with extremely expensive commitments of a social nature, made a decisive attempt at financial stabilisation.

One of the peculiar features of social policy within the new socio-economic system has been the change in the relationship between the Federal central government and the regions, as regards the distribution of powers to tackle social problems. Until recently in Russia, the State remained the chief determinant of social policy, but the potential of the Federal budget is extremely limited. In this situation, therefore, the State is taking on the function of redistributing resources, and is gradually moving to a policy of transferring responsibility for solving social problems onto the regions, while also introducing compulsory payments into extra-budgetary funds (including the Pension Fund and the Employment Fund). In recent years, therefore, responsibility for tackling the overwhelming majority of social problems has in fact been transferred to local authorities, although this has not meant that the necessary financial provision has been strengthened: 70 out of the 89 members of the Russian Federation depend on the support of the Federal budget.

Table 7.1   **Expenditures on social goals (per cent of GDP) ***

| | *Years* | *Total* | *Source of financing* | | |
			Federal budget	*Territorial budget*	*Extra-budgetary funds*
Housing &	1994	4.60	-	4.60	-
utilities	1995	3.66	-	3.66	-
Transport	1994	-	-	0.56	-
	1995	-	-	0.75	-
Education	1992	3.58	1.21	2.37	-
	1993	4.03	0.76	3.27	-
	1994	4.36	0.81	3.39	-
	1995	3.40	0.52	2.88	-
Arts &	1992	0.61	0.31	0.30	-
culture	1993	0.61	0.41	0.41	-
	1994	0.73	0.47	0.47	-
	1995	0.42	0.35	0.35	-
Health	1992	2.45	0.27	2.18	0.00
	1993	3.58	0.34	2.82	0.42
	1994	4.09	0.37	2.76	0.96
	1995	3.41	0.21	2.33	0.87**

Pensions	1992	4.83	-	-	4.83
	1993	6.06	-	-	6.06
	1994	5.92	-	-	5.92
	1995	5.33	-	-	5.33
Employ-	1992	0.06	-	-	0.06
ment and	1993	0.22	-	-	0.22
unemploy-	1994	0.38	-	-	0.38
ment	1995	0.33	-	-	0.33
Other,	1992	1.16	0.09	0.26	0.81
social	1993	1.51	0.19	0.36	0.96
	1994	2.39	0.16	1.04	1.19
	1995	2.25	0.23	1.02	1.00
Total	1992	12.69	1.88	5.11	5.70
	1993	16.01	1.49	6.86	7.66
	1994	17.78	1.66	7.76	8.45
	1995	15.14	1.03	6.58	7.53

* This table does not take into account all socially directed expenditure headings. In particular there is no precise data on subsidies to municipal housing and public utilities, and public.
** Estimate

Stroyev, Speaker of the Upper House - the Council of the Federal Assembly - has talked about the demarcation of rights and responsibilities in social areas between the Federation and its members:

> The new social and political situation has made the distribution of obligations and powers between the Federal and regional authorities an issue of paramount importance, and the same is true of their distribution between the State, on the one hand, and NGOs and private individuals, on the other. (Stroyev, 1997, p.5).

Moreover, as the author notes, the consequences of market transformation have to some extent already altered the model of interrelationships between authorities, because this model is, in the final analysis, determined by the restructuring of property relationships.

Restructuring has, in its turn, had an impact at three levels: Federal State property, State property of the members of the Russian Federation, and the property of local self-governing authorities (municipal property). Theoretically, each of these ought to have become the main provider of social protection to the population at the corresponding level. 'What has actually happened?' asks Stroyev:

> In 1995/6, local and provincial administrations were forced to take on additional social functions. Federal central government set in motion a programme for handing over social institutions to the municipalities; it proposed that regional financial resources should be allocated to these aims and, in the case of shortage of such funds, help should be supplied from Federal sources. (ibid., p.6).

A question on the distribution of powers to tackle social problems between the centre and the regions was put to those who took part in the survey at both stages of our research (in 1996 and 1997), and the following trend was noted. In 1997, the majority of respondents (62.9 per cent) spoke out in favour of broadening the regions' potential. In 1996, only 43.6 per cent had come down in favour of the powers of the regions. This kind of distribution of responses demonstrates both a drop in confidence in central government and the social policy actors' awareness of the possibilities and prospects of alternative subjects tackling social problems.

At the same time, the background conditions to this are that neither the outlays provided for nor the Federal adjustments to regional and local budgets are sufficient, while private structures and NGOs have not been able to acquire a mastery of the application of capital to such a huge sector in such a short time.

Although social programmes have been adopted by the State Duma, funding considerations mean that the majority of them cannot be implemented in the near future, as Melik'yan, then Minister of Labour, declared in an interview with the newspaper *Finansovye izvestiya* on 1st October 1996. Having touched on the issue of employment, Melik'yan noted that the efforts of the government to try and apply a brake to the process of releasing labour had hindered the restructuring of industry and prevented wages from increasing (Goryacheva, 1996).

A Description of the Situation in the Social Sphere

The fact is that almost all attention has been focused on attempts at economic transformation, and solutions to social issues are being postponed to an unspecified future time: the negative consequences of these socio-economic policies are immediately apparent. The most noticeable feature of Russia's present social situation is the impoverishment of the country's population, with very many indicators showing a steep drop in the standard of living.

By way of example, we can look at how current economic policy has been reflected in the structure of consumption of the Russian family. First and foremost, statistics show a growth in the proportion of expenditure on food and a corresponding decrease in the share of expenditure on non-foodstuffs. However, a reduction in consumption of many particular food products can be noted. The calorific value of the daily food intake per head of population fell from 2,527 kilocalories in 1991 to 2,200 kilocalories in 1996, while the proportion of animal produce in the total calorie content of the daily food intake fell from 35 per cent to 29.9 per cent (Institute of Economics, 1998, pp.46-47).

The prices of such foodstuffs as fish, milk, bread and pasta have seen an especially large increase:

Table 7.2   Food price increases (annual per cent)

Type of food	1991	1992	1993	1994
Frozen fish	4.6	260.0	2,178.0	7,350.0
Milk	2.0	74.7	1,050.0	4,073.3
Wheat bread	2.5	107.5	1,165.0	4,185.0
Pasta	3.4	150.0	1,130.0	4,806.0
Poultry	4.1	59.1	678.5	1,720.3
Pork	6.3	113.0	1,162.0	22,860.8
Beef	6.7	96.5	957.0	2,254.8
General price index	2.7	72.1	677.6	2,236.2

Source: State Committee for Statistics of the Russian Federation: *Report on human resource development in the Russian Federation: collected statistics,* Academia, 1997, p.23-4.

Until very recently these were the four leading items in the food intake of low-income households, so this has entailed a change in the composition of the diet of poor sections of the population and a reduction in its quality. This, in its turn, has had a negative impact on other aspects of human resource development, such as health and aptitude for training. This deterioration in the quality of nutrition between 1990 and 1994 is a likely contributor to the 22 per cent increase in gastrointestinal diseases and a 44 per cent increase in endocrine and immune system diseases and metabolic disturbances (*Russian Statistical Yearbook*, 1995, p.170).

Differentiations between the structure of consumer expenditure across income groups within the population became more marked. In 1996, in the lowest income decile of households, according to data from Russian State Committee for Statistics research, 55 per cent of expenditure went on obtaining food, while in the highest income decile the proportion was 29.1 per cent (Institute of Economics, 1998, p.47).

Table 7.3   **Food consumption (average per person per year, in kg)**

Type of food product	1990	1997
Bread	97	118
Potatoes	94	125
Vegetables	85	80
Fruit, including soft fruit	37	25
Meat	70	45
Eggs (number)	231	180
Milk and dairy products	378	220
Fish	15	8
Sugar and confectionery	32	23

Source: State Committee for Statistics of the Russian Federation: *Report on human resource development in the Russian Federation: collected statistics,* Academia, 1997, p.23-4.

The 1990s have seen a sharp fall in sales of many domestic appliances. So, for example, in 1990, 234,200 televisions, 84,000 fridges and 145,600 vacuum cleaners were purchased in St. Petersburg, but in 1994, the figures for these goods were 51,600, 22,300 and 22,300 respectively (Muzdybaev, 1995, p.204). Moreover, the purchasing power of the Russian population is falling continuously: for the period from the fourth quarter of 1997 to April

1998, purchasing power across the country fell by 17 per cent (*Izvestiya*, 15 April).

Basic public utilities have become considerably more expensive. From 1990 to 1994, the growth in prices for these was 6,000 per cent. From 1992 onwards, the cost of services has been increasing at a far higher rate than that of consumer goods. This trend also continued in 1995, with services provided by local authorities - gas, hot water, central heating, sewerage and rented housing - in particular becoming more expensive (*The socio-economic position in Russia in 1995*, 1995, pp.165, 254).

The physical volume of fee-paying services has dropped sharply: in 1995, it was 24 per cent of the 1990 level. It is true that in 1997, a growth of 3.7 per cent was noted in this indicator; however, within the structure of fee-paying services, the proportion of individual consumer services diminished and the proportion of municipal housing and public utilities, medical, and communications increased (Institute of Economics, 1998, p.47). This list of fee-paying services could be extended to include the introduction of an additional subscription payment for receiving public service television broadcasts and of a fee for crossing State borders, as well as the ending of indexation of cash incomes and savings for Russian citizens.

As a result, Russia's Human Development Index, based on the indicators of average life expectancy, education and GDP, fell from 0.848 in 1992 to 0.78 in 1996, which suggests that Russia no longer numbers among developed countries which typically have an index above 0.9.

The increasing severity of the social policy measures now being put into practice could not but tell on the situation in traditional areas of social activity. Thus, negative trends in the education system are evident: the destruction of the educational capacity of Russia is now plain for all to see. Over-production of some specialists and under-production of others, lack of demand for knowledge and experience, the deteriorating occupational and skills structure of the workforce, obsolete knowledge, the falling prestige of education - all these are losses sustained by society as a result of past negative processes and today's critical situation in the economy. 'The projected sharp reduction in numbers of students entering the daytime departments of higher educational establishments and the increase of 25 per cent in the ratio of students to each lecturer will result in a 45 per cent cut in higher education' (Smirnov, 1996).

One of the intractable causes of the crisis in education is the sharp fall in the volume of financing. Expenditure on education from the Federal budget was cut from 5.85 per cent in 1992 to 3.48 per cent in 1997.

Consolidated expenditure on education in percentages of GDP was respectively 3.56 per cent and 3.97 per cent. Less than half the demand for education resources was satisfied. In addition, funding cuts have led in their turn to the direct collapse of health care in Russia. It was assumed that transferring health care onto an insurance basis would change the direction of funding flows. However, rather than generating additional funding, it has led to substitution of extra-budgetary resources for budgetary ones (30 per cent of all extra-budgetary expenditure). Over five years, real funds have been cut by 21 per cent and now represent, according to various estimates, between 2.3 per cent and 3.2 per cent of GDP. Annual *per capita* expenditure is about $50 (Institute of Economics, 1998, p.27).

Both official statistical data and the results of public opinion surveys bear witness to the deteriorating social situation. In particular, joint research by VTSIOM and Strathclyde University in early 1995 revealed that 78 per cent of respondents were not satisfied with the their family's economic position, with 62 per cent considering it to be worse than five years ago (*Report on human resource development in the Russian Federation: collected statistics,* Academia, 1997, p.27). Thus, social policy in Russia in the mid-1990s has been notable for a sharp increase in the severity of its measures. Among the consequences of the policy being conducted are a fall in living standards for the huge mass of the population, growing income differentiation, a sharp reduction in the volume of available social goods and growth in unemployment.

To provide a comparison with this official information, we will now turn to the survey of social policy actors that formed part of our research. In the course of these interviews, we discussed the issue of the impoverishment of broad sections of the Russian population. We were interested in how far those taking part in the survey were starting to play an active role in tackling social issues, what they personally, their enterprises or establishments were doing, and what the respondents knew about measures being taken at Federal, regional, city or territorial district levels to tackle social issues as they arise. So, one of the interview questions was phrased as follows: 'Do you know anything about actual anti-poverty programmes?', but 80 per cent of company directors and 40 per cent of all respondents replied 'no, not really'.

The Issue of Social Guarantees

One of the main provisions of the 1993 Constitution of the Russian Federation declares that Russia is a Social State. This presupposes (among other things) the formation of social policy and, correspondingly, of a concept of a Social State with distinctly expressed priorities. There should also be a system of social guarantees and ways of implementing them, given that it is precisely such a system which fulfils the conception of a Social State.

What, then, is really happening? In pre-reform Russia, social affairs had the outward appearance of being adequate. The socialist State was oriented towards a paternalist model and everything associated with it; and a system of social guarantees existed (their low level is a separate matter).

Social guarantees are also being proclaimed nowadays. However, substantial changes have taken place in the system of guarantees. For example, the right to work has been replaced by a guarantee of assistance in finding a job, the level of the various individual guarantees has fallen and they are less widely available. But, at the same time, there is now freedom of choice, which did not exist in the USSR. The fact that freedom of choice has appeared is a gain, but the level of guarantees has fallen and some guarantees have been completely lost - and these, naturally, can only be seen as losses. As social policy changes, it is gradually taking on features characteristic of a liberal economic model, far removed from the model of a universal Welfare State. State support is for a limited number of the population, primarily those who are genuinely unable to provide for themselves - the disabled, pensioners, children (although only children from certain families). In other words, there is a distinct trend towards targeting social assistance; means-tested benefits for the poor, but for everyone else, the State now only aims to provide an enabling function.

Movement towards this liberal model appears to be widespread now. Supporters argue that the model has advantages when compared to the Keynesian one. However, it requires particular conditions if it is to be realised in contemporary Russia: phased implementation of the relevant reforms and corresponding preventive measures (the introduction, for example, of a benefit for the poor, tackling the issue of the minimum wage and the Subsistence Minimum, bringing in pension reform and reforms in education, health care and housing).

Some things are already being done, but much (and, obviously, much that is fundamental) remains to be done. Moreover, attempts to meet the social objectives laid down are rather more aimed at adaptation to the market situation, and are far from providing for the welfare of the Russian people. In the context of implementing the liberal model in Russia, social transformation processes cannot proceed at a forced pace. The country is still not ready to carry out these reforms: they cannot be implemented in a hurry. Housing and pension reform may be realised in conditions where there is a comparatively low inflation rate. Inflation growth in Russia has come to a halt, but at the same time we should not forget the high level of debt. In other words, Russia has somehow kept to the formally required level of inflation growth, but only from an external point of view: in fact, economic conditions in Russia are far from achieving the situation in which the country could zealously apply itself to building a liberal model in this way.

For example, there are a lot of unresolved problems with the extra-budgetary social funds. As Smirnov and Maleva note, the Pension Fund is in a very difficult position:

> In 1995, in the aim of providing State pension payments on time, 1,000 billion roubles of temporarily unused Employment Fund resources and 2,000 billion roubles of banking sector credit reserves were diverted to fund Pension Fund outlays. The systematic indebtedness of the Federal budget for payments made by the Pension Fund to those entitled to Federal pensions has aggravated the situation. Calculated to March 1996, uncancelled debt for 1992-1994 was 1,600 billion roubles, and for 1995 - 3,000 billion roubles. In 1996, no provision was even made in the Federal budget to reimburse 11,300 billion roubles to the Pension Fund. (Smirnov and Maleva, 1997, p.30).

Moreover, it should be taken into account that wage levels in Russia do not yet allow people to enter the new markets. At existing wage levels, the majority of the population cannot provide their own social protection through the social funds system, and so they need State support. In addition, and more importantly, they cannot put their new-found freedom of choice into effect: fee-paying medicine is replacing free medicine, surgical operations are now becoming practically unobtainable, few people can pay for treatment in a sanatorium or top-level treatment centre, and it is becoming increasingly impossible for either adults or children to go away on holiday during their time off work or study. Anyone may choose any school for their child, however far from everyone can actually put this right into practice. Its is hardly surprising therefore that the majority of respondents gave a positive response to the question about preserving the practice of granting free services.

Social policy in Russia is gradually acquiring multiple providers, but this process is still only just beginning. In these conditions - the conditions of transition to market relations - social policy must combine both traditional methods of tackling social problems (meaning well-developed methods, typical of the country concerned) and new approaches, using the experience of countries that have been through the stage of adapting to a market economy.

A perception of the paternalistic role of the State as the main social guarantor is fully-formed and strong in the consciousness of Russians, and this means that the State cannot consider itself free of obligations to provide social protection to the citizen, even though it has now adopted the role of mere 'legislator, laying down rules, or mediator' (Sharonov, 1998, p.63). Nowadays, the State's role in tackling social issues and in providing social protection to the Russian population should not be shrinking but actually growing. The majority of Russians are acutely in need of social assistance and - for various reasons - are not able to 'get in on' the new market relations. Obviously, it is simply impossible to make a lightning transition to a new system and a new social model, and this is all the more true in the conditions of a 'crisis social formation' (to use Lapin's terminology (Lapin, 1992, pp.10-11)). Some time will have to elapse, during which new mechanisms for regulating social affairs will take shape; but in the meantime, the old mechanisms are proving inappropriate for the new system (which itself is still in the making).

However, over a period of 70 years, a stable ordering of roles became established in Russia: as Roik writes 'the State as monopoly employer' gave rise to the function 'State as monopoly distributor of social payments' (Roik, 1997, pp.62-3). This in its turn led to the formation of stereotypes in the public consciousness, which practically ruled out any responsibility on the part of employees and employers, as well as negating the importance of their joint efforts to create specialised social protection institutions - compulsory and voluntary social insurance, which in their turn are necessary elements in forming a liberal social protection system.

The predominant public attitude is still that absolute power (legislative and executive) belongs to the State, that all aspects of life for the country's population fall within its competency, and that it should manage all public institutions. From this certainty stems the absence of any demands for systematic evaluation of social and occupational risks for various categories of workers, for actuarial calculations to determine insurance contributions, for the development of a medical and social infrastructure, for the restoration of legal rights at work for everyone, and for services to establish levels of need for social assistance.

Therefore, there is a contradiction between initial principles and real results. Absence of feedback from those who are the direct objects of current social policy, lack of initiative and of active participation in the reform process and the protracted - and perhaps unavoidably sluggish - process of social change (expressed in the psychology of dependency on the State) all mean that the existing system of social guarantees, subsidies and payments is simply an unregulated aggregation of legislative standards. This does not meet the demands of the present social situation, and in many respects continues the traditions of a socialist model of distributive relations.

According to the Constitution of the Russian Federation:

In the Russian Federation... State support shall be provided for the family, for maternity, paternity and childhood... State benefits and other guarantees of social protection... shall be established. (Article 7, paragraph 2).

Everyone has the right to protection and to medical assistance. Medical assistance in State and municipal health care facilities shall be free of charge to citizens.... (Article 43, paragraph 1).

At the same time, statistics show that:

Child mortality increased by 7.5 per cent between 1990 and 1996. According to State Committee for Statistics forecasts, low birth rates and high perinatal mortality mean that, by the end of the century, the pre-school cohort in the Russian Federation will be 1,195,000 fewer in number. Since 1994, the proportion of children suffering from rickets has increased by 20 per cent and from forms of eczema, by 23 per cent. Almost 10 per cent of children under one year old have detectable anaemia, while 20 per cent of pre-school children have some kind of chronic illness. One in 50 babies born in 1993 died during the first year of life. Because of the absence of balanced, chemically and ecologically pure food products, the number of children with birth defects has risen - by 53.5 per cent between 1990 and 1993. This is directly related to the inferior diet of pregnant and breast-feeding mothers. It is no coincidence that, in 1994, almost a third of pregnant women were suffering from anaemia caused by this poor nutrition, as against 25 per cent in 1993 and a total of 16.6 per cent in 1991. (*Chelovek i trud*, vol.5, 1997, p.34).

A telling comparison is that, in 1995, life expectancy for Russian men was 58 years, three years less than in India, ten years less than in China and six years less than in Russia at the start of the period of transition. Reform of the system of social guarantees is undoubtedly one of the most urgent problems for social policy, which is today undergoing a general process of reform.

Table 7.4   **Total number of births, 1989-1998 (million)**

Year	Births
1989	2.161
1990	1.989
1991	1.795
1992	1.588
1993	1.379
1994	1.408
1995	1.364
1996	1.305
1997	1.230
1998	1.240

Source: UNDP, 1999b.

Recent Russian Interpretations of the Social Situation and Social Reform

The sharp deterioration in the social and economic position of the Russian population demands decisive shifts in ideas about the aims, criteria and mechanisms, according to which the social sphere will function during the course of Russian economic reforms, as well as in the corresponding fundamental changes and renewal of social policy itself.

It was a mistake to assume that social affairs could wait until after the period of economic hardship, and that this quiescence, in its turn, would allow economic reforms to go through rapidly and successfully. As the process of economic reform has dragged on, the lack of systematic structure to current social and economic policy, and the hopelessness of social policy measures that are primarily directed towards alleviating the social consequences of economic transformation, are being felt all the more strongly.

Russia embarked on reform as 'a society where the State had large-scale commitments, with a mechanism for "extricating" resources from production in order to fund these commitments' (Ulyukayev, 1997, p.10). Proceeding from data which summarise social and economic practice in a number of countries over a long period of time, Ulyukayev constructs his argument on the thesis that there is a close correlation between economic growth and processes of democratisation, drawing on Lipset (1960), Huntington (1991), Boron (1995) and Alesia and Perotty (1997).

Movement towards forming a market economy has demanded corresponding democratic (liberal) reforms and, particularly, reductions in the State's social commitments. Ulyukayev draws attention to the fact that this measure is inevitable, given the chosen direction of reform, but also notes that any review or contraction of the State's social commitments is extraordinarily difficult to accomplish, from a political point of view: 'Such measures are realistic only when a particular political "window of opportunity" opens' (Ulyukayev, 1997, p.11).

In Russia, the first of these 'windows', according to the author of this article, was in 1991-4. During this period, a great deal of success was achieved, but this did not affect the area of social reform:

> It was as if some kind of informal political contract was made - the reformers received freedom of action in the economy in return for their tacit agreement to preserve, in the main, the structure and mechanism of the State's social commitments. The window gradually 'closed' as all the forces of reform were thrown into achieving financial stabilisation, and, obviously, further attempts to tie the realisation of social reforms to this were counterproductive - neither one nor the other was achieved. (Ulyukayev, 1997, p.12).

According to 'first wave' reformers, a second 'window of political opportunity' opened a little way in 1997, as a consequence of crisis in the Russian model of nomenklatura-monopoly capitalism, which is burdened by protectionism and 'by the native stains of socialism' in relation to the State's social commitments. These reflections from the radical democrats' camp suggest both a continuity of severe policies in regard to social matters in Russia, and the prospects for possible transformations.

Shmelev also dates a new stage in Russian economic reforms from early 1997. Unlike Ulyukayev, his perception of the prospects for market reform in Russia is rather pessimistic:

> As a result of the unjustifiably severe - one could even say fanatical - monetary policy of the government and the Central Bank, the country's economy has gone into deadlock, and until it breaks out of the vicious circle of general non-payment, normal market motivations will not come into play, and effective stimuli and levers will not start to work... The main reasons for the general payments crisis were: prolonged artificial shortage of money in the economy; deliberate non-payment for State orders; delays in paying pensions and wages to staff in the budget-funded sector; lack of efficiency in the newly-developed taxation system; involuntary flight by more than 40 per cent of the Russian economy into the shadows, i.e. completely outside the scope of

tax; unrestrained price increases in natural monopoly outputs and in transport tariffs; domestic producers' slowness to adapt to competitive market conditions; non-payments by CIS partners; and the unforeseen extent of corruption, abuse and organised crime. The chain of non-payment can be broken only where it was principally formed: in the relationship of the budget to all the rest of the economy. That must be the Number One economic objective. (Shmelev, 1998, p.4).

In Shmelev's opinion, actions undertaken by the present reform Government can be expected to show material results only after the year 2000 (i.e. after the Parliamentary and Presidential elections). However, over the next three to five years, all the framework reforms (including social ones) will lead to an inevitable increase in social tension in Russia. In conclusion, Shmelev looks at the objectives of this new stage of the reforms, interpreting them critically from the 'new reformers' standpoint, and anticipating 'a social reform which transfers the main burden of social security expenditure and social and medical insurance from the Budget onto ordinary citizens' (ibid., p.6).

Abalkin, Director of the Russian Academy of Sciences' Institute of Economics and a member of the first generation of Russian reformers, sees the situation similarly. Abalkin (1998, p.3) notes:

Today Russia is faced with the need for serious, fairly profound adjustments to the direction of social and economic policy... Discontent with the outcomes of the way the reforms have been conducted in Russia is growing, and increasingly critical assessments of their social impact have led to acute problems. Danger signs are appearing - the repudiation of radical transformations and a return to the past.

Abalkin highlights a number of acute social problems, which have been aggravated by mistakes made during Russia's social and economic development and require urgent resolution:

- the problem of restoring the social status of work and its remuneration;
- the rise of unemployment and fall in labour force participation;
- the demographic crisis;
- the damage of science, education, health care and culture as a whole.

In Abalkin's opinion, Russia has long since fallen behind other countries that can claim to have given social priorities special importance during their development:

> According to the latest data, budgetary expenditure on key aspects of social affairs is as follows (in per cent of GDP): expenditure on science in the USA is 2.54 per cent, in Germany - 2.26 per cent, in France - 2.34 per cent, and in Russia - 0.53 per cent in total; expenditure on education in the USA is 7.6 per cent, in Germany - 4.1 per cent, in France - 5.7 per cent, and in Russia - 3.7 per cent; outlay on health care in the USA is 14.1 per cent, in Germany - 8.6 per cent, in France - 9.8 per cent, and in Russia - 2.5 per cent. (ibid., p.8).

Addressing the experience of countries which have undergone profound economic transformations, Abalkin notes that success is possible only in the presence of one indispensable condition: to be precise, where the results of reforms reflect the interests of broad strata of the population and receive their support. From this, it follows that the level of a country's development is directly dependent on investment in the social sphere. 'This means science, education, culture, health care and other related areas. Anyone who invests resources in achieving goals in precisely these areas is looking to the future' (ibid., p.5).

A new conception of transition to a socially-oriented, highly-efficient market economy is being put forward, and this includes:

- raising the quality of life for the population ;
- raising the quality of the environment;
- creating a mixed, socially-oriented economy;
- renewal of State regulation of economic and social processes;
- strengthening the infrastructure;
- promoting a stable and trustworthy financial and banking sector;
- reliable social partnership between workers, employers and the State.

(ibid., p.6).

This programme, put forward by one of the ideologues of socio-economic transformation in Russia, undoubtedly demonstrates an awareness of the vital need to re-think the situation. Nevertheless, a distinct accent on the senior, leading role of the State in tackling social problems is discernible: the need for social policy to acquire multiple actors, so essential in the present conditions, is practically ignored - it is not 'in the frame'.

The Russian government's official position, as shown in proposed State programmes, now also appears to be moving towards a socially-oriented economy. Thus, the Deputy Minister for the Economy, Sharonov, evaluating new approaches to reform in the social sphere and proposals for adjusting current social policy, picks out the following distinctive features of the new model, while noting its moderately liberal character:

- renouncing paternalism: the State is ceasing to strictly determine either the behaviour of the individual in the social sphere or exactly what set of services the individual may or should receive;
- de-nationalising social affairs and freeing the State from the function of granting the citizen direct social services: as applied to many types of social services, this means the State is ceasing to be the provider, who grants these services to the consumer; in some cases, the State will adopt the role of legislator, only laying down the rules, and in others, will become an intermediary between consumer and provider;
- forming a market in social services, with real, nascent competitiveness between producers, pre-supposing an improvement in the quality of the given services and a reduction in the costs of producing them.

(Sharonov, 1998, p.63).

This 'moderately liberal' approach could hardly be called 'new', even in the Russian situation. The State has been vigorously striving to throw off the mantle of social guarantor for a number of years.

It is also notable that the majority of official statements in this area have the - enviably constant - shortcoming of confusing two essentially different problems. On the one hand, it is proposed to take more actively liberal approaches to social policy reform, while on the other, the grounds for introducing innovations are that expenditure of Federal budget resources is difficult to control.

Sharonov also writes about absence of purpose and about non-transparency of transfers allocated for social needs, emphasising that the regions have a vested interest in this situation. He proposes the fundamental measure of handing social policy over to municipal control, or - to put it another way - advocates what has been defined above as renunciation of paternalism by the State, or redistribution of its functions in regulating social affairs. But first of all it will be necessary to take measures to strengthen, or even just organise, control over expenditure of the Federal budget contributions at a regional level.

Yet another of the 'arguments' put forward by this representative of the 'new wave of young reformers' is:

> At present, we have 156 types of subsidies, benefits and social payments in operation, which are intended to reach 100 million people - almost two-thirds of the population of the Russian Federation. Total expenditures on these goals last year (1997) were 350 trillion unrevalued roubles. There are methods which allow us to determine the effectiveness of similar outlays from the point of view of whether the poorest and most needy sections of the population are really receiving them. Therefore, in Russia, roughly 18 per cent - 20 per cent of the total amount of social subsidies and payments go to these sections of citizens. In developed countries, the analogous indicator is 45 per cent - 55 per cent. (ibid., p.64).

If this is really the situation, then the question inevitably arises again: why does the State want to shed practically all responsibility for allowing social crisis to occur (apart from periodically drafting yet another up-to-the-minute concept of social reform), instead of strengthening its controlling function? Why has it renounced the functions of social guarantor, which must inevitably be carried out during this transition period, and handed them over for management by local authorities? Why has it put the citizen - the new subject of social policy - on the road to free competition, even for social services?

Notwithstanding the promising outlook and all the attractions of liberal reforms in both the economy and the social sphere, such precipitate approaches do not inspire confidence in the real possibilities of implementing the plans outlined. Serious financial transfusions are necessary, and these require serious programmes and the commitment of time. Therefore, social policy reforms should be starting from a gradual, carefully considered improvement of the current position and amendment of its various elements. In other words, for the time being, it is a matter of adjusting details.

The desire to reach an outcome, when one has hardly embarked on something, is still a traditional Russian trait. According to the position taken in the Constitution, Russia has already been a Social State since 1993. However, a public opinion survey carried out in 1996 by the Socio-Political Research Institute, as part of its monitoring study of the movement of Russian society towards a Social State demonstrates that Russia has still not yet found the right path. The State does not guarantee observance of many of the norms of democratic society: equality of all citizens before the law (85 per cent of respondents thought that the State does not guarantee this), personal safety (92 per cent), human rights (84 per cent), social guarantees (86 per cent), freedom of political choice (91 per cent), tolerance of other people's opinions (53 per cent) and freedom of speech (36 per cent) (*Chelovek i trud*, 12, 1996, p.18).

Turning to the results of our own research we found that the majority of participants in the survey thought that this legislative instrument was premature. Thus, one is left with the impression that the liberal approach provides a convenient mask for politicians currently in power in Russia. Their liberal ideas are merely rhetorical. Having failed to justify themselves or obtain any positive results in the area of economic transformations, the instigators of the liberal approach to reform in Russia have switched their attentions to the social sphere.

In our view, given Russia's present social and economic position, realisation of the liberal model must be seen as some kind of distant goal, a possible future line of development, which pre-supposes serious reconstruction of the system of funding the social sphere and the introduction of new mechanisms of support and assistance for Russia's population: the creation of a system of extra-budgetary funds, the redistribution of functions between Federal and regional authorities, and so on. It should also be noted that, in conditions of contemporary economic instability, the conduct of social policy according to the requirements of a liberal model could well provoke significant growth in social tension and worsening social crisis, with telling effects on the demographic situation, and the health of the Russian people.

Section II - Debates on Employment Policy

The labour market policy of any State, especially one conducting economic reforms or in transition to market relations, inevitably represents a key direction in its new social policy. Therefore, in any analysis of the way social problems are being tackled in Russia, we should pay special attention to the Russian labour market situation. In this section, we attempt to analyse basic approaches to the formation of employment policy and also particular aspects of the way it is conducted in the cities that we studied.

The formation of a labour market requires appropriate employment policy alongside reconsideration of decades-old mechanisms for tackling related problems. Has Russia adopted a new kind of reproduction of human resources and a new system of employment, in order to ensure a qualitative shift in the level of economic growth? Is there a new conceptual approach to the issue of employment becoming established in contemporary Russia? What influence do specific aspects of regional labour markets have on the conduct of employment policy? How should Russia tackle the problems of supporting groups which are suffering from the labour market crisis?

The Nature of Social Policy in the Area of Employment

In many respects, the nature and priorities of the employment policy being conducted by the State are predetermined by the liberal direction of reforms. Thus, among the outcomes of measures taken have been an expansion in forms of labour activity and an increase in the scale of self-employment across the Russian population. At the same time, the primary reform strategy has been directed at tackling a number of related economic objectives, leaving social ones practically untouched. However, as Kosmarsky and Maleva note:

> in one sense, the position in the social sphere has exerted an influence on the choice of macroeconomic strategy - it is a social criterion that has dictated the pace of reforms. This meant choosing between two alternatives - either the stringent version, cleansing the economy by bankrupting unprofitable enterprises, with a consequent sharp upsurge in unemployment (in this scenario, Russian economists were forecasting possible open unemployment of 4-7 million in the first two or three years; ILO experts gave estimates of 6-7 million); or the version involving support for inefficient production, preserving high formal employment and averting simultaneous mass redundancies. As is well-known, in practice, the line followed was the second one. (Kosmarsky and Maleva, 1996, p.6).

In this view, the government could not bring itself to make any other choice, if it wanted to avoid open social and political crisis, which might put an end to transformation just as it began. However:

> the policy of supporting the existing level of employment or slower rates of growth in unemployment, accomplished by using subsidy schemes - with loans and grants to unprofitable producers - has led inevitably to the emergence and reproduction of high latent unemployment. The two most widespread forms of this in Russia are sending staff on compulsory unpaid (or part-paid) leave and applying various short-time working regimes. By the summer of 1992, when the country's economy underwent its first payments crisis, the partially unemployed already numbered about 2 million people. And other, hidden, negative labour market processes have unfolded steadily,

despite numerous shifts in the paradigm of credit-financed and budgetary policy. (ibid., p.6).

The conclusion may be drawn from this that the high level of hidden unemployment in the Russian labour market has been caused by the conscious choice of a macroeconomic strategy. The negative economic and social consequences of this phenomenon are very well-known: the preservation of a large number of inefficient jobs, the reduction of real incomes for people in formal employment, the weakening of incentives to high productivity, and so on. However, Kosmarsky and Maleva continue:

> moreover, from the point of view of certain government functions, yet another, less obvious, effect has been achieved: under current legislation, the registered unemployed have become the object of social protection, but - as a result of this choice of policy - several million people, who are formally employed but lack a permanent source of income from work, find themselves outside the framework of social assistance and, in principle, are not the object of State social policy. (ibid., p.6).

Employment policy and relevant ways of tackling labour market problems in Russia depend directly on the macroeconomic situation and on changes in the structure of production, and these define labour market policy as subordinate to policy relating to financial and economic structures. Moreover, the 'social bloc' within the government (including the Ministry of Labour of the Russian Federation, the Ministry of Social Protection, the Federal Employment Service, the Federal Migration Service, and others) lacks the potential to influence the scale of employment and unemployment directly; its sphere of influence is limited by prescriptive safeguards and by the regulation of specific labour market processes.

Change in the structure of employment is substantial, and includes a fall in the economic activity of the population, a sharp increase in the scale of informal employment, a reduction in employment, sharp growth in registered unemployment, an increase in the gap between registered and total unemployment, the growing scale of hidden unemployment, the increasing duration of unemployment, change in socio-demographic characteristics of the unemployed, and negative social consequences of labour market tension (unemployment and poverty, a fall in the standard of living and people's incomes, and so on).

One particular feature of the employment policy being conducted by the Russian government - and of its overall social policy - is the transfer of responsibility for tackling social issues to the regions. In the context of the liberal direction of the reforms being carried out in Russia, the State has shown tendencies to minimise its own functions in providing employment, to try and extricate itself from tackling social objectives and transfer these to the regions. This was a result of both the general strategy for social policy in the 1990s and, in particular, of underestimating the importance of employment as an integral area of the economy (Institute of Economics, 1998, pp.31-2).

A detailed analysis of the specific regional features of the cities which form the object of our research is presented in Chapter 5. As far as the labour market situation is concerned, difficulties are being aggravated by the fact that, among the most significant characteristics of the Russian labour market in the years 1992-7, regional problems are central:

- tendency of regional labour markets to develop in different directions;
- growing problem of providing work in differing regions;
- increasingly different rates of unemployment between regions.

In evaluating the regional labour market situation in the cities which formed the object of our research, we could distinguish these regions as comparatively comfortable. For example in December 1997 in the Northern Caucasus the registered unemployment rate was 20.4 per cent of the active population (see Table 3.1, p.64); in July 1997 this was 0.8 per cent for Moscow, 1.3 per cent for St. Petersburg and 2.2 per cent for Voronezh. Between August 1996 and June 1997, there had been a change in the number of job-seekers in Moscow from 53,900 to 65,300, in St. Petersburg from 53,500 to 54,600, and in Voronezh from 32,600 to 28,700. In fact, Moscow's unemployment rate is the lowest in the country. Comparison of these statistics reveals a substantial difference in the rate of unemployment in the three cities. We should note that there has been no upsurge of social instability in these regions during the years of reform. This reflects the labour market situation and, at the same time, determines the nature of current employment policy and its objectives.

In the course of our research, we analysed regional programmes which contribute to employment policy, compared the outcomes of implementing them, and considered particular features of financing them. This revealed marked differences between regions, both in their labour market position and in local authority policies for tackling employment problems and finding people jobs.

Employment Policy Programmes

In all the three cities we studied, the employment policy of the authorities is determined, at a strategic level, by national labour market policy. Analysis of employment promotion programmes in Moscow, St. Petersburg and Voronezh shows that the main directions of work in support of employment, which lie within the competence of the local authorities, have been shaped by the Federal programme. However, essential differences between the labour market positions in these three cities make their mark on specific programmes of work for the Employment Services. The most successful labour market has formed in Moscow. The unemployment rate is insignificant, and rapid growth in non-State structures is fairly successfully absorbing any suitable workforce. According to the assessments of most of the Moscow respondents, there was no observable increase in unemployment in 1996-7, although many people in the politicians group noted that Moscow also ran the risk of hidden unemployment, especially in the form of prolonged delays in paying wages.

Official statistical data indicate that the position in St. Petersburg is also fairly favourable, even showing a certain tendency towards reduction in the number of officially registered unemployed. In 1995, the official unemployment rate was 2.2 per cent, but by the end of 1996 it had fallen to 1.8 per cent, and by mid-1997 to 1.3 per cent (*St. Petersburg*, vol.3-4, 1996, p.111). It is notable that local forecasts of growth in unemployment in St. Petersburg had not been realised: in his interview given early in 1996, the Chair of the St. Petersburg Employment Committee forecast a growth in the number of unemployed to 80,000 people, but in reality, by the end of the year, the number of unemployed was fewer than 50,000. The main reason for the inaccuracy of this forecast was the significant increase (by 14.2 per cent) in the number of employees working part-time at the initiative of their management: they formed 9.8 per cent of the total number of employees. All sectors of the city's economy, with the exception of public bodies, saw cuts in staff numbers during 1996 (*St. Petersburg*, vol.3-4, 1996, p.70). A comparison of the dynamics of change in numbers employed in the State and non-State sectors does not show a significant growth in employees in the latter. This real growth in hidden unemployment was noted by nearly all the St. Petersburg respondents. At the same time, high-ranking officials consistently drew attention to the increase in illegal employment.

Of the cities in our research, Voronezh is in the most difficult position. Unemployment continued to grow over the period 1995-7. In 1995, the officially registered unemployment rate was 2 per cent of the economically active population, in 1996 - 2.8 per cent, and by the end of the first half of 1997 - 2.2 per cent. Judging by statistical information, compulsory partial employment was not as widespread in Voronezh as in St. Petersburg: it affected 6.2 per cent of employees; although it is true that the Voronezh Employment Service referred to the incomplete nature of the information provided by enterprises. The Voronezh respondents considered the change in the composition of the unemployed to be a notable feature of the 1997 scene: among those who lost their jobs, there was an increase of skilled workers with narrow occupational specialisations, who would be very difficult to re-skill - both because of their low occupational mobility and because of insufficient resources for retraining.

Comparison of the reasons given by the Chairs of the Employment Committees in Voronezh and St. Petersburg for such differing labour market situations reveals them to be surprisingly similar:

> the general economic situation, political instability, lack of investment in physical production, the insignificant efforts of the State to restructure the economy (St. Petersburg).

> a fall in production, the non-payment crisis, the absence of conditions for investment activity and of a clear policy for converting the defence sector, the disproportionate prices of industrial and agricultural production, lengthy delays in paying staff in the budget-funded sectors and in all social payments (Voronezh).

These assessments reflect real macro-economic processes and the weakness of national policy. The processes which exert an influence on the labour market situation are similar; differences in outcomes are more connected with particular features of the existing employment structures and of segmentation of the labour market in the cities concerned. The economy of St. Petersburg is multi-functional, more open and more competitive across different types of production, - even if only on the domestic market - and this offers greater potential for finding a job or changing one's type of work than does the economic structure in Voronezh, with a high proportion of military-industrial enterprises and lack of competitiveness of the output of most non-military enterprises, whether on foreign or domestic markets.

Despite such significant differences between their actual labour market situations, a comparison of the Employment Programmes devised by the Moscow, St. Petersburg and Voronezh governments for the period 1995-7 shows that their general directions were very similar: employment promotion, restraining growth in unemployment, measures to prevent mass redundancies, vocational training and retraining, and promoting employment for certain sections of the population, especially those who need social protection. There are separate sections covering employment creation and preservation of jobs; promoting self-employment and the development of entrepreneurial activity; promoting the organisation of public works' schemes; and providing careers guidance services and socio-psychological counselling to maintain the motivation to work. However, a more detailed analysis of the programmes and activities of the Employment Services exposes specific differences.

In Moscow, the priorities in employment policy for 1997 were, in our view, very little different from the 1996 priorities: restraining mass redundancies of staff and the pace of growth in officially registered unemployment; and providing targeted assistance to members of such socially vulnerable groups as young people or women, who have lost their jobs. However, evaluating actual employment promotion activities, our respondents noted the creation of jobs in small businesses as being the highest priority. At the same time, this points to the expansion of Employment Service bodies in the city's districts, and to the intensification of contacts and joint activity with employers, culminating in monthly thematic conferences involving employers in the Administrative Districts. But this activity, in the opinion of those taking part in it, is rather more like education about the position in various branches of industry, the possibilities offered by the Employment Services and the legislative framework of its activities than a concrete attempt to find ways of supporting employment. A number of Moscow respondents actively discussed the question of what should be considered 'a suitable job' in the Employment Services process of dealing with an unemployed person. In particular, the legislation stipulates that any job proposed to the unemployed person by the Employment Services must match his or her qualifications and offer pay no lower than that in his or her last job. In the opinion of representatives of the Employment Services, it is essential to introduce changes into the legislative framework defining 'a suitable job'. The spectrum of opinions was fairly wide: 'any paid work should be suitable for an unemployed person' (middle-ranking official); 'if, in the course of six months, an unemployed person has not agreed to the jobs offered or to retraining, then any paid work should be considered suitable for him, and if he refuses it, his benefit payments should be stopped' (high-ranking official).

In St. Petersburg, both in the stated employment policy objectives for 1997 and in the respondents' evaluations, the chief feature is a major push towards co-operation with employers, an activity which is proving very productive. From 1996, when the city's Employment Service declared this work to be a high-priority direction, there have been attempts to extend links with enterprises, especially in the non-State sector, to expand the direct services offered to employers by the Employment Services, and to provide financial support to employers. According to St. Petersburg Employment Service officials, this initiative has found its highest developments in new 'appropriate technologies' and in work with specific enterprises which are cutting staff. The essence of one such scheme is that the enterprises offer people 'voluntary release': in other words, they do not pay them the three months' severance benefit. The money thus saved goes partly on re-training the staff released and partly on the purchase of equipment for those who would like to start their own businesses. Re-training of this group of workers is generally fairly clearly targeted towards available vacancies or real prospects for new jobs that may open up. But it cannot be said that there have turned out to be many budding entrepreneurs: in the pilot project carried out in the city in 1997, fewer than 10 per cent of those released under this scheme tried to start their own business. However, in the opinion of the Chair of the city's Employment Committee, this new mechanism, which is still under development, enables employment to be maintained and the resources of enterprises, the city budget and the Employment Fund to be spent more rationally.

The establishing of a data bank on 'critical zones of the labour market', undertaken by the St. Petersburg Employment Committee jointly with the Centre for the Strategic Analysis of Social Processes, could be considered another attempt to create an 'appropriate technology'. Four groups in the economically active population are included in this 'critical labour market zone': people who are officially registered as unemployed; those who are not working, are not officially registered as unemployed and whose families have a *per capita* income below the Subsistence Minimum; those who are on short-time working, do not have any additional earnings, and have a *per capita* income below the Subsistence Minimum; and those who are fully employed but have wages below the Subsistence Minimum and have no additional earnings. In the first half of 1997, the number of those who found themselves in the critical labour market zone fluctuated between 10,000 and 420,000 people and was about 17 per cent of the economically active population; in the first half of 1996, it had been a little higher - in the order of 20 per cent to 24 per cent (*St. Petersburg*, June, 1997). Information obtained by the monitoring scheme, on the dynamics of change in the groups which fell into the critical labour market zone, their demographic structure, their socio-occupational status and their real material circumstances has been used to create specific targeted programmes of support, with fairly precise goal-oriented aims and directions.

The more difficult Voronezh labour market situation and the lack of clear prospects for restructuring the city's economy have compelled the local authorities there to make fairly extensive plans for the creation of temporary and seasonal jobs (in 1997, over 12,000) and of public works schemes to give work to the unemployed who are not in receipt of benefit (about 8,000). Those who took part in our survey consistently drew attention to the necessity for and importance of expanding counselling programmes for those who have lost their jobs.

Analysis of the main directions of the Federal Targeted Employment Promotion Programme in 1996-7 and the Employment Programmes of the three cities shows that both Federal and local authorities are trying to carry out fairly active policies in the area of employment. However, in reality, judging by the opinions of our respondents, the nature of employment policy differs in essence between the cities we studied. Most officials and politicians who expressed a view on this issue considered that Moscow is in a special economic situation, and that this offers the possibility of conducting active employment policy in the capital. However company directors considered that employment policy was passive and compensatory in nature, and could not be anything else while there was no normal reproduction of jobs. Trade unionists held more or less the same attitude, and neither group had seen any recent change for the better.

The views of our St. Petersburg respondents on the nature of employment policy remained practically unchanged between the two stages of our research. Noting that the City Government which was newly-formed in 1996 had more sensible policies in this area, most of those taking part in the survey thought that it would be possible to talk about active employment policy only when a revival and growth in jobs had begun:

> In unstable economic conditions, there can be no active employment policy. Today, just like a year ago, no government body is able take on responsibility

for devising this policy painstakingly and in detail - it simply cannot be done (Deputy Chair of Employment Committee).

At the same time, respondents in the group of officials noted that certain elements of active policy had been strengthened, such as training unemployed people in methods of independent job-seeking. The opinion of directors of industrial enterprises in St. Petersburg was harsher than in Moscow:

> There is not even any kind of properly thought-out system for supporting employment. What the Employment Service does is, of course, essential - we can't leave people who have lost their jobs without any material support; but the Employment Services cannot solve the problem of finding people work unless there is a growth in jobs on the labour market (Director of 'Star', a joint-stock company).

> I can't even hazard a guess as to what employment policy is; I can only see that the authorities and the trade unions are conducting a policy of prolonging a hopeless situation - and their actions can only be damaging. Employers have been trying to behave in some way actively, but their interests and potential are simply left out of the equation; many of them have just given up and let themselves be carried along by the current (Director, 'Signal' Research and Production Group).

Trade union leaders here supported the use of a protectionist policy in relation to domestic producers, with consequent preservation and expansion of employment.

Textual analysis of the interviews with Voronezh respondents shows that any discussion of the nature of employment policy inevitably turned into complaints about the extremely difficult position in industry, followed by assertions that, in this situation, there was potential for no more than a compensatory policy to provide families with incomes at survival level. It was extremely difficult to retrain or get people into jobs because of the constriction of the labour market. At the same time, most respondents who expressed an opinion on this issue noted that some directions of work in the Employment Services, such as psychological counselling, were being strengthened. Employment Services data show that more than 50 per cent of the registered unemployed considered that both material support and counselling on rehabilitation were of equal value to them.

The academic literature of recent years and the programmes of political movements have fairly often raised the issue of the need to develop and use standard social indicators as criteria in the current transformations. This can be seen especially clearly in the programme of the 'Yabloko' group, a political movement with a social democratic orientation. By and large, our respondents supported this approach. Representatives of the Moscow trade unions argued for two social indicators - the correlation of the average wage in the budget-funded sector with that in productive branches of industry, and a socially acceptable level of unemployment. Judging by the Federal Employment Promotion Programme for 1996-7, the government deliberately held the registered unemployment rate for 1997 within the limits of 4.9 per cent to 5.6 per cent. In the cities we studied, the rate was significantly lower. It should be pointed out that, to most respondents, the standard social indicators, in particular of socially acceptable levels of unemployment, was most often viewed within a paradigm of social stability, rather than within the framework of, for instance, social reproduction:

> I think that an unemployment rate of 10 per cent already means a very tense situation, while at 15 per cent it is most likely there would be social unrest. (Senior Deputy Chair, Trade Union Federation of St. Petersburg and Leningrad Province).

Russian Federation Ministry of Economics analysts suggest more stringent standards and consider that, across Russia as a whole, we should be looking at a socially-tolerable scale of unemployment measuring 7-8 per cent. They argue their position on the basis of the nature of the Russian model of the labour market; in particular, that it has specific characteristics such as a high degree of collectivism, which is a traditional means of ensuring mutual support between workers, varying speeds of movement towards the market by different sectors of the economy and a patchy approach to the market in different regions. A number of respondents based their discussion of the socially-tolerable limits of unemployment on the inefficiency and weakness of the system of social protection:

> With the present system of social protection and low benefits, even a small growth in unemployment is intolerable (Deputy Head of the Committee for Labour and Employment of the Moscow City Government).

Almost no one could bring themselves to forecast the unemployment situation, even for the near future, because of the lack of clear prospects for economic and industrial policy. Evaluating the situation, directors of industrial enterprises in Moscow and St. Petersburg said that, in their view, the process of mass redundancy had already been and gone in a lot of enterprises. Voronezh respondents, however, did not express any such certainty.

The Functions of Social Policy as it Relates to Employment

Overall, analysis of the structure of the Employment Programmes in our three cities and the Employment Act of the Russian Federation suggests that these documents are consistent with a functional paradigm of social policy as it relates to employment: maintaining social stability, providing motivation to work, stimulating those who have no job or who have lost their job to agree to low-paid work (which is considered preferable to remaining unemployed and living on benefit), retraining or increasing skills to match the requirements of the labour market, meeting the interests of socially-vulnerable groups and implementing support for them, and achieving control over State expenditure.

First, let us highlight the function achieved most successfully in all three cities, one which can be fairly directly evaluated: *ensuring social stability*. Unemployment as such has not been the cause of mass protests in any of the three cities we studied. Individual actions, usually organised by the trade unions, were connected in St. Petersburg with delays in paying wages; while in Voronezh, according to local authority assessments, the reason for a 'march of the empty pots and pans' action was the grave position of the population in an overall sense: low incomes, with delays in paying pensions, benefits and wages. The level of social tension and the potential for a dangerously explosive situation was assessed by our respondents as fairly high, but overall, mass protests associated with unemployment have not been observed.

It is more difficult to assess whether the function of *providing motivation to work* has been achieved. When we discussed this question with our respondents, at least two sides to the issue were highlighted. On the one hand, there was coercion ('positive motivation') through the need to meet stringent legislative conditions to gain unemployed status, the reduction of the period of receipt of the initial rate of benefit (75 per cent of the average wage over a three-month period), and stringent conditions for choice of work. On the other hand the issue was formulated as the need for the Employment Services themselves to use their forces to maintain motivation to work - primarily by means of active attempts on the part of the Service's staff to find a job suitable for the person, by means of retraining related to labour market demand, by means of training unemployed people in more effective methods of independent job-seeking, and through psychological counselling.

In the majority of cases, the Moscow respondents - with the exception of company directors - supported more active interventions by the Employment Services, noting that current transformations in the organisation's structure and the expansion of territorial employment promotion bodies to include careers advice and psychological counselling in their structure are yielding positive results, supporting motivation to work and a growth in the number of people finding work. It is notable that, in the opinion of almost all the respondents who work in the Employment Services at various levels, the attitude of most Muscovites who have lost their jobs is usually an active one:

> although, of course, in practice we do have a hard core of people who are consciously trying to live on benefit, by getting a job for a very short time in order to renew their right to Unemployment Benefit (Head of the Moscow Committee for Labour and Employment).

Evaluating the overall situation in Moscow, we can say that our respondents were very little exercised by the problem of motivation: perhaps this attitude was connected with the fairly favourable labour market situation in the city and with the low unemployment rate.

Among the St. Petersburg respondents, the prevailing opinion was of the need to strengthen methods of coercion through stringent employment law and labour legislation. This attitude could be seen especially distinctly in the judgements of officials of high and middle rank, company directors and some politicians. Several arguments lie at the basis of this attitude. First and foremost, the presence of contradictions in labour legislation: when releasing someone due to staff cuts, the enterprise gives three months pay as a severance benefit, while the Employment Services are obliged to pay - and do pay - Unemployment Benefit from the day of release. About 25 per cent of the city's unemployed have been released under such staff cuts schemes and gone on to gain unemployed status and receive benefit. This situation, in the respondents' opinion, does not stimulate the unemployed person to make any active effort to look for work; moreover, it created raised expectations for any vacancies offered. Respondents saw the solution to this as lying 'in increasing the stringency of conditions laid down in the legislation for granting and paying benefit', and some of them mentioned wider use of the Employment Service's power to withdraw unemployed status, where the claimant refuses vacancies offered at lower wages than he or she has received at the previous workplace.

The second argument was that a fairly significant section of those with unemployed status and in receipt of benefit are in fact working - more often in the shadow economy, but sometimes in temporary or casual jobs. There are no statistics on these phenomena, but material from our survey of unemployed people in the city shows that they are very widespread. Trade union leaders were more inclined to the opinion that the Employment Services need to work more carefully with the unemployed, mainly by retraining them for occupations required on the labour market; at the same time, this group of respondents thought that this would become possible only when the capacity of the labour market expands. In Voronezh, practically all the respondents who discussed this question (more than half) felt that it was necessary to make the conditions for gaining unemployed status and receiving benefit more stringent, in order to strengthen motivation to work.

Another peculiarity in the attitude of our Moscow respondents was found when discussing the issue of the possibility - or the necessity - where there are no suitable vacancies, of motivating the unemployed to agree to low-paid jobs or vacancies which do not match their skills. The more-or-less general attitude was expressed in the following:

> It is absolutely impossible to make a Muscovite work for 300-400 roubles, and quite a lot of vacancies are being offered with pay at precisely that level (Employment Service manager).

It is no coincidence that a lot of migrants have come to work in Moscow from nearby countries, where a person's economic situation is significantly worse. The main argument behind our respondents' attitude is that the pay levels offered are considerably lower than the Subsistence Minimum for Moscow. A number of them, particularly trade unionists, insisted that the approach to fixing the minimum wage should be revised: the amount should be no lower than the Subsistence Minimum, and this standard amount should be included in the Wage Rates Agreement. The St. Petersburg trade unions are also trying to defend this position, although they have not yet been successful.

The St. Petersburg social policy actors who took part in our research thought that it would be both useful and possible to make conditions harsher for the unemployed in their choice of work, including in relation to the amount of remuneration. The main argument for this position is the fall in Employment Fund resources (there were delays in payment of benefit in the city in 1997).

The Voronezh respondents working directly with people who have lost their jobs used a number of examples to demonstrate how, as the duration of unemployment increases, there is a lowering of expectations both in the parameters of social status and in relation to the amount of pay. Moreover, some of the Voronezh respondents thought it possible to increase motivation to take a low-paid job by using the following technique: a defined compensatory amount could be granted for a certain period of time, out of the Employment Fund, to allow for adaptation and possible promotion at the new place of work or to look for another more highly-paid job.

Overall, it can be said that most of the Employment Service staff and the company directors we surveyed, in all the cities, thought that an unemployed person should agree to work for any wage and in any job, and that the position laid down in the Employment Act, on the need to offer the unemployed person 'work suited to his or her level of skills and knowledge', is unrealistic in present conditions.

Judging by our interview materials, social policy actors in St. Petersburg and Voronezh were very concerned about issues of training, re-training and increasing skills to match the requirements of the labour market. In evaluating the system of training and re-training itself, most St. Petersburg respondents defined it as ineffective in integrating unemployed people into the world of work, despite the significant efforts of the city's Employment Services in this sphere. The main obstacle to organising a successful re-training system was thought to be not so much lack of resources (although 1997 saw a substantial cut in funding for these purposes by comparison with 1996) as the absence of a development programme for the city and a properly thought-out industrial policy. The comment of a Member of the St. Petersburg Legislative Assembly can be seen as typical:

> We should not let anything and everything be up for grabs; we need to make sure that training and re-training match the occupations that are in demand and will be required in industry. The city needs an economic and social development programme and a by-law on working out forecasts and plans for this development.

The attitude of the trade unionists also seemed fairly coherent: the intention of the previous city government to turn St. Petersburg into a financial, cultural and tourist centre is hardly realistic in the near future. The city remains a large industrial centre, and is also strengthening its role as a transport centre. Primary demand for occupations in the market infrastructure has been more-or-less saturated, and the training system should help to re-structure the city's economy while preserving its high industrial potential. It should be said that most respondents thought that the present city government, formed after the 1996 elections, has engaged more with the strategic problems of developing St. Petersburg's industrial potential. In 1997, the 'Development Strategy Concept for the City' was worked out; however, the general situation was still assessed as unsatisfactory.

Issues of training and re-training workers are even more heightened in Voronezh. The city has a fairly highly-developed system of higher and secondary education; however, its present structure remains more-or-less the same as in the pre-reform period. It is feeling its way towards some minor changes - and, judging by our respondents' unanimous statements, a forecast of the city's development is essential. It will be very difficult to accomplish this: most enterprises see no prospects for their own development:

> The local authority's attempts to determine the requirement for staff potential from directors arouses, to put it politely, a smile. The most usual answer to this question is: 'There's nothing you can do. I don't know what's going to happen to me tomorrow, and today you are asking me about some kind of staff training, some kind of forecast of staffing requirements...' (Chair of Labour and Employment Committee, Voronezh Provincial Administration).

Of course, Voronezh Employment Centres have programmes for developing vocational training; however, even on paper, actual funding is provided under only one heading - organising training for 6,000 unemployed people in occupations which enjoy labour market demand. In fact, it became clear from the texts of the interviews that re-training through the Employment Services offers a slim chance of obtaining work; more often, informal contacts play the main role.

Is employment policy being implemented in keeping with the interests of socially vulnerable groups? In the Employment Programmes of all three cities, as in the Federal Employment Promotion Programme, a special section is highlighted: 'Social integration and support of citizens with special needs', in accordance with Article 13 of the Russian Federation Employment Act. This provides for support to citizens with limited capacity for work; citizens discharged from military service and members of their families; the long-term unemployed; for promoting youth and women's employment; for work for serving and released prisoners; and for establishing job quotas.

In point of fact, the Moscow respondents, in assessing employment programmes, focused their attention mostly on work with citizens who are especially in need of social protection. Judging by these assessments, serious re-structuring of the bodies that deal with employment problems is being carried out in Moscow. There is a significant expansion of functionally directed structures to work with specific groups who have lost their jobs and are in the highest 'risk zone'. A youth employment centre, 'Outlook', has been created to tackle youth unemployment; among other things, it meets the costs of supervising young people during their period of adaptation at an enterprise, out of Labour and Employment Committee funds. The President's State Services Academy and the Women's Enterprise Academy have opened the 'Women's Business Centre', to help women setting up their own business; it allocates subsidies, gives direct help in registering small businesses and managing affairs at the initial stage, and is devoting more attention to developing homeworking. The Centre for Retraining Armed Services Personnel has been opened, as has the Centre for Practical Co-operation with Entrepreneurs, using resources allocated for the creation and preservation of jobs. The functions of the State Enterprise 'Labour', which organises public works' schemes, have been expanded: under a Decree of the Government of the Russian Federation, the 'Federal Programme for Promoting Employment of Pre-release Prisoners' enables the enterprise to draw people in this category, whose sentences will end before the year 2000, into various types of work. A Home Visits Programme, taking in mainly disabled people, is also in operation.

In St. Petersburg, there are also special employment promotion programmes for these groups, and work directed at finding them jobs or re-training is being carried out. With the support of the Federal Employment Service, the 'Youth Training' programme ran from 1994-7, organising temporary employment for school and college leavers. However it cannot be said that they took in a wide circle of young people: in 1996, 1,700 people aged 14-26 were directed into youth training, and in the course of the year about 25 per cent of them got permanent jobs. However, the results of work within this programme were being claimed as very effective by the Federal Employment Service, even in 1994, and the St. Petersburg experience was recommended to be disseminated to other regions. The

'Choice' Young People's Careers Guidance and Employment Promotion Drop-in Centre was created to offer careers guidance and counselling to young people in the city. The city authorities rate the work of the specialised Youth Employment Exchange very highly; its work in organising regular fairs of vacant jobs and study opportunities is considered especially effective. The 'Women's Employment Promotion Programme' has been in existence since 1993: in particular, this provides for financial assistance to create jobs for women, especially those in need of social protection.

However, Employment Committee data indicates that this work was more successful in 1994 (630 jobs were created for this group); in 1995-6, the process slowed down because of the deteriorating financial position of enterprises and of Employment Service itself. The Women's Homeworking Exchange was created in 1994; in 1996, it arranged training for 210 women and work for 130. This activity was maintained in 1997; however, the results were more modest because of the reduction in funding for the programme. With the aim of training homeworking specialists and of helping women's social adaptation, the 'Reticella' educational and rehabilitation centre was organised. Co-operation with the international 'Women and Management' institute was directed at supporting entrepreneurial initiatives and creating new jobs for women. Within this framework, 'Women's Project' exhibitions were organised, where the projects of women leaving higher education, mainly those who had not managed to find work, were presented. The majority of those presenting their projects have received support from various interests, including the St. Petersburg Employment Committee. Unemployment among those disabled people who have the right to work and are looking for a job is far higher than the average unemployment rate for the city. Thus, in 1995, 64.8 per cent of the total number of unemployed people found a job, but only 22.3 per cent of disabled unemployed people. In order to increase the effectiveness of assistance to this group, the City's Centre for the Rehabilitation and Employment Promotion of the Disabled was created in 1994. The allocation of quota jobs for people with limited capacity for work does not have a substantial influence on the process of finding them work at present. Such groups as lone parents and parents of large families caring for children or disabled relations are small in number, as are refugees and forced migrants. However, it seems from the reports of the Employment Committee that a separate register of these groups is kept; activity in trying to find them jobs takes into account specific features of their situation, since the majority of the unemployed from these groups are socially deprived and restricted.

Analysis of Voronezh programmes to support citizens with special needs shows that these take in all the groups provided for by the legislation. However, resources are provided only for the experimental development of an occupational rehabilitation system for disabled people and the creation of temporary jobs to get young people into work. All the remaining areas are covered under 'developing measures to find people work and carrying out consultations on issues of labour legislation'. In the opinion of those taking part in our survey, work with groups of citizens with special needs is made extremely hard by the difficult economic situation.

The Problems of Financing Employment Policy

The way in which the labour market has formed in Russia is inevitably reflected in the system of financing existing employment policy. The source of financing for employment policy is the State Employment Fund, which is a national extra-budgetary fund. Contribution rates are laid down by the 1996 Federal Act on Insurance Contributions to the Russian Federation Pension Fund, the Russian Federation Social Insurance Fund, the Russian Federation State Employment Fund and the compulsory medical insurance funds. Insurance contributions are deducted from the wages fund by enterprises and organisations.

Financing employment policy and the work of the Employment Fund is not only one of the most difficult areas, but also very contentious. First of all, it should be noted that, in contemporary social and economic conditions in Russia, the rate of insurance deducted depends not only on the requirements of employment policy as such but also, in many respects, on the size of the tax burden as a whole. Against the background of a constantly shrinking tax base and a lack of trust in the authorities, a high level of taxation creates a situation in which even insurance deductions are perceived as a tax burden and a method by which the authorities divert resources to their own advantage. As a consequence of this, there is a constant push towards reductions in insurance contributions for the Employment Fund, as long as taxes which ensure direct receipts into the Federal Budget are also increasing. Under the legislation in force in Russia, Employment Fund resources are de-centralised, with most of them at the disposal of the regions. Only 20 per cent are redistributed by Federal bodies. As a result, resources tend to concentrate in regions that are relatively successful, but remain in severe deficit in the problem regions.

Over a number of years, the system of financing existing employment policy has in many respects been conditioned by an orientation towards carrying out active measures of labour market regulation. The advantages of choosing precisely this strategy have been outlined by the former head of the Federal Employment Service, F. Prokopov (1998). In his opinion, 'successful output' would be an impact on registered unemployment in Russia, leading to its reduction, and for this the rate of expenditure on active measures, according to his evaluation, would have to be more-or-less 0.02-0.03 per cent of GDP for each percentage of total unemployment. This means that, in 1996, such expenditure should have been 5,000 billion roubles, or 0.26 per cent of Russia's GDP. International comparisons provide evidence on financing labour market policy. In European countries with experience of conducting labour market policy, the share of GDP expenditure on 1 per cent unemployment in 1993 ranged from 0.16 per cent in the UK to 0.55 per cent in Denmark. In the USA, it was equal to 0.1 per cent. In countries with transitional economies, 'unit outlays' are significantly lower: moreover, Russia has shown the lowest indicators - 0.04 per cent in 1994, 0.06 per cent in 1995 and 0.04 per cent in 1996. In 1993, expenditures of GDP allocated per 1 per cent unemployment in Bulgaria were 1.2 times higher than in Russia; in the Czech Republic, 2.8 times; in Hungary, 6.5 times; and in Poland, 3.6 times higher (Prokopov, 1998, p.30). What is more, Prokopov notes a trend towards reducing the proportion allocated to 'active' measures in Russia from 71.3 per cent in 1994 to 34.1 per cent in the first half of 1997. In the opinion of the article's author, cutting expenditure on vocational training for the unemployed, on public works' schemes and on other forms of active employment policy brings in its wake a reduction in the number of unemployed people involved in these programmes: in 1997, for example, the average monthly number of people trained was more than three times lower than in 1995, while the number participating in public works schemes was 1.6 times lower.

Different points of view regarding the role of active measures in labour market policy in Russia are held:

In 1995-6, writes Zaslavsky, 'more than half the resources of Federal employment promotion programmes were targeted towards maintaining jobs and other measures regarded as active employment policy, but the effectiveness of their use has fallen year on year. So, of the 260,000 additional jobs that it was envisaged the programmes would create by 1996, 38 per cent were created, while only 14 per cent of the staff formally covered by relevant measures actually received compensation for wages. As a result, the growth in unemployment has not been halted, and in a number of regions of the country, a chronic situation has arisen, with outstanding benefit payments owed to the registered unemployed. (Zaslavsky, 1998, p.86).

The analysis carried out by Chetvernina and Lakunina (1998) shows that, from autumn 1995, serious problems arose in connection with the formation of employment funds in the regions and with cuts in the Federal section of the Employment Fund, whose resources are redistributed to regions with a high unemployment rate. In practically all the regions, a cut in the receipts of regional employment funds has been observed over the last two years, caused by a fall in production and a reduction in the share of enterprise incomes going on tax. The decision of the national parliament, the Russian Federation State Duma, to reduce the rate of contributions from 2 per cent to 1.5 per cent from January 1996 further increased the deficit of the Employment Fund by a substantial amount. At the same time, employers' debts of the insurance contributions that should have been transferred to the Employment Fund started to grow. By 1 October 1997, these stood at 3,500 billion roubles across the whole Russian Federation. Moreover, a large part of this debt was attributable to 14 donor regions: for example, Moscow employers owe 2.3 times as much as the sum total owed by employers in such depressed regions as the Pskov, Ivanov and Vladimir Provinces.

The absolute reduction in monetary receipts into regional employment funds has led to an increase in the proportion of expenditure that has to go on paying Unemployment Benefit: over 9 months in 1995, expenditures on payment of Unemployment Benefit were 29.2 per cent of all Employment Fund expenditures, but for the corresponding period in 1997 they were 56.8 per cent.

The deficit in regional employment funds has also brought in its wake a reduction in receipts into the Federal part of the Employment Fund. Receipts are significantly lower than the rate laid down in the legislation (20 per cent). The rate deducted for the Federal part of the Fund on average across Russia was equal to 12 per cent for nine months of 1995, but only 3.8 per cent for the same period in 1997. As a result, by autumn 1997, the regions were in debt to the Federal part of the Employment Fund to the tune of over 500 million roubles, with the main debtors, as before, being the donor regions with a low unemployment rate. Thus, in the course of the last three years, the Belgorod and Smolensk Provinces and the Sakha Republic (Yakutiya) have become long-term debtors. The registered unemployment rate in these regions remained below 1.4 per cent throughout the 1990s, while deductions from their regional funds into the Federal part of the Employment Fund, for nine months in 1997, were 5.5 per cent (2.4 per cent for all 1996) for the Sakha Republic (Yakutiya) and 0.1 per cent (1 per cent for all 1996) for the Belgorod Province. In 1997, Smolensk Province did not transfer any money at all into the centralised part of the Employment Fund, while in 1996 the percentage deducted was 6.7 per cent.

Meanwhile, the need to build up the centralised part of the Employment Fund is growing. Firstly, the number of subsidised regions is increasing: over the last two years it has grown to 14 Federation members. Secondly, the growing deficit in regional employment funds and the benefit payment debt have made a number of regions completely dependent on receipts from the Federal part of the Employment Fund, which has become the main source of minimal benefit payments. However, by no means all those in need can count on this minimal assistance. Thus, 40.5 per cent of those who got any benefit in March 1996 received it at a level below the minimum wage; another 38.1 per cent received from one to three times the minimum remuneration; 8.9 per cent got less than the Subsistence Minimum for their region; and 12.5 per cent received a sum between the Subsistence Minimum and the average wage. However, 54 per cent of the unemployed who had a right to benefit did not receive any at all (Zaslavsky, 1998, p. 124).

As a result, it has now become the case, in most regions, that the unemployed cannot even count on a minimum benefit, even though, for a third of the unemployed, benefit is the most important - and often the only - source of existence. In this situation, active forms of labour market policy are proving to be, in principle, inaccessible to most of the Russian unemployed; this even includes vocational retraining, since the unemployed often have no means of meeting transport expenses. Obviously, in a period of economic decline, priority must be given not to high-cost and ineffective active policies, but to the kind of passive labour market policy which is being conducted in market economy countries. Therefore, it is necessary to separate sources of financing for active and passive employment policies and to identify their quantitative proportions within the total budget (ibid., p.127).

Particular Features of Employment Policy Finances

In conversation with our respondents, we discussed issues of financing employment policy, transparency of information on expenditure of resources, the various headings under which they are used, and the possibility of and necessity for inter-regional redistribution.

The results of our survey turned out to be contradictory. Thus, those representing Moscow and St. Petersburg enterprises thought that reducing deductions into the Employment Fund from 2 per cent to 1.5 per cent had been useful. Most of the Moscow directors were in favour of generally leaving this money in the control of employers, since the expenditure of these resources at enterprises would be more targeted towards the interests of the specific enterprise. The Voronezh directors, however, were unable to come to an opinion on this issue.

Employment Service respondents thought that reducing deductions into the Employment Fund was irrational. The main argument of the St. Petersburg respondents was the fact that the Fund's resources are hardly sufficient to pay benefits (during 1996 there were delays in paying benefit there), and very little is left for programmes of active assistance to the unemployed, especially re-training and vocational training; and this, in its turn, could lead to an increase in the number of registered unemployed.

Members of all respondent groups were united in their attitude to the issue of increasing Federal centralisation of some Employment Fund resources. This opinion came down to the fact that financing is more effective at a regional level. The remarks of the Moscow respondents (Employment Services officials, representatives of political parties and movements, and others) on this issue were particularly acerbic; while the Voronezh respondents were more careful in what they said.

It should be noted that the separation of areas of competence in employment policy between Federal and regional authorities (although no different from other spheres of government in this respect) is a sharp one, and so has proved to be extraordinarily difficult for our respondents. We attempted to clarify whether they thought that redistribution of powers and legislative reinforcement of them is needed, and whether resource provision should be strengthened at regional or, on the contrary, at Federal level. Overall, Moscow respondents spoke out in favour of separate spheres of influence, with stronger regional components. Although they acknowledged the key role of the Federal authorities in tackling social problems, including employment problems, the St. Petersburg respondents evaluated the Federal authorities' actions negatively:

The Federal authorities have a clear-cut policy - to exterminate everyone physically, almost literally (Director, 'Signal' Research and Production Group).

Some people noted that the role of local authorities in social policy is badly defined in legislation, but that, in many respects, it is they who should take moral responsibility for the position of the population.

Comparison of the Structures of Expenditure on Employment

Over recent years there has been a significant redistribution of resources between expenditure headings in the Federal Employment Fund budget. Analysis of Employment Fund expenditure shows that, over three years, the most significant growth was in the proportion of expenditure used to pay Unemployment Benefit. A similar picture can also be observed in the expenditures of the three cities we studied. The main reasons for this state of affairs are the reduction of the proportion of deductions into the Employment Fund from 2 per cent to 1.5 per cent of the total volume of the wages fund, in the growth in the number of unemployed and in the significant increase in the average wage of those who become unemployed. Employment Services staff in both Moscow and St. Petersburg noted a new trend towards the emergence of a fairly large category of people who have an insignificant length of service at their last workplace but a high wage. According to the respondents' assessments, this is a manifestation of behaviour consciously intended to enable the claimant to get a high rate of benefit without making a permanent commitment to a place of work. The respondents' views on spending Employment Fund resources rationally were one of a few areas where differences emerged between the 1996 and the 1997 interviews. In the 1996 interviews, practically all the trade unionists, directors and politicians thought it necessary to increase the proportion of resources spent on retraining and raising skills levels. But the overall deterioration in the funding position, including the reduction in receipts into the Employment Fund, and the absence of clear ways forward to economic re-structuring led them to change their attitude. Re-training remained a high-priority area, but only if there were to be an economic upturn. In 1997, the chief target was considered to be cutting the length of delays in paying Unemployment Benefit.

Because of the particular gravity of the position in Voronezh, all the respondents there put strong emphasis on this problem. The economic situation in Voronezh is such that, according to those taking part in the survey, only 16 per cent of enterprises are paying taxes. An absolute majority of enterprises were debtors to the Employment Fund, even in 1996. Delays in payments of benefit lasted anything up to four months. It cannot be said that the local authorities are not trying to change the situation. In 1997, a regional decree was adopted, giving deductions into the Employment Fund the status of top-priority payments. However, because of the crisis situation of most of the city's enterprises, the decree has not changed things for the better. The most frequent solution has been the payment of benefit in the form of foodstuffs, received by the Employment Service from enterprises to set against their debts.

St. Petersburg respondents more often drew attention to the expenses involved in maintaining the Employment Service itself; it is true that, in suggesting that these were too large, they were relying mostly on information from previous years, when the proportion of spending under this heading was more than 20 per cent of all Employment Services expenditures (1995). Moscow respondents took a more favourable view of the formation, expenditure and control of Employment Fund resources. Staff of the various sub-divisions of the Moscow Employment Service described a fairly stringent and effective system for controlling Employment Fund expenditure. The trade union leaders took a special position on the issue of distribution of Employment Fund resources, the essence of which was that 'equal participation of the State, employers and trade unions is essential', both at the decision-making stage and in the process of administering the expenditure of resources. The technical details of this approach, in their opinion, should be carried out within the decision-making and monitoring framework of the Tripartite Agreement.

New Debates on Reform of Employment Policy

Analysis of the academic literature for 1996-8 enables us to draw the conclusion that the problem of reforming labour market policy is becoming increasingly topical; at the same time, these issues are being discussed more actively in the press. However, the multiplicity of approaches, conceptions and opinions does not make it possible as yet to pick out any one general structural trend in proposed reform of social and labour relations. Discussions centre mainly around the nature of policy as it is currently being conducted.

Over all the years of reform in Russia, national employment policy has been distinguished by an orientation towards active ways of tackling labour market issues. Evidence of this is provided both by official documents and by the statements of officials who represent the State institutions which are directly responsible for formation of this policy in Russia.

In 1996, the Russian Federation's Federal Targeted Employment Promotion Programme for 1996-7 was adopted, and the section entitled 'Labour market policy' laid out the main objectives of national employment policy. First and foremost were envisaged an investment policy and support of entrepreneurship:

> an increase in investment activity directed towards creation and modernisation of jobs is envisaged as one of the economic priorities for 1996-7 ...

> ...Increased employment must be achieved through a balanced investment policy, which takes into account the necessity for capital inputs both into the leading-edge sector of the economy and into areas of traditional employment, while stimulating fuller use of existing jobs and the development of small businesses. (*Official Journal*, vol.20, 13 May 1996, Art.2357, p.5059).

Two years later, in the new version - the Russian Federation's Federal Targeted Employment Promotion Programme for 1998-2000 - job creation continues to be seen as one of the main economic priorities and one of the main objectives of national employment policy (*Official Journal*, vol.33, 17 August 1998, Art.4005, p.7699).

Accordingly, as we have already commented, a budgetary policy is also being formed to fund employment promotion and get people into work (Prokopov, 1998, pp.30-1). Thus in 1998 an orientation towards active labour market policy still remained the defining one in Russia. This was indicated in an Institute of Economics programme report (1998) which listed two key objectives:

> reorientation of policy towards an active stance, to provide employment and seek more finance to assist the badly-off;

> measures favouring the formation of conditions in which potential for work and business activity by citizens can be used to their fullest, stimulating behaviour appropriate to a competitive market environment. (pp.33-4).

However, in the academic literature, alternative points of view are also examined. Thus Chetvernina and Lakunina (1998), Fellows of the Institute of Economics of the Russian Academy of Sciences, consider the use of active labour market policy to be unfounded. At present, there are not enough financial resources for employment policy to be directed exclusively towards active measures: more attention should be paid to passive employment policy. Turning to the issue of reforming the existing system of paying Unemployment Benefit, Chetvernina and Lakunina propose the introduction of a new system of unemployment insurance. In the authors' opinion, in order to implement this, a single Russian national Employment/Unemployment Insurance Fund would have to be created, which would accumulate tax receipts from all the regions and redistribute financial resources to the regions depending on their economic situation.

The object of social insurance should be the wage-earning citizen who has paid contributions into the insurance fund. Thus, young people who had never worked, housewives, refugees from other countries, and so on, would be excluded from the scope of passive assistance, although they would have a right to register as unemployed or to make use of the Employment Services. In addition, members of each of these named categories could be covered by special national programmes, implemented through the Employment Services, or helped through relevant departments. The basis of this insurance should be a national extra-budgetary social insurance fund for unemployment (presently the Employment Fund), whose resources would be accumulated Federally and redistributed between regions depending on their unemployment rate. The sources for formation of the social insurance fund for unemployment would be deductions in unequal proportions from employers, the State and employees. The amount of benefit could be 60 per cent of the average wage at the last place of work.

The most important aims of an insurance system were highlighted as:

unemployment benefit should allow a family sufficient means to prevent a sharp fall in their standard of living if one of their members becomes unemployed;

granting of benefit should allow someone who has lost their job to concentrate on looking for a new one;

benefit must be paid to employees from those sectors which previously received subsidies and grants from the budget, but have recently been deprived of them and forced to re-organise;

these unemployment benefit payments should automatically provide a financial stimulus for the development of the economy, increasing the purchasing power of the population during a period of sharp fall in demand.
(Chetvernina and Lakunina, 1998, pp.127-28).

In his discussion of the contemporary labour market paradigm, Zaslavsky also states that:

> the transfer to a system of social insurance for waged employees, organised on social partnership principles and used to further material support to the unemployed for a period while they find work, may become an effective form of regulating unemployment... To a certain extent, a system of social insurance should replace the declining extra-budgetary State employment funds, which have come under the control of the executive authorities. (1998, p.94).

However, Prokopov stresses that moving over to an insurance system does not bear much relation to the reality of Russian transition economy conditions. In his opinion, the existing system of deductions from the wages fund is more acceptable. In the plan he puts forward, he argues for an 'optimal' budget for the Employment Fund which requires a certain critical mass of expenditure on running programmes and offering services to achieve a noticeably positive result. His main focus is on adjusting the active part of the programme:

> replacing enterprise subsidies to support jobs with expansion of programmes for training unemployed people;
>
> limiting subsidised employment by using programmes of temporary employment (public works schemes);
>
> vocational training for occupations in demand on the labour market, targeted at young people;
>
> expenses for the organisation of intensive consultation work within the framework of 'job-seekers' clubs'. (1998, p.94).

Thus, the issue of the nature and priorities of current labour market policy continues to be discussed and remains a long way from being finally resolved.

Part III

Surviving Poverty and Unemployment

8 Welfare, Resources and Household Survival

Жизнь прожить не поле перейти
To get through life is not to cross a field

We have looked at the issue of household circumstances and survival strategies and of employment through the prism of two alternative approaches existing in contemporary sociology. One considers separate individuals either as elements of a social system (structure), whose actions are determined through their place in a system of socio-economic relations, or as elements of a cultural system within the framework of which they act under the influence of the norms and rules which have come to exist in the given culture. The other views them as active social subjects, 'rational actors', who bring into play all their numerous resources in pursuit of their own aims but take account of the rules determined by the limits of the specific situation within which they have to act.

What was the main factor determining our respondents' action strategy and their coming to occupy a certain status (including their employment status) - structure or action? system or actor? To what extent should the subject under study be cultural processes shaping behaviour, or situational constraints and possibilities which a rational actor is in a position to utilise, or, indeed, some kind of personality characteristics capable of leading to certain models of individual action? The events of recent years in Russia have provided a unique opportunity for examining these viewpoints as they apply to the conditions of a society in transformation, in which the confrontation between system and actor has been driven to extreme forms. For a significant proportion of the population of Russia mechanisms for determining behaviour through identifying oneself with a group have been disrupted, and for precisely this reason the role of other factors is increasing. So, what factors do govern the behaviour of Russians today? How are they affected by the simultaneous transition to a market economy and reconstruction of social policy, with its rejection of the Soviet model of 'a universal Welfare State'? Why is it that, under similar circumstances of threatened or real unemployment, some people become entrepreneurs and enter the 'upper' class, while others tumble to the 'bottom'? What mechanisms function during all these processes, and especially in the shaping of social groups which were entirely or almost entirely absent in Russia just ten years ago (the long-term unemployed, the poor, entrepreneurs)? What are the particular socio-economic or cultural features of the present situation in Russia: are constraints on their action the main determinants of the behaviour and the status of actors (and if so, in what way do they constrain the actors' freedom of action); or is the main factor the actors themselves, with their individual actions and particular features of their personalities?

We aimed to answer these questions through our research. We also intended to analyse the self-identification of the unemployed in terms of their social status and to test the hypothesis that being unemployed in Russia does not assign one to the lowest status level. In addition, one of the main aims of the study was to analyse the features of unemployment and poverty in Russia, and the general and specific characteristics of these conditions in comparison with unemployment and poverty in Western European countries. Finally, we also considered it important to establish what role unemployment benefit and other social subsidies play in determining the stance of an actor; whether poverty and the situation in their households push people back to work more quickly; and what general role aspects of social policy - as it is being implemented - play in the actual circumstances and behaviour of Russians today.

To meet these aims, we set ourselves three blocks of objectives during the course of our research. One block related to issues of the dynamic of change in the material circumstances of 'labour market crisis group' members; the second related to the change in their employment status; and the third was to do with which actual factors shape these dynamics, and what is the most important factor in determining the behaviour and the status niche of group members.

First Block

• To provide a detailed description of the composition, objective circumstances and social self-assessment of people who are in a crisis employment situation, including their values; to compare this description with the positions adopted by the rest of the population, analysed according to an overlapping methodology using data from representative national surveys by the Russian Independent Institute of Social and Nationalities Problems (RIISNP); and to compare groups of respondents differing in employment status and place of residence, in terms of their material circumstances and the way these were changing, their structure of consumption, their forms of social participation and their values;

- To provide a description of 'the poor'; to gain a more accurate understanding of the concept of 'poverty' ('a certain level of income', family/household 'resources' or 'accessibility of forms of social participation approved by society', as applied to the socio-cultural specifics of Russia) and its relationship to the respondents' labour market niche - in particular, the relationship with unemployment;
- To reveal the models of survival chosen by respondents and to make an analysis of the 'success' of these strategies;
- To identify certain 'social types' among members of labour market crisis groups, in terms of the 'core' and 'periphery' of groups, and to illustrate each type using real examples.

Second Block

- To explain the reasons for entry into labour market crisis groups and the employment strategies utilised by the respondents;
- To analyse the expectations and aspirations of members of labour market crisis groups and their impact on choice of behaviour strategy;
- To establish the direction of labour flows (State or private sectors of the economy, and which specific sectors), the willingness of respondents to follow the demands of the labour market, the activity and independent initiative of an unemployed person searching for work, and their capability to adapt;
- To establish the 'success' of the activities of people who have found work after a period of unemployment: are those questioned happy with their new work; does it correspond to their usual occupation; are they satisfied with the pay; on balance, have their material problems within the family been solved?

Third Block

- To analyse the reasons for choice of a certain survival strategy and labour market behaviour strategy, including: objective factors associated with features of local labour market; composition of households, including the presence of children under 18 and other dependants; the presence of certain resources and the comparative significance of different types of resources in price terms;

- To establish to what extent survival and employment strategies are a consequence of rational choice or of specific cultural factors, and what considerations lie at the root of that choice;
- To reveal whether a 'culture of poverty' or 'dependency culture' exists in Russia, and whether it is in fact the cause of poverty, or whether the relationship is the inverse of this;
- To establish the role of different stratifying factors in the new socio-economic conditions, and to identify 'winners' and 'losers' at this stage of the implementation of reforms in Russia;
- To find out which is most important - structure or action, system or actor.

A separate word needs to be said to the effect that pursuing these aims, as an objective in itself, required the development of a research methodology which would enable the aims to be attained while ensuring that the results would be comparable with data from studies conducted in Western European countries, in view of the difference in cultural traditions and living standards. The way in which we dealt with this is described in Chapter 4. As regards the other objectives, Chapter 8 gives the results of work on objectives from the first block, as well as that part of the third block which is thematically linked to them. Chapter 9 gives the results of work on the second block of objectives and that part of the third block arising out of the issues examined in that chapter.

Material Circumstances of Respondents from 1996-1997

The question of the respondents' material circumstances constituted a separate research problem. Although the literature contains a large number of criteria of poverty, when used in specific sociological studies in Russia these methods have turned out, one after the other, to be insufficiently reliable. As shown by the data from our - and other studies - conducted in this area, respondents often assess their own material circumstances inappropriately: for various reasons, they are either not entirely sincere, or are inconsistent, or very subjective and imprecise (see Table 8.1).

As we can see, respondents with the same level of income (which, incidentally, was so low that 80 per cent of it must clearly have been inadequate even to secure the most modest diet) spend such widely differing proportions of it on food that, in many cases, either the data on *per capita* income or else the data on the proportion spent on food must be wrong - although in the majority of responses a correspondence can be observed between them.

Let us begin with a look at how the material circumstances of the respondents changed over the period of observation. The basis for comparison will be a group of questions that was repeated in both stages of the research, coupled with the respondents' own assessments of the changes in their position during the course of the research.

Table 8.1 Distribution of 1996 respondents by per capita income and proportion of outgoings spent on food - n (per cent)

% on food	<0.2	*Per capita income in millions of roubles*						*Total*
		0.2-0.4	0.4-0.6	0.6-0.8	0.8-1	1-1.5.	>1.5	
< 30	-	4 (6)	-	1 (4)	-	1 (8)	2 (20)	8 (3)
30-50	3 (10)	9 (12)	11 (20)	10 (36)	9 (45)	6 (50)	7 (70)	55 (24)
50-80	15 (45)	30 (41)	29 (53)	14 (50)	6 (30)	5 (42)	1 (10)	100 (43)
>80	15 (45)	30 (41)	15 (27)	3 (10)	5 (25)	-	-	68 (30)
total	33 100	73 100	55 100	28 100	20 100	12 100	10 100	231 100

The dynamic of change in the respondents' material circumstances during the year that had elapsed between the surveys contained contradictory features. Judging by *per capita* income, a certain improvement in the position of the overall body of respondents could be seen. In 1996, the median value of [monthly] *per capita* income was roughly 350,000 roubles, whereas in 1997 it was 500,000 roubles. In comparison with mean Russian *per capita* income figures, in both cases this was a little below half the mean Russian monetary income levels

(*Russia-1997*, 1997). If we look at what lies behind these general figures, however, we can see that in all three cities there was a slight rise in the number of people with *per capita* income below the Subsistence Minimum.

We took as a basis for the Subsistence Minimum a figure of 400,000 roubles, which was better for our calculations, even though for March/April 1997 – i.e. when the second phase of the survey was carried out – it was 410,000 roubles according to the State Committee for Statistics data (*Russian Economy in the first six months of 1997*, 1997, p.70). Our figure practically matched data on the Subsistence Minimum originating from the Centre for Macro-Economic Strategies of the Russian Academy of Sciences (*Argumenty I fakty*, Vol.24, 1997, p.1) and statistical summaries from the Institute of Economic Problems of the Transition Period.

The total figures were as follows: Moscow - 40 per cent (32 per cent in 1996), in St. Petersburg - 29 per cent (23 per cent in 1996), and in Voronezh - 80 per cent (69 per cent in 1996). As regards those who are very poor, with a *per capita* income less than half of the Subsistence Minimum, in Moscow and St. Petersburg their numbers had fallen by 1.5-2 times over the year, so that they came to constitute 8 per cent and 4 per cent of respondents respectively, while in Voronezh the figure had risen by 3 per cent to 37 per cent.

Table 8.2   Respondents by size of per capita income in 1997 - per cent

Income per Family member	*Moscow*	*Voronezh*	*St. Petersburg*	*Total*
<0.2 mln r.	8	37	5	14
0.2-0.4 mln r.	32	43	24	32
0.4-0.6 mln r.	27	15	25	24
0.6-0.8 mln r.	11	2	22	12
0.8-1 mln r.	13	3	8	9
1-1.5 mln r.	4	0	10	5
>1.5 mln r.	5	0	6	4
total	100	100	100	100

As may be seen from the table, in spring 1997, it was only in Voronezh that the group with income of less than half the Subsistence Minimum constituted a significant proportion of the respondents. As regards the other groups ('badly-off' - from 0.5 to 1 times the Subsistence Minimum; 'averagely well-off' - 1 to 2 times the Subsistence Minimum; and also 'well-off' and 'prosperous' - over twice the Subsistence Minimum), Moscow and St. Petersburg accounted for a little over 20 per cent of successful respondents, whereas in Voronezh virtually all the respondents who were not 'poor' fell into the category of 'badly-off'. It should be added that there were only two people in Voronezh whose income exceeded the mean *per capita* income for the city (approximately 620,000 roubles), and there were no 'prosperous' people (>2.5 times the Subsistence Minimum) there at all; in St. Petersburg, where the mean *per capita* income for the city at the time of the survey was over 1.1 million roubles, there were just five people with more than the mean *per capita* income for the city, while 12 (16 per cent) fell into the category of relatively prosperous people. In Moscow, however, where mean *per capita* incomes were at that time around 4 million roubles, none of the sample attained that level, while the proportion of relatively prosperous people was 9 per cent.

Thus, the crisis employment groups investigated actually represented the deprived section of society only in Voronezh. In St. Petersburg and Moscow, although the great majority of respondents also did not belong to the most flourishing strata of society, in fact distribution in terms of *per capita* income revealed only a few isolated poor people, while about one-quarter were badly-off. Overall it could be said that, the distribution of the sample across levels of welfare in Moscow and St. Petersburg corresponded to representative samples of the *ordinary* Russian populace, even though distortions in mean incomes arise from the concentration of the new Russian élite in Moscow and St. Petersburg, and the high proportion, in comparison with other regions, of relatively prosperous people. Thus in March 1997, at the same time as the second stage of our study was being conducted, according to data from a representative national survey by RNISINP, 45.1 per cent of respondents had an income below 300,000 roubles, that is more people than in our sample had an income of less than 400,000 roubles. By contrast Voronezh provided a picture of a 'social sink', not just in relation to the city itself but also average figures for the whole of Russia.

If we assess redistribution of the population in each city between the different prosperity groups, we see that in all cases there has been an erosion of the boundaries within the basic 1996 group - the badly-off, who have between 0.5 and 1 times the Subsistence Minimum per person. The size of this group across the whole sample had fallen from 44 per cent to 23 per cent. One-third of the group had moved into the category of poor people, while the majority (two-thirds) had moved into the 'averagely well-off' category. All three cities also saw a rise in the relatively successful strata, who have over twice the Subsistence Minimum per person.

This picture of changes in the circumstances of respondents indicates that, in Voronezh alone, exclusion had risen over the year, and isolated examples of people who managed to pull themselves out of this sea of deprivation and poverty only serve to confirm the general rule. This is also borne out by analysis of changes in property at the disposal of the families. In all the cities without exception, property at the disposal of the respondents had increased. In Moscow and St. Petersburg, the number of apartment owners had risen by six per cent; the number of people with a *dacha* had risen by six to seven per cent in all cities; and more than 50 per cent of respondents in each of the cities had been making expensive purchases, including a personal computer (nine Muscovites and two in St. Petersburg) and a car (one each in Moscow and St. Petersburg and three in Voronezh), or had incurred other significant expenses (apartment repairs/decoration, repairs/decoration or construction of *dacha*). True, nearly the same number in all the cities (45-49 per cent) replied that they had not managed to do anything of this sort, and in fact it is this section of the respondents who may, in our view, be referred to as living in poverty or being badly-off.

On the other hand, of those whose property had not increased during the intervening year, 60 per cent owned no real property, whereas this figure was below a half for the respondents overall. If, however, we consider the interdependence of the respondents' incomes and their property, it appears that among the two low-income groups one-and-a-half times more respondents had various types of real property than among the five higher-income groups: this phenomenon was associated with the co-existence alongside the 'old' poor of the 'new' poor.

The 'new' poor are a new phenomenon in post-Soviet Russia: there was nothing like them in the USSR. They consist of large sections of skilled specialists and blue-collar workers who have secondary vocational or even higher education, are middle-aged or elderly and, prior to the reforms, belonged to the best-off strata among the population. Being members of a socially strong section of the population, these strata used to be active champions of reforms. However, in the current conditions of deep crisis, specific features of their occupational skills and spheres of employment (in enterprises formerly in the military-industrial complex, in cultural, educational or scientific establishments or in health care within the budget-funded sector) have doomed a large mass of people in these strata to a catastrophic fall in their standards of living and to lower status employment.

So the poor who had not just low incomes but also a low level of property ownership were primarily those who, over our year of observation, were not able to permit themselves any outlay except on day-to-day needs. In our view, this showed that using income level as the criterion of poverty is not justified as a tool in analysis of poverty, under Russian conditions at least. Understanding poverty as a characteristic of the respondents' property/income circumstances brings us somewhat closer to understanding the essence of this phenomenon, but this too failed to provide an exhaustive answer to the question as to whom we might consider poor in contemporary Russia, since their inadequate assessment of their own income overlaid the co-existence of 'new' and 'old' poor, and confused the picture.

At the same time, under conditions where there are no settled strata with their own standards of consumption, and where there has been a unique kind of 'revolution of aspirations' in the last few years, the subjective side - respondents' assessment of their own circumstances - was just as important as the objective aspect of material circumstances in understanding the actions taken by the respondents and their chosen behaviour strategies and in evaluating their effectiveness. Thus, when we analysed levels of correlations using the CHAID system (Magidson J., 1993), using 'tree-select' with a p-level of 0.5 or more, it transpired that, in all the accumulated data, first place in terms of significance for assessing their own material circumstances went to the response to the question of what material circumstances the family found itself in compared to others around it. One group comprised those for whom it was better or the same, and the other group comprised those for whom, on their own assessment, it was worse. *Per capita* income level was only in sixth place of significance, after the respondents' assessment of whether they were able to dress well, the proportion of income going on food, the dynamic of change in material circumstances, and other factors.

Thus, the main factor influencing a person's perception of his own material circumstances as 'bad' and creating a corresponding incentive to change them was comparison of one's circumstances with one's neighbours'. In this light, let us look at the three cities with regard to respondents' assessment of their own circumstances.

In Moscow, the number of those who considered their own circumstances worse than others' rose from 31 per cent to 47 per cent during the year of observation. There was a corresponding rise in the number of those who assessed their material circumstances as bad (from 43 per cent to 56 per cent) and those who thought that their circumstances had deteriorated still further when compared to the previous year (from 47 per cent to 65 per cent). This undoubtedly reflects the vast gulfs between incomes and consumption levels that have become so glaringly evident in Moscow in recent years. In St. Petersburg and Voronezh, the index for assessment of one's own circumstances as worse in comparison with that of others remained at the same level as the year before. Correspondingly, the assessment of one's own material circumstances remained at the previous level in St. Petersburg, while in Voronezh the assessment of one's own circumstances as 'bad' rose by roughly a quarter, and exceeded half the respondents. Clearly, the rise in negative assessments of one's own welfare in Voronezh was influenced by the absolute impoverishment of the Voronezh respondents, as mentioned above, even though the relative proportions for *per capita* income remained at the level of the previous year.

In addition, the subjective social mood of the poorest section of the respondents had deteriorated. The figures for the change in material circumstances and expectation of a continued deterioration clearly marked out the most deprived group from the total sample, even using such incomplete criteria as *per capita* income or proportion of outlay going on food (Tables 8.3 and 8.4). This was one of the important things that stimulated us to test whether persistent poverty was forming during the course of re-structuring of Russia's economy, and to establish whether or not economic deprivation was also accompanied by social deprivation.

This was in fact why, although analysis of *per capita* income, proportion of family budget spent on food and assessments made by the respondents themselves of their material circumstances (in general; in relation to others; over the last six years; over the last year; for the year to come) gave what would appear to be fairly full material on the circumstances of the respondents, the 'loose ends' found in this information obliged us to seek a more precise set of characteristics for the group of 'poor' people.

Table 8.3 **Change in material circumstances, 1996/7, for respondents with various proportions of outgoings spent on food - n (per cent)**

Per cent of outgoings spent on food

Material circum-stances	<30%	30-50%	50-80%	>80%	Total
worse	2 (26)	13 (23)	41 (40)	45 (64)	101 (43)
same	3 (37)	31 (54)	42 (41)	19 (28)	95 (40)
better	3 (37)	13 (23)	20 (19)	5 (8)	41 (17)
total	8 (100)	57 (100)	103 (100)	70 (100)	238 (100)

Table 8.4 **1997 prediction of change in material circumstance by proportions of outgoings spent on food - n (per cent)**

Per cent of outgoings spent on food

Material circum-stances	<30%	30-50%	50-80%	>80%	Total
worse	1 (12)	5 (9)	10 (10)	19 (27)	35 (15)
same	3 (36)	41 (72)	74 (73)	44 (64)	162 (69)
better	4 (52)	11 (19)	17 (17)	6 (9)	38 (16)
total	8 (100)	57 (100)	102 (100)	69 (100)	236 (100)

We were also encouraged in this direction by our desire to check the applicability of Townsend's concept of poverty to the Russian situation; this concept regards poverty as a level of welfare at which a person does not just consume fewer of some goods or other, including spiritual values, or utilise lower-quality products and services - though these are important. The main thing that distinguishes Townsend's understanding of poverty and brings it into line with the way the vast majority of Russians understand poverty is that it perceives 'poverty' as lack of potential to lead the life the majority of people live in that society - a restriction of forms of 'social participation' and a minimisation of the types of social bond that are typical in the conditions of the given society. In this interpretation, poverty becomes a complex, integral indicator which describes a particular group identifiable in society and co-existing in parallel with the way of life and culture of the majority of members of that society.

This aspect of our study concerns the special part that poverty is playing in the re-formation of a stratification system in Russia. The poor in Russia are not, after all, a stratum differing from others, with a different way of life and type of reproduction. The question of markers of a particular way of life among the poor is one that is so far only partly resolved. Bearing in mind, therefore, that in their responses to direct questions concerning their material circumstances the respondents were guided both by their perceptions and by actual income figures, we attempted to separate out which particular questions were the 'nucleus' of the set for material welfare and which were 'threshold' questions to establish the boundaries of between levels - which by no means always corresponded with the breakdown by *per capita* income levels. This way of looking at the question enabled us to analyse whether there were, among these 'thresholds' or within the 'nucleus', indicators pointing to the formation of a particular stratum of poor people with their own particular way of life, which differed from that of the majority of the population, and their own structure of consumption.

Inter-correlation and factor analysis showed that in Russia today there are property/income strata for whom way of life and social participation differ not just quantitatively, but also in terms of quality characteristics. Of the 27 questions associated with the material circumstances of the respondents in the 1997 survey, just 17 fell within the most significant category (with relationships with at least nine other questions in the material circumstances block, i.e. one-third of the questions in that block). The others were 'peripheral' indicators. It should also be pointed out right away that, of all the questions in the survey, the greatest statistically-significant relationship with the questions of the material welfare set was found to be that of the question on the proportion of outlay going on food in the household's structure of expenditure - a question which effectively synthesised information on income level and on family expenditure priorities. In this respect, it was a far more 'operative' question than that of *per capita* income, which did not even make it into the 'top twenty' of questions with the highest number of statistically-significant relationships with the material welfare set. In stratifying our sample in terms of structure of consumption and forms of social participation, therefore, we made extensive use of the question on proportion of income going on food as a control question.

Of these 17 questions, some were significant as 'thresholds' between the way of life of different strata only for the higher property/income strata, while others were significant for lower strata; yet others were of importance for various strata, but the frequency of performance of a certain action differed in them, and changes in the way of life of the respondents were reflected as they moved to another group (for example, 'I used to spend money on newspapers and magazines, but now I can no longer afford to', 'occasionally I can afford to spend money on that', 'I regularly spend money on that' or 'I don't spend money on that because I don't need it'). Questions which were of significance for certain groups of respondents, for example those with children who were minors, stood rather on their own. At the same time these 'special' questions showed a very high heuristic significance, since the respondents skimped on their children last, and questions on whether paid sessions at clubs for children or new clothes for them could be afforded were very clear 'threshold' questions for this section of the respondents.

Among the questions on structure of consumption, the following were the most important in establishing which stratum the respondents belonged to: possibility and frequency of buying of fresh meat, purchase of clothing and footwear, delicatessen meat or fish, use of paid medical, educational or other services, and the presence of real property. Here something in particular needs to be said about the question on the presence/absence/ impossibility of acquiring expensive equipment (domestic, video, audio) or of making other high expenditures (repairs/decoration of apartment, building of *dacha*). It was shown by processing the sample data (and this will be partially expounded below) that the response that there had been no such outlay during the year demonstrated a very high level of heuristic significance in identifying levels of material prosperity. It was a threshold indicator dividing the successful and non-successful sections of the respondents (as replies to other questions from the material circumstances set show, respondents often feel themselves that they are 'successful' or 'not successful' precisely by consideration of this threshold). It may be that the role of this indicator (within it, the element of not being able to afford to buy domestic equipment is of particular importance) is associated with the novelty of most types of domestic equipment in the Russian consumer market and the readiness of Russians to skimp on something else so as to acquire domestic equipment for the house. The lack of potential to make such a purchase is the clearest possible evidence that there is nothing to skimp with; beyond this, we can only talk of different depths of poverty - from the badly-off to the indigent. Other threshold indicators are the lack of potential to buy fresh meat or clothes for the children; these factors are a symptom of being indigent rather than just badly-off or poor.

As regards way of life and social contacts ('forms of social participation'), analysis of all the survey questions relating to various forms of social participation showed that the most common types of non-work social contacts in Russia are contact with relatives (64 per cent) and with friends (63 per cent). For comparison, 26 per cent of the respondents went to church, and 15 per cent went to sports clubs of all types taken together. Clubs, as places of social contact, were even less popular. The number of responses where respondents had been obliged to cease going to such places because of lack of money was correspondingly so minuscule that it did not constitute a basis for any real conclusions.

So, bearing in mind that the vast majority of respondents (85 per cent) maintain their most socially-significant contacts by visiting or being visited (since cafés and restaurants are expensive and there is no tradition of this kind of outing), it is not surprising that finding it impossible to make such contacts was among the most important 'thresholds' of poverty.

It was in fact inability to visit people (it is not done to arrive 'empty-handed') that distinguished the poor from the badly-off, in much the same way as inability to buy newspapers and magazines or clothing. So, if poverty and indigence are divided by the possibility of at least occasionally buying fresh meat, fruit, sweets or clothes for one's children, then the badly-off and the poor are divided primarily by the 'thresholds' of social participation. For the badly-off this participation is restricted - they can only occasionally afford to invite guests round, visit as guests, buy clothing, newspapers or magazines or go to the theatre or cinema - but for the poor, these forms of social participation are essentially never possible.

For all these three least well-off strata, it is also impossible to acquire luxury foodstuffs, to visit cafés or restaurants, to take trips out of town, to utilise paid social services, tourist travel and certain other features of consumer behaviour or forms of social participation. But we do not propose to cover these in detail because of the high percentage of 'I don't spend money on that because I don't need it' responses - for example, concerning the possibility of buying imported cigarettes, where almost 60 per cent of respondents gave this answer. Besides, in all of these strata a markedly smaller percentage of respondents had any real property at all when compared to the average for the sample, and this was what clearly delineated the poorest groups of respondents (as isolated by us) from the 'poor' as identified using the formal marker of assessing one's own *per capita* income level.

Without dwelling in detail on the distinguishing features of other property/income strata, we would just comment that while the badly-off and the averagely well-off were divided primarily by whether they could or could not make relatively expensive purchases, the well-off and prosperous were divided from the averagely well-off chiefly by the frequency rather than the fundamental possibility of carrying out actions of one type or another. Thus the well-off and prosperous could afford to make regular purchases of fresh meat, sweets and fruit, and they all also bought luxury foodstuffs, which the averagely well-off could only afford to do occasionally. They also had no financial restraints as regards visiting or receiving visitors, they regularly purchased newspapers and magazines, and there was no skimping at all on children's needs.

The clearest threshold characteristics of the level of welfare are presented in Table 8.5. By way of explanation we should say that among the 25 people from three cities who could no longer afford to buy meat, half (12 of them) were people for whom over 80 per cent of income went on food. There were equivalent significant shifts for other consumer items. Bearing in mind the particular features of the structure of consumption and savings in different families, these thresholds naturally do not have any absolute significance, but their relationship with a certain level of welfare came out fairly clearly in the course of the research. From now on, therefore, we shall use the most general characteristics in creating typologies - although not all of these characteristics have to be present in each individual person. Thus a member of the 'poor' group may buy newspapers regularly but never buy meat, while most people in that group occasionally buy meat but do not buy newspapers, and so on.

Incidentally, when we analysed the degree of correspondence between the respondents' purchases and the proportion of the household budget going on food, we again ran up against the phenomenon of people purchasing expensive equipment, computers and cars (the table contains only some of the respondents' replies concerning their various purchases and outlays) when they apparently spent over 80 per cent of their income on food. We would not go so far as to say that they all deliberately deceived the interviewers. Judging by the reactions of many people during the survey, this was the first time they had thought about how much they spent on food, and the figures they gave at this time were rather 'off the top of their heads', as also were the data on *per capita* income. Unfortunately, this is a problem common to research in Russia, and many interviewers complain of difficulties in obtaining relevant information from their respondents. Underestimates may be as much as 40 per cent, and reflects not so much a desire on the part of the respondent to misrepresent his or her income, as the specific Russian income structure.

Table 8.5 Shifts (thresholds) in consumption, by per cent of outgoings spent on food, across sample as a whole - n

Response variables	*<30%*	*30-50%*	*50-80%*	*>80%*	*Total*
Cannot afford to spend money on meat, though used to	-	4	9	12	25
Cannot afford to go visiting on special occasions, though used to	1	3	7	12	23
Cannot afford to invite people round to visit, though used to	1	6	21	32	60
Have not acquired any expensive equipment	5	15	46	46	112
Have acquired domestic equipment	2	28	37	8	75
All respondents	9	56	120	110	295

Analysing all the data obtained shows us that the real distribution of respondents by groups with differing levels of welfare (including varying levels of potential for social participation) looks somewhat different from the distribution obtained using the criterion of *per capita* income or proportion of income spent on food. Moreover, taking into account features of the structure of consumption, we think the least well-off group should really be called 'indigent' rather than 'poor'.

Table 8.6   Distribution of respondents by structure of consumption and social participation

indigent - 8-10 per cent (20-24 people) - never buy meat, sweets or new clothes for children, never go visiting and never receive guests;

poor - 10-11 per cent (24-25 people) - can only rarely afford to buy meat, fruit, sweets, clothes, do not go visiting, do not buy newspapers, do not pay for private lessons for their children, and only rarely buy them new clothes;

badly-off - 25 per cent (about 60 people) - do not buy domestic or other expensive equipment, can never afford luxury foods, and feel seriously constrained in purchasing clothes, going to theatres, concerts or the cinema and buying newspapers or magazines;

averagely well-off - 34-35 per cent (80-85 people) - this is the group where free money starts to appear, and, depending on family priorities, the variability of outlay and savings strategies increases: some save on clothing, others on domestic and other equipment, others again on food, etc.; in general the whole group experiences constraints in buying certain products, especially luxury foods, going to the theatre, taking tourist trips and buying clothes;

well-off - 10-15 per cent (28-36 people) - experience constraints in the acquisition of very expensive things, like cars or computers, in visiting cafés or restaurants or taking tourist trips, but make almost no economies on food or domestic equipment;

prosperous - 10-12 per cent (24-28 people) - can afford many expensive purchases, but basically they have all the expensive kinds of equipment already; depending on family priorities they regularly buy luxury foods, go to restaurants, go on tourist trips or make expensive purchases, although even they cannot afford all kinds of outlay at once without economising on something from among their desired expenditure.

Taking into account the distortions created by the respondents in the income data, we could say that the boundary between the badly-off and the averagely well-off lies at the level of the median *per capita* income value (in 1997) of 500,000 roubles, and slightly above the Subsistence Minimum of 420,000 roubles (although, as our experience shows, respondents do not usually include in their *per capita* income calculation one-off additional earnings, child allowances, grants and so on; they list only their wage for their main job, income from additional jobs and pensions). In Moscow and St. Petersburg, this boundary was slightly higher, and in Voronezh slightly lower. The threshold between averagely well-off and well-off, on the other hand, was fairly clearly 800,000 roubles.

Having constructed a welfare index which could vary from 1 to 10 depending on the number of property/income strata identified, we considered the issue of social morale and life attitudes among members of each stratum. As our analysis revealed, the differences between them were simply astounding. Among the two poorest strata, 64 per cent of the respondents thought their lives were basically not going well, and only two per cent thought they were fine; while among the two best-off strata just four per cent had a poor opinion of their own life and 30 per cent thought it was fine. The rest thought life was satisfactory. Assessing different ways of achieving their aims, only 14 per cent of members of the poorest strata thought the most effective way was to come to a direct arrangement with those on whom the solution to their problems depended, while among the best-off strata 47 per cent adhered to this view. Meanwhile 43 per cent of the poor and only 9 per cent of the well-off and prosperous expected State help in solving their problems.

In many cases there were even starker differences between members of the poorest and the richest groups. Among the indigent, 92 per cent indicated that their life had deteriorated during the last year, and no-one thought it had improved. Among the prosperous, on the other hand, five per cent reported a deterioration in their life, with 42 per cent pointing to an improvement. Correspondingly, 23 per cent of the indigent (and none of the prosperous) thought that their state of poverty allowed them to accept aid from anyone willing to offer it. Their own poverty-stricken circumstances, on the other hand, were usually attributed by them to external factors. 31 per cent of them thought that their poverty-stricken circumstances depended solely on the economic situation in the country, and none of them thought they themselves were the cause. And in this they were right, in the sense that before the economic reforms their poverty, thanks to the way social policy was run in the USSR, would not have been so profound. Among the prosperous, though, the position was reversed. 74 per cent of them were convinced that their material circumstances depended primarily on themselves, and none thought that the main factor was the situation in the country. Correspondingly 46 per cent of the indigent (and only five per cent of the prosperous) were entirely in agreement that the State should look after everyone not in a position to look after themselves. On the other hand, 23 per cent of the indigent were not in agreement with this, nor were 79 per cent of the prosperous (the rest were 'don't-knows'). It is hard to say what is dominant - expectations of paternalism or a feeling of inability to cope with the situation, but 77 per cent of the indigent (against three per cent of the prosperous) did not feel that things were going their way, while 46 per cent (zero per cent) thought that life was not worth much. Given this feeling, it is not surprising that 39 per cent of the indigent thought it would be easier to die and escape all one's problems, while not one of the prosperous felt that way.

It may be that the gloomy subjective social mood felt by the indigent was coloured by problems of health and a degree of social isolation, as these things come through quite clearly for them. 39 per cent of the indigent and five per cent of the prosperous assessed their own health as bad. Nor is this surprising, if we remember that 54 per cent of the indigent (and not one of the prosperous) complained of headaches. As regards social contacts, none of the indigent was able to spend time going out with friends for entertainment, while 26 per cent of the prosperous spent their leisure time that way. For the indigent, however, contacts with neighbours at home were particularly important (77 per cent), as these did not require any special outlay, while only 10 per cent of the prosperous had any social contact with their neighbours.

Thus analysis of the figures for indicators such as the dynamics of change in material circumstances, subjective social mood, the specific nature of forms of social participation and the health of members of various welfare groups enabled us to establish that there were perceptibly deeper gulfs between them than those arising out of analysis of *per capita* income. The differences between the two poorest and the two best-off groups were particularly visible, and in particular the gap between the indigent and the prosperous groups. This enables us to state that persistent poverty has begun to be created in contemporary Russia, and moreover that the people in this situation have certain fairly distinctly-expressed features in their way of life and personality characteristics.

At the same time, poor people who are currently experiencing major constraints on their structure of consumption and social participation, but who form part of the 'badly-off' group, hardly differ in terms of their views and subjective social mood from the better-off respondents. In view of the fact that, as our observations over the year showed, this group has a tendency to dissipate (it had shrunk by half over the year), it may be assumed that in Russia there will soon have formed a group of poor people who are quite distinct from the rest of the population, comprising both 'old' and 'new' poor; while the rest of the population, one way or another - possibly by changing their demands and their view of the world - will adapt to the new conditions and create new living standards. The question of who will become the 'new' poor and why deserves special attention, and will be analysed later in this chapter.

Before moving on to this, however, in view of the differences between the situations in the cities studied, we must also demonstrate the extent of regional differences in this matter.

Table 8.7 Regional differences in the structure of consumption and social participation - n (per cent)

	Moscow	*Voronezh*	*St. Petersburg*
indigent	10 (10)	7 (12)	2 (3)
poor	11 (11)	8 (13)	6 (7)
badly-off	26 (26)	16 (27)	19 (24)
av. well-off	27 (27)	24 (40)	30 (38)
well-off	15 (15)	3 (5)	14 (17)
prosperous	11 (11)	2 (3)	9 (11)
total	100 (100)	60 (100)	80 (100)

As can be seen, there are very similar proportions of the badly-off group in all the cities; a concentration of 20-25 per cent mainly in the two poorest groups, although the depth of poverty varies; and perceptible regional differences in the proportions of the two best-off groups. Even in our sample, which covered only respondents unfavourably placed in the labour market, the numbers in these two groups exceeded 25 per cent in Moscow and St. Petersburg, and in Voronezh were four to five times lower than in St. Petersburg. On the other hand, on more detailed analysis of the situation for specific people in each city, the differences in the proportions of the two poorest groups as between Moscow and St. Petersburg turned out to have a relationship with specific structural features of the households within them. In Moscow there were more one-parent families and families with a large number of dependants, where there was a high family dependency ratio (ratio of number of dependants/number of employed), which, as we shall show later, had an instant effect on the proportion of poor families.

We can conclude from this analysis of the respondents' material circumstances during 1996-1997 as follows. First, the dynamics of change in the respondents' material circumstances over the past year were very clearly regional in nature. In Voronezh there was a relative and absolute deterioration in the respondents' circumstances, in comparison both with respondents in Moscow and St. Petersburg and with inhabitants of Voronezh generally. Respondents from the labour market crisis groups in Voronezh really did represent the most deprived section of society. In Moscow and St. Petersburg, a slight increase in the group of poor people was accompanied by an erosion of the group of badly-off and a rise in the group of averagely well-off. Overall, using the *per capita* income criterion, the group with income below the Subsistence Minimum constituted around 45 per cent, including 14 per cent with income less than half the Subsistence Minimum. The data obtained testified to the increasing polarisation of Russian society, which is causing the abyss between the really poor and the rest of the population to become even deeper and more and more difficult to bridge.

Second, analysis of the material situation as well as the income situation showed there to be a large group, comprising almost half the respondents in all the cities, members of which were not able to acquire any new property for their household. The majority of respondents without any real property was also concentrated in this group. This meant that, in respect of these people, it was applicable to apply a criterion of poverty of simultaneous low *per capita* income and lack of the types of property most commonly owned in that society. The numbers of poor people in this definition constituted about 25 per cent of the sample. At the same time, even the application of this dual criterion of poverty could not eliminate many 'loose ends' in the respondents' replies.

Third, such contradictions were removed with the aid of Townsend's interpretation of the concept of poverty. This showed firstly that Russians for the most part have an intuitive interpretation of the concept of poverty, exactly along the lines of Townsend's (not having the potential to 'live like everyone else'). In addition, having adapted his concepts to Russian socio-cultural and economic conditions and having operationalised them on the basis of a detailed analysis of the sample, we were able to model the 'ideal types' of members of various property/income strata.

Fourth, in the course of this analysis it was demonstrated that among the 'ordinary' population of Russia today there really are different property/income strata, which differ not only in quantitative terms, but also in the quality characteristics of their ways of life and social participation. The relative size of these strata differed widely between regions, but taken as a whole, the proportion of people in profound poverty or indigence - using Townsend's definition - was around 20 per cent of those in our study. Of course, it must straight away be said that the limited and specific nature of the research sample prevents these results from being extrapolated to Russians as a whole.

Fifth, nevertheless, the results of the research do enable us to state that there is evidence in contemporary Russia not just of incipient persistent poverty, but of a fairly distinct specific way of life and personality characteristics among the representatives of these poor. This applies to that section of the Russian population which fell within the two poorest groups in our research. At the same time, the badly-off, who also experience substantial constraints in their structure of consumption and social participation, differ very little in their views and subjective social mood from the better-off respondents. Since there is a trend towards erosion of the badly-off as a group, we suggest that it will not be long before a group of poor people will be created in Russia, who will differ quite markedly from the rest of the population, and will consist of 'old' and 'new' poor; some of the badly-off will move into this group, while the rest of the population will somehow, perhaps by altering their aspirations and ideas, adapt to the new conditions, and new living standards will be shaped. The question of who is becoming the 'new' poor and why requires particular examination, and will be analysed later in this chapter.

Household Composition and Unemployment as Causes of Poverty

What is the cause of poverty and is there a relationship between unemployment and poverty? All who have studied this problem agree that the answer to this question is obviously 'yes'. From the results of the first stage of our research, however, we had the impression that this relationship is by no means simple, and for the second stage we decided to investigate this question in detail. We were primarily interested in finding out which of our respondents were in the most deprived groups, what kept them within these groups, what survival strategies they chose and in what way these strategies differed from the strategies of other respondents.

Let us examine the issue of who fell into the most deprived groups, beginning with the unemployed. However, to avoid the danger of 'blurring' regional specifics, which were very distinct in this case, we shall have to analyse the data separately for each city.

Moscow

Of the 30 registered unemployed in 1996, 20 described themselves as still unemployed in 1997 (the rest had found work). Among them were 14 unemployed officially registered with the Employment Service, three who were in fact unemployed, but who had for various reasons taken themselves off the Employment Service register, and three more who also described themselves as *de facto* unemployed, although one of them had successfully applied for retirement pension, while the other two had become registered disabled. In 1997, a further 14 people had been added to this group - eight registered unemployed and six *de facto* unemployed, of whom two were pensioners. Finally, there were ten people who had found work, in two cases self-employment. All these groups, totalling 44 people, became the object of our special analysis of the nature of relationship between unemployment and poverty.

The results of analysis of the distribution of these 44 people between the various property/income strata are shown in Table 8.8. This table also gives a comparison of the status of these people in terms of the two poverty criteria - *per capita* income below 400,000 roubles, and the mixed criterion developed by us during the research adjusting for the structure of consumption and social participation.

It should be pointed out that the 17 poor people in the left-hand column of Table 8.8 and the 16 in the right-hand column are not one and the same set of people. These are figures which partially overlap, but the degree of non-coincidence is nevertheless fairly significant. The 16 genuinely poor included ten who were formally poor (four from among the indigent and six from the 'poor' group); two more had 'slipped down' from the 'badly-off'; and a further four had been added to this grouping from apparently perfectly successful groups.

Meanwhile, seven of the group of formally poor people had transferred to other groups: three to the badly-off and four to entirely successful groups. This occurred because of sources of income available to the respondents which were not taken into account in assessing *per capita* income, or because of peculiarities in outgoings governed by the situation in the household (for example, material circumstances were worse for the disabled or for alcoholics than for others with the same actual income).

Table 8.8 Distribution by level of material welfare among the unemployed in 1996 and 1997 in Moscow (44 persons)

Material circumstances	per capita income	Adjusted for consumption and participation
indigent/ poor	17	16
badly-off	14	9
averagely well-off	10	13
well-off /prosperous	3	6

Who in fact falls into the categories of 'indigent' or 'poor'? An exhaustive list of all the social types is: single women of pre-pension age in poor health; one-parent families with children under 18; and families of the disabled. The general statement may be made, on the basis of our research, that in Moscow it was the composition of the household, not unemployment, that was crucial to poverty; since, firstly, families with this household composition were basically among the poor even before unemployment reared its head, and secondly, two-thirds of the members of this group said that for one reason or another they were actually not interested in finding work.

An example of the realities of finding work for most of the members of this group of long-term unemployed is provided by respondents from families that were similar in type, who during 1997 had made the transition from unemployed to the category of those who had found a job. These were two women, both in one-parent families with children under 18 (in one case one child, in the other two). Not being able to take jobs in the private sector (where the workload is large and incompatible with their family responsibilities, and where there is little enthusiasm for employing single mothers with children under 18), both took jobs at budget-funded institutions (teacher and social worker). In both cases, because of rates of pay in budget-funded sectors, the *per capita* income in their families was 250,000-300,000 roubles; i.e. in Moscow terms, they were still 'poor' in the formal sense, just like those who remained unemployed. In reality, though, one (the one with two children) is in an indigent situation, whereas the other (with one child) belongs to the badly-off.

Among those who had recently become unemployed (i.e. during the period between the two stages of the research), those who were 'poor' were members of one-parent families with children under 18. Finally, among the *de facto* unemployed there were two who were poor - a young woman not seeking work because of family circumstances, and a young man who had found a job during the year, but was out of work again. They had both been in the insecure employment group in 1996.

Thus the overall picture for poverty among the groups was as follows.

Table 8.9 Distribution of poverty across groups of unemployed in Moscow (n)

Material circum-stances	Long-term unemp (1996-1997)	Official unemp 1997	De facto unemp 1997	Unemp who found work 1996	Total
indigent	6	-	-	2	8
poor	5	1	2	-	8
sub-total	11	1	2	2	16
total	20	8	6	10	44

As may be seen from Table 8.9, the main bulk of the group of poor people was made up of long-term unemployed, although the long-term unemployed accounted for only 45 per cent of the whole of this sample of 44 respondents. At the same time, taking the Moscow sample of 100 people as a whole, when we analysed it from the point of view of structure of consumption, not only overall but also for each individual separately (in order to test the methodology of assessing poverty using the mixed criterion of structure of consumption plus social participation), we found only 22 people who were poor; i.e. of the 56 people who did not enter into this particular analysis, only six were indigent or poor. Looking at this from a different angle, if we consider the poor in the entire Moscow sample, exactly half (11 out of 22) were long-term unemployed, while another five were people with some kind of experience of unemployment. The remaining six were: a single middle-aged female pensioner; a man (a fitter) with three dependants, who was under threat of redundancy in 1996, had then suffered a spell of unemployment, subsequently found a job but had been released (bearing in mind that his trade is generally in short supply, this makes one wonder whether there were discipline or alcohol problems in his case), but had found another job by the time of the 1997 survey; two single women with children; and two single middle-aged women. As a general statement, the overwhelming majority of poor people in Moscow were 'old' poor, whose family circumstances and health would have placed them under threat of poverty even in the pre-reform period.

So what survival strategies did these people employ? Among the indigent, the most common survival strategy was to sell property (half the respondents), followed by eating into savings, borrowing money and earning money on the side; much less common was receipt of help from others, income from letting property, work in several different places and self-sufficiency in food grown at a *dacha*. Thus of 25 responses on how to alter one's circumstances for the better, only nine might be considered constructive, the rest being either passive ('we get help from others', 'we borrow', - when you look at the respondents' circumstances, the latter can only be seen as a disguised form of aid), or destructive ('we are eating into our savings', 'we sell property').

Among the group of poor people, eating into savings was placed first, followed by self-sufficiency in food grown at the *dacha* (four responses), then receipt of help from others and additional earnings. Next came sale of property and 'no attempt to improve our position', then borrowing money and sale of vegetables from the *dacha*. Of 20 responses, eight involved constructive actions, while the remaining 12 were destructive or passive. In both of these groups, exactly half of the respondents were trying to take some kind of constructive action to alleviate their situation, and the other half was not doing so.

We tried to determine the types of economic activity of the most deprived section of our Moscow respondents according to the classification proposed by Rose (1993a) in his 'Barometer' study conducted in Russia in the 1990s. Rose identified four basic types of economic activity: 'protected' - among ways of getting income are wages from job, social assistance at place of work, pensions, growing food, help from friends; 'entrepreneurial' - income from extra employment and various one-off jobs; 'socially vulnerable' - wages, social assistance at work, pensions and benefits are the only sources of income; 'marginal' - growing food, help from friends and relatives, and upkeep of the home are the only types of economic activity. According to Rose, the 'protected' type of economic activity is most common in Russia (43 per cent), followed by the approximately equally-common 'entrepreneurial' and 'socially vulnerable' types (23 and 22 per cent respectively), with the list being completed by the 'marginal' type (12 per cent).

From analysis of the 22 people who fell into the indigent and poor group out of the Moscow sample as a whole, nine, i.e. 41 per cent, belonged to the marginal type (which had accounted for 12 per cent in Rose's national study); a further two (nine per cent) belonged to the protected type, which Rose found to be the most common type in Russia at 43 per cent; four (18 per cent) were vulnerable (22 per cent in Rose's study), and seven (32 per cent) of the 'poor' respondents featured economic activity of the entrepreneurial type (23 per cent of Rose's sample). Thus in the group of poor people the main types of Russians were almost un-represented, whereas the two polar groups, which were less characteristic of the Russian population as a whole, were commonly found. One section was frankly marginal, comprising only unemployed people, and long-term unemployed at that: they were mainly one-parent families. The second section was making active attempts to escape from the situation of poverty, and comprised largely so-called 'new' poor people (six out of seven people with an entrepreneurial type of economic activity were from among the 'new poor'). At the same time it needs to be said that the 'old' and 'new' poor were roughly equally represented among the marginal type (four 'old' and five 'new').

We think that the marginal group of poor people, who are essentially not seeking work and are not capable of either working effectively or choosing any kind of effective survival strategy, reflects a social type that is frozen in this position by predominantly external factors - one-parent family, children under 18, poor health, various combinations of these - which engender dependence on sources of income not associated with their work activities. Even in these conditions, of course, given certain personality inclinations and features, at least an averagely well-off existence is possible, and there are examples of this even in the Voronezh sample, despite the seriousness of the situation on its labour market. This is more the exception than the rule, however, and for most people who have these particular external factors, they are in fact crucial.

The ways in which survival strategies in the groups of indigent and poor differed not only from Rose's data on types of activity among

Russians, but also from the chosen survival strategies of other respondents from our Moscow sample as a whole, were very striking (Table 8.10).

As we can see, almost all the respondents from the Moscow sample who had sold their property were among the indigent and poor (seven out of eight), along with almost half of those who had eaten into existing savings (the remaining poor apparently had no savings anyway). On the other hand, virtually no-one with secure secondary employment fell into the indigent and poor groups. In addition, while constructive and active types of survival strategy were predominant among the Moscow sample as a whole, survival strategies among the indigent and poor - although generally more varied as between individual respondents - were more likely to be of a destructive nature.

Table 8.10　Selected survival strategies, Moscow - n (per cent)

Response variables	*Whole sample*		*indigent/poor*	
We are providing ourselves with some foodstuffs	27	(27)	5	(23)
We have several jobs	25	(25)	2	(9)
We are using existing savings	20	(20)	9	(41)
We have had to borrow money	15	(15)	5	(23)
We take any chance to earn extra	14	(14)	7	(32)
We are not doing anything	13	(13)	2	(9)
We get help from others	10	(10)	5	(23)
We rent out property	8	(8)	2	(9)
We are selling our belongings	8	(8)	7	(32)
We are involved in small-scale trading or re-sale of goods	5	(5)	-	
We are selling excess produce from our *dacha*	4	(4)	1	(4)
Total	149	(149)	45	(205)

A quite different picture of survival strategies was manifested by the six people who, while forming part of our sample of 44 unemployed (or formerly unemployed, in the case of the 1996 survey), also belonged to high-income groups. None of them had dependants, all were actually in work, three had full-time work which they referred to as a reason for not seeking a job (one had his own business, a second worked in several places and had additional earnings, and a third - a woman of pre-pension age - had well-paid work as an administrator), and a further two were young men with secure sources of income (renting out real property, trade) who worked in various places simultaneously. The last one was a single woman of pre-pension age with poor health, who was quite astutely taking advantage of a particular aspect of Russian legislation to remain formally unemployed until she reached pension age, even though she had a *per capita* income of 1.3 million.

In four of these cases we can see how personality features can overcome, in an entirely rational way, unfavourable external factors arising out of a system of economic relations in no way within the control of the respondent, while in a further two cases (the young men with additional earnings), we see how the system of socio-economic relations in Russian society itself is being utilised successfully to select a structure of employment that is optimal for the person in question. All six are also very astutely taking advantage of the existing social security system.

Finally we can consider 'badly-off' and 'averagely well-off' unemployed Muscovites. The variety of social types here is much greater, as too is the variety of survival strategies employed, according to each person's available resources and personal preferences. These include single unemployed women who have additional earnings, married women, who partially provide the family with food grown at a *dacha*; middle-aged married women with additional earnings; and married women with children under 18. Basically, apart from unemployment benefit received (or other benefits, including pensions), they had income from economic activity and their real *per capita* income was over 400,000 - though it did not reach 800,000 roubles.

This review of the life and survival strategies of our respondents makes it clear that, apart from large families, one-parent families, households containing disabled people or single-person households where the person is just unwell, Moscow offers quite a lot of potential for a person to feed themselves without becoming poor, even without a full-time job - although a person in this situation may experience a sense of social insecurity and psychological discomfort in this situation. For single people or members of households with no dependants, the crucial role is played not so much by objective factors set by the external situation, as by features of their own personality, about which we shall talk in more detail later. True, the presence of certain resources (a *dacha* where one may provide oneself with food), or real property which may be rented out, gives some additional advantages here, but for the great majority such things are not crucial.

St. Petersburg

In St. Petersburg there were 13 long-term unemployed, of whom six were still officially registered unemployed, and seven were now *de facto* unemployed but had been registered with the Employment Service in 1996. Two of them were in the indigent or poor category: one (a woman) was the head of a one-parent family with a child under 18 and the other (also a woman) was a middle-aged disabled person from a large family with a high family dependency ratio. In both cases passive, non-constructive actions were chosen, belonging to the marginal type of economic activity (renting out property owned, borrowing money).

In terms of their lifestyle and structure of consumption, a further three people were in the badly-off category. These were: the head of a two-parent family with two dependants; a young married woman with a small child who was not seeking work because of her family circumstances; and a young married unskilled man with additional earnings, who had changed his job more than once during the course of the year, which suggests there might be problems with discipline or alcohol.

Six of the long-term unemployed in St. Petersburg met the standards of the averagely well-off. Among them were: a young stevedore living with his parents, who had also been released from work several times during the year, but was working in several places while retaining unemployed status; middle-aged and elderly men in families without dependants; a middle-aged woman from a large family with a low family dependency ratio, who was deliberately doing nothing to improve her material circumstances; and a young man (under 21) living with his mother, who had found a job but lost it again during the past year.

Finally there were two respondents from among the long-term unemployed who belonged to the 'well-off' and 'prosperous' categories. They were both married women with no children.

In St. Petersburg, there were just five new unemployed, either officially or *de facto*. These were people of a type already familiar to us from the Moscow sample - a middle-aged single or a young married man engaged in small-scale trading or with other additional earnings; a single woman with a young child not seeking work because of her family circumstances; a married woman from a large family with no dependants, receiving unemployment benefit while awaiting a pension and with additional earnings. Of this group, just one single middle-aged man belonged to the 'poor' category: his additional earnings and his trading were clearly not going too well, resulting in his being obliged to sell some of his property. Of the rest, one man was badly-off, two were averagely well-off and one (a single woman with a child who was renting out property) was well-off.

The fates also positively beamed upon those previously unemployed in St. Petersburg who had found work. Of the 12 who had done so, not one was living at the level of either indigence or poverty, although three were at the 'badly-off' level. For all these three, in the final analysis this was linked with a combination of their family circumstances and the situation in their sector of the economy. One was a married man, a low-paid specialist in the mass culture sector, with a child under 18, and although he tried to earn some extra money, this was not enough to lift his family out of the badly-off category. The second was a young married man with two small children, a computer operator, who was also making active efforts to improve his circumstances (a bit of incidental trading, growing vegetables at his *dacha*), but this had little impact on the situation. Finally, for the third man, who was in a highly-paid occupation (builder) and had three dependants, even doing more than one job at once did not help him to raise his family up out of the badly-off category.

The main body of those who had found work, however, were either among the 'averagely well-off' (4) or among the 'well-off' and 'prosperous' (5). The latter five people (with one exception, where the level of welfare in the family was associated with other family members' income) were people with professions that were in short supply and attracted good pay - an administrator, a charge-hand engineer, a sales manager and a book-keeper. The only explanation for their temporary unemployment could have been a desire to spend a few months on benefit as a sort of 'holiday' and to return to work after a few months when the benefit level fell. In this respect, the situation in St. Petersburg was radically different from that in Moscow, where most respondents' level of welfare bore little relation (even for those in the best-off groups) to their particular skilled occupation, and mainly arose out of the general and somewhat mysterious formula 'we take advantage of every opportunity to earn extra'. Given that such activity is not sanctioned by law in the eyes of the tax inspection and other authorities, what lay behind this form of words in each individual case could not, of course, be ascertained, but there were some respondents who used this phrase while having difficulty staying up in the 'badly-off' bracket, while others went on tourist trips and bought computers and cars.

To conclude this review of material wellbeing among respondents from the St. Petersburg sample, we should also observe that of the remaining groups considered, there were six people who fell into the 'indigent' or 'poor' categories. These were: a single female pensioner; a single middle-aged man with the unpromising - in Russia's current conditions - profession of botanist, who had remained in the group of people in insecure employment; a married woman with five dependants who, despite being a qualified chef and also engaged in small-scale trading, was not in a position to ensure her family an appropriate standard of living; a middle-aged woman who was a radio engineer belonging to the group in insecure employment, and had two dependants in her household; and two middle-aged family men.

Thus in St. Petersburg, as in Moscow, a relationship could quite clearly be made out, not so much with employment/unemployment as with the family circumstances of the respondents and the composition of the household. The presence of a well-paid skilled occupation that is in short supply (in St. Petersburg) or secondary employment (in Moscow) is capable of exerting considerable influence on the respondents' material circumstances, but with a family dependency ratio of more than 1:1 it can make the family at best averagely well-off, and only in a few unique cases can it make them well-off. In any event, there was not one person in the group of 'prosperous' people in our study, from any of the cities, who had more than one dependant, and there was only one of the 'well-off' who had two dependants.

From the point of view of types of economic activity in operation, the picture in St. Petersburg was generally similar to that in Moscow.

Voronezh

The situation in Voronezh was totally different. The poorest long-term unemployed here included not just one-parent families, married women with small children and disabled people. Of the six people in the group of indigent and poor long-term unemployed of Voronezh, only two (a man from a one-parent family with a child and a single woman with children under 18) fell into the category of 'old poor'. The others were the 'new poor' - people who essentially can make their lives reasonably bearable in

Moscow and St. Petersburg, whereas in Voronezh some of them tend to hit 'rock bottom'.

Among the more successful Voronezh long-term unemployed, numbering seven in all, the same survival strategies were being used as in Moscow: for example, married women staying at home with young children are partially self-sufficient in food, and try to earn a little on the side while eating into their savings; or else they are partially self-sufficient in food and trade in vegetables. However, while such a strategy provided a *per capita* income of 400,000 in Moscow, in Voronezh it provided less than 200,000. Once again, we encounter the type of a married woman of pre-pension age, member of a household where there is one employed person per dependant, self-sufficient in food and trading in what she grows at the *dacha*. As a result, in terms of structure of consumption and lifestyle, two of the respondents were in the badly-off group, and five in the averagely well-off group. Of the long-term unemployed in Voronezh, only one - a failed entrepreneur with steady additional earnings - was in a genuinely favourable situation.

The predominance of 'new poor' among the long-term unemployed in Voronezh was also perceptible in the diffusion of various types of economic activity in this group. The entrepreneurial type of economic activity was top of the list (nine out of 13), while others were forms of the marginal type of activity.

We see a similar picture to Moscow and St. Petersburg when we analyse the Voronezh respondents who had become registered or *de facto* unemployed during the past year (12 cases). Here again we found the one-parent family and the single disabled person represented. Married women stayed at home with the children and did not all seek work. Mention has already been made above of the other social types represented in this group. Three of the 12 new Voronezh unemployed belonged to the 'poor' and 'indigent' categories. None of them was seeking work, citing the particular nature of their skills as their reason, and while the one-parent family among them may be described as representing the 'old poor', the two others were from the 'new poor' (Table 8.11).

Self-sufficiency in food was a strategy chosen by almost all the new Voronezh unemployed: in four cases, they also sold food they had grown and had additional earnings; in three cases, savings had been eaten into, while the same number had borrowed money; one woman had rental income from her real property and received help from others. In all, six people employed marginal strategies, while six, despite a considerable degree of marginality, displayed elements of entrepreneurial activity.

Table 8.11   Distribution of poverty across groups of unemployed in Voronezh - n

Material circum- stances	Long- term unemp (1996- 1997)	Official unemp 1997	De facto unemp 1997	Total
indigent	2	-	-	2
poor	4	1	2	7
sub-total	6	1	2	9
total	13	17	8	38

Taken overall, of the 25 registered and *de facto* unemployed in Voronezh in 1997, nine were in the category of poor and indigent, six were badly-off, nine were averagely well-off and one was well-off, using the mixed criterion of structure of consumption, forms of social participation and *per capita* income.

To complete the picture for Voronezh, it should be said that two of the 1996 unemployed had found work, and by the time of the 1997 survey one of them was working, while the other had joined the group in insecure employment. They both belonged to the 'averagely well-off' group and were engaged in the entrepreneurial type of economic activity. There were six people in the 'poor' category who did not fall into any of the other groups in the foregoing analysis. Three of them were one-parent families with two or more children under 18; one was a one-parent family with one child; one was a two-parent family with a ratio of three dependants to two employed people; and one was a two-parent family with a child. It was largely their particular family circumstances that had pushed them into the poor group.

We can now summarise the conclusions of our analysis of the relationship between poverty and unemployment within the overall framework of our research. First the poor and the unemployed are mutually overlapping sets; they do coincide for the most part, but they are not identical.

Second, in Moscow, St. Petersburg and to some extent Voronezh, the primary cause of real poverty, and especially for profound poverty, was the respondents' family circumstances. These circumstances prevented people from taking their place as effective employees on the labour market, and kept them among the unemployed; and in those cases where respondents from 'risk group' families actually found work, they mainly stayed in the 'poor' category anyway, or at best moved up to be among the 'badly-off'.

Third, there were significant regional differences between the poor. In Moscow and St. Petersburg, the only addition to the traditional types of the 'old poor' was the single middle-aged person with health problems, while the 'new poor' were actually the 'badly-off', whose situation before the reforms was substantially better than now, with the result that they perceive their current circumstances as a disaster. In Voronezh, on the other hand, people perfectly well able to work had fallen into the 'poor' category - including people with families where there were other employed people and where the family dependency ratio did not exceed 1:1.

Fourth, analysis of real material circumstances enabled us to identify certain social types among our respondents, which correlated with their place in the stratification system. As far as the long-term unemployed were concerned, these types were: one-parent families with small children; single people of pre-pension age, often in poor health; married women with pre-school children; middle-aged and elderly married women either from families without dependants where the husband worked, or from large families (4-5 members or more) where several members worked.

Distinct social types were also discernible in terms of the material circumstances criterion. Thus, the indigent and poor were represented by five main types:

- one-parent families with children under 18
- families with children under 18 where parents were disabled
- single people of pensionable or pre-pension age in poor health
- families of suggested alcoholics
- members of families with a high dependency ratio on the employed.

All these types appeared among the registered or *de facto* unemployed, and even those who belonged to the group in insecure employment did not have any real occupation. The only exception was the suggested alcoholics, of whom there were two in the study.

Moving on from the poor to the badly-off, the list of social types is enlarged by the categories of: young married women with small children; married middle-aged women in poor health in a two-person household, the second of whom was always employed; middle-aged single people with relatively normal health; one-parent families where the adult member of the family worked; and some two-parent families with two children. In general, one might say that almost no-one was in a position to keep a family with more than one dependant per working member in the 'well-off' or 'prosperous' category. One dependant per two employees was the maximum ratio enabling the majority of families to be among the well-off or averagely well-off. In some isolated cases, the ratio was one dependant per employee, but not more.

Fifth, given identical household composition in the same city, occupational status could, as a rule, only exert influence as far as placing the household in the badly-off or averagely well-off groups was concerned. Only in St. Petersburg, among people in households with no dependants and with a fairly limited range of occupational statuses, could a relationship be traced between the occupational status of the respondents and their position in the well-off or prosperous strata. In almost all other cases, the respondents' material circumstances were governed not so much by occupational status as by the effectiveness of the survival strategies they employed.

Sixth, the survival strategies used by the poor to improve their material circumstances were more varied than the strategies of all the others. They contained more passive or destructive types of action, however, and active or constructive types of action were more rarely encountered. Among the 'old poor' the marginal type of economic activity was more commonly found, with destructive or passive forms of behaviour, than among the 'new poor', for whom constructive or active types of activity dominated (with attempts to earn extra money and engage in small-scale trading, including sale of produce from a *dacha*), belonging in Rose's (1993a) classification to entrepreneurial types of economic activity. This pattern, however, was perceptible more as a trend than as a strong relationship.

Household Survival Strategies

In the earlier sections of this chapter we have made a detailed analysis of the material circumstances of the households surveyed, and of the interdependence of poverty and unemployment. In the course of our analysis we became convinced that, although the majority of the poor were in fact unemployed, and most of the unemployed were poor or badly-off, the cause of poverty lay not in the simple fact of losing one's job, but rather in the respondent's characteristics as a person, which were in turn linked with their household composition and health. Furthermore, their current circumstances are, in most cases, a result of an entirely conscious and rational choice, since many unemployed people openly admit that they are not interested in finding work (22 out of 31 registered unemployed people stated various reasons why they were not interested in working).

In analysing these issues, problems of household survival were also partially touched on, as were the resources used to survive. These are so important, however, that they need special consideration. How do unemployed people manage to survive, given the pitifully low unemployment benefit that most of them receive?

In tackling this question, it is worth comparing our data with the results of Dean and Taylor-Gooby's research into unemployment in England, in order to help us gain a more detailed understanding of the circumstances of unemployed people in Russia. To start with, in terms of both numbers and actual employment status, the sub-sample of unemployed people in the second phase of our research was fairly similar to the English sample, although various types of partial employment were more prevalent among the Russian unemployed. In fact, 79 per cent were fully unemployed in England and 65 per cent in Russia; six per cent of the English unemployed had unregistered employment and seven per cent in Russia; and partial employment or additional earnings were enjoyed by 15 per cent of the English respondents and 28 per cent of those in Russia. Thus, additional earnings were a source of livelihood alongside unemployment benefit for one in four Russian unemployed people and one in seven in England.

A second important difference between the circumstances of the unemployed in Russia and those of their English counterparts is the potential to draw on help from friends and relations to relieve those circumstances. In contrast to England, traditions of solidarity and mutual assistance are very strong; and the list of those on whom one can count for help is much longer among Russians Table 8.12).

What is obviously making itself felt here is a different structure of social contact and of forms of social participation, which characterises the unemployed in Russia. The lives of 20 per cent of the English unemployed were totally devoid of social contact, whereas in Russia the equivalent figure was only 1 per cent. But then, regular contact with friends and relatives without organised forms of recreation (such as clubs) or involvement in public life (political, religious organisations) were typical of only one-third of the English unemployed and of half of the Russians. A lifestyle in which contact with friends and relations was accompanied by participation in the activities of religious and, to a much lesser extent, other social organisations was substantially more common among the Russian unemployed (26 per cent as against 16 per cent in England).

Table 8.12 Social resources of unemployed people in Russia and England - n (per cent)

Whose help they can count on	Russia		England	
	Persons	per cent	persons	per cent
Parents/grandparents	125	52	22	26
Brothers/sisters	81	34	5	6
Sons/daughters	33	14	9	11
Former spouse	17	7	1	1
Friend	103	43	7	8
Neighbours	31	13	-	-
Colleagues	58	24	-	-
Boss	12	5	20	24
No-one	45	19	2	2

Moreover, for the majority of the Russian unemployed, in contrast to their English counterparts, the current situation is still not 'extreme', and they have certain reserves to fall back on even if their present sources of income dry up. There were 62 per cent in Russia as compared to 52 per cent in England who would approach friends or relations or find themselves a job. Meanwhile, roughly equal proportions of respondents (19 per cent in England and 21 per cent in Russia) could not give a definite answer as to what they would do in the event of their present income being lost, and there was also an identical proportion who would give preference to actions such as 'I would sell my possessions or live on my savings' (nine per cent in each case) or 'I would commit suicide' (one per cent in each case). On the other hand 12 per cent of the unemployed in England would resort to crime or prostitution, and seven per cent would ask for charity, whereas the corresponding figures in Russia are only three per cent and two per cent, i.e. four times fewer. We should add that Russians were provided with a certain 'safety margin' by their housing circumstances - there was not a single homeless person among them, whereas in England the figure was 11 per cent - and about a third owned their own, albeit very modest, accommodation (in England none of the respondents owned their own accommodation).

Thus both the extent of social contact and the closely-related social resources at the disposal of Russians, coupled with their particular housing circumstances and the possibilities of finding a job, enabled them to have somewhat more confidence in their circumstances than their English colleagues. Although their level of income placed them in worse circumstances (40 per cent of English unemployed people were able to buy newspapers regularly, for example, and only 18 per cent of Russians), this correlated with the lower standard of living in Russia among the population at large as compared to England.

Having considered the specific nature of sources of survival for the Russian unemployed in comparison with their colleagues in England, let us now look at how their circumstances differed from those of other Russians. The basis we shall use for this comparative analysis is the data obtained by Rose (1993b).

Taken overall, the circumstances of the members of our 'labour market crisis groups' were significantly worse than those of the average Russian as presented by Rose's data. In his research, for example, the material circumstances of 20 per cent of respondents were better than five years previously; but in our sample, only 9 per cent were in this situation. The comparatively worse circumstances of the members of labour market crisis groups in our sample were obviously explained by the substantial differences between their sources of income. Thus, help from friends and relatives constituted a source of income for one in twenty of Rose's respondents and for one in four in our research. Benefits and pensions were valuable as sources of income for 22 per cent in Rose's sample and 48 per cent in our research. Although the role of unemployment benefit was relatively minor for most of the respondents, two facts were of fundamental importance: 1) among the registered unemployed, the number for whom the benefit played an important part in their income or constituted the basis of household income increased by one-and-a-half times over the year, rising to 58 per cent of all registered unemployed in 1997; 2) of the 18 unemployed people, for whom unemployment benefit played an important part or was the basis of income in 1997, two-thirds were long-term unemployed who had also been unemployed in 1996. Moreover, in 1996 too, benefit had played an important part or been the basis of income for half of them. We may therefore talk of a particular stratum developing among the unemployed, comprising people living on benefit and not wishing to find a job.

The scale of this phenomenon is not all that great, however, since the number of people for whom benefit played an important role in family income constituted only one-fifth of the long-term unemployed. But if we also add in those long-term unemployed who receive assistance from relatives, the number of people living not on earnings but on State benefits of one kind or another or on money provided by friends and relatives comes up to about one-third of the long-term unemployed. At the same time, such a life is the result of conscious choice for most of them, since it is impossible for them to radically alter their circumstances by finding a job, or because various factors mean they are unwilling to find work - it is not the consequence of a dependency culture. For such respondents, poverty is definitely not a factor pushing them towards finding a job, since for them (as we demonstrated in the previous section of this chapter using specific examples and consolidated figures concerning the composition of the poor) finding work in the current labour market situation would not mean any perceptible change whatever in their circumstances. It is no surprise that 89 per cent of them named poor pay at the jobs on offer among the reasons why they had turned down work. Most typical in this respect were the circumstances of single mothers with children under 18 and of single middle-aged women or women coming up to pensionable age with poor health who, as we showed above, constitute the main body of the poor long-term unemployed. Young married women with small children in the badly-off category are in a similar situation; for them too, their current employment situation is a result of rational choice.

When discussing details of survival strategies for members of labour market crisis groups, we must not forget also that the large amount of free time at the disposal of unemployed people and people in insecure employment gave rise to additional earnings over and above their main wages or salary: these were a source of income for 39 per cent of our respondents, compared to only 21 per cent of Russians in Rose's research. At the same time, the number of households and the spouse's employment status in the samples for the two studies were virtually identical, and the average Russian actually had more children under 18 than those in our research. Thus, the above-mentioned differences between sources of income in our data and in Rose's were not connected with characteristics of the households: they arose out of the respondent's own employment situation.

Comparison of our respondents' survival strategies with those adopted by their English colleagues and by ordinary Russians shows that Russians in this situation, especially the long-term unemployed and people who had spent some time on unpaid leave, have a fairly characteristic structure of survival strategies, in which additional earnings and help from various sources feature large. The main source of this help is relations and friends, although for roughly one-third of the long-term unemployed the benefits they receive also play an important part. Assessment of the part played by various social transfers in family income might be substantially higher if the respondents included in their calculation those types of benefit they receive not as unemployed people, but as ordinary Russian citizens, since Welfare State traditions that still prevail in Russia mean that the most meaningful social transfers are received by the public at large, and not just the poor. Two-thirds of housing maintenance costs, including the provision of electricity, more than half of telephone rental charges and all the cost of local telephone calls, as well as two-thirds of the cost of travel on public transport, are paid for by the State and municipal authorities. In total, this amounts to roughly 500,000 roubles per household (1997), and still excludes free education, health care, pre-school facilities and all kinds of benefits and payments in kind (for example, child benefits, which have up to now been received by all parents without exception, free breakfasts and dinners at school, free text-books, subsidies for children's music schools, and so on). Therefore, the relatively modest payments that our respondents were receiving as unemployed people were not such as to create any 'dependency culture' among them over and above what might be present among the general public.

At the same time, wide dispersion of the standards of living across our sample - even those with similar household composition - forced us to look at the question of differences between the comparative effectiveness of various survival strategies in improving the material circumstances of the respondents. Let us first, however, list the strategies we have in mind. By way of hypothesis, we identified the following possible survival strategies for unemployed people and those in insecure employment:

- registered unemployment with receipt of corresponding benefit plus various types of additional earning;
- receipt of unemployment benefit and of other types of income which do not lead to a reduction in the respondents' economic potential

(i.e. property, financial resources, etc. which do not derive from the sale of possessions or from 'eating into' savings);

- receipt of unemployment benefit plus drawing on savings or sale of possessions;
- the three variants mentioned above, but without unemployment benefit (for the *de facto* unemployed and those on long-term unpaid leave);
- steady full-time employment (unregistered employment), which might be accompanied by formal unemployed status or being on long-term unpaid leave. Nine of our respondents were in this situation.

As our research showed, each of these strategies did actually exist in its pure form in the sample. At the same time, in the great majority of cases these strategies were combined in various permutations. In addition, where a household had other members, there was also the possibility of surviving on their earnings, including pensions (which were as high as 1.5 million roubles in some cases), and their other sources of income.

In view of this variety of possible strategies, our initial objective was amended, and an attempt was made to determine the effectiveness of the elements built into the strategies rather than the strategies as a whole; these elements included the main types of income received and the ways in which they were obtained:

Table 8.13 Main sources of household income - n (per cent)

Different sources of income	*Whole sample*	
Wages of other family members	144	(61)
Casual earnings	93	(40)
Pension	83	(35)
Smallholding, garden, allotment (incl. at *dacha*)	72	(30)
Help from other relatives	50	(21)
Personal savings	26	(11)
Student grant	22	(9)
Maintenance for a child	17	(7)
Single parent's allowances	9	(4)

Analysis of the sample revealed there to be just two significant factors affecting income/property stratification (leaving aside the actual fact of finding a job, which of course in most cases had a noticeable impact on the material circumstances of the respondents): the respondent or other family members working on a permanent basis somewhere other than in their main job; and the presence of pay received by other family members as a steady source of income in the household.

Let us next look in turn at each of these factors, beginning with finding a full-time main job. About half the respondents had experienced a change in status and type of employment during the year between the surveys; and these changes were very unevenly distributed. Overall, it could be said that those who were working at the time of the first survey, albeit in insecure employment, were for the most part working (and often more securely) at the time of the second survey.

Meanwhile, those who were unemployed at the time of the first survey mostly continued out of work. We shall deal with how respondents found work in more detail in Chapter 9, but for now we should just say that, in the vast majority of cases, whether or not the respondents found work was determined solely by their desire to do so, which was linked in turn to what they required in a job, to their health, family situation and so on.

However, as a form of income, the wages of other family members were no less important to the respondent's material circumstances than getting a job. The absence or presence of other family members' wages had an impact not only on the level of welfare of the family generally, but also on the dynamic of change in this level:

Table 8.14 Change in households' standard of living in relation to the presence of wages of other family members - n (per cent)

Material circumstances	Wages of other family members present	No wages from other family members	Total
deteriorated	54 (38)	46 (50)	100 (43)
unchanged	59 (41)	36 (39)	94 (40)
improved	31 (21)	10 (11)	41 (17)
Total	144 (100)	93 (100)	237 (100)

This is somewhat of a given, bearing in mind that we have already concluded it is the family dependency ratio that is of crucial importance to the material circumstances of a household - the number of employed people to the number of dependants in the family.

Finally, one additional important factor in determining the material circumstances of households was whether household members had several jobs. A total of 75 respondents were active in this way (including steady involvement in small-scale street trading). One-third of those with secure secondary employment indicated that their circumstances had improved over the intervening year, and less than a quarter said they had deteriorated (the corresponding figures for those not holding down two or more jobs simultaneously were 12 per cent and 48 per cent).

Such forms of relatively stable employment as small-scale trading and self-employment were also fairly effective, especially for those who had not yet reached pension age. Of those who had been involved in street trading, one-third had managed to improve their material circumstances over the previous year (as against 16 per cent across the rest of the sample), and only 20 per cent thought that their standard of living was worse than other people's (as against 41 per cent across the rest of the sample). In this respect, involvement in street trading produced more perceptible results than the sale of food grown at a *dacha*. This latter was, in the main, an activity of those whose standard of living had fallen over the last year, and who themselves assessed their circumstances as bad.

This brings us to the question of types of action that were not effective in terms of their results, despite being widely used by the most deprived contingent of the respondents. These were primarily elements in the survival strategy which were associated with use of existing family possessions. In the previous section of this chapter we have already pointed out, taking the Moscow sample as an example, how widespread was the sale of possessions in an attempt to improve one's material circumstances, especially among indigent and poor people. The same trend can be seen in the sample as a whole. In all three cities, in terms of assessment of one's own circumstances as compared to those of others, two-thirds of the group of people selling their possessions referred to their standard of living as worse than other people's and described their material circumstances as bad (the equivalent figure for the sample as a whole was just over 40 per cent). Moreover, there was no-one who said that their standard of living was better than other people's or that their material circumstances were good. The highest percentage of those selling their possessions comprised people who were finding it impossible to put up with things any longer (22 per cent, as against 11 per cent of the rest). To sum up, then, all indicators showed that virtually everyone choosing this type of action was in dire circumstances. There was a total of 18 people selling possessions in the three cities studied. The 18 who were renting out property were enjoying distinctly better circumstances; but, although this measure was more effective (especially in Moscow and St. Petersburg, where rents are much higher than in Voronezh), respondents generally adopted it only when their circumstances had taken a turn for the worse, and not just to obtain extra income.

The second type of action which is also chosen by members of the most deprived groups is drawing on savings. True, in order to select this type of action they had to have savings. This alone suggests that the group who ate into their savings were already in somewhat less severe circumstances than those who sold possessions. Looking at all the factors together, including structure of consumption, lifestyle and *per capita* income, one could say that those who drew on their savings were people who had become impoverished recently, rather than people who really belonged to the poorest strata, and this was why they had a fairly stark view of their own circumstances. In line with this assessment, two-thirds of them (compared to 39 per cent in the rest of the sample) indicated that their circumstances had deteriorated during the past year. This was substantially more even than among those who had sold possessions, where only half said that their circumstances had deteriorated. The number who had eaten into savings was 32 (26 indicated savings as a source of family income). In contrast to those selling possessions, these were mainly 'new', not 'old' poor.

The deterioration in their circumstances in recent times ranks them alongside groups of people who had borrowed money to improve their circumstances (39 people) or who had received help from others (49). Among those who had borrowed money, almost two-thirds indicated a deterioration in their circumstances during the past year, compared to over half of those who had received financial help from relatives. At the same time, these types of income were conditional not only on the respondents' real level of welfare, but also by their level of expectations and their relatives' standard of living. In the poorest group, with an income of 200,000 roubles or less per person, almost half received help from relatives (42 per cent). But even in the relatively affluent group with an income of between 600,000 and 800,000 roubles, one in five was receiving similar assistance. There were even people with a *per capita* income exceeding 1.5 million roubles who were still receiving help from relatives.

The third type of activity which requires special comment is one-off additional earnings. The highest incidence of this type of activity was chiefly among those who thought that their standard of living was worse than other people's (43 per cent, compared to 37 per cent in the rest of the sample). The special feature of additional earnings as compared to all other survival strategies, though, consisted in the extraordinary heterogeneity of the actual material circumstances of those adopting this strategy. Dispersion was from indigent to prosperous, i.e. additional earnings were resorted to by members of all property groups (albeit to varying degrees). Taken overall, however, the effectiveness of additional earnings was substantially greater than that of sale of possessions or drawing on savings.

The prevalence of additional earnings clearly correlated with employment status. They were most common (two-thirds of the group) in the group with insecure employment, for whom this was a conscious survival strategy, in contrast to finding a job with steady employment. Next came the *de facto* unemployed (53 per cent of the group), some of whom, in objective terms, also belonged to the group with insecure employment; it was just that their compulsory unpaid leave had continued for so long that they had begun to class themselves as unemployed. Among the registered unemployed and those who had found work after a period of unemployment, one-third of respondents had some one-off additional earnings, as compared to one in four of those who had found normal employment without any period of unemployment. This is in line with other Russian Independent Institute of Social and Nationalities Problems (RIISNP) data for national samples.

The most common form of activity - self-sufficiency in foodstuffs grown at a *dacha* - was evenly distributed across all the groups identified in terms of their material circumstances. This leads us to suppose that it is less indicative of economic need than of socio-cultural traditions among Russians.

To conclude this review of the effectiveness of the survival strategies deployed, brief mention should be made of those who made no effort whatsoever to improve their material circumstances. This group mainly comprised the most affluent respondents. Thus, from the point of view of survival strategies, the 'well-off' and 'prosperous' grouping broke down into two uneven sections - some (the great majority) tried to earn as much as possible, holding down several jobs and having additional earnings, while others (roughly one in ten) did not try to do this. Having what by Russian standards was a good *per capita* income (1-1.5 million roubles), they stuck with this and were generally quite happy. One distinctive feature was the comparative youth of those who had an active drive to achieve and which of this group had additional earnings. Men were more common among them; they had a higher standard of education and, especially, a higher skills level. By contrast, in the 'averagely well-off' and 'badly-off' groups, education and skills were unrelated to material circumstances, while in the two poorest groups, those with higher education were 1.5-2 times less than for the sample as a whole.

Different survival strategies were thus quite closely associated with certain types of actor. We have discussed their features in relation to their property circumstances. But gender differences also had a significant bearing on the selection of a strategy. Among men there was a higher proportion oriented towards active forms of action, while among women the greater proportion used various passive forms of obtaining income. Thus 48.5 per cent of men and 32.6 per cent of women did work on the side. Meanwhile 26.1 per cent of women (14.1 per cent of men) took assistance from relatives, and 35.5 per cent of women (23.2 per cent of men) were working towards self-sufficiency in food. Unemployment benefit played quite an important part in income or constituted its basis for 40 per cent of the women who had ever received it, but for only a quarter of men.

In conclusion of our examination of the comparative effectiveness of survival strategies and the question of who uses them, we would like to emphasise that the relationships given above form a closed list. In the array of information analysed, there were no other correlations of any significance whatever between survival strategies and questions from the block on material circumstances or on types of actors which have not been mentioned above.

To sum up, then:

- The great majority of respondents took a broad range of actions which comprised their survival strategy, obtaining income from widely differing sources;
- The effectiveness of these strategies depended primarily on the effectiveness of the various types of action undertaken by the actor. The most effective strategy was to receive several secure salaries. This was done in three main ways - permanent employment of the respondent, permanent employment for other members of the household, and secondary employment for the respondent or members

of the family. Forms of the latter could vary, to include holding more than one job, self-employment and street trading;

- The prevalence of different sources of income and of different ways of obtaining them depended on the level and dynamic of change in the respondent's material welfare, the presence of particular resources, and the respondent's gender;

- Forms of survival strategy associated with dissipation of existing economic resources were common first and foremost among the most deprived section of the respondents. The sale of belongings was characteristic of people in absolute poverty, while drawing on savings, loans and receipt of help from others were characteristic of people whose descent into poverty was relative in nature;

- The selection of survival strategies was linked to the particular features of the resources at the disposal of the respondents. There was a particularly clear relationship to be traced between economic resources and such strategies as drawing on savings and partial self-sufficiency in food; there was also a relationship between social resources and the receipt of help from others or money loans; and there was a relationship between personality resources and steady employment in all its variants. However, survival strategies other than employment were not very effective and had no perceptible impact in improving respondents' material circumstances.

Resources and Household Status: Personality Effects Where Structure is Fluid

The issue of what part various resources play in the stratification process is a key problem in contemporary sociology, both in Russia and abroad. The tradition, which dates back to Weber, of considering the economic, power and socio-cultural potential (resource) has been modified in the conceptions of contemporary sociologists into an enormous number of sets of various types of resource which determine the status niche of an individual in the social field.

In non-Russian sociology, one of the most popular conceptions of the part played by various resources in stratification is that of Bourdieu. In Russian sociological literature, on the other hand, it is Shkaratan who has offered the most comprehensive views on resources significant in stratification. We have reviewed and compared these models in Chapter 4 (pp.107-110).

Analysis using the methodology described in Chapter 4 revealed the following. Firstly, and not surprisingly, our 'welfare threshold' characteristics are most closely related to our integrated criterion of welfare (which primarily takes into account the structure of consumption and lifestyle, and also to some extent socio-psychological discomfort and forms of social participation). Secondly, many questions concerned responses which were a consequence, not a cause, of the respondent's being in a certain status niche (for example, responses to questions related to having small children, including help looking after them and so on, reflected the fact that the material circumstances of respondents in families with small children were usually worse than on average across the sample). Thirdly, when such 'thresholds' and 'consequences' items had been removed, it became clear that, in the Russian situation, the most important characteristics which influenced the respondents' circumstances and were important in determining the comparative significance of 'situational' and 'personality' factors were the following (given in descending order of significance and without taking into account the direction of the relationship: the number of relationships with the questions that fell into the block of 27 questions under analysis are shown in brackets):

- (highest ranking) proportion of outgoings spent on food (20);
- not owning any real property (16);
- agreeing with granting concessions to private business to help overcome unemployment (14);
- the 'interest level' of the current job and the *per capita* income (13 each);
- such personality characteristics as: more than three rejections of jobs following interviews with employers; the presence of expectations of paternalism (12 each);
- work in heavy industry and the defence industry, which are experiencing a crisis; the desired amount of wages as an aspect of the respondent's level of aspirations (11 each);
- mass redundancies at the respondent's place of work; holding down several jobs; non-receipt of salary over the past six months; certain aspects of health and the respondents' references to their health as an obstacle to obtaining a good job; neighbours - at home rather than at the *dacha* - forming a constant circle of informal social contact;

confidence in the role of retraining as an important way of overcoming unemployment; rejecting a job because it does not match respondent's qualifications/skills (10 each);

- age; complaints about the stressful nature of the job; complaints of headaches; lack of any form of concession or other forms of social assistance at the respondent's workplace or that of family members; friends at work forming the stable circle of informal social contacts; being in an occupation in which it is impossible to find work; lack of desire to seek work and, at the time of the 1996 survey, lack of concern about getting it; conviction that age is a restricting factor on obtaining a good job while a high skills level helps in finding one; and finally the conviction that the non-scientific intelligentsia are the grouping which has suffered most under the economic reforms in Russia (9 each).

If we try to systematise this ragbag of various indicators, we see that, with the exception of the proportion of expenditure going on food, which is an integral characteristic of welfare and lifestyle for the household generally, the other characteristics fall into groups as follows. Of Bourdieu's categories of classification, economic resources are of the greatest importance for Russia, including:

- presence of real property, utilisation of which may not provide any direct economic benefit, but has generally been a sign of persistent poverty or of a family having been badly-off since pre-reform days, and indirectly confirms that the family lacks any hidden potential to improve its circumstances; the fact that these really are people whose material circumstances were not good even before the reforms is clear from the age composition of the grouping, if nothing else - 50 of the 91 people without any real property were aged over 40;
- level of *per capita* income;
- the sector in which the respondent works and whether there were mass redundancies at their place of work in the six months before the survey: this is a specific form of economic resource associated with the features of our respondents' labour market niche;
- the possibility of receiving more than one income from stable secondary employment;
- non-receipt of salary at the main place of work during the last six months.

Symbolic resources were generally without significance, and social resources were virtually insignificant. To be more precise, two-thirds of our respondents indicated that the social resource of 'contacts and connections' played a part in obtaining a good job; but it was a specific feature of our sample, into which fell - by definition - people who in the vast majority of cases had no such connections, that we could not establish any effective role for this resource. As to distinguishing between people who had either relations or friends as their main circle of social contacts, the percentage of each group who had managed to find work over the year of observation was almost exactly the same. It would appear that social contact mainly with relations reflects, in a concentrated form, a more traditional and patriarchal, non-urbanised lifestyle, and is typical of a type of person with a less mobile psyche, who finds it more difficult to adapt to the changes of recent years. Social contact with friends correspondingly typifies a more urbanised and mobile lifestyle and individual, and therefore the circle of social contact is more a feature of personality than of social resource.

Finally, cultural resources also had no great significance - or, to be more precise, it was the respondent's skills (but not their education) that were significant. Moreover, it was not the level of skills that was significant, but rather their particular characteristics, such as the respondent's trade or profession. Furthermore, only a very narrow range of occupations played a positive role in stratification, and mainly only in St. Petersburg. For the rest of the respondents, occupation was often a factor that made it more difficult - or even impossible - to find work 'in one's usual occupation': which was, not surprisingly, a consequence of the restructuring of the Russian economy.

The main mass of factors which determine the status niche of our respondents, though, failed altogether to fit into Bourdieu's classification, or more precisely could be assigned to what he called habitus and left out of his classification of resources.

Shkaratan's conception of resources, on the other hand, contained a large number of resource types which were on the list obtained as a result of processing our research materials. Thus, the following coincided with his resources connected with the household: level and type of income, ownership of real property, the opportunity to choose various household survival strategies and the opportunity to use various forms of social support. In resources connected with the respondent's environment, it was 'contacts and connections' (with the same amendments as applied to Bourdieu's social resources). The resources which he classified as respondent-related resources could effectively be split into two groups.

Some were objective in nature. For our sample, the significant ones were age, health and the sector where the respondent worked (here the only significant aspect was whether they belonged to the sectors worst affected by crisis, for example the heavy and defence industries). Others, meanwhile, related more to the socio-psychological sphere, and it was specifically these which gave Shkaratan's conception the edge where heuristic potential was concerned. This means above all what Shkaratan termed 'potential for active mobilisation of one's own resources', and included level of aspirations, willingness to change the conditions and content of one's activities, and the existence of secondary employment. In point of fact, behind such characteristics as three or more rejected job offers, lack of desire to change one's occupation when there are no jobs in it, and stating a desired level of pay, there actually lies a willingness to change the conditions and content of one's activities and a certain level of aspirations. Much has already been said above concerning the role of secondary employment as a very important resource in a survival strategy, and it was ranked seventh.

There were also some other socio-psychological characteristics which turned out to be significant. Foremost among these was the 'market orientation' of the respondents, which indirectly indicated their degree of adaptation to market conditions. There was also the presence of expectations of 'paternalism' - the Russian equivalent of 'dependency culture'. For Russia, this issue is not discussed in terms of 'dependency', but in terms of 'paternalism', since a centuries-old tradition has led to the great majority of the population being convinced that the State is obliged to look after them, and this point of view is also still enshrined in the minds of the political élite (the 'compensatory' function of social policy). The watershed lay between the position 'my material circumstances are dependent solely (or largely) on the economic situation in Russia' and that of 'my material circumstances are dependent solely (or largely) on me'. This block of questions on expectations of paternalism also covered varying attitudes to registration with the Employment Service (ES), in the event that a respondent lost their job again. Here the divide lay primarily between those who would go to the ES because they needed the unemployment benefit and those who would not do so because they felt that additional earnings would provide them with far more money than benefit would and that the ES had been set up for those not in a position to help themselves. The hypothesis put forward at the outset that values would also feature among the factors of greatest significance was not confirmed in practice. Values did figure among statistically significant factors, it is true, but they ranked only 16th in significance (out of a possible 21), and the only one that was significant even to this minor extent was the value of individualism in contrast to the conformist value 'it is better to live like other people than to stand out from the crowd' and of wage levelling in contrast to equality of opportunity.

Nevertheless, we can use these values to demonstrate how even such statistically weak dependencies operated on the central questions of the block on material welfare. We can start with attitudes of individualism/conformism and examine them through the prism of the question on *per capita* income (Table 8.15).

While conformist values are somewhat more widespread among the low-income groups (up to 600,000 roubles per person, i.e. up to one-and-a-half times the Subsistence Minimum) than those of individualism, from the 600,000 threshold upwards we begin to see a rise in individualistic values, and in the most affluent groups (with an income in excess of 1 million roubles, i.e. 2.5 times the Subsistence Minimum) the ratio of individualistic to conformist attitudes becomes 10:1. We have no reason to suppose that this is a consequence rather than a cause of belonging to a given group. Why not? Well, firstly, such attitudes are fairly persistent, and the majority of members of the low-income groups commented that they had previously lived much better, and indeed recent downward social mobility was typical of their situation. Thus these attitudes had been shaped under different conditions and were not simply associated with belonging to lower strata.

Table 8.15 Per capita income of those espousing individualistic/conformist values (millions of roubles per person)

Income	Stand out from the crowd	Live like other people	Total
< 0.2	15	15	30
0.2 - 0.4	34	40	74
0.4 - 0.6	27	28	55
0.6 - 0.8	16	12	28
0.8 - 1	9	11	20
1 - 1.5	10	2	12
> 1.5	10	0	10
Total	121	108	229

Secondly, analysis of data from representative surveys of Russians by RIISNP showed that downward or upward social mobility in the under-30 age groups was related primarily with place of residence (in the capital, a major city, a medium-sized town, a small town, a village or a hamlet). For the 30-40 age group, it was associated with values; and for the over-40 age group the relationship was with mobility of the psyche and with values (Tikhonova, 1997a). Bearing in mind the age characteristics of our sample, we have no particular reason to be surprised at the importance of values.

The same jump is also shown by the values attributed to equality of income versus equality of opportunity. Starting from an income of 600,000 roubles, the ratio of supporters of an equal opportunities society to supporters of an equal income society, which had up to this point risen steadily from 1.5 to 3, suddenly jumps to a ratio of 4:1 in favour of the former, while in the more affluent groups with an income exceeding 1 million roubles it reaches 6:1.

In this respect, one feature of Russians generally and of our respondents in particular needs further comment, although it has no direct connection with the issue of resources; because without appreciating this feature, it is impossible to understand either the behaviour of many unemployed people, or their apparently absurd rejection of jobs offered (even in cases where the respondent would agree to change his occupation), or their own assessment of their material circumstances. This feature is the non-economic nature of the way they think. We shall not especially dwell here on the reasons why they have this characteristic, discussed in depth elsewhere (Tikhonova, 1996b, 1997b, 1997c, 1997d; Tikhonova and Shchepurenko, 1998); we shall restrict ourselves to stating that the preconditions for it are related to an issue of civilisation, to the fact that Russia has not as yet been through the capitalist stage of development, with its inherent dominance of economic values. There is just one fact that we shall highlight here - that a substantially higher proportion of our respondents were bearers of a non-economic mentality/habitus, with its dissociation of economic circumstances and interests, on the one hand, from values on the other, than was the case in representative surveys of the Russian population conducted by RIISNP. Thus when more affluent Russians were asked to express a preference between interesting work and pay, as pair values, the results were different from those of our respondents.

One would expect the value attributed to pay in low-income groups to be greater than the value attributed to the content of work. Among the indigent and poor, however, the ratio of those choosing interesting work over pay was 1.3:1. Among the badly-off this ratio was 1.5:1. Meanwhile, in the affluent groups of respondents who had nonetheless found their way into employment crisis groups, this ratio was 1.1:1, and for a representative survey of Russians in March 1997 it was 0.5:1. These results match data from Chernina's (1994) investigation of unemployed people in Novosibirsk, which demonstrated the role of 'interesting work' specifically for the poorest contingent of the unemployed. Thus, just as there are groups with different types of value systems among the Russian general public, among our respondents too the picture was mixed, although the ratio of representatives of different value systems for Russia as a whole and among crisis groups within the population was directly inverse.

To complete our review of the role played by different resources, let us look at what caused the dynamic of change in the material circumstances of the respondents over the year between the surveys. We can start by saying that it was governed by very much more rational factors than those we have looked at above or which governed their material circumstances generally. Thus, the factors which caused changes in the respondents' material circumstances included virtually the entire list of changes to their employment status.

In descending order of significance and covering both direct and inverse dependencies, they took the following form: finding work (among those who had found work there were almost three times more people who recorded an improvement in their material circumstances than among those who had not found work), having additional earnings, starting to receive a pension, successful start-up of a business, having secondary employment, being made redundant more than once during the year, and successful completion of re-training courses. Among non-economic factors, significant relationships included the respondents' conviction that they are playing an important part in things (direct dependence), the existence of a psychological barrier in job-seeking, the presence of more than three unemployed people in the respondent's immediate circle, and one's customary social circle consisting of relations (inverse dependence). In addition, there was a very clear difference between age groups, in both material circumstances and their dynamic of change.

Age was also very closely linked with a certain level and type of aspirations, with the degree of mobility of the psyche, and with the capacity to adapt to new realities. In the under-40 age groups, therefore, between 35 per cent and 42 per cent thought that life was reasonable and they could get by perfectly all right, while only 3.5 per cent felt they could not carry on any longer in their present circumstances; whereas in the 41-60 age groups the picture was the reverse. Only about 15 per cent felt that life was quite bearable, while about 20 per cent felt they had come to the end of their tether and could no longer put up with their circumstances. Age differences were even more clearly apparent in assessment of the dynamic of change in material welfare. The 51-60 age group were 'losers', and the 26-30 age group were 'winners' (see Table 8.15), while the most affluent circumstances according to the integral criterion of comparing one's circumstances to those of other people were found among those in the 31-40 age band.

These, therefore, are the main results of our analysis of the comparative significance of different types of resource in determining the respondents' level of welfare and its dynamic of change. But there was another, no less interesting aspect to the question - which factors played a crucial part: those linked to 'situational' variability, or those linked to 'personality' variability? What was the most important thing - the objective situation associated with the individual's place in the social system and prescribing actions of a certain type, or the respondent's personality features, which govern the actions of a rational actor?

If we look at our results from this angle, it is clear that limitations arising from the objective situation of the individual were few. To begin with, household composition was one of these 'objective' factors. A high family dependency ratio meant relatively less good circumstances for those respondents, while certain types of household (one-parent families with children, single women coming up to pensionable age, and so on) showed a tendency to concentrate among the poor and the long-term unemployed. At the same time, if we disregard single people and one-parent families, our sample was generally in line with household structure for Russia, and therefore being a member of any other type of family could not affect either the respondent's falling into a crisis group or his level of welfare. Thus, an important characteristic of the respondents' objective situation such as the composition of their households operated as a determining factor for only a very narrow range of people, and even then could be traced rather as a strong trend than as a strict rule. For others, meanwhile, it left fairly wide room for manoeuvre.

In the second place, in a situation where the economy is being restructured, the sector the respondent works in is an important characteristic: however, this was only of significance in two cases - for those employed in a) heavy industry, or b) the defence industry, both of which are experiencing a crisis. Those who did not wish to leave these industries had a relatively lower level of welfare than the rest. The importance of this factor, however, was in no way self-contained: after all, in 1996 the number of respondents working in these industries was 62, whereas by 1997 it had dropped to only 28. This question will be dealt with in more detail in Chapter 9; the only important point that we want to make here is that the labour market in contemporary Russia presents fairly broad possibilities of finding work for those who are prepared to exercise occupational mobility and to change the conditions and content of their activities.

In the third place, other situational limiters which influenced and helped to determine levels of welfare were mass redundancies at the respondents' enterprises and long-term failure to pay wages, for example working at an enterprise which was in crisis. And indeed, analysis of the composition of the group of people who had not received wages for some considerable time shows that more than half of them were on compulsory unpaid leave or *de facto* unemployed (the majority of whom were also on unpaid leave, but for such a long time that all contact with their enterprise had effectively withered away). We have already discussed in our treatment of survival strategies what it is that keeps people at such enterprises and why they do not try to find work elsewhere, and we shall return to this question in Chapter 9. Let us just say for now that it is a fully conscious and rational choice, arising out of the personal predilections of the respondents.

Let us now summarise what has been said:

- Taking all resource characteristics into account, we may state that it was the features of the respondent's position on the labour market that were of crucial importance in determining the status niche of members of those strata which found themselves victims of economic restructuring or of the increasing demands placed on employees in a market economy; and the most important of these features were those associated with particular aspects of the respondent's personality. If we draw on Bourdieu's classification, then the only components which came into operation were those of economic potential linked to the individual's position on the labour market, and in fact only a very restricted number of them. Standard of education and skills level, for example, were of no significance. Trade or profession was important for a narrow range of specialist and white-collar occupations. On the other hand 'habitus', which Bourdieu failed to include in his list of resources at all and which played no particular part in stratification, was significant. If we go to Shkaratan's classification, the category of greatest importance in actual stratification was the potential for effective utilisation of one's own resources;

- Among the main types of resource governing the level and dynamic of change in material circumstances, apart from the respondent's position on the labour market, a crucial part was also played by personality factors. Primary among these were the ones which enabled a person to adapt to the labour market, and to accept the new 'rules of the game'. The general statement may be made that those respondents who had lower potential to adapt tended to 'get stuck' in the groups of unemployed and employees in insecure employment. Despite a progressive deterioration in their material circumstances, they could not or did not want to accept the realities prevailing in contemporary Russia or to change the level and nature of their labour market aspirations, and in most cases hid behind references to their skills and to lack of jobs on the labour market. At the same time, the level of their job expectations was excessive. This led to their occupying a lower status niche across the entire range of significant factors;

- Differences between levels of ownership in households had almost no significance in determining the level of welfare of individuals, since the property resource very rapidly broke down in conditions where income was insufficient. Although during the early stages of a change in status, it constituted something of a reserve for the family to draw on, in the days of the USSR the amount of possessions held by the majority of Russians was so small and it was oriented so much towards personal consumption, that it had absolutely no perceptible impact on family circumstances. Respondents resorted to utilising possessions as a source of income only in case of extreme need or when their material circumstances had taken a sharp turn for the worse, but this use still did not enable families to break out of their state of poverty;

- Analysis of the comparative significance of 'situational' variability, reflecting the place of the individual in the socio-economic system, and 'personality' variability, reflecting the individual personality traits of the actor, and above all socio-psychological traits, revealed the crucial importance of the role of personality factors in determining the welfare of an individual. Of course we are not talking here about élite strata, who occupied a privileged position in the socio-economic system in pre-reform Russia and still do so now. Our conclusion applies only to that section of the population which did not belong to the privileged strata of pre-reform Russia, that is ordinary Russians.

9 Unemployment and Employment Strategies

Не имей сто рублей, а имей сто друзей
You don't need a hundred roubles if you have a hundred friends

In discussing the reasons why people fall into particular groups in relation to labour market crisis - referred to from now on as 'crisis groups' - we can distinguish between objective causes, subjective causes (as perceived by the respondent) and the official causes which are reflected in relevant documents. The last two groups of reasons will be reviewed in this section, and in the next section we will look at the objective causes of employment crisis.

The simplest picture is presented by official reasons for dismissal. In answering the question on this, most unemployed respondents in the first phase survey, as well as those who had found work after a period of unemployment, presented themselves as 'classically' unemployed in the sense that they had lost their jobs as a result of staff cuts (40 per cent), liquidation of the enterprise (7 per cent) or the end of a temporary contract (5 per cent). At the same time, almost half of the respondents (44 per cent) were people who gave the official reason for leaving their own job as 'voluntary'.

Subjectively, unemployed respondents, as well as those who had found work after a period of unemployment, connected their job losses with the problems faced by their sector or their enterprise (although in a number of cases there were no objective bases for this), and in the final analysis with the reforms currently under way in Russia. And in one particular sense they were right, since before the reforms it was seen as extraordinary for any employee to lose his job, and they must rarely have been affected by it. Nevertheless, it is true that a number of respondents gave fairly serious personal reasons as the cause of leaving their jobs such as poor relations with management, health reasons, and heavy family responsibilities. In all, these three reasons were cited as the causes of their having such serious employment problems by 30 per cent of unemployed respondents and 25 per cent of those under notice of redundancy.

A year later most of these people were registered as unemployed (twelve people) or were *de facto* unemployed (ten people). A particularly high percentage of those who cited health reasons as the real cause of leaving their

315

jobs were unemployed (70 per cent). Noticeably smaller, but still fairly large, was the percentage of unemployed people among those whose reason for employment crisis was conflict with management (42 per cent) and only 31 per cent of those who gave their family situation as the cause of their employment problem were unemployed. Thus, those who, in 1996, had linked their worsening employment problems with re-structuring of the economy, crisis in their sector or the position of their enterprise, had in the main been successful in finding work (26 per cent of them are registered unemployed or *de facto* unemployed, while 58 per cent have full-time employment). Those who had a personal basis for their worsening employment problems, especially poor health and difficulties in getting on with management, had remained or become unemployed.

It is necessary to say a few words separately about the reasons why people in insecure employment find themselves in crisis. The overwhelming majority of respondents from this group also gave the reason as the difficult position into which their enterprise had fallen, and many added to this the difficult position of their sector as a whole. This largely corresponded to reality, since they worked in sectors which were experiencing a crisis. The members of this group form the 'backbone' of any large enterprise. Their education, their length of service in their usual occupation, their experience of work as skilled specialists in white- or blue-collar jobs, the significance of work to them, their disciplined attitude, sex and age - all these were advantages displayed by this group in comparison with others.

Turning to the issue of the respondents' labour mobility (Table 9.1), the first thing to emphasise is that the changes within the groups demonstrated that the respondents' labour mobility was very high. Both the registered unemployed and those who had found work after a period of registered unemployment had a fairly large stable core which still existed a year later. In the registered unemployed group, this core was almost half (44 per cent), and, taking into account the *de facto* unemployed, was over 60 per cent. Among those who had found work (after a period of unemployment) in 1996, three-quarters of the group were still in stable work in 1997.

In the insecurely employed group, this core also existed, although it was relatively small - below 30 per cent - and it included both people in genuinely insecure employment and the *de facto* unemployed who had not broken off links with their enterprises. These were the oldest, most highly skilled specialists working in science, education and the military-industrial complex, whose characteristics were outlined in the description of the sample in Chapter 4. Only one in eight of this group had become unemployed and about half (30 people) are now working successfully - 22 of these had changed their workplace in order to get a job, and the circumstances of the rest at their enterprise had stabilised. Thus, in the insecurely employed group, the respondents' situation had turned out more successfully than for the registered unemployed.

Table 9.1   Redistribution of 1996 respondents from 1996 to 1997 - n (per cent)

1996 groups	*Unemployed (n=70)*	*Insecurely employed (n=58)*	*Redundancy (n=55)*	*Found work (n=55)*	*Total (n=241)*
1997 groups					
No reply	-	1 (2)	-	-	-
Unemployed	31 (43)	8 (13)	5 (9)	3 (6)	47 (19)
Insecurely employed	2 (3)	11 (19)	11 (19)	3 (6)	27 (10)
Redundancy	-	1 (2)	1 (2)	1 (2)	3 (2)
Found work	21 (29)	26 (43)	19 (33)	38 (67)	104 (43)
De facto unemployed	15 (22)	5 (9)	2 (4)	8 (15)	30 (12)
Normally employed	-	4 (8)	19 (33)	2 (4)	25 (10)
Self-employed	2 (3)	2 (4)	-	-	4 (3)

The situation in the group under notice of redundancy had turned out even more successfully. Either immediately or after an interval (in the first three months of unemployment, benefit is paid at 100 per cent of wages at the last workplace, so many people do not look for work immediately), two-thirds of this group had found work and only one in ten was unemployed (registered or *de facto*). Of course, this successful outcome is very relative: 31 people out of 170 who had been working in 1996 were now unemployed, while another 45 retained insecure labour market status. However, their situation was still qualitatively different from that which can be observed in the 'registered unemployed' group.

In all, over the time between the surveys, from all the groups taken together, 108 people changed job (45 per cent of the whole sample), i.e. the labour mobility of respondents was very high. Indirectly this yet again confirms that a fairly large number of job opportunities (but not of 'good' jobs!) is offered by the Russian labour market as a whole.

However, the overall picture of the dynamic of change in the respondents' employed/non-employed status alters fundamentally when viewed across the three cities. The most successful was the position in St. Petersburg, and the most difficult was the position in Voronezh. In St. Petersburg, almost half of those who had previously been unemployed had now found work (12 people, or 48 per cent), while in Voronezh only one person had managed to find work (7 per cent). Even more of those under notice of redundancy in St. Petersburg had found work - 13 people (87 per cent). This may indicate that, across the sample as a whole, the greatest success of all in finding work was in posts for skilled workers, of whom there were more in St. Petersburg.

The distribution of workers across sectors, forms of ownership and size of workforce at enterprises shows that the main flow of recruitment in 1997 was towards large (> 1,000 employees) joint-stock enterprises. This was particularly typical of St.Petersburg, where it was a new 1997 trend, since in 1996 recruitment went mainly towards large state enterprises. SMEs came a close second there in 1997, as they had done in 1996. However, the main body of the unemployed would either prefer to work in a State enterprise (25 per cent) or could not generally determine their preference (42 per cent). Not one person wanted to work in a large joint-stock enterprise, and only 16 per cent of the unemployed would like to work in private enterprises. Among those who had found work, on the other hand, although many also could not determine their preference, 28 per cent aspired to work in private and joint-stock enterprises.

From the point of view of redistribution of staff across sectors, the main outflow was from heavy industry and the defence industry (in 1997, 28 people worked in those sectors, as against 62 in 1996), while recruitment was above all towards trade (36 people in 1997, as against 22 in 1996) and also, although to a lesser extent, towards municipal housing and public utilities, transport, the construction industry and budget-funded sectors, from which there was also a large outflow of staff. In the sample tracked by our study, trends in redistribution of labour between sectors fully coincided with trends recorded by labour market statistics for the cities in the study.

What then, were the methods used in looking for work? Just as the survival strategies used varied greatly, there was great diversity of job-seeking strategies:

Table 9.2   Ways of looking for work - could choose more than one answer (%)

	Unemp-loyed	Average
I have applied to the ES	90	72
I am looking at advertisements	70	69
I am actively approaching relations	66	71
I am going directly to the enterprise	26	25
I am advertising myself	6	5
I am looking for work abroad	0	0
I am going on re-skilling courses	6	3
I am trying to set up my own business	3	7
I am doing casual work	20	26
I have used a private agency	10	9
Other	0	0

Detailed analysis of job-seeking strategies, shows that the unemployed preferred passive job-seeking strategies, for example, waiting for the Employment Service (ES) to suggest suitable work or reading job vacancy adverts, while 15 per cent generally did not do anything to seek work of their own accord. Those who had found work had sought it more actively - they more often applied to enterprises personally, placed job search adverts, asked for help from people they knew in finding work. However, in reality, there were actually only two main ways of finding work - finding work on the recommendation of people one knew, including former workmates (almost half of all those who had found work), and finding work through the ES (about a third of those who had found work).

In this connection, it is necessary to say something about respondents' assessments of the activities of the ES. In assessing various aspects of the ES's work, respondents were consistent in their responses to different questions. We should note straightaway that the attitude of ES staff towards respondents was on the whole assessed positively – two-thirds rated it as 'good' or 'excellent'. Practically no-one complained that they had been refused payment of benefit. Among the complaints, there were responses which demonstrated lack of understanding of the actual point of unemployment benefit, such as 'they told me that they couldn't accept my sick note'. And although, in addition, there were some respondents in the 1997 *de facto* unemployed group who complained that they had been taken off the unemployment register without warning, a check on this revealed that these were people whose period of unemployment was longer than a year and who had not been to the ES at the right time to sign off. However, the complicated procedure for claiming benefit (and above all the queuing at ES offices to make one's claim), given the relatively small amount of money involved, meant that, in total, about half of those who had ever been in receipt of benefit were happy with this area of the ES's activities, and another quarter were unhappy.

Positioning payment of benefit at the beginning of our analysis of the activities of the ES is not random; responses showed that their work has now been reduced mainly to the payment of benefit. Although most people did not apply to the ES so much to get benefit as in order to find suitable work or to get retrained (69 per cent), in practice the ES in its present form fails to meet these other aims. Although it does somehow manage to get some people jobs (we should remember that one-third of those who found work actually did so through the ES), the situation with retraining has been worse. And although, in a number of cases, the impossibility of the applicant getting work in his previous occupation was immediately clear, retraining had been suggested to only 17 respondents. This is related to the current ES practice of sending people for retraining generally only after they have been unemployed for a year. In addition, retraining is rather cut off from real life. Both the ES, which organises courses without taking into account real market demand for certain trades or professions, and the respondents themselves, whose aspirations to change occupation had little direct relationship to the problems of finding a job, were at fault in this.

In general, there was a fairly actively declared thrust towards changing occupation in both 1996 and 1997 - about half the respondents said that they would like to re-train. Moreover, out of the 44 per cent who wanted to change their occupation in 1997 (including 57 per cent of the unemployed), the majority could name the trade or profession that they wanted to enter, while many were even able to indicate the wage (as a rule, a high wage) which people currently working in this occupation command. But practically all these occupations are connected with skilled white-collar work, with about half wanting to enter jobs in the financial sector and the rest wanting to acquire the professions of computer programmer, P.A. to a managing director, fashion designer, simultaneous interpreter, lawyer, film or video camera operator, veterinary surgeon, economist, sociologist, psychologist, psychiatrist, trader forecaster, and so on. All these occupations demand several years familiarisation and then several more years to become proficient to the point where one can command the wage estimated by the respondents, and consequently such occupations are undoubtedly without prospects for most of our respondents, since the majority are no longer young. It is difficult to describe such 're-training' plans as anything other than detached from real life.

It is true that some people chose an occupation on a more realistic basis, naming trades such as plumber, vehicle fitter, driver, welder, carpenter and other blue-collar occupations with high pay levels. But since responses in this group also included ideas such as 'vehicle fitter or manager', we were forced to suppose that, at least for some of those who were set on blue-collar occupations, they were more in the way of hopes than real plans.

As far as jobs were concerned, the ES had mainly suggested to respondents either jobs which didn't suit them in terms of pay or jobs not commensurate with their skills. It may come as a surprise that, despite the allocation of colossal funds in Russia for the creation and preservation of jobs, the ES had not offered help in attempting to become self-employed, such as business start-up, to any member of the unemployed group, or those who had found work or those under notice of redundancy. Indeed the number of people in our sample who had tried to start up a business at their own risk was only a few dozen. It came as a revelation to most respondents that the ES has a general duty to assist in this.

As a result, in 1997, less than two-thirds of respondents would be prepared to register with the ES if they were to lose their jobs. The main motive which determined their intention to apply to the ES was 'I need unemployment benefit' (112 people), but the hope of finding a new job through the ES was held out by half this number - 57 respondents, who actually gave this as an accompanying motive to the receipt of unemployment benefit. At the same time, of those who would not apply to the ES if they were unemployed, almost all gave as their reason that the ES would not help them find a job and that they could manage to earn more than unemployment benefit by virtue of additional earnings. Thus, the respondents clearly defined the role of the ES, not as an organisation for job-seekers, but as a body for the payment of unemployment benefit.

In concluding this review of the issue of the respondents' labour mobility, it is essential to point out that such mobility is not limited only to finding a job. As answers to the 'respondent's diary' questions showed, over the year of observation six people had successfully started their own businesses, 16 people had tried to start one but without success, 16 people had completed re-training courses, and another ten people had started such courses; six people had been on public works schemes, 11 people had changed their place of work more than once over the previous year (of whom four were unemployed at the time of the 1997 survey), 11 people had taken retirement pension and three people had moved onto invalidity benefits. 64 people had regular additional earnings, and 97 people had found one new job (including 7 people who continued to sign on as unemployed). Thus, the respondents' labour mobility was not only high, but also fairly diverse.

In relation to this, it is worth devoting some attention to more general matters that relate closely to the respondents' employment. First and foremost is the regional differentiation of forms of labour mobility. For example, public works schemes were mentioned in Voronezh and St. Petersburg but were entirely absent from Moscow, since they are very unpopular among Muscovites; on the other hand, the proportion of those in Voronezh who had found more than one new job and then left it in the course of the year between the surveys was noticeably higher than elsewhere. This was mainly connected with the lengthy delays in payment of salaries at Voronezh enterprises (which is less typical of Moscow and St.Petersburg), as a result of which those who depended on having a job with real wages were forced to look for new jobs. At the same time, in Moscow and St.Petersburg, additional earnings and work in one's own business were much more widespread.

Secondly, there is the lack of effectiveness of retraining for the unemployed. Training them through courses which enabled them to gain new qualifications did little to help the respondents find work: less than half of those who completed courses found work, since their retraining was carried out without taking into account the particular features of the labour market or the needs of the unemployed - including wage levels. The foregoing review of respondents' desires for retraining gives us some understanding that attendance on such courses was, for a significant proportion of the unemployed, the only possibility of further preserving their status as unemployed, and was not a step towards a new job. In any case, 25 per cent of respondents who completed courses openly admitted that they were not interested in a job or could not go out to work because of their family circumstances.

Thirdly, self-employment is very widespread. It includes, firstly, the 12 people who had their own business in 1996 and were still running it in 1997 (one of the 'hidden' 1996 entrepreneurs had been unsuccessful and closed down his business during the year), and another six entrepreneurs who joined their ranks during 1997; secondly, five other people who described their status as 'self-employed' in 1997; thirdly, a significant proportion of those who marked 'additional earnings' as a form of employment income over the previous year (this usually meant various kinds of private repair, painting, decorating and building work which is not recorded anywhere). In this regard, the most important point to note is that people who are in some form of self-employment are gradually being concentrated among the unemployed (registered and *de facto*) and people in insecure employment (especially those on compulsory leave). So, in 1996 only one 'businessman' belonged to the unemployed group, and most of them were on unpaid or part-paid leave. By 1997, however, they had noticeably reinforced the ranks of the unemployed - out of those 18 people who admitted that they had their own business, six were registered unemployed at the time of the second survey, three were *de facto* unemployed and three more were on compulsory leave. Eight people were employed and running a business in parallel. The overwhelming majority of the group of businessmen was among the 'well-off' and 'prosperous' respondents (13 people out of the 18). Unemployed people who were really entrepreneurs or at least self-employed were the section of the unemployed discussed in Chapter 8, who were actually affluent. Other types of self-employment were also widespread: in the first instance, among people in insecure employment and, to a lesser extent, among the unemployed we discussed in our outline in Chapter 8 of the additional earnings situation especially as it applied in Moscow. What is more, many were quite satisfied with the way their situation had turned out. For example, when asked whether they were satisfied with their present job, almost half the respondents in insecure employment answered 'yes', and only a third gave the response 'no' to this question.

In this regard, we should point out that even though the actual finding of a job depends above all on the respondent and not on the state of the labour market, remaining successfully employed and being satisfied with the new job are linked, in the first instance, to the possibilities offered by the labour market and by its breadth, which give not only diversity of choice of various employment strategies but also diversity of choice of jobs which match the respondents' needs. For example, it was a result of objective differences in the state of the labour market that 63 per cent of those in St. Petersburg who had found work after being unemployed were happy with their job, while in Voronezh the figure was only 43 per cent. Moreover, the most noticeable influences on satisfaction with a job were how interesting the respondents found their work (one of their most important values), their readiness to accept a lower status on finding work, and the status of their trade/profession and particular post.

The issue of status is linked with the fact that the main body of respondents had found work in lower status posts - very significantly lower for some. So, among those who had held managerial posts in 1996, 41 per cent remained managers and another 30 per cent were in skilled specialist posts. 29 per cent of former managers were in blue-collar posts, including five per cent, i.e. one person, who had even become an unskilled labourer. We can also observe a similar picture when analysing the jobs found by skilled specialists: 46 per cent of them had found work at a lower status, with 21 per cent going into blue-collar jobs. 23 per cent of those categorised as 'white-collar workers' went into blue-collar jobs. Overall, it can be said that it was easier for skilled blue-collar workers to find work which preserved their professional status, while finding work was hardest of all for unskilled blue-collar workers. As for the rest, the general mass of them found work fairly easily, but at a lower professional status.

Furthermore, as the 1996 survey showed, 40 per cent of respondents were then privately willing to reduce their status in order to find work, while the other 60 per cent would not agree to this. It is therefore unsurprising that, after finding work with lower status, their level of satisfaction with the job varied - among those who had privately been agreeable to a drop in status in 1996, 59 per cent were satisfied with their jobs. Among those who had been psychologically unwilling to accept this, satisfaction with the job was only 37 per cent.

As far as 'interest value' was concerned, in general this was one of the central features of work for our respondents. We have already mentioned this overriding preference for interesting work even to the detriment of earnings, in Chapter 8 during our discussion of particular features of the values of members of crisis groups. But a full understanding of the role that this characteristic of work plays for them is possible only by looking at what they value and what they are unhappy with in their present job. In assessing this, the main thing for most respondents was, firstly, the undemanding nature of the work, and secondly, its content. At the same time, among the things they liked in their work were that it was clean or physically light: the percentages of those satisfied with it in those respects were 83 per cent and 79 per cent. The percentages of those who were satisfied with their work on the grounds that it was interesting or varied were respectively 76 per cent and 71 per cent, while the average indicator for general satisfaction with their present job was 48 per cent across the sample. As to the influence of earnings and of the level of security on satisfaction with work, then although respondents always mentioned low earnings as the most important reason for refusing a job and the most important aspect of a new job, the only relationship between satisfaction with the present job and indicators of material welfare was recorded in the two poorest groups, where the proportion of people satisfied with their jobs was only 20 per cent. Members of all the other groups, from the badly-off to the prosperous, were satisfied with their job to practically the same extent (in all of them, the proportion of those satisfied was about 50 per cent of the group), while the chief significance for them was precisely the undemanding nature of the work and its content.

So we can conclude:

- Subjectively, respondents from all groups basically related the reasons for their falling into the crisis groups not to themselves but to the situation of their enterprise and the economy as a whole. In formal terms, the largest group was formed by those who had lost their jobs through staff cuts, while in fact, according to the 1996 survey data, the main bulk of the unemployed and those under notice of redundancy lost their jobs in the course of fairly large-scale, but selective, staff cuts at large enterprises which had been compelled to reduce labour force surpluses during transition to the market;
- The labour mobility of respondents was high and diverse, although each 1996 group had a fairly large stable core which still existed a year later. The unemployed had found work much more rarely than members of other groups. Regional differences between those who found work were very significant, although general tendencies in other respects remained the same;
- In accordance with current re-structuring, the main outflow of employees was from heavy industry and the defence industry, while people found jobs mainly in trade, municipal housing and public utilities, transport, the construction industry and the budget-funded sector. Furthermore, if in

1996 the main flow of recruitment was towards small and medium enterprises, then in 1997 the largest flow of those who found work was towards large joint-stock enterprises - a fact which, obviously, is related to the start of an upturn for some industrial enterprises. This is evidenced by the improvement in circumstances at their enterprises for a section of the 1996 respondents from the group in insecure employment, who by 1997 already had full employment at their enterprises;

- Despite the diversity of approaches used in seeking work, there were really only two ways of finding a job - finding a job on the recommendation of friends, including former work colleagues, and finding work through the ES;

- The functions of the ES at present are less helping with finding work than paying benefit. On the whole the ES is coping successfully with this function, even though the amount of benefit and the actions necessary to receive it arouse some discontent among the unemployed;

- The various forms of labour mobility, the poor effectiveness of retraining, and the lack of understanding on the part of the ES and those in crisis groups of the meaning of retraining in a situation where the economy is being re-structured, are all salient features; as is very widespread self-employment, which for many is a consciously chosen, though officially unrecorded, employment strategy;

- For the majority of respondents, satisfaction with a new job is linked with three factors. One of them, systemic in nature, related to the objective possibilities of the local labour market, and gave rise not only to the possibility of rational choice of a particular employment strategy (for example, additional earnings instead of full-time work in Moscow), but also to satisfaction with the new job. The two others related to a number of personal resources at the disposal of respondents: on the one hand, willingness to reduce their status and to change the nature of their activity because of the limits of the labour market; and, on the other, the role of the 'interest level' of the job - for many respondents, this 'interest level' was able to reconcile them with low earnings and reduced status.

Reasons For 'Getting Stuck' in Employment Crisis Groups

In the previous section, we analysed the reasons why people fall into groups that are in crisis in the labour market. However, the reasons for falling into a certain employment crisis group may differ from the reasons why someone remains in that group for a long time. Thus, the data cited above had not helped to answer the question why people with the same occupational characteristics in one case find work and in another case remain unemployed, even though - at least for some of them - finding work would significantly improve their material circumstances. But after analysing the data, the picture of choice of particular employment strategies and 'getting stuck' in crisis groups becomes clearer.

We should immediately stress that in attempting to isolate a relationship between employment status and age, sex, objective indicators of state of health and particular features of objective occupational status, we revealed no statistically significant relationships between respondents' membership of particular groupings and their current employment. This allows us to assert that, in general, there are practically no objective obstacles to finding work for people in crisis groups, although to find a job which corresponds to the respondent's wishes across a whole set of factors is indeed impossible for many people.

Analysis of the degree of correlation between employment status (depending on the year of observation) and the responses to all the questions on both phase questionnaires, indicated that there were two variables out of several hundreds analysed which were very significant (p-value 35 and 18). These were the sector of the economy in which the respondent was working in 1997, and employment status during the first phase of the research. So further confirmation was obtained, firstly, that the redistribution of labour between different sectors during the course of market reforms was the most significant 'systemic' factor assisting in resolving employment problems; and secondly, that there was a tendency for respondents to be 'frozen' in a group with a particular employment status, so that the unemployed who did not find work in the first few months after losing their jobs became the long-term unemployed. Even if they did get work after two or three years of unemployment, this job would turn out to be only short-term, and after it ended they would very rapidly fall back among the numbers of the unemployed (this also applied to the insecurely employed group). However, we have already looked at both these trends in the previous section. The next most significant group of factors (p-value from 10 to 5) which had an influence on the employment status of respondents in 1997 included two types of variables: 1) job refusals and 2) reasons why the respondent was not seeking work. Both these groups in fact demonstrated that the respondent had not found work either because of excessive aspirations or generally little interest in having a job - or both these factors together. Given that it is these factors which also reveal the reasons for 'getting stuck' in crisis groups, they merit detailed examination.

The question of what respondents value in a job, what kind of requirements they bring to the job, and what in the final analysis leads them to be satisfied with a job, is of particular interest in this connection. With the primary aim of obtaining an answer to these questions in the course of the research, an attempt was undertaken to reveal the labour values of the respondents. We note that, according to the data of a number of pieces of research, including RIISNP research, the Russian population, like the populations of other countries, considers work to be secondary in life to the family. However, the distinctive nature of Russians lies in the fact that Russia has seen one of the largest ruptures between the subjective importance of family and work anywhere in the world (Magun, 1995). This is linked with the relatively low significance of labour values in the Russian mentality: in our survey, 26 per cent of respondents in the imagined situation of receiving a large inheritance or a big win would prefer not to work.

A hierarchy of labour values was defined on the basis of a list of 23 labour values, covering practically all their main categories - material and spiritual, individual and social, indirect and direct, 'internal' and 'external', describing both what people put into work and what they get out of it:

Table 9.3   Labour motivations and job satisfaction in 1997 (per cent)

	satisfied with jobs	*all respondents*
Varied work	52	27
Useful work	42	34
Work that takes 'nous'	42	17
Work that is not too tiring	53	11
Can improve skills and qualifications	69	16
Good pay	45	74
Convenient shifts, flexible hours	60	20
Well-organised work	42	18
Good working conditions	45	32
A regular flow of work, making fairly even demands on me	24	10

Good safety techniques	36	5
Getting on well with workmates	53	41
Getting on well with management	45	17
Interesting work	51	42
Work does not damage my health	41	15
Concern/provision for employees' domestic needs	50	6
Undemanding work	43	10
Chance to display initiative	54	17
Fair appraisal of workers	39	11
Full use of knowledge and abilities	56	16
Prospects for career development	64	14
No fear of redundancy	31	19
Chance to make useful contacts	60	10

This hierarchy was measured at both stages of the research and displayed very great stability: only on three out of the 23 points did the results change quite noticeably over the year. The significance of good pay rose from 57 per cent to 74 per cent, the significance of the chance to improve one's skills fell from 33 per cent to 16 per cent and the significance of well-organised work fell from 28 per cent to 18 per cent.

As we can see, across the whole sample, the first place in the hierarchy of labour values was held by high pay, and this also sharply increased its lead over the year of observation. As a result, in the overall hierarchy, wages significantly outstripped the other factors which had been in the top three (shown in italics) - the values relating to 'interesting work' and 'good relations with workmates'. At the same time, values such as 'potential to show initiative', 'potential to improve one's skills' which characterise the presence of a drive to achieve, come at the end of the list and even lost some of their popularity over the period of observation. Moreover, although most respondents noted the importance of contacts and 'who you know' in getting a good job, the potential for acquiring connections at work which would be useful in future was an also-ran in this hierarchy.

Overall, people who valued the significance of good pay highly were also far from indifferent to the conditions in which they had to work, at the same time scorning those labour values which presupposed high dedication to work, initiative and responsibility. Conversely, those who had an active drive to achieve were less worried by the size of the reward for their labour. So, among adherents of high pay, 38 per cent noted the significance of working conditions, and for those for whom the size of the wage did not appear among the most important features of a job, working conditions were important only for 16 per cent. The parallel indicators for the importance of possibilities to display initiative were respectively 13 per cent and 30 per cent, for improving skills – 14 per cent and 24 per cent, and for the potential to acquire useful connections and contacts - 7 per cent and 18 per cent.

On the other hand, satisfaction with the job and success in finding work was much higher for those who had expressed a drive to achieve. Among those for whom a drive to achieve was important, satisfaction with the job is significantly higher than across the sample as a whole.. As to the significance of a drive to achieve in finding work, it was noticeable that the unemployed demonstrated a two or three times lower preoccupation with possibilities for self-fulfilment at work, for displaying independence and initiative, for improving skills and for professional development, than those who had found work: they also have a noticeably clearer orientation towards such values as 'good pay' (92 per cent of the unemployed and 72 per cent of those who have found work), undemanding work (21 per cent and 8 per cent respectively), 'good relationships with management' (26 per cent and 15 per cent) and 'fair appraisal of staff' (17 per cent and 9 per cent), as well as towards other values which characterise a comfortable job.

Thus, people who have successfully overcome a crisis period in their working life demonstrated a much clearer aspiration to have a job which gives them the potential to use their knowledge and abilities to the full and to develop initiative and enterprise. They also attach substantially greater significance to the possibility of improving their skills and, in the final analysis, of moving up the job ladder. The leanings of those who have found new jobs towards such labour values as 'prospects for career development' were expressed three times more often than in the unemployed group, and regression analysis revealed this indicator to be one of the main variables by which this group differs from the unemployed.

The particular features of labour motivation and the significance of various characteristics of a job also affected the respondents' aspirations in relation to the job. These aspirations were rather high for the present state of the labour market. More than half the respondents were looking for work which had to be in their usual occupation (the sole exception here was the respondents who had started working normally again during the year of observation, without a period of unemployment - about 60 per cent of them were willing to change occupation to find work).

The overwhelming majority of respondents would not agree to poor working conditions (a 'dirty' job), 87 per cent to poor relations with workmates, two-thirds to inconvenient working hours or boring work, and more than half would refuse a job at a long distance from home.

Added to these requirements - meaning that the job they would agree to take should be in every respect comfortable - was the requirement for high pay. Moreover, the level of pay requirement was also excessive. Only 23 per cent of respondents would agree to wages of less than 800,000 roubles (mainly in Voronezh, where the average wage for the city is a lot lower than in Moscow and St. Petersburg), while more than half aspired to pay of over one million roubles. Furthermore, 90 per cent said that they would not agree to a low-paid job even if all their other job requirements were met.

The aspirations of the unemployed were also very great, and in a number of cases even exceeded indicators across the sample as a whole. Suffice it to say that a review of responses to this question in 1996 shows that two-thirds of those unemployed in 1996 were still refusing to find work with lower status in 1997. Status turned out to be the restraining factor on finding work even for many indigent and poor people, especially single middle-aged people among the 'new poor'. Furthermore, less than a quarter of the unemployed who fell into the two most deprived groups expressed a willingness to work for pay of less than one million roubles, even if the job was suitable on all other points. There were some, even among the poorest, who gave as the limit below which they would not agree to go out to work - a wage of three million roubles. The lack of desire of two-thirds of the unemployed to reduce their job requirements if they could not find work within another year was also surprising.

In this regard, it will be enough to adduce just one example from the 1996 survey, which in its various facets form a prism reflecting the most striking features of unemployment in the cities studied (sex, age, skills and education). In addition, the household composition and the material circumstances of this respondent place her among the most deprived and those most in need of a job, making her typical of the two poorest groups among the unemployed. An unemployed woman of just over 40 years old, a computer programmer by profession, she has higher education to postgraduate level and speaks English and Japanese. She became unemployed following the reorganisation of a large State enterprise. She has had 18 years work experience (13 of these in her last job), with jobs as a systems programmer, lecturer in a college of higher education, translator from English and Japanese. She enjoys good health. She has had no work since May 1995: she is prepared to accept a whole range of negative aspects of a job (such as a long way from home). At first sight, it seems incredible that a person with such potential has not found work on the Moscow labour market.

The situation becomes even more improbable once you know this respondent's replies relating to her attitude to unemployment and her material circumstances. She finds unemployment extraordinarily difficult to cope with, and fairly regularly has thoughts of suicide. Her material circumstances appear to be simply catastrophic. Her main family income is unemployment benefit, which has already been reduced to the minimum because of the length of her period of unemployment: this represents an income of 41,000 roubles per month per head. Taking prices into account, this buys only 300 grams of bread a day and nothing more. She has five square metres of living space per person in one room in a communal flat; her only 'expensive' possessions are a small fridge, already over six years old, and two small rugs of the same age. She has no allotment, nor does she carry on any individual occupational activity either for herself or for sale. Her household consists of two people, the respondent herself (head of the family) and an eight year old daughter. The child does not have a father, and the mother does not get any maintenance for her.

However, a more detailed analysis revealed the following. Her material circumstances were indeed very difficult, one of the most difficult across the whole sample, but they were better than the respondent herself assessed them to be. In indicating her *per capita* income, the respondent took into account only unemployment benefit. In fact she also received lone parent child benefit and a municipal subsidy towards the cost of municipal services and housing; she was getting help from relatives, former work colleagues and friends; and she also had occasional earnings (most probably as a translator). Consequently, the family could still afford to pay for the child's music lessons and to use private medical services. But she had had no holiday, done no work on her flat, nor even bought any new clothes in the previous year. This may not have been starvation, but it was a completely poverty-stricken existence.

Unemployment is indeed difficult to live with, so difficult that people can get into an intensely neurotic state and become extremely frustrated, which can have a strong effect on their reactions. For example, she refused a second interview, despite the fact that she would be paid for it. In this case, one could perhaps even say that the shock of unemployment had been so strong that it had brought about a certain psychological shift which now prevented the respondent from tackling her problems. She was the type of person who, in extreme conditions, was not able to tackle her problems herself: she had clearly expressed expectations of paternalism. Her responses to the questions on values (a section in which the respondent writes directly on the questionnaire) showed a severe crisis of values, the result of a conflict between her own system of values and the new realities of life. She revealed a sense of complete frustration and an accompanying 'mish-mash' of ideas. She gave mutually exclusive answers to the same questions: in particular, she was both convinced (completely unjustifiably) that her life would soon improve and that she would probably never find the work she was looking for. She could not relinquish her standard of expectations from a job: her willingness to retrain took the shape of a desire to become a lawyer, which was completely unrealistic.

So what kind of job was this respondent seeking and how did she set about looking? First it must be said that she was a very active job-seeker, using almost all the methods listed on the questionnaire. Secondly, she had had more than one interview (systems programmers are in fairly short supply on the Moscow labour market - and her language skills were another plus). But she had failed to get any of these jobs, because - as she herself says - of her sex, her age and her appearance. Most probably personnel officers shied away from her for three reasons: 1) she is a single mother, which means she is entitled to a large number of privileges as an employee and could get an unrestricted number of sick notes, amounting to as much as 100 per cent of her working time in a year; 2) highly inappropriate behaviour, which was evident both in her written answers to the questionnaire and during the interview, and which all personnel officers - in view of the way in which current employment legislation tends to favour the employee - are keen to avoid; and 3) the issue of the level of pay. This problem was a real stumbling block: with qualifications like hers - even as a single mother and a not entirely adequate person - the respondent could have found work paying at least $100 - $150, which (taking into account her various social benefits and occasional additional earnings) would provide her with a perfectly tolerable standard of living. But she had aspirations to earn $2,000 a month and she did not want to abandon any of her job requirements, even given the threat of complete destitution for herself and her child: and finding work at even 10 per cent of that wage would certainly be problematic for her.

One could adduce a fair number of such examples. However, they all demonstrate one thing - the noticeable differences between the unemployed and people who have found work, among whom such social types are almost completely absent. Analysis of the situation of those middle-aged unemployed people who - judging by their responses - had maintained appropriate behaviour, but who nevertheless did not want to go out to work, demonstrated the same thing.

In this connection, we would also like to draw attention to one factor that is very important for an understanding of the position of unemployed Russians. Many of them are former specialists or white-collar workers. Before the reforms they had fairly high status and an affluent way of life, and taking into account that the overwhelming majority of these people are middle-aged and even older, they already have a formed and defined personal identity, and a corresponding level of aspirations. In recent years, all this has been destroyed. Bearing in mind that the attitude of Russian society towards the unemployed is generally completely loyal and sympathetic (only 11 per cent of a national sample responded to a RIISNP survey in December 1996 by saying that the unemployed were made up primarily of poor workers, and the rest linked unemployment with the objective difficulties experienced by Russia in recent years), being unemployed does not reduce their social status: for Russians, this is not measured by their position as an unemployed person, but by who they were until they became unemployed. For these people to go as far as renouncing their habitual work activities in favour of lower status and in general changing their whole habitual way of life would constitute a very serious cause of inner turmoil and a great sacrifice. So the price they name for this sacrifice (their desired pay level) is excessively high. Often it is such that finding work at that pay level would be unrealistic in practice - and the question falls of its own accord. At the same time, their present experience is painful for them, and the impossibility of meeting the standards of consumption they had previously, while they also see that for most other people around them such standards have risen further (we should recall that comparing themselves to others is the main thing by which Russians identify themselves), engenders in them a feeling that their position is catastrophic and a simultaneous unwillingness to reduce their aspirations.

The impossibility of finding a new permanent job with the high pay they desire has predetermined for many of those in insecure employment and for some of the unemployed the preferability of doing various kinds of temporary or casual work for additional earnings or of living on other sources of income (help from others, or unemployment benefit). Additional earnings were much more widespread among people in insecure employment who, on the one hand, had a lot of free time and on the other, preferred this survival strategy to finding work, since they did not want to reduce their status or to change their occupation. Thus such earnings were, on the one hand, a cause (as an alternative to permanent employment) and, on the other, a consequence of the absence of secure employment for the respondents. An orientation towards receipt of assistance was to a great extent typical of the unemployed.

The fact is that, when someone is really willing to change their occupation and the nature of their work, it is possible to be successful in getting back into a job, and this was clearly demonstrated by another case, from St Petersburg. Both as a person and in the way she found her job, she presented a completely typical portrait of those of our sample who had returned to work. She was a married woman of about 45, with a twelve-year-old child; at the time of our first survey, she lived with her aged parents in two rooms of a communal flat. Her husband was the only one receiving a real wage (1,700,000 roubles a month): she herself had already been on compulsory leave for more than six months by the time of the survey, while her parents received a total pension of 560,000 roubles a month between them. Thus the dependency ratio within this respondent's family was very high; despite her attempts to earn extra money, the fact that she received some benefits, and the fact that a part of the family's living space was rented out, resulted in the family being categorised as 'badly-off' on our welfare index. She assessed their material circumstances as 'satisfactory', although she indicated that there was only enough money for everyday expenditure and that it was already becoming difficult to purchase clothing. Over the year before the first survey, the family had bought only clothes and the only fee-paying social services they had used were medical ones; all the family's relatively expensive belongings (fridge, washing machine, furniture, colour TV, stereo, piano and carpet) had been purchased before the reforms. So, measured by these facts, her assessment seemed to be completely accurate. The family did not own any kind of real property. In a word, both before the reforms and during the survey period, this family was neither in the most prosperous nor the poorest section of society.

She assessed her own health as 'satisfactory'; and, on the basis of the General Health Questionnaire, this turned out to be really the case. However, she was paying the price for stresses associated with work and with the family's worsening situation: headaches, sleeping badly, tension, feeling the need for a pick-me-up, as well as some other indicators, all showed an unfavourable impact on her nervous system. At the same time, her replies to questions of a general nature demonstrated her fairly stable mental state.

She was typical of the sample as a whole in her values: she preferred to have a clear conscience in her dealings with the authorities, valued interesting work above good pay and freedom over material prosperity. However, she was trying to live like everyone else, without standing out from the crowd, and was a supporter of an equal income society rather than an equal opportunities one.

She saw no way of protecting her own interests in contemporary Russian society. Consistent with having grown up in a paternalistic, conformist setting, she did not agree with the statement that her material circumstances depended first and foremost on herself, and thought that her friends and relations ought to help her solve her problems. On the whole, she also believed that the state should help all those in need, regardless of the reasons for their poverty. Her confidence was relatively high, but although she thought that things would soon improve for her, she did not feel that she herself was playing an important role in them. Like other respondents with the same general outlook on life, she suggested that the state ought to combat unemployment by giving subsidies to state enterprises, although, in addition, she thought that concessions to private business to create jobs also seemed to be a promising measure.

She was an engineer by occupation, and the post she held was that of senior design engineer; she had higher education and over 25 years' length of service behind her. She loved her occupation, which she had worked in all her life, and she said that, in the imagined situation of receiving a large inheritance, she would prefer to continue in the same occupation, but look for a new place of work. However, she was also attached to her actual job (in a large privatised enterprise with over 1,000 workers), where she had worked for more than 15 years: she was hoping that the situation there would stabilise and she would be able to return. Therefore, she was seeking work without any inner conviction of a need to do so, although she looked through advertisements and also asked people she knew for help in finding a job.

Possibly because of this, she allowed herself fairly high job requirements: as we have already said, this was fairly typical of a significant number of respondents. Her desired salary level was about 1,500,000 roubles, although she herself understood that she could not really aspire to more than 1,000,000 on the current labour market. The only disadvantages she was prepared to accept in a post were that it might be uninteresting, intensive or very responsible. At the same time, she had given herself six months to look for a suitable job, and was ready to change her occupation if she had not found anything suitable at the end of that time. She indicated that the occupation which she would like to retrain for was that of 'computer specialist'.

A year later, she had found a new job and joined the 'well-off' group. This was demonstrated not only by the fact that she had been able to acquire several consumer durables and a computer over the period between the surveys, but also by the fact that it was now possible for her to use a broader range of fee-paying social services. In addition, she and her family had moved to a separate privatised two-room flat, acquired with assistance from her husband's work.

(The family numbered 4 people at the time of the second survey, as her father had just died - meaning that the family dependency ratio had fallen to 1:1.) Her husband's salary had risen markedly (to 2,700,000 roubles), and she herself had found a job that even paid the salary she had wanted. Taking into account her mother's pension, local council subsidies and child benefit, the family's total income was nearly 5,000,000 roubles a month.

Although in 1996 she had looked to the future pessimistically, expecting the family's position to deteriorate in future, it is not surprising that by 1997 she had become more optimistic. One of the main bases for this optimism was her success in finding a job. True, this had actually meant changing her occupation: she now defined herself as a 'print worker'. She had acquired these new skills in 1997, through taking up a senior post in a small private enterprise. In practice, she had got this job following her first interview with any potential employer, and acquaintances had recommended her for it. She was happy in her new job, and had no plans to change it, since - although she found it tiring - she valued it for its 'inherent interest', high pay, good working conditions and because she got on well with the management, as well as feeling it offered her potential for self-fulfillment and was socially useful.

She was also happy with her life overall, and the successful resolution of her difficult problems, along with a job in the private sector of the economy, had led to a marked increase in her self-confidence and notable shifts in her psychological portrait. By the time of the 1997 survey, she already not only thought that things would soon improve for her, but she was also sure that she herself would play an important role in this. In line with her new views, she felt that her material circumstances depended mainly on her; the state ought not to help all those in need, but only those who could not provide for themselves for objective reasons (such as the disabled, and pensioners). She now had the feeling that she was in a position to take responsible decisions herself; her assessment of her own health had improved, and her need for a pick-me-up had disappeared. She also saw ways of protecting her own interests, among which were applying to the courts and attempting to come to a direct arrangement with those who could solve her problem, in return for an appropriate payment. Moreover, the conviction that it was better to live like others had been replaced by the belief that it was better to be an outstanding individualist, and the ideal of an equal incomes society had made way for the ideal of equal opportunities. There was also now no question of subsidies to state enterprises as a means of combatting unemployment, and preferential credits for unemployed people to start their own businesses now appeared alongside concessions to the private sector for job creation.

The striking differences between the long-term unemployed and those who have found new jobs as typified by these two respondents led us to attempt to record them systematically. This was managed partly using the 'PRA index' ('actual potential to adapt'). In the first phase of our research, the index had already shown the extraordinarily poor ability of the overwhelming majority of respondents to adapt to the situation that has arisen on the Russian labour market in recent years (Table 9.4).

As we can see, the basic pattern is fairly rigid: in all cities, the high RA index of those who had found work after a period of unemployment exceeds that of the unemployed by several times (in Moscow - 3.2 times; in St. Petersburg - 2.3 times; in Voronezh - 8.3 times). At the same time, a low PRA index was actually typical of the unemployed, and less typical of those who had found a job (in Moscow the low PRA index is found twice as frequently for the unemployed as for those who found a job; in St. Petersburg - 1.5 times; in Voronezh - 1.6 times). Thus, in the first phase of the research, our hypothesis of the significant role played by personality characteristics in determining the general employment situation - and in the formation of long-term unemployment in particular - was confirmed.

Table 9.4   PRA index in various respondent groups in the three cities studied, in 1996 (per cent)

	Unemp- loyed (n=70)	Insecurely employed (n=58)	Redund- ancy (n=55)	Found work (n=55)	Total (n=241)
Index level		*Moscow*			
Low	46	43	8	22	30
Average	47	38	68	23	52
High	7	19	24	55	18
		St. Petersburg			
Low	29	50	41	19	34

Average	63	36	32	62	49
High	8	14	27	19	17

Voronezh

Low	67	36	31	42	44
Average	33	50	63	50	49
High	0	14	6	8	7

A year later, the figures from this index were again confirmed. And again most of the respondents with a low PRA index found themselves in the registered unemployed group (36 per cent); and only 9 per cent of the unemployed had a high PRA index. On the other hand, the 1996 situation of those who had found work was also confirmed - their PRA index was on average much higher, and 19 per cent of them had a high PRA index. In addition, respondents who had had a low PRA index in 1996 had been less successful in finding work over the course of the year of observation than those with a high PRA index. Finally, respondents with the least effective survival strategies found themselves concentrated in the group with a low PRA index. For example, they were one-and-a-half times less likely to be in steady secondary employment than the average for the whole sample, but one-and-a-half times more likely to have borrowed money. Furthermore, the psychological state of the respondents with a low PRA index demonstrated that, regardless of their unwillingness to make any concessions in order to get a job, they found their present position quite hard to bear. More than half of the group of respondents who said they had been bad-tempered and more than a third of those who thought that coping with their problems was beyond them, were also respondents with a low PRA index. However, their assessment of themselves was very high. Not one respondent with a low PRA index simultaneously stated that he always thought of himself as a worthless person, and only seven per cent replied 'quite often' to this question.

Thus, the unemployed differed significantly across a whole range of parameters from those who have found work. Furthermore, these parameters were connected in general with an unwillingness to accept the new reality of the labour market in Russia - more precisely, with the very existence of this market and its 'rules of the game', including mechanisms for determining the value and cost of labour. So it is not a chance factor that the picture of reasons for finding work and causes for refusal to work of the Russian unemployed was found to be essentially different from that of, for example, their English colleagues, who have grown up in social conditions where a labour market - with accompanying unemployment - has existed for hundreds of years. Thus, in the Dean and Taylor-Gooby research which we have already mentioned, the unemployed gave self-esteem above all as the main motivation in their attempts to find work (more than half the English unemployed referred to this motivation). Self-esteem as a motivation for finding work was significant for only a quarter of the Russian unemployed, whose main motivation was material factors.

Correspondingly, Russians placed unsuitable pay levels at the top of their list of restrictions on finding work, while for their English colleagues this reason occupied only third place (see Table 9.5). On the other hand, the English named family problems as restricting their finding work three and half times more often than Russians. In addition, the Russian unemployed named as restrictions on obtaining work - the absence of suitable jobs on the labour market (39 per cent) and lack of job search skills (18 per cent).

Table 9.5   Comparison of motives for seeking work, unemployed people in Russia and England - n (per cent)

Motive for seeking work	Russia		England	
Pressure from ES	5	(2)	2	(2)
Material factors	48	(24)	23	(27)
Self-respect	45	(23)	45	(53)
No reply	100	(51)	15	(18)

Obviously, this specific structure of job aspirations also explains, to a major extent, the present status of the long-term unemployed, although it was the unemployed who had had the most interviews with potential employers. 70 per cent of the unemployed had had three or more interviews with employers, and 26 per cent of the registered unemployed had had even more than ten. Among those who had found work, the majority had had only two or three interviews with employers, including the one for the job which they had then taken. However, the outcomes of these interviews were very different in the different groups. Almost half of the unemployed, for various reasons, themselves refused the job offered after being sent for interviews by the ES (in half the cases, because it did not correspond to their usual occupation; among other responses were 'because of my age', 'because of my children', 'the hours didn't suit me', 'the employer hadn't been paying any wages for a long time', 'I didn't suit the job and the job didn't suit me', 'I don't like shop work', 'it wasn't white-collar work, it was heavy manual work'). But in most cases, the employer had refused them after these interviews. Cases where the employer had refused someone who subsequently found work were relatively rare (27-28 per cent). Thus, the situation of the long-term unemployed differed noticeably from that of those who had found work, in the sense that half the unemployed, when offered a fairly large number of jobs, themselves did not want to go out to work, while the other half had been categorically refused by employers. Moreover, the latter situation sometimes even manifested itself as being taken on and then rapidly fired: among those who were registered unemployed, the proportion of those who had changed jobs more than once during the year between the surveys was approximately twice that in the other groups.

This is the picture given by detailed analysis of job refusals and their relationships with employment status. As regards the reasons why a respondent was not seeking work, then in descending order of prevalence these were: 'my health prevents me', 'it is difficult to find work matching my skills' (half the unemployed in 1997 were those who in 1996 thought that their finding work was hampered by particular aspects of their knowledge; among those who had found work this indicator was 18 per cent), 'it is difficult for me to overcome the barrier that I have to find work myself, when I don't know where to go or what to do in order to find work', 'family obligations do not permit me to look for work', 'I do not know anyone who could help me find a job', 'I'm not interested', 'there is no relevant information', 'there are too many people with my specialist skills' and other reasons, including hopes of finding work at one's old enterprise.

The third most significant group of factors correlating with the respondents' employment status included indicators of the respondent's flexibility in relation to their job requirements, and particular features of their labour motivation. Among the former were the length of time which might make them alter their job requirements (most of those who had found work wanted less than six months for this, while two thirds of the unemployed considered that even a year of unemployment would not make them give up their requirements), and their willingness to travel a long way to a job in another part of the city. While among all those who had found work 55 per cent were willing to work a long way form home, among the registered unemployed, only 25 per cent were. The labour motivation factors were above all typical of the insecurely employed group. 65 per cent of that group were sure that work should be important to people, and the percentage of adherents to the importance of high pay was very small.

Finally, the fourth and fifth most significant groups of variables included socio-psychological characteristics ('habitus') of the respondents, including their understanding of realities in Russia today, their psychological state, their inclination to maintain a particular circle of social contacts, etc. In analysing these, it was revealed that the unemployed were in the main less inclined to change the content of their habitual activities than those who had found work, and less certain of their strengths. Among them, the belief was widespread that their problems should be solved for them by someone else. Overall, those who had found work were more inclined to depend on themselves and more certain of their own strengths. The certainty that their material circumstances depended in the first instance on themselves was expressed by 44 per cent of those who had found work and only 19 per cent of the unemployed. Correspondingly, willingness to find work on losing their present source of income was expressed by half of those who had permanent jobs at the time of the 1997 survey and by only 20 per cent of the unemployed. Among methods to help them solve their problems, 38 per cent of those who had found work named attempting to come to a direct financial arrangement with those on whom the decision depended, while among the unemployed only 17 per cent named this method (really the most effective in contemporary Russia). Moreover, the 17-20 per cent who replied positively to the questions listed above were in general the most affluent section of the unemployed, for whom the status of unemployed person was only a cloak for their unregistered employment.

Thus, among the main reasons for workers 'getting stuck' in employment crisis groups were the following:

- The particular features of the contemporary Russian labour market, where because of on-going re-structuring of the economy a strong imbalance has existed for five or six years between demand for labour in various occupations and employment in various sectors. In addition, in 'successful' sectors, the level of requirements from staff is growing, as a result of which they are being replaced by workers from other sectors, with a simultaneous reduction in status both for those released and for the new staff taken on. As a result, those workers who have refused to change the habitual content of their labour activity (whether changing the nature of activity, occupation or sector), have significantly fewer chances of successfully finding work after falling into an employment crisis group;

- Long membership of a particular employment crisis group on the one hand increases the probability that the person will remain in this group because he gets used to a particular way of life and adapts to it, and on the other hand is in itself a consequence of particular personal characteristics;

- Among these particular personal characteristics the most important are the respondent's willingness to work and the level of his job aspirations. Most respondents from the registered unemployed and the insecurely employed groups were not interested in getting a permanent job: firstly, because their present status was for them only a cover for their real, unregistered employment, including private enterprise; or secondly, because either health or family situation did not allow it. The family situation does not strictly speaking limit finding work, but can further the choice of a particular employment strategy that takes into account the composition of household and the respondents' level of job aspirations. Thirdly, people are not interested in getting a job because of the nature of their job requirements, and it is these which, in the final analysis, are decisive;

- Aspirations in relation to work, for the main body of respondents and especially for the unemployed, were patently excessive given the current Russian labour market situation. Most of them would like to work near home, in their usual occupation, in comfortable working conditions, in an undemanding job with a good atmosphere and working relations and with a high level of pay. Willingness to reduce the level of job requirements, even if only by travelling further from home to work, noticeably increased chances of finding work;

- 'Drive to achieve' labour values were also-rans as far as labour motivation indicators were concerned, although they were noticeably more widespread among those who had found work than among the unemployed; and among those who were satisfied with their present job, they even worked their way forward to a place among the front runners. Overall, the main factors playing a significant role in creating job satisfaction were working conditions and the content of work, and - for the two most deprived groups - income level;

- The nature of the aspirations of the Russian unemployed in relation to work and their perception of restrictions on finding it differed significantly from analogous indicators for the unemployed in Britain. The nature of these differences demonstrated the unwillingness of the Russian unemployed to seek work in labour market conditions and their perception of unemployment above all as an absence of the necessary means for living, and not a qualitatively different social status;

- Our attempt to record the particular psychological characteristics of our respondents using the PRA index showed that, even in a relatively small sample of respondents, statistically significant differences exist between the unemployed and those who have found work. Moreover, analysis of the dynamic of change in the respondents' employment status over the year of observation showed that the PRA index level of respondents in 1996 had a noticeable influence on change in their employment status. This led us to a more attentive examination of the issue of the particular personality characteristics of the unemployed.

Particular Personality Characteristics of the Actors as Factors in Their Employment

It has been shown above that employment status was chosen by the actors on a completely rational basis, taking into account a whole range of factors - household composition, the presence of other resources and the possibilities of using various survival strategies, the significance of various job requirements and their willingness to moderate these, including changing the content of their productive activities, as well as their degree of adaptability to the realities of contemporary Russia. Overall, one could say that the main thing was their desire to work - as a rule, anyone who wanted to work had the possibility of doing so, although (depending on the state of the local labour market and the sector where they had worked before) often with reduced status, a shift in content of activity, and - in a number of cases - a change of occupation.

This conclusion, however, did not explain three overridingly important facts. Firstly, it remained incomprehensible why employers did not want to have anything to do with the majority of the unemployed, and refused their services. Even if we suppose that often the refusal to hire for a job was at the request of the worker himself - because he didn't want to find work - nevertheless, it was hardly necessary for the enterprise to meet such a request halfway. There was indirect corroboration of the fact that those who had found work were the kind of staff who, to a large extent, suited employers: not only had they found work, but also there were approximately three times as many people among them who would have been willing to stay at the job they had

had before their period of unemployment, if they had been able to agree a change in their occupation or post or lower basic pay. So, the proportion of those who had no possibility of remaining at their old job was 89 per cent of the unemployed in 1997, and only 63 per cent of those who had found work.

Secondly, it was not clear why the unemployed themselves did not want jobs and stated overtly excessive job requirements, when a significant section of them did not differ from those who had found work in either household composition or skills or other characteristics.

Thirdly, taking into account the particular features of the labour markets in the three cities, the position of people in employment crisis in Moscow seemed surprising. Even in St. Petersburg - less favourable from the point of view of possibilities of finding work - only 18 people out of 80 remained registered unemployed or *de facto* unemployed, while the rest had found normal jobs. In Moscow, this indicator was 34 out of 100 respondents. Such a position supports our hypothesis that unemployment can be varied in nature, and that in St. Petersburg unemployment is, in the first instance, linked to on-going re-structuring and has a less 'persistent' character; while in Moscow, where labour market conditions are more favourable, it is caused above all by personal factors relating to the unwillingness of the unemployed person to get a job or the impossibility of him doing so for some kind of personal reasons. To a certain extent, the role of personal factors in unemployment was also confirmed for Voronezh, where almost three-quarters of those who were working in 1996 had, after receiving notice of redundancy, gone straight into a new job without any period of unemployment, at the same time as almost all those who were unemployed had remained so. But the proposition that the main differences between the behaviour of the unemployed in Moscow, St. Petersburg and Voronezh lay in their particular personality characteristics had yet to be tested.

The desire to explain these three facts led us to analyse this type of resource more fully, and this not only showed its significance as applied to choice of survival strategy and level of material security, but also revealed the presence of personal resources ('habitus') in an analysis of the dynamic of change in employment status. We compared the respondents from employment crisis groups with the position of respondents in the RIISNP national representative surveys, and also compared the various employment crisis groups with each other.

Table 9.6   **Values of Russians (RIISNP data, March 1997) and of respondents in labour market crisis (April 1997) (per cent)**

Values	Russians overall	Respondents in labour market crisis
Equality of opportunity	60	70
Equality of incomes	37	25
Interesting work	31	56
The most important thing is how much a job pays	64	41
Being different from others	35	53
Living like others	59	45

As we can see, the differences between respondents from the employment crisis groups and other Russians were as high as 1.5-2 times. Moreover, both the two-stage research we are describing here and the RIISNP monitoring research confirm the non-random nature of these gaps. According to some values, the positions of respondents from the employment crisis groups changed over the year, but by no more than 6 per cent (the number of those who considered that the main thing in a job is that it should be interesting, which was almost two-thirds of the sample in 1996, fell), while according to others they remained generally stable. The values of other Russians were similarly stable, with some also falling, only more strongly (the above example value fell from 45 per cent in 1996 to 31 per cent in 1997). Thus, our respondents changed together with the whole population, but they continued to demonstrate a fairly original type of value, where a greater role was played by 'income interests', with equalising and conformist attitudes less widespread than among average Russians. This could hamper their adaptation to contemporary realities.

On the socio-psychological level, there were other differences between respondents from the employment crisis groups and the national Russian sample. In spite of what would seem to be their difficult objective position, less than half of them were pessimists. The certainty of people from the employment crisis groups that justice would triumph in the end looked unrealistic. One in four of them at both stages of the survey considered the most productive means of defending their interests to be application to the courts (only one in 20 of Russians overall). At the same time, the proportion of those who believed that there were simply no means of defending their interests was only 22 per cent of respondents from the employment crisis groups, as against 53 per cent of Russians in general.

The data we have are, of course, inadequate to resolve the question of the particular socio-psychological characteristics of members of employment crisis groups, and especially of the unemployed. But they do allow us to confirm that very serious bases underlie Gordienko, Pshevnev, and Plyusin's (1996) research data on the particular socio-psychological characteristics of the unemployed. This issue is extraordinarily important, in the first instance, in order to improve the operation of the ES, which up to now has not taken this phenomenon into account in its work and has, on encountering the manifestly differing specific psyches of unemployed people, placed a completely incorrect interpretation on them.

At the same time, in many characteristics where we expected to encounter differences between respondents from the employment crisis groups and other Russians (understanding the main objective of State social policy as providing for all the needy up to a necessary social level; willingness to submit to the authority of managers; and so on), we did not discover any, at least across the sample as a whole. However, on analysing the differences between the unemployed and those who had already found work at the first stage of the research, these were found to be very great - and these were not only differences in the level of aspirations in relation to work and in labour motivations.

The most typical feature of those who had fallen into employment crisis groups, especially the long-term unemployed, was the absence of sufficient realism and adequacy in assessing oneself, one's life as a whole and one's labour market situation. This inadequacy was linked, obviously, with poor ability to adapt to the new reality that has arisen in recent years in Russia, and with the gradual withdrawal into a 'desired' reality, as a defensive reaction of the psyche to the overload of the recent years.

There is evidence of withdrawal into 'desired reality' in the fact that, in responses to questions of a general nature relating to assessment of their future, the unemployed at both the first and second stages of the research were more placid by nature, more inclined to expect that 'everything will be resolved of its own accord', and noticeably more optimistic than those who had found work. And although, over the period of observation, the respondents' optimism diminished practically by half, it was still the case that in 1997 36 per cent of the unemployed (as against 28 per cent of those who had found work) considered that their immediate future prospects promised them an improvement in their lives. 61 per cent of the unemployed and 57 per cent of those who had found work were certain that if they just put up with a little more, then life would somehow come right. At the same time, in responses to concrete questions about their future (such as the dynamic of change in their material circumstances, or possibilities of finding work), the unemployed fully demonstrated their distinct understanding of the lack of prospects of their position.

Lack of adequate assessment of their situation and of themselves could also be seen in other responses given by the unemployed. So, for example, in 1996, 50 per cent of unemployed Moscow respondents declared that they did not feel supported by their friends and family, although most also indicated that help from family and friends was a main source of income for them. According to the data from the RIISNP representative survey of Russians, carried out in October 1995, only 19 per cent of Russians in general did not feel supported by their friends and family. Thus we can see that a particular lack of gratitude to friends and family and a demand for excessive attention for themselves was typical of unemployed Muscovites to a much greater extent than for Russians in general and other Muscovites in particular.

Another noticeable difference from average indicators for Russia was the tendency of people from the employment crisis groups, and above all of the unemployed, to display lack of a disciplined attitude. So, in December 1996, according to data from the RIISNP surveys, less than 60 per cent of people did not agree with the opinion that managers 'should be obeyed regardless of whether you are sure they are right or not'. In our 1997 research, this indicator was 96 per cent of the unemployed (78 per cent of those who had found work): and only 13 per cent of the unemployed thought that a disciplined attitude helped one obtain a good job. At the same time, according to the data of the RIISNP research carried out in 1996 among small business people in a number of cities in European Russia, including Moscow, over 40 per cent indicated that a disciplined attitude was the most important characteristic of an employee. ES staff and other groups surveyed for this project as 'policymakers' also assessed it more highly. Unemployed people's assessment of the role of initiative and of putting oneself into the job, as factors in getting a good job, was also very low (15 per cent and 17 per cent respectively), while one in three of those who had found work considered them important.

Thus, the long-term unemployed differed from those who had found work not only in terms of their level of aspirations but also their psychological type in general. They typically gave unrealistic assessments of the situation in Russia, of their own prospects, of methods of realising their interests, of the needs of employers in relation to employees and of the value of their own labour, as well as displaying a lack of flexibility. It is possible that this not only hindered those of them who nevertheless were interested in finding work from choosing the most acceptable of the possible jobs, but also scared off employers, who as a rule refused to hire them after interview.

However, the main body of the unemployed, including the hidden unemployed, did not strive to change their attitude to themselves or to life, since despite the dramatic tension of the situation they found themselves in, it had not developed into a tragic one because of the existence for most of them of alternative survival strategies and employment strategies (which we have discussed above in connection with the problem of the 'price of sacrifice' and the level of aspirations). It is possible, however, that this was also connected with widespread expectations of paternalism among the unemployed. So, members of the unemployed group and those who had found work were sharply differentiated by their beliefs as to whom their material circumstances depended on (on themselves: 44 per cent of those who had found work and 19 per cent of the unemployed; on the situation in Russia: 38 per cent of those who had found work and 53 per cent of the unemployed) and by their perception of the possibility of influencing what happens in their lives (42 per cent of those who had found work and only 24 per cent of the unemployed considered that they were playing an important role in things, while 39 per cent of the unemployed and 12 per cent of those who had found work were certain that putting right the problems that had arisen was beyond their capacities). As a result of the conviction that nothing could depend on them, however hard they tried, even the manifestly unsuccessful position in which the unemployed found themselves did not encourage them to reduce their assessment of themselves or their self-esteem. 81 per cent of the unemployed did not consider themselves worthless individuals, and only two per cent (one person) was firmly convinced that he was a worthless person.

Here we would like to focus on something which is very important to an understanding of the position of the unemployed: the problem of 'dependency culture', which when applied to Russian conditions is very closely linked to expectations of paternalism, although paternalism comes out more as its 'ideological justification' than as its real cause, which we will try to indicate below.

In general, one objective of our research was to look at whether there is a phenomenon in Russia which is analogous to what has been given the name in Western sociology of 'the dependency culture'; but neither the data from the first stage of the survey nor analysis of the data from all the questions in the block on the problem of 'dependency' in the second stage questionnaire gave any serious basis for considering that a similar phenomenon does exist in Russia. Sometimes, the individual figures seemed to suggest something similar, but more detailed analysis using pair correlations demonstrated that, in every case, the issue was something different, and we anticipated that because of the small size of all social benefits, there is no 'dependency culture' in Russia.

However subsequently we encountered this phenomenon in our analysis of a group which had been revealed, independently of our original objective, to have more than three unemployed people in their immediate circle. Having originally observed it as noticeably differing from the total sample, we thought that this group (which consisted of 61 people) must be a concentration of the most deprived respondents and a focus of various types of social exclusion. For example, half of all those who indicated that they spent more than 80 per cent of their total income on food were found to be concentrated in this grouping.

However, on more detailed review, it turned out that nothing was so simple. Although this group actually consisted in general of unemployed people and the percentage within it of people from the poorest strata was somewhat higher than the average across the sample, nevertheless its main specific feature was found not to be this, but to be the quite distinct life position of its members. Moreover, this specific feature was not so much linked with particular individual characteristics of their values or of their psychological state - where it was almost untraceable (the sole exception was greater anxiety, more depression and a greater tendency to hypochondria than across the sample as a whole) - as with the phenomenon of 'dependency culture' exactly as it is interpreted in the western sociological tradition, although in Russian terms this would conventionally be described rather as a semi-deliberate dependent position. The corresponding emphasis, therefore, was not on the formation of dependency on social assistance, but on the completely rational - although possibly not always sustainable - exploitation by members of this group of the State, of the various social funds and of those around them, including family and friends: it was this which allowed us, conditionally, to call this group 'dependent'.

We should immediately note that members of this group understand that this approach is proving less and less effective for most of them. Our research data show that their position in relation to all the rest of the sample actually deteriorated in all the cities, and especially in Moscow (71 per cent of them noted a deterioration in their material circumstances, as against 47 per cent across the whole Moscow sub-sample) where the typical features of this group were generally most strikingly revealed (which, obviously, also told of the differing fates of people like our respondents in Moscow and St. Petersburg). They expect an even greater deterioration in the future, and pessimism in assessing their prospects is almost twice as widespread among members of this group than on average among the respondents. This may also cause some greater depression in their psychological state. And here they are right, since life in Russia is now so hard, and Russians have to struggle so vigorously for even a possibility of preserving their standard of living, that social dependency - which used to be viewed with equanimity - has begun to give rise to increasing resistance and condemnation both by the authorities and by society.

After this preamble, we will try to illustrate in figures why most members of this group are bearers of the 'dependency culture' ideology, while they are not objectively people in a difficult or hopeless position (although there are also some of them who are, especially in Voronezh).

However, above all we should note that members of this group do not differ from the structure of the sample as a whole in sex, age, particular occupational characteristics or skills level: in fact, they stand out as surprisingly precise representatives of the sample. Across all the most important resources at their disposal, respondents with more than three unemployed people in their immediate circle differed from others first and foremost in that their health was, according to their own assessment, noticeably worse than that of people who did not have any unemployed people in their immediate circle: among the former, 21 per cent complained of poor health, and in the latter group, six per cent. 13 per cent of the former group and 25 per cent of the latter considered their health to be good. Moreover, it is possible that this is a consequence of their general hypochondria. Their other types of resources surprisingly exactly replicated that of the sample, with the exception of sources of income, which will be covered below.

Only 13 people in St. Petersburg fell into this group, while in Moscow and Voronezh the number was found to be identical and almost twice as large - 24 people in each city. So, in order to emphasise some particular features of this group, the author conducted an analysis of its position separately for each city and from now on will compare Moscow and Voronezh, in the example of which both the main particular features of all the group and the range of specific differences are evident.

In terms of the structure of consumption and way of life, although the proportion of the two poorest groups among the 'dependent' exceeded the average indicators for each city, earlier (before the reforms) these people had regarded themselves as completely successful to a much greater extent than the other respondents. So, for example, in Moscow, 62 per cent of this group bought cold meats or delicatessen fish products (as against 39 per cent on average for the city) and 70 per cent in Voronezh (50 per cent on average for the city). Another evidence of their previously very affluent position was the property which their family had acquired. Suffice it to say that in Moscow 42 per cent of respondents in these groups had a three-room flat, while the average was 31 per cent, and in Voronezh the corresponding indicators were the same, but with a small excess for two-room flats. At the same time, the property indicators gave indirect evidence of the fact that these are in principle the 'new poor', since the amount of possessions they had previously acquired was generally fairly large. In Moscow and Voronezh, out of 48 people, only five had children under 18 in the family (two large families in each city, plus a one-parent family in Voronezh). Thus, out of the 48 people who made up the 'dependent' group in the two cities, only five people were in that unfortunate stratum where their objective position could well explain the 'dependency culture'. There were no two-parent families with one or two children under 18 in this group.

In the group we are describing, forms of social participation and social contacts in general were very distinctive. In Moscow, this group contained most of the people who had attended youth organisations, played in an orchestra, taken part in amateur dramatics, or attended meetings of political parties in the last three years - eight of the 12 people across the whole Moscow sample to whom this applied. Overall, almost all this group took part in various forms of such activity. Relatively less widespread were church attendance and sports club membership (twice as rare as across the whole Moscow sample), and also various forms of evening classes (two and a half times rarer). In Voronezh, the use of all these forms of spending leisure time was generally less widespread, although there also the number who attended evening classes was several times less than the average for the city, while twice as many usually spent time going out with other people for entertainment.

In general it could be said that members of this group love life and know how to enjoy themselves - they don't shut themselves away to work or study. Most of them have continued to attend these organisations, and the number of those who had stopped going to them because of lack of money was even slightly lower in percentage terms than in Moscow as a whole (20 per cent and 22 per cent respectively).

Other data also say something about the greater attraction of a comfortable life for members of this group than for other respondents, and about their lower 'drive to achieve' motivations. So, for example, in assessing various aspects of work, the Muscovites, and also in some of the questions the Voronezh respondents, displayed relatively lower interest than others who took part in the survey towards aspects such as content, social usefulness, potential for displaying initiative and using knowledge and ability. The relative egocentrism and 'self-satisfaction' of the members of this group were especially noted in relation to such aspects of work as getting on with workmates, which is generally extraordinarily important for Russians. Among members of the group we are reviewing, getting on with workmates was found to be important for only 20 per cent, but 32 per cent overall for Muscovite respondents, and 49 per cent for Voronezh respondents. But then convenient shifts, well-organised work and not having a tiring job had relatively greater significance for them than for other respondents.

The structure of permanent social contacts in this group was fairly unusual. Contacts with old friends and - even more so - former and present workmates were relatively unimportant for members of this group. Social contact (taking into account that in their immediate circle there were more than three unemployed people) took place in what one might call 'their own circle'. In this, contacts with relations and various neighbours predominated - neighbours at home (54 per cent as against 40 per cent of those who have no unemployed people in their immediate circle), neighbours at the *dacha* (25 per cent and 17 per cent respectively) and at 'garage clubs' (10 per cent and five per cent respectively).

But the main thing was the number of replies from respondents in this group, especially in Moscow, which allowed us to assert that they generally perceive their dependent position as a proper one. They do not try to get work, and most of them know, even when unemployed, how to make sure their lives are no worse than other people's. According to their employment status, these people, as should be expected, are concentrated in general among the registered and the *de facto* unemployed, and also are on unpaid or part-paid leave. Moreover, a year ago more than half of them had also been unemployed or on leave. They were not especially seeking a job - half of this group in Voronezh and more than half in Moscow were not interested in working. Among the few who were nevertheless working anyway, four people in Moscow and one in Voronezh were intending to give up work.

Most 'dependents' in both cities were sure that they would never find work (to be more precise - for Muscovites, as opposed to Voronezh respondents, this meant not work in general, but a job that they would be willing to take). Among the reasons which hinder their finding work we can list particular characteristics of their knowledge, experience and skills, the burden of family responsibilities, and poor health.

Given the fact that more than half of them in Moscow and a third in Voronezh considered that no period of unemployment would make them change their list of job requirements, while to find a job meeting their requirements is practically impossible, we conducted an analysis of the ideas of respondents from the 'dependent' group about how they intend to survive. From this it became clear that the predominant element was a dependent tendency, accompanied by a simultaneous conviction that nothing depends on the respondents themselves. In answering the question 'who, in the first instance, should help you to tackle your financial problems and employment problems?', less than half the Moscow respondents and only one in four in Voronezh replied 'myself', although over the whole sample this response was chosen by more than half the Muscovites and almost half the Voronezh respondents. Among the other responses the predominant ones were 'the State' - one in four Muscovites and almost half the Voronezh respondents - and 'friends, relations and acquaintances'. To the control question 'On what does your financial position largely depend?', 28 per cent of dependent group members in Moscow and 32 per cent in Voronezh (as against 17 per cent on average for Moscow and 28 per cent for Voronezh) replied 'on the country's economic situation and nothing else. However hard I try, very little depends on my own efforts'. Almost as many considered 'largely on the country's economic situation, although my own efforts do count for something'.

The conviction that nothing depends on themselves, in combination with a firm - although not always well-founded - certainty on the part of three-quarters of this group in Moscow and almost 60 per cent in Voronezh, that their material circumstances are worse than other people's gave them the moral bases for using all possible types of help. In any case, a third (as against 12 per cent across the sample) of Muscovites from this group were willing to accept help from anyone without reference to their level of poverty, and somewhat more than a third were willing to do so if their material circumstances became more difficult. Furthermore, a quarter of Muscovites (as against nine per cent across the sample) considered that 'it is the responsibility of the State to provide for those who need support, so I could apply to relevant State organisations for help'. Another quarter was certain that the family and relations should fulfil this obligation. In Voronezh, these indicators were somewhat lower, but also noticeably exceeded the indicators across the sample as a whole. Possibly because of such arrangements as 'free gifts', this group experienced the loss of possibilities of using social services at the enterprise as much more painful than others did - above all, the right to free or subsidised use of holiday centres, children's summer camps, medical services and sporting facilities. In any case, two-thirds of this group in Moscow said the loss of this right was important for them (45 per cent across the Moscow sample).

In addition, it should be said that many of them had succeeded in realising their dependent tendency. A third of respondents from this group in Moscow (as against 20 per cent across the sample) and 40 per cent in Voronezh (as against 35 per cent across the sample) indicated help from relations as a source of income. But then, additional earnings were one-and-a-half times less widespread in this group than on average among Muscovites. Only half the members of this group in both Moscow and Voronezh did not receive any kind of help from the State or charities in cash or kind (on average across the Moscow and Voronezh samples, more than two-thirds of respondents did not receive such help). Moreover, among kinds of such help were subsidised health care, public transport and a number of other subsidies and payments. In Moscow, the predominant forms of survival strategies which this group listed from the possibilities given (in diminishing order) were: 'we borrow money', 'we receive help', 'we provide ourselves with some foodstuffs', 'we are using up our savings' and 'we have more than one job'. In Voronezh also, the predominant forms, in diminishing order, were: 'we provide ourselves with some foodstuffs', 'we borrow money', 'we are using up our savings' and 'we receive help'. Each of these survival strategies received no less than 20 per cent support. The 'we borrow money' strategy was especially interesting, given the situation that people were sure that their position would not improve in future. In fact, this was a somewhat masked form of the 'we receive help' strategy.

Thus:

- The core of the unemployed and insecurely employed groups (especially those who had been on compulsory unpaid leave for a long time) was very distinctive in its socio-psychological characteristics. Its members, who had belonged to the most affluent stratum of society before the reforms, had chosen a way of life for themselves where their circle of permanent social contact was limited to neighbours and relations, and the role of friends was relatively small. Furthermore, they chose above all to maintain social contact with those neighbours and relations who were also not working. A drive to achieve was not widespread in the group, but an orientation towards comfortable working conditions in a job was overtly expressed. Forms of leisure activity connected with study or re-skilling were practically absent, but various forms of entertainment and hobbies were widely represented. In practice, they were not seeking work, and the respondents themselves explained this by the difficulties of their situation. Dependent tendencies and expectations of paternalism were widespread. The members of this group displayed great egocentrism and the overwhelming majority of them had no children (the exception were a few households consisting of large and one-parent families);

- In the current economic conditions in Russia, the position of this group is deteriorating, relatively speaking, which allows its members to consider that those around them (from the State to their friends) are obliged to maintain or at least help them. This conviction is displayed both in their tendencies towards believing that someone should provide for them and in the concrete survival strategies that they choose. In most cases, they are actually successful in finding a source of means of subsistence apart from wages, although the number of them who - according to objective reasons - can count on help from elsewhere (large and one-parent families or disabled people) is very small in the composition of the group and does not exceed the indicators for the sample as a whole;

- The deterioration in their material circumstances and their understanding of the lack of prospects of their chosen position in contemporary economic conditions arouses pessimism and hypochondria in members of the 'dependent' group. However, most of them are not able to reconsider their employment position, or do not want to. This is connected with their particular individual features, including their excessive requirements in relation to work and their lack of willingness to reduce these.

Conclusion - The Role of Systemic and Personality Factors

So, who are the new deprived groups who have appeared in the structure of Russian society as a result of the re-structuring of the economy and its transition to market lines? What role do systemic factors connected with the re-structuring of the economy and with current social policy play in their choice of survival and employment strategies? And what role is played by personality factors arising from the particular individual features of the actors? Should individuals be seen as components in a system (whether socio-economic or cultural) or as rational actors - as the two main lines in contemporary sociology would have it?

The two main chapters of this section have, in point of fact, been devoted to answering these questions, so there is no need to repeat all their arguments here. However, we can reproduce briefly the main conclusions of our research:

- The re-structuring of Russia's economy and its transition to market lines have hit the majority of the population hard. Crisis phenomena on the labour market (unemployment, insecure employment, mass redundancies, etc.) have affected the majority of the population to some degree or other. Furthermore, various types of employees have suffered from the transition to the market in different ways. Some - for example, employees in industry or science - have suffered from the decline of their sector. Typical outcomes for them have been mass redundancies due to staff cuts, and insecure employment in all its forms. Others - employees in municipal housing and public utilities, consumer services, and trade - have suffered from the increased demands placed on the workforce in market conditions. There are various reasons why they might lose their jobs, but there is a complete absence of insecure employment (hidden unemployment) in this grouping;

- The results of our research have shown that *different types of unemployment co-exist in Russia at present*, and that in principle these demand a variety of administrative solutions to improve employment - all the more so because the different types interact differently within each region. The main reasons for the existence of different types of unemployment are:

    i) The restructuring of industry. Over half of industry was previously directed towards the requirements of the military-industrial complex; at the same time, a significant section of civilian enterprises was not competitive. Mass redundancies have already taken place in industry, and there will be more. Those cities where the labour market is less diversified, and where SMEs - which create new jobs - have developed more slowly, have fared worst. In our research, Voronezh provided a graphic example of such a city. The main outflow of labour has been from heavy industry and the defence industry, while recruitment was above all towards trade, municipal housing and public utilities, transport, the construction industry and the budget-funded sectors;

ii) Cuts in budget funding to a number of sectors, particularly culture, education and science. These have led to redundancy for some sections of staff in these sectors, and to a sharp growth in insecure employment for others. These problems affected all regions in proportion to the number of people working in budget-funded sectors there, but in rich regions like Moscow the wages of budget-funded sector employees are paid on time, while in subsidised regions such as Voronezh they are months late. As a result, there is a large group of highly skilled specialists who have been forced to change their occupation, although often they have not been formally unemployed. Many of the youngest, most highly skilled and mobile members of this group have entered the kind of new highly paid occupations which did not exist before. However, they have found this process fairly painful and usually continue to identify with their old occupations;

iii) Changes in demands on employees in the transition to a competitive economy, especially in those sectors where staff are in direct contact with clients - trade, the service sector, municipal services and utilities. In these sectors, as the market system has developed, staff have been replaced on a massive scale. However, as the results of our survey show, the experience of redundancy does not force a person to re-consider his or her attitude to work. So, of those who had lost jobs in the service sector, some of the unskilled workers had been forced to change their place of work more than once, because the employer was not pleased with their work;

iv) The formation of a labour market, in place of the labour shortages of a planned economy. A real labour market gives people a certain degree of 'training' as independent actors on that market - an idea of the approximate value of their labour, the habit of job-seeking, the ability to correctly present themselves as meeting the employer's requirements, appropriate behaviour in the case of unemployment, and so on. In Russia, however, where over the course of 70 years there was no labour market, and for 60 years no unemployment, the population has in practice totally lost these habits. Unemployment in these conditions frequently appears to be not so much the consequence of an objective absence of jobs as the consequence of people not being psychologically prepared to change to the type of employment that predominates in a market economy: these are, as it were, systemic factors which have filtered down to the 'personality' level. Moscow is a striking example of this phenomenon: the demand for staff with almost any skills and occupation substantially exceeds the number of unemployed people. However, the fact that a section of the population was not psychologically prepared for the demands made on employees by a labour market has led to the formation of long-term unemployment even in Moscow. This last cause of unemployment was typical of all three cities studied, although to varying degrees;

- The labour mobility of respondents over the year of observation was high and diverse. Despite the diversity of approaches used in seeking work, there were really only two ways of finding a job - finding a job on the recommendation of friends, including former workmates, and finding work through the ES - although the functions of the ES at present are not so much helping job-seekers as paying benefit. On the whole, the ES is coping successfully with the latter function, although the amount of benefit and the steps necessary to receive it arouse some discontent among the unemployed;

- In each of the groups that are distinguished by their type of employment, there is a fairly large stable core which is preserved and forms 'persistent' or 'long-term' unemployment or insecure employment. This core has fairly marked specific socio-demographic or other characteristics, including way of life and circle of social contacts. Random members of the group who do not correspond to its particular typical characteristics do not, as a rule, stay long within it. As a result, although the renewal of the composition of groups is continuous, a section of the new members fairly quickly leaves the group just as another section, to a large extent corresponding to the social type characteristic of the group in question, 'gets stuck' in it. On this level, we can talk about the formation of at least two - up to now - fairly stable strata in the new social structure of Russia: the long-term unemployed and the insecurely employed. Long membership of a particular employment crisis group on the one hand increases the probability that the person will remain in this group because they get used to a particular way of life and adapt to it, and on the other hand is in itself a consequence of particular personal characteristics;

- Among these particular personal characteristics the most important are the respondent's willingness to work and the level of their job aspirations. Most respondents from the registered unemployed and the insecurely employed groups were not interested in getting a permanent job: firstly, because their present status was for them only a cover for their real, unregistered employment, including private enterprise; or secondly, because either health or family situation did not allow it. The family situation does not strictly speaking limit finding work, but can further the choice of a particular employment strategy that takes into account the composition of household and the respondent's level of job aspirations. Thirdly, people are not interested in getting a job because of the nature of their job requirements, and it is these which, in the final analysis, are decisive;

- Aspirations in relation to work, for the main body of respondents and especially for the unemployed, were patently excessive given the current Russian labour market situation. Most of them would like to work near home, in their usual occupation, in comfortable working conditions, in an undemanding job with a good atmosphere and working relations and with a high level of pay. Willingness to reduce the level of job requirements, even if only by travelling further from home to work, noticeably increased chances of finding work. Variations in the level of aspirations of the long-term unemployed and those who had found work after a period of unemployment were very great, as were variations in flexibility of attitude to these aspirations. It was as if they had focused within themselves all the variations in psychological type of the unemployed and those who had found work. Typical of the long-term unemployed were inadequate assessments of the situation in Russia, of their own prospects, of methods of realising their interests, of the needs of employers in relation to employees and of the value of their own labour, as well as displaying lack of flexibility. It is possible that precisely this inadequacy not only hindered those of them who nevertheless were interested in finding work from choosing the most acceptable of the possible jobs, but also scared off employers, who as a rule refused to hire them after interview. These particular features of the unemployed were distinctly displayed in Moscow and less distinctly in Voronezh;

- For the majority of respondents, satisfaction with a new job is linked with three factors. One of them, systemic in nature, related to the objective possibilities of the local labour market, and gave rise not only to the possibility of rational choice of a particular employment strategy (for example, additional earnings instead of full-time work in Moscow), but also to satisfaction with the new job. The two others related to a number of personality resources at the disposal of respondents: on the one hand, willingness to reduce their status and to change the nature of their activity because of the limits of the labour market; and, on the other, the role of the 'interest level' of the job - for many respondents, this 'interest level' was able to reconcile them with low earnings and reduced status. In addition, for the two most deprived groups there existed a statistically significant relationship between job satisfaction and income levels;

• The nature of the aspirations of the Russian unemployed in relation to work and their perception of restrictions on finding it differed significantly from analogous indicators for the unemployed in countries with a long-established labour market. The nature of these differences demonstrated the unwillingness of the Russian unemployed to seek work in labour market conditions instead of a labour-shortage economy and their perception of unemployment above all as an absence of the necessary means for living, and not a qualitatively different social status;

• The predominance of women with specialised secondary or higher education stood out as a specific feature of the long-term unemployed group. Members of this group were generally in the 41-60 age cohort. Another particular and typical aspect of the group was found to be its members' previous employment - those who were 'stuck' in the long-term unemployed group were not so often employees of large industrial enterprises or institutions as of small businesses in trade or catering. Their circle of social contacts was typically first and foremost relations and neighbours, and on the level of general social well-being they are typically pessimistic, lost, and feel that they are unable to manage their own lives. Some complain about their health. Their values demonstrate the existence of notable differences from other groups. We also confirmed Chernina's (1996), and Gordienko, Pshevnev, and Plyusin's (1996) data on the poor assessment by the unemployed of their qualities as workers, and also on the high proportion of people with rigid and inflexible psyches which make it difficult for them to adapt to the new conditions.

Overall, the material circumstances of this group are worse than others, although there are members of it at all levels of welfare. The least well-off long-term unemployed are the 'old poor' - one-parent families with children under 18 and the families of disabled people. Among the badly-off and the averagely well-off, the so-called 'new poor' predominate. For those who are in the well-off or prosperous strata, unemployment is generally only a cloak for their real work activity, which they are usually conducting in the shadow economy.

Analysis of the real circumstances of the households of the long-term unemployed enabled certain social types of respondents to be identified, which correlated strictly with their employment status. These types were: heads of one-parent families with small children; single people of pre-pension age, often in poor health; married women with children of pre-school age; middle-aged and elderly married women either from families without dependants where the husband worked, or from large families (four to five members or more) where several members worked. Presumed alcoholics and people who had been in breach of labour discipline did not belong to the long-term unemployed group but to the group who had changed jobs more than once over the year of observation. However, the main body of those who had changed jobs more than once during the year had done so as a result of delays in being paid at their new job. This was especially typical for Voronezh;

- Typical particular features of the long-term insecurely employed group are the broad representation of men, its relative middle age, its high skills level, and its long service at the enterprise - which was as a rule large or medium-sized and in the area of science, scientific services, education and industry (heavy industry or the defence industry). In other sectors, insecure employment leads to fairly rapid change of job. From the point of view of the circle of social contacts, typical features of this group were the very high importance of friends at work and friends in general, as well as the high importance of getting on well with workmates among the main job requirements. Among values, as with the long-term unemployed, the great importance of the level of interest inherent in a job was a specific factor. Most employees in insecure employment were family people with grown-up children. There were practically no really poor people in this group, since the presence of wages of other family members, and also active work activities on the part of the insecurely employed in the shadow economy - which was considerably more important to them than to the general body of the unemployed - creates quite a bit of potential for supporting an average standard of living.

Overall, it could be said that the policy of preserving a section of the most skilled staff at an enterprise, even if they are sent on compulsory leave or kept in conditions of partial employment, is justified, since it has both allowed enterprises to keep a skilled workforce until the situation stabilises and allowed employees to remain working where they want to work, even at the price of certain sacrifices. For those who have found other work, this period has turned out to be a period of adaptation to new labour market conditions and has been more merciful than simple dismissal;

- The core of the groups of long-term unemployed and those who had been insecurely employed for a long time formed a very distinctive group, distinguished by its fatalism and by a conviction that nothing depended on them. Its members, who had belonged to the most affluent stratum of society before the reforms, had chosen a way of life for themselves where their circle of permanent social contact was limited to neighbours and relations, among whom they chose above all to maintain social contact with people who were also not working. In practice, they were not seeking work, and the respondents themselves explained this by the difficulties of their situation. Dependent tendencies and expectations of paternalism were widespread.

In the current economic conditions in Russia, the position of this group is deteriorating, relatively speaking, which allows its members to consider that those around them (from the State to their friends) are obliged to maintain or at least help them. In most cases, they have actually been successful in finding a source of means of subsistence apart from wages, although the number of them who - according to objective reasons - can count on help from elsewhere (large and one-parent families or disabled people) is very small in the composition of the group and does not exceed the indicators for the sample as a whole. Members of this group are not willing to reduce their excessive requirements in relation to work. As applied to the members of this group (and only to them) we can talk about the formation of a distinctively Russian version of the 'dependency culture' - a form of social dependency which appears, with a discriminating marker, when people fall into employment crisis groups;

• Our research showed that, in Russia today, it is generally impossible to study the problem of poverty on the basis of the respondents' own assessments of their material circumstances, and that this is related to the absence among ordinary Russians until recently of strata which are essentially differentiated by standards of consumption. The percentage coincidence of the respondents' own assessments of their position (including their level of income and the proportion of their expenditure that went on food) and their real level of welfare was less than 50 per cent. Russian sociologists have already proposed various means of measuring material welfare linked to various indices. The method developed here was a particular modification of this approach and involved assessing the level of welfare through an integrated criterion of the structure of consumption and way of life, based on revealing certain 'threshold' values. This criterion, which broadly comes under the umbrella of Townsend's ideas, demonstrated the applicability of his concepts to the Russian situation.

The problem of the genuinely poor in Russia today does not lie in the fact that they have a low *per capita* income, but that in principle they are deprived of the potential for the way of life that most of their fellow citizens lead. This fact is connected not only with the structure of consumption but also with restrictions on social participation, with a specific type of social contact, and with the choice of destructive or passive survival strategies that are not typical of the rest of the population. The position of this group continues to deteriorate, relatively speaking, and in the future they expect it to deteriorate further.

Using this definition, poverty is a characteristic of about 20 per cent of our sample. And even in Voronezh, where the situation has been much more unfortunate, the proportion of was still only 25 per cent. Another 25 per cent were badly-off: people who also experienced certain restrictions on their social participation and their way of life, but whose situation had not yet become persistent in character, while their survival strategies were more rational and constructive in nature. Unlike the poor, this group was unstable in composition. Over the year between the surveys, the number of badly-off people fell markedly, with two-thirds of them moving into the category of the averagely well-off, while the rest joined the ranks of the poor.

The largest section of people in the crisis groups (a little over a third) were in the averagely well-off group, and the remaining 20-25 per cent were 'well-off' or 'prosperous', for whom economising did not mean a lower quality of life or limiting social participation, but only meant setting out priorities in purchasing and buying each item in turn;

- The poor and the unemployed are mutually overlapping sets; they do coincide for the most part, but they are not identical. The primary cause of real poverty, and especially of profound poverty, was the respondents' family circumstances. These circumstances objectively prevented the people concerned from taking their place as effective employees on the labour market, and kept them among the unemployed; and in those cases where respondents from 'risk group' families actually found work, they mainly stayed in the 'poor' category anyway, or at best moved up to be among the 'badly-off', since they had been forced to take low-paid jobs.

The poor, then, were represented by five main types: one-parent families with children under 18; families with children under 18 where one or both parents were disabled; single people of pensionable or pre-pension age in poor health; families of supposed alcoholics; members of large families with a high family dependency ratio.

Moving on from the poor to the badly-off, the list of social types is enlarged by the categories of: young married women with small children; married middle-aged women in poor health in a two-person household, the second of whom was always employed; middle-aged single people with relatively normal health; one-parent families where the adult member of the family worked; and some two-parent families with two children. In general, one might say that almost no-one was in a position to keep a family with more than one dependant per working member in the 'well-off' or 'prosperous' category. One dependant per two employees was the maximum ratio enabling the majority of families to be among the well-off or averagely well-off. In some isolated cases, the ratio was one dependant per employee, but not more.

The survival strategies used by the poor to improve their material circumstances were more varied than the strategies of all the others. They contained more passive or destructive types of action, however, and active or constructive types of action were more rarely encountered. Among the 'old poor' the marginal type of economic activity was more commonly found, with destructive or passive forms of behaviour, than among the 'new poor', for whom constructive or active types of activity dominated (with attempts to earn extra money and engage in small-scale trading, including sale of produce from a *dacha*);

- The role of current state and local authority social policy in the survival of the poor and unemployed is close to nil. Those transfers which they received along with all the rest of the population, such as housing benefits, utilities and transport, were of fundamental importance. Benefits as such, targeted on the least affluent section of the population, were so insignificant that they had almost no effect on either their standard of living or their behaviour strategies. The main thing for most people was the product of their own economic activity or the help they received from sources other than the State. The sole exceptions were a few of the least affluent unemployed people - the heads of one-parent or large families - who had no forms of constructive activity;

- There were significant regional differences between the income and property status of populations. The proportion of well-off and prosperous people in the capitals was four times greater than in Voronezh, and of the poor - four times less. In the capitals, the 'old poor' predominated, while in Voronezh there were almost as many 'new poor' as 'old'. Moreover, in Moscow and St. Petersburg, the only addition to the traditional types of the 'old poor' was the single middle-aged person with health problems, while the 'new poor' were actually the 'badly-off', whose situation before the reforms had simply been noticeably better than now; but in Voronezh people who were perfectly well able to work had fallen right down into the 'poor' category - including people with families where there were other employed people and where the family dependency ratio did not exceed 1:1.

Given identical household composition in the same city, occupational status could, as a rule, only exert influence as far as placing the household in the badly-off or averagely well-off groups was concerned. Only in St. Petersburg, among people in households with no dependants and with a fairly limited range of occupational statuses, could a relationship be traced between the occupational status of the respondents and their position in the well-off or prosperous strata. In almost all other cases, the respondents' material circumstances were governed not so much by occupational status as by the effectiveness of the survival strategies they employed;

- The effectiveness of these strategies depended primarily on the effectiveness of the various types of action within them. The most effective strategy was to receive several secure salaries. This was done in three main ways - permanent employment of the respondent, permanent employment for other members of the household, and steady secondary employment for the respondent or other family members. Forms of the latter could vary, to include holding more than one job, self-employment and street trading. Absence of permanent main and secondary employment depended not so much on the state of the regional labour market as on the personal aspirations of the respondent. Thus it was particular features of the respondent's position on the labour market which were decisively significant in determining their new status niche when they fell victim either to economic restructuring or to increased demands on staff in market economy conditions: it was this position which allowed adaptation to the labour market, to acceptance of the new 'rules of the game'.

Forms of survival strategy associated with dissipation of existing economic resources were common first and foremost among the most deprived section of the respondents, and may be viewed as destructive in that the overwhelming majority of respondents had acquired possessions exclusively for their own personal use. Only being in the deepest poverty could compel respondents to start selling their possessions, but the economic impact of this was close to nil. Sale of possessions was characteristic of people in absolute poverty, while drawing on savings, loans and receipt of assistance were characteristic of people whose descent into poverty was relative in nature;

- Thus, the personal characteristics of our respondents exerted a huge influence on their employment status and their income/property status, and through those also on individuals' general status niche. Furthermore, this influence was greater, the broader the labour market and the quicker the pace of development of the private sector in the region, because this gave a broader spectrum of choice of potential behaviour strategies when difficulties with employment arose. And the broader the spectrum of choice of potential behaviours which did not correspond to standards from previous life experience, the larger the role which personal factors started to play, and above all - socio-psychological factors.

This allows us to draw a final conclusion which offers a distinctive answer to the question of what is the main thing - the system or the actor, social relations or social action. This conclusion falls within the broad sociological tradition which perceives separate individuals as active social subjects, 'rational actors' who put all their multiple resources to use in pursuit of their own aims, but taking into account those rules which are laid down by the concrete situation within which they have to act.

The spectrum of possible actions for someone in contemporary Russia is laid down by the objective situation. But for most of the population, even in relatively depressed large cities, the spectrum of possibilities is fairly broad, although for most of the population these opportunities do not correspond to their own wishes. Within the limits of this spectrum of actions, a person is free to choose, and in doing so they are completely governed by rational considerations. These considerations are far from always subject to the logic of economic expediency, and are as diverse and many-sided as are people themselves. For some people, preserving status is more important than material prosperity; for others, the most important thing is family and children; for a third group - their own health; while the members of a fourth group do not want to leave their favourite occupation even though there is no demand for it after economic restructuring - and so on.

In carrying out this act of choice - the choice of a survival strategy which will in essence define their place in the newly-forming society - in a situation where there is a fairly wide spectrum of possibilities, a person is above all governed by their personal notion of what is important and what is not, what they will agree to do and what they will never accept.

From this results the enormous role of personal factors in determining their new status niche.

Thus, in discussing the role of systemic factors in the process of stratification, it is essential to talk not so much about crisis in different sectors or enterprises during restructuring, which most of the population are managing to cope with more or less successfully on an individual level. The main thing is the fact that the transition to a market economy demands a new manner of thinking and a new method of assessing oneself and the world around one, a new understanding of the value and effectiveness of various survival strategies, of qualities desired and encouraged by society which are qualitatively different from those it valued previously. Systemic factors appear as a framework, a restricting device, a social imperative that the economy demands of the population. Personal factors determine a person's ability to conform to this imperative and correspondingly to use this ability to occupy a defined place in the new Russia. They do not exist separately from one another, but where the spectrum of possibilities is broad enough and the person is free to choose, personal factors can be of decisive importance. Perhaps this freedom of choice and the right to this freedom also explain the amazingly long-suffering nature of Russians during the course of the experiment that fate has been conducting on them for the last few years, and which is so agonising for most of them.

Part IV

The State of Russian Welfare

10 Social Policy and Social Order

Кошке игрушки, а мышке слезки
Toys for the cat, tears for the mouse

At the end of the 20th century, a new world has taken shape, whose key features have been very well described by Manuel Castells in his book, *The Information Age: Economy, Society and Culture* (1998). In his conclusion, he writes:

> A new world is taking shape in this end of millennium. It originated in the historical coincidence, around the late 1960s and mid-1970s, of three independent processes: the information technology revolution; the economic crisis of both capitalism and statism, and their subsequent restructuring; and the blooming of cultural social movements, such as libertarianism, human rights, feminism, and environmentalism. The interaction between these processes, and the reactions they triggered, brought into being a new dominant social structure, the network society; a new economy, the informational/global economy; and a new culture, the culture of real virtuality. (vol.III, p.336).

Among the phenomena which paved the way for this new world, Castells lists the fall of the soviet empire, the disappearance of communism and the end of the cold war. It is difficult to argue with such an obvious conclusion. However, this makes it all the more comprehensible that those living among the ruins of the fallen empire and the scattered illusions of a communist paradise would like to find their place - a well-deserved place - in the information age, the global economy and the network society. Of course, one must concur with the conclusion that the populations of territories which have nothing of value or interest to offer to the dynamics of global capitalism will not be able to join in this new life, or enter this new world. But all the same - is there a chance for Russia, and for Russians? Let us turn to further reflections by the same author:

> The restructuring of statism proved to be more difficult, particularly for the dominant statist society in the world, the Soviet Union, at the centre of a broad network of statist countries and parties. Soviet statism proved incapable of assimilating informationalism, thus stalling economic growth and decisively weakening its military machine, the ultimate source of power in a statist regime. (Ibid., p. 337).

Castells' statements about the new Russia, scattered around the book, might perhaps be defined as optimistic. He thinks that the new Russia will most likely be kept outside the European Union because of the West's historical fears, but will, nevertheless, no longer wish to tolerate its humiliation, and will revive its power as a strong nation, through reliance on its own human resources (ibid., pp 26-36, 356).

Our research took place during years of crisis in the systems of both state and society in Russia, years when hopes for rapid, positive reforms had, on the whole, been left behind. The text of this book was written largely after August 1998, when what remained of public trust and respect towards the post-Communist authorities finally crumbled to nothing. The main, and completely rational, reasons for this lay in the population's deteriorating standard of living (especially in the provinces), in falling social guarantees alongside a growing tax burden, and also in manifestations of social inequality which had become open and even blatant. All this led to a sharp reduction in the social base for liberal democratic reforms. Anything achieved by the reformers came to be wholly dependent on the goodwill of the President's immediate circle and of financial and political groupings close to the President. Alliances and compromises had to be made with these forces, whose interests had nothing in common with either market-competitive expectations or with the democratic hopes of the population.

Among the economic consequences of the policy of compromise from 1995 onwards, we should highlight the growth in corruption, which in recent years has developed into a stable system of relations in Russia. The main peculiarity of recent interactions between entrepreneurs and officials has consisted in the fact that it has now become - in contrast to the unstable situation of 1992 to 1994 - long-term in nature. Specific 'relational contracting' has been formed, and this no longer just comes down to a simple exchange of services between officials and business. Rather, it entails mutual strategic and tactical support within a framework of prolonged co-operation: individual officials are increasingly starting to move into the role of *business partner* in relation to particular entrepreneurs. One result of such a symbiosis has been the loss of national economic efficiency at the macro level - since the losses to society repeatedly exceed any advantages to be obtained from particular firms and particular officials maintaining 'relational contracting' (Radayev,1998).

As a result, the ultimate aims of the reforms - the creation of a competitive market economy and the construction of a democratic society in Russia - have not been achieved. Moreover, circumstances at the beginning of 2000 seem to be immeasurably more difficult than on the eve of the reforms, at the end of 1991. Even though the problems to be tackled are just as difficult, the Russian economy now has far fewer domestic resources at its disposal; and the possibilities of any outside assistance are almost completely exhausted.

Russia has joined the ranks of those countries with low life expectancy, a weak economy and huge social and economic differentiation within the population, and it has one of the highest levels of corruption in the world. At the same time, Russia remains a country uniquely rich in natural resources, with competitive human capital, first-class scientific education and a partially intact experienced workforce within the high-tech sector of the military-industrial complex. Over the years of reform, the exceptional adaptability to market economy conditions of a significant section of the population and a high level of survival-directed activity have been demonstrated. This forms the background to the situation in relation to social policy issues, both those of resource provision and those connected to its directions and methods of implementation.

Social policy in Russia has undergone very significant changes during the years of reform. As was shown in detail in Chapter 2, social policy in the USSR was interpreted as a system of organisational measures, directed at transforming the social sphere in specific ways (increasing the scale of residential building, the numbers of doctors and teachers, and so on). At the same time, the system of social protection - the most important section of social policy - meant primarily the right to work, provision of a state-guaranteed pension and a system of administratively regulated prices, ensuring the accessibility - at least in terms of price - of basic goods and services, free education, health care, sport and many other forms of leisure activity, as well as free allocation of housing. All this enabled social policy in the USSR to be viewed as a peculiar version of the Western Welfare State.

However, in its basic principles, this was an entirely different type of welfare state from its Western analogue. Whereas, in the West, citizens could obtain the goods provided for them by law through the institutions of civil society, in the USSR, because of the absence of a civil society, they were deprived of this possibility and became 'state-dependent workers'. Nevertheless, at the same time they perceived all and any social goods as constituting the *raison d'être* of the state's activities, its inalienable and obligatory function, which would be fulfilled independently of its having any economic potential; and, to a significant degree, this notion was also shared by the political élites, which, although they never neglected their own interests, still declared 'increasing the welfare of the Soviet people' to be one of the most important objectives of the state.

Somewhat anticipating the analysis that follows, it should be noted that this belief, accompanied by an absence of any institutions of civil society, rebounded painfully on Russians during the reform years, leaving them completely helpless before a state which was suddenly refusing to pay its 'social dues' to its own citizens. The young Russian state was already resolved, even in the first year of its existence, on this default - possibly the most important the country has seen, in terms of its scale; moreover, not only did such actions fail to alert advocates of the reforms in Russia and in the West, they even aroused warm approval from such quarters, which convinced the new political élites of Russia that they were acceptable. In the light of this, the 1998 default should be hardly surprising. However, the declarative and illusory nature of this objective was no secret to many Russians. It is no coincidence that over half of our respondents thought there was no difference between the society that existed before perestroika and contemporary Russian society, in terms of whether the state took equally good care of all its citizens.

Nevertheless, the presence - though limited - of a whole range of social goods and subsidies, which were universal in nature, and an even greater number of targeted ones (in the sense that they went to people working in a certain place) enables us to distinguish the pre-reform model of social policy in Russia as an independent, fourth type of welfare state alongside the three types of 'welfare capitalism' described in Esping-Andersen's (1990, 1999) model of welfare state classification. The particular features characteristic of this type were state regulation of all aspects of life in society, limited stratification, high bureaucratisation, and also the receipt of subsidies primarily through the system of production collectives (the workplace).

In the preceding chapters of this book, we have also noted that, having won mass support primarily by using slogans about the struggle against privilege and about greater social justice, individual freedoms and equality of opportunity for all, the ideas of economic reform were at first compelled to hide their true nature behind the mask of a 'social state' - which was exactly how the Russian state was described in the Constitution of the Russian Federation. However, for most of the political élites, the true nature of the new Russian state was, from the very first, no mystery, and here their interests differed radically from the position of the 'first wave' of democrats, who took part in the Gaidar government. Having done all the difficult, dirty work, these 'high-minded' democrats were, in point of fact, completely ousted by the old *nomenklatura*: for the latter, reform simply meant that it became possible to throw off the yoke of their obligations to take care of the people at a time of sharply increased personal appetites and new living standards, on the one hand, and of a sharp cut in incomes from export of natural resources (along with a fall in oil prices on the world markets), on the other. At the same time, no one made any official change in the social obligations of the state to its citizens, and, although 'second-rank figures' constantly attempt to repudiate the idea of the 'social state' on the basis of lack of economic resources, not one remotely outstanding political figure or party has done so - partly because of the constant election campaigns in Russia throughout the years of reform.

As a result, a paradoxical situation has arisen in Russia today. Formally, Russia is a welfare state in a variety of ways, and, in reality, various systems of social subsidies and payments do exist, covering two-thirds of the population in total. Again formally, in terms of constitutional guarantees, the right to work also continues to exist, as do state-guaranteed pension provision and free education, health care and housing allocation. In a number of regions, even the system of administratively regulated prices continues to exist, ensuring the accessibility - at least in terms of price - of basic goods and services. However, at the same time access to work and to remuneration for labour of more than a quarter of the economically active population is being infringed, the huge mass of the population is becoming monstrously impoverished, a significant proportion of young people are turning out to be not only uneducated but even illiterate, and free, guaranteed medical care has been replaced by the need to wait years for a free operation. The housing queue has not moved for decades. And all this is taking place against a backdrop of not only 'new Russians', but also ordinary state officials blatantly 'throwing money about' and of large-scale illegal export of capital abroad: an estimate of the volume of this, far from being the highest, is about $300 billion over the reform period.

Under these conditions, should we conclude that Russia is a 'social state', where the reason for the ineffectiveness of current social policy is simply lack of money? Of course not. As our research showed, the main reason for Russia's being considered merely a formal 'social state' and for the seemingly fantastic inefficiency of the country's current social policy is the inherent contradiction between the formally declared and the real aims of this policy. And if we look at the real aims - rather than the formally declared ones - then this policy, although it bears no relation to a welfare state, is nevertheless very effective. Given that this is the key to understanding the whole area of social policy issues in Russia, we should elaborate on what we mean.

Real versus formal welfare

As has already been noted in Chapter 6, three quarters of the social policy actors surveyed thought that Russia was not a social state, and only 19 per cent were convinced of the opposite. Almost 40 per cent said that ensuring social stability was the main aim of social policy being implemented in Russia today, while 28 per cent said it was to defend the interests of the élite. Since, from the point of view of the contemporary political élite of Russia, social policy is necessary only in so far as it prevents citizens from hindering the realisation of its own plans and interests, then defending élite interests amounts to the same thing as ensuring stability in society. Thus, in the final analysis, over 65 per cent of our respondents thought that the main aim of social policy was to ensure stability in society in the interests of the ruling élite.

In those groups most closely connected with the practical implementation of social policy (middle-ranking officials and trade union leaders), about 90 per cent of respondents shared this position, with most of them (about 70 per cent of these groups) putting the main emphasis on ensuring social stability. The overwhelming majority (over 80 per cent) of those respondents - politicians and the management élite - who were more familiar with the real mechanism of power, in particular the mechanism of decision-making on social issues, also saw these as being the main aims of social policy, but they placed their chief emphasis on defence of élite interests (over 50 per cent). As to possible social policy aims, such as helping the most deprived sections of the population, supporting the economically active population and preserving Russia's human resources, these figured noticeably only in the replies of high-ranking officials, a third of whom regarded the chief objective of social policy as targeted social assistance, and about another 10 per cent - as supporting the economically active population.

Thus the main aim of the social policy being implemented in Russia today is, in the opinion of all those connected with its implementation, to ensure stability in society in the interests of the élite, and not in any way to target help towards the most deprived people. Having recalled this key conclusion, more detailed grounds for which have been provided in the preceding sections of the book, let us continue our analysis.

What, then, would most tend to destroy the social stability which the Russian élite would like to preserve? Obviously, it is less likely to be the further impoverishment of socially deprived sections of the population than the main mass of Russians being deprived of customary goods. The fact is that, up to now, according to both statistical and sociological research data, children and pensioners have suffered most from the reforms. This opinion was also shared by those of our sample who were members of groups affected by labour market crisis: at both stages of our research, about two-thirds of the respondents named pensioners as being among those social groups in the most difficult position. But vulnerable social strata (which include, alongside elderly people, lone mothers, disabled people, and so on) are much less capable of active social protest than the rest of the population. Our research also gave clear confirmation of this: in the first stage of the research, a total of five per cent of the members of labour market crisis groups viewed meetings, demonstrations and similar things as means of defending their interests, and in the second stage, only three per cent; however, among the most socially deprived groups, no one at all favoured such courses of action. If we then take into account that the most deprived groups have no access to such methods as strikes or the creation of independent trade unions (which garnered up to 25 per cent support over the course of the survey), because of their displacement from the labour market, then no real forms of protest at all remain at the disposal of these groups, in conditions where the relevant institutions of civil society are absent.

Thus the authorities need have no fear of any real protest from this group of Russians, which could endanger the ruling élite. It is this which provides the obvious explanation for the equanimity with which our survey respondents viewed social policy, and for the attitude they took to their own stewardship - at best, that of 'tender-hearted auntie', which we have already mentioned in the previous chapters of this book.

The situation in relation to the remaining, relatively successful section of the population is quite different. The 'tobacco riots' in Moscow in 1991, the closure of railways and airlines in various regions of Russia in 1998, the mass protests in Moscow and St Petersburg at attempts to introduce timed charging for telephone calls, and finally the landslide growth of non-payment for local public utilities, as prices for these have risen, have all shown that, in principle, Russians are capable of active social protest - but only when the rights and subsidies, which, from their point of view, are most vital to them, are affected. Moreover, this protest usually takes one of two main forms: mass sabotage (as in the case of non-payment for local public utilities, which was spread equally across all the main population groups, not only the most deprived) and spontaneous - or, more precisely, extra-institutional - revolt. Both of these forms represent a very serious danger to the ruling élite, under conditions of crisis in the economy and of strong social tension (Lang-Pickvance, Manning and Pickvance, 1997; Manning, 1998).

So, given that complete neglect of the position of ordinary Russians by the authorities could really lead to active social protest from them, what are the key principles of state social policy for these people, which - even if largely intuitively - today's political élites in Russia are finding themselves compelled to take into account?

Popular views of state welfare

First and foremost, at least judging by RIISNP representative national surveys (and the same position is typical of the members of labour market crisis groups we surveyed), is that the state should satisfy the requirement, under the 'duty' model that prevailed until recently, to take care of all the poor, not only those who are, for objective reasons, not in a situation to provide for themselves (pensioners, the disabled, and so on). It is true that the number of adherents of this position is gradually falling (with the number reducing from 73 per cent to 63 per cent over the year of observation of respondents from labour market crisis groups), but nevertheless there were still more of them than of proponents of targeted social assistance.

This view of the functions of the state is connected with two circumstances, to which we would like to draw attention. Here we have in mind the conviction of many Russians, especially those working in the state sector and members of socially vulnerable groups, that their material circumstances and solutions to their employment problems depend solely or primarily on the state. As our research showed, being in difficult material circumstances does not make people change their outlook on this issue (47 per cent thought this, in both the 1996 and 1997 surveys). This does not mean that people are not willing to make independent efforts to find earnings or casual income: as we have tried to show in the chapter devoted to household survival strategies. Rather it reflects the objective impossibility of improving their position by means of finding work independently, given the present state of the labour market in Russia, for the majority of those members of vulnerable social groups (lone mothers,

mothers with many children, disabled people, elderly people in poor health, and so on) who find themselves in conditions of employment crisis, and for many residents of the depressed regions. Members of socially strong groups are largely ready to tackle their problems only or chiefly on their own, and they formed about 40 per cent of our sample; the remainder found it difficult to define their position.

Half of all the respondents at both stages of the research were unable to name any means of standing up for their interests, and only about 20 per cent selected 'applying to those state or voluntary organisations which are responsible for the services that should be tackling your problems'. Thus, for the majority of members of socially vulnerable groups (especially in the non-Moscow sample), the act of putting their trust in the state is simply a result of the genuine hopelessness and impossibility of tackling their problems independently: expecting help from a source, which you know cannot provide it, must arise simply from complete hopelessness.

It should be noted that, from the other responses to this question, about 30 per cent of respondents selected the answer 'attempting to come to a direct arrangement with those who can solve your problem, in return for an appropriate payment', while one in four thought that applying to the courts was a fairly productive way of standing up for their interests. (Up to three responses could be selected in reply to the question about ways of defending their interests.) Unlike all the above responses, which maintained a steady position at both stages of the survey, means of fighting for one's own interests such as taking part in meetings, demonstrations or strikes, creating independent trade unions or engaging in party political activities lost half their adherents over the year, and by 1997 these numbered only 20 per cent in total.

We should highlight the following aspects of the more specific views of Russians affected by the employment crisis, on how employment policy in Russia should be structured. Firstly, from their point of view, people who cannot find any kind of work should be the ones considered unemployed. Only 10 per cent of respondents thought that a job offered should have to be in the person's normal occupation, while 21 per cent believed that all those who are not receiving a regular wage, including people with insecure employment, ought to be considered unemployed.

Secondly, in finding people work, the person's sex and age ought not be taken into account (87 per cent and 73 per cent of the sample held these views respectively). However, state of health ought to be taken into account - most of the respondents at both stages of research thought that, where there is a shortage of jobs, disabled people ought to live on benefit while citizens capable of work should be given jobs first.

Thirdly, three quarters of respondents were convinced that all workers should receive benefit if they lost their job, regardless of the size of the income of other family members.

From this it can be seen that the views held by most people on social policy in general and, in particular, on the kind of employment policy needed in Russia today are very far from either traditional welfare state social policy or liberal social policy; they are a somewhat contradictory conglomeration of levelling ideas, inherited from the past, and those adjustments which have had to be made to such ideas under the influence of reality in Russia today.

Thus, both among social policy actors and in the consciousness of ordinary Russians, two models of social policy have collided. One of these outwardly recalls the concept of a welfare state but, in fact, simply reflects the interests of the ruling élite in maintaining power and attempting to support accustomed living standards for the basic mass of the Russian population: it is being built on ideas of the universalism of social support and ensuring consensus between the public and the main élite strata, although, under conditions of progressive deterioration in the position of the Russian population, this consensus is very unstable. This position seems to manifest selfishness, since Russians are attempting to slow down the fall in their standard of living, even at the expense of the poorest strata. In fact, however, this is not so, since most Russians feel sure that, if the little money allocated to social needs were not being stolen, then there would be enough for everyone. It is no coincidence that 51 per cent of respondents in our sample thought that current social policy in Russia was ineffective because officials are stealing a significant proportion of the resources allocated to social policy and so, in practice, these are not reaching the general public.

The second model arises out of rational-idealist and humanist considerations of helping the poorest people, and is shared by some of the senior figures of the political élite and (judging by RIISNP research data) by some of the most successful sections of the population, the number of whom is relatively small.

This means that, at least in 2000, social policy in Russia will, as before, be mainly an attempt to preserve the semblance of a welfare state for all - even though it is completely impossible to realise this objective - while at the same time disregarding the higher speed of deterioration in the position of the weakest social groups. This, as before, will create the illusion of an ineffective social policy.

Given the real reasons for this pseudo-ineffectiveness, it is not surprising that, to the actors and the objects of social policy, they appear to be qualitatively different. For the social policy actors, the chief reasons for its ineffectiveness appear to be lack of resources and inappropriate distribution of competencies between Federal and local authorities; while, for the objects of this policy - judging by our respondents' answers - 'even the government does not know how modern social policy ought to be formulated, nor what the main spending priorities should be'. 58 per cent of respondents selected this position from the response variables offered. It is obvious how, to the objects of social policy, there can appear to be a contradiction between the officially declared aims of social policy and the real mechanism for conducting it, about which we have already talked above. Seeing the scandalous irrationality, from the point of view of its declared aims, of many actions undertaken within the framework of social policy, people react in the only way available - they start to think that those who are conducting the policy do not themselves know what they want.

And actually, it is difficult, from a common sense point of view, to explain a system in which there is no money to pay unemployment benefit or to provide credit for unemployed people to start their own small businesses, but, on the other hand, the main purpose of resource expenditure in many towns has become to stimulate the preservation and creation of jobs at large and medium-sized enterprises. Even in Moscow, out of the 1.2 billion roubles of projected Moscow City Employment Fund income in 1996, 624 million roubles - a little over half - were to be allocated to 'creation of new jobs', that is financing various enterprises and organisations, primarily state or privatised ones, at the expense of the Employment Fund - an original manner of redistributing state resources to the advantage of managerial élites. Moreover, the respondents themselves considered this approach to combatting unemployment to be not very effective - in 1997, only 28 per cent supported the idea of granting subsidies to state enterprises to preserve jobs. Noticeably more popular were the ideas of granting concessions to private business for job creation (41 per cent) and improving retraining schemes (38 per cent), while equally popular was the idea of granting preferential credits to unemployed people to start small businesses (27 per cent).

In this regard, let us recall that among our survey groups affected by the labour market crisis, several dozen people had tried to start up their own business, but only about 10 per cent of respondents' attempts had been successful. We also note that, according to data from an RIISNP monitoring survey of small entrepreneurs, about 10 per cent of small entrepreneurs in Russia had started up their business in order to avoid unemployment. Moreover, not one person in our sample had received any credit to start his or her own business.

Of the other possible reasons for social policy being ineffective, in second place (51 per cent) came the view that 'officials are creaming off a significant proportion of the resources earmarked for social policy, so that in practice these do not get through to the general population', which - as we saw in the example of transferring resources to ineffective enterprises - corresponds absolutely to reality; other large sections (36 per cent) went for 'too few resources are earmarked for social policy' and 'there are not enough trained specialists for all the state services which deal with social policy problems to work effectively' (20 per cent).

As far as the work of Federal and local authorities is concerned, about 10 per cent of respondents at both stages of the survey assessed it as 'goo' or 'very good', and 40 per cent to 50 per cent as 'poor' or 'very poor'; moreover, their evaluation of the Federal authorities was more negative than of local authorities.

We should also add that, in analysing both the social policy actors' responses and those of the objects of this policy, we were not able to record any significant differences between the positions of the various political parties and movements. In the actors' interviews, the link between their ideas about existing and necessary models of social policy and their social and professional status was more readily traceable than the link with their political views. About a third of the ordinary Russians believed that social issues could be best tackled by Yavlinsky's 'Yabloko' party or by Zhyuganov's Communist Party. (Although it has to be said that many of those who held this view voted for other parties in the Duma elections.) The nine remaining political parties mentioned in the questionnaire (the Agrarian Party of Russia, 'Women of Russia', Gaidar's DVR, Lebed's Congress of Russian Communities, Zhirinovsky's LDPR, Chernomyrdin's 'Russia - our home', and others) garnered about another third of the responses in total. Finally, a little over a third of the respondents (37 per cent) thought that there was no party in Russia capable of tackling current social problems.

However, it is not only political parties and movements, but also trade unions, for which this would seem to be the main function, that are incapable of defending the interests of ordinary Russians.

Table 10. 1   **Do the trade unions give real help to the unemployed/ those threatened with unemployment? (per cent)**

	1996 survey	*1997 survey*
Yes	0	1
Most probably, yes	0	21
Most probably not	19	44
No	43	34
Don't know	38	0

However, over the period between our surveys the respondents' position in relation to the trade unions became noticeably 'warmer' and the uncertainty in attitudes to them disappeared. In 1996, the number of positive assessments of the role of the trade unions was precisely zero, but by 1997 almost a quarter took this view. At the same time, the number of those who assessed the work of the trade unions negatively also increased, so that instead of 62 per cent, there were 78 per cent. Such a picture is, obviously, a reflection of the trade unions' initial attempts to step into the role less of 'distributor' of goods and services than of 'defender' of working people - but also of the relative lack of effectiveness of these attempts.

The need to change their basic function relates not so much to the fact that, during a worsening economic crisis, the requirement for 'defensive' functions grows, so much as with the fact that the 'distributive' function is gradually falling away to nothing: either the trade unions will find themselves another 'ecological niche', or they will simply die out because they are not needed.

Our research data also provide fairly sharp evidence, in particular, of the fact that the 'distributive' function of the trade unions is dying out - the extent and significance of social subsidies received through the workplace reduced over the year of observation, by between one and a half times and twice in total, and lost any real significance for most of our respondents. Thus, for example, in 1996, 38 per cent of respondents received medical services through the workplace, but by 1997 only 17 per cent did so. 17 per cent of the 1996 respondents or their children had taken advantage of subsidised visits to holiday homes, children's holiday camps or tourist resorts, or had made use of workplace sporting facilities; but by 1997, it was only 9 per cent - and so on. Moreover, in 1997, 54 per cent of respondents had already ceased to receive any social subsidies, goods, services or additional pay through the workplace.

Actually existing welfare

Moving from a general description of the aims, effectiveness and subjects of current social policy in Russia, from the point of view of both the actors themselves and the objects of this policy, to an evaluation of the real consequences of how it is being conducted, we see the following picture.

The vague consensus between the authorities and the public, which we have already discussed as it applies to social policy aims, takes on a real, material form in the very complex and resourceful model of survival, which is being used by most of the Russian population today. It is precisely this model which ensures the relative stability of the social and political situation in Russia, and therefore the authorities are inclined to close their eyes to many of its particular features, which 'don't fit' into the liberal model of social policy.

The main feature of this model is that it offers people the possibility of surviving in conditions where there is an almost complete absence of real 'live' money. This a very real problem within the Russian economy, with its widespread practices of barter and mutual payments: in our research 13 per cent of respondents indicated they had received wages not in money but in goods and foodstuffs obtained by barter at some time over the last three years; moreover, 16 per cent of all those working had not received wages in the six months before the survey, while 32 per cent had received part payment. Even if money actually appears - whether in the form of wages or social payments - a significant part of it simply disappears on its way to the population, as it passes through the hands of individual officials. This disease, which was also typical of Russia in the past, has flourished so virulently in recent years that to change the situation would require enormous political will and several years of tireless work on the part of the government. In these conditions, which the present Russian government understands only too well, all it can do is to attempt to maintain political stability by supporting the model of survival, which is the most recent response to the situation.

Survival without money can be achieved in two different ways. One of these depends on the authorities, and simply boils down to the fact that they should satisfy the most basic needs, free or practically free of charge, if only at the most minimal level, to keep the population alive. This relates mainly to subsidising charges for public utilities, which allows free or almost free use of heating, electricity, water supply, and so on. The only public utility which is strictly charged for is the telephone, which is incomparably less important in Russia than, for example, heating the home.

As a result of charging for the use of telephones, the practice of giving up exchange telephone services has become fairly widespread, even in Moscow. However, attempts to take the next step and introduce timed charging for telephone calls arouse strong resistance from the public - and, moreover, from those sections of the public which are capable of active protest - and so it has not been implemented up to now in the vast majority of Russian regions.

In addition, free state education and health care have been preserved, although in most cases they are inferior in quality to fee-paying services; all the same, they allow a significant section of the public to fulfil these social needs, even if only at the most minimal level. Transport services are also subsidised, and without this, the wages of many categories of workers would not even be enough to cover travel to work. Since there is support for the acceptance of basic social goods being provided free of charge, the possibility arises of providing a number of important subsistence necessities without asking money for them, or for a charge that is purely symbolic by comparison with their real cost.

On the other hand, the consensus between the authorities and the public, which ensures relative stability in society - despite many months of non-payment of wages, pensions and child benefits and a seemingly complete absence of means of existence - has been preserved by the public itself converting demand and exchange of goods and services to demand and exchange in kind, and by the rise of a 'collective survival' model. Thus, for example, almost 40 per cent of our respondents engaged in various kinds of work on their own account (sewing, knitting, renovating flats, mending cars, and so on). In a number of cases, such services were found not to be for strangers but for acquaintances, and not for money but on the basis of mutual service - in other words, barter at an individual level. Moreover, for 22 per cent of respondents, or half of those who generally did this, the results of such individual work were very important in maintaining sufficient income for the family.

We do not propose to examine here the issue of how effective this model is in tackling social problems. It goes without saying that its long-term consequences will be monstrous, involving a sharp fall in the population's standard of health and level of education, a shrinking base for reproduction of the highly skilled and qualified workforce, and a general fall in the quality of Russia's human resources. However, this issue of consequences is not a particular theme of our research. We merely wish to point out that any attempt to change the existing situation in society - whether in the form of 'municipal reform' or attempts to put a stop to 'shadow' employment, and so on - before the economic position enables people to receive a regular wage sufficient to guarantee them at least their present extremely low level of consumption, is fraught with very serious social and political consequences, which could be so destructive that they would lead to the same net economic effect as separate measures to 'rationalise' the use of resources allotted to the social sphere.

Therefore, since there is no visible improvement in the economic situation as yet, the destruction - even the partial destruction - of the existing model is a thing of the future. It is not so much a matter of whether this model of social policy - or any other - is effective, so much as whether there is a physical possibility of choosing any alternative social policies. From this point of view, we can recall the conclusion drawn in Chapter 3 that there is close interdependence between, on the one hand, extant models of social policy and, on the other, the state of the labour market and production relations overall. The present state of the Russian economy and the country's established system of production and socio-political relations leave practically no short-term prospect for change in the model of social policy that exists today.

From the point of view of tackling any of the specific objectives of social policy (helping vulnerable social groups in the population, ensuring maximum employment, creating incentives for people to go out to work in the case of job loss, and so on), this model is ineffective, since making any impact on these objectives depends, to no small extent, on distributing flows of money towards defined 'social targets' - which it is impossible to ensure in conditions where demand in Russia has been 'converted' to demand in kind. It is no coincidence that, for most of our respondents, social benefits have not played any significant role, because of their low levels and (in Voronezh) because of delays in paying them. Thus, unemployment benefit had some degree of vital significance for only a third of those who had ever received it. Moreover, even social assistance from the authorities to specific population groups is increasingly often given in kind and not in cash - for example, food at free canteens for the poor, the right to free travel, free tickets to children's theatres, free food items in short supply, and so on. But these subsidies in kind are not so large that they could in any way have a noticeable influence on people's behaviour, in view of our findings concerning the real determinants of employment and survival strategies, given in chapters 8 and 9, devoted to an analysis of the situation of households.

As we have seen, social policy is inseparable from the economic situation in a society, and from trends in development of the national economy. Understanding this is the first important pre-condition for making an accurate assessment of the 'corridor of opportunity', within the limits of which a range of social policy variants, that are actually feasible, can be accommodated. The second pre-condition is understanding how far the scope of this policy includes the interests and requirements of the country's social strata. And, finally, the third pre-condition is the nation's existing experience of ways and means of implementing social policy.

If we take into account all three of these pre-conditions in the forms in which they are established in Russia at the beginning of 2000, then, obviously, we must proceed from the understanding that social policy, in the long-term, will have to be directed towards the circumstances of the two-sector economy which is taking shape.

The survival economy and the development economy

Dogmatic liberal reform policy has precipitated both vulnerable social groups and strong groups, who represent the economic and social base of any contemporary society and accomplish productive work, amongst those who have suffered.

Such a significant proportion of the Russian population belongs to the first section, that it does not even seem possible to conceive of paternalistic methods that would be adequate to support them. We should simply recall that, according to calculations adjusted on the basis of the Russian Longitudinal Monitoring Survey investigation, the proportion of families below the poverty line in November 1996 was no less than 36 per cent. In addition, it is essential to remember that no calculation of the proportion of poor people and of the extent of poverty takes into account the level of education and the need to make good the occupational losses of those categories in the population who have been called 'the new poor'.

This could obviously be a matter of deploying a survival policy addressed to the great mass of the population, in several intersecting planes. This policy must help - or, more precisely, it must underwrite - Russian households, so that the majority of them can simply survive the most difficult period that lies ahead, until industrial and agricultural production can be revived. It is important to give citizens incentives to provide for themselves and to help each other, where they do not have sufficient incomes for their physical and social reproduction. In other words, the state has an obligation to help households survive by becoming self-sufficient in food. This assumes that the state will provide incentives for the organisation of mutual help between neighbours, and promote the acceptance of pensioners working in the 'neighbourhood economy' (looking after children, and so on), promote sale at wholesale prices - or, if necessary, give out free - seeds, breeding birds, and so on, help with the repair of flats and houses, and supply fuel. In all these cases, local authorities will play the decisive role, relying on the material resources of fellow-citizens, based on the principle of 'house to house', 'family to family'.

Help for residents of large and medium-sized towns has become especially important. Their allotments and small-holdings are often too small and much too far from where they live, sometimes to a point that makes them practically useless for cultivation. Inefficient agricultural enterprises should be deprived of enough land to meet this need completely, and the land should be rapidly transferred to people living in the suburbs nearby. It is also essential to provide transport subsidies to citizens for travel to their allotments and small-holdings.

All these measures are temporary, extraordinary and non-market in nature: however, they are the only way to help the majority. For this majority, the economic activity which, of necessity, forms the daily round of their economic and social life, is directed towards survival. The problem here lies in the fact that, unlike other countries with a similar economy, Russia must perforce involve in her economy - and will have to continue to do so for a significant period of time - educated people, who represent human and cultural capital that, if there were the investment resources, could be applied in the other sector of the economy - the development economy.

This is the sector that will determine the country's future and its movement towards a market, information economy. In the particular situation of contemporary Russia, this will be possible only by the creation of a small number of enclaves of accelerated development. A base does exist from which to tackle this strategic objective, although it has also been reduced to a semi-ruined state.

In the second half of the 20th century, having embarked on the struggle against the USA for world domination, the Soviet Union stimulated accelerated development of the defence industry. The result was that most of the country's skills and innovative potential became concentrated in the military-industrial complex. Thus, by the mid-1980s, over 3 million people were working in science and scientific services, of whom about 80 per cent were involved in the military-industrial complex. Moreover, 82 per cent of the military-industrial potential of the USSR and about 80 per cent of military-industrial complex enterprises were in Russia. Russia was also the chief military-industrial base for the whole world of 'real socialism'; but, at the same time, outside the military-industrial complex, Russia contained only some non-systemic elements of the civilian economy. So, for Russia, unlike the other former republics of the USSR or the former Central European satellites, saving the military-industrial complex meant saving the national economic system as a whole, along with the particular features of its human resources. The most educated and occupationally advanced Russian workers were concentrated in the military-industrial complex, and it was they who were the most active supporters of the market economy, a state based on the rule of law, and modernising the Russian way of life (Shkaratan and Galchin, 1994; Shkaratan and Fontanel, 1998).

A number of analysts and researchers have seen military-industrial enterprises and their staff as the lever which will facilitate modernisation of the country's economy. Of course, this presupposes the realisation of a conversion programme, the disaggregation of gigantic defence plants into smaller units and the privatisation of a significant number of these. However, the outcome has been different: the military-industrial complex has not been transformed, but has collapsed, taking with it many of the elements of an information economy, of high-tech and of advanced urban culture, since it was in the defence industry that indigenous town-dwellers were concentrated. The military-industrial complex was a supporting structure of the former USSR, such that to some extent the long hoped-for process of demilitarising the economy has also become a process of de-urbanising the Russian way of life.

Many defence industry workers from the proto-middle class fell into the 'new poor', a historical phenomenon previously unseen, at least on such a scale. One difficulty still lay in the fact that they did not identify with their occupation, but with the enterprise or branch of industry. Thus, the collapse of the organisations with which people were accustomed to identify led to the collapse of the contacts that integrated them into the world of work.

Where are these people now? Many of them, mainly aged under 35, now work in Western countries; others have changed their occupation and were among the first to move into the financial and banking sector or the new political establishment; the majority eke out the pitiful existence of the semi-unemployed. Thus, in 1996, pay in the science and scientific services sector was 81 per cent of the average for Russia, while in the former defence industry, it was 64 per cent of the average industrial wage.

Our conversations with directors of enterprises in both 1996 and 1997 confirmed that the first to be released were highly skilled and qualified young workers with the best prospects, that is the most economically active section of the enterprise's personnel, who have skills which it is important to preserve. Those who left the enterprises became small traders, ancillary workers in the service sector, and so on. Few of them were able to find jobs in their normal occupations. Meanwhile, there are some industries where it is impossible to train staff in a short period of time, so that accumulated experience plays an important role - for example, the aviation industry.

Raw materials capital has now taken the place of the military-industrial complex in the Russian economy, partly through close co-operation with Western transnational corporations. The influence of the military-industrial complex before the August 1998 crisis has been broken. The leading banks, commodity and insurance structures are working on raw materials. The average wage in the oil extraction industry was 278 per cent of average Russian earnings, and in the gas industry, 383 per cent. However, the human resources which predominate in these raw materials sectors are fundamentally different from those in the military-industrial complex on the eve of its failure: as a rule, they are 'peasant-workers'. Therefore, further destruction of the military-industrial complex means that Russia will be pushed out onto the raw materials periphery of the world system.

To transform Russia into a high-tech country with a really competitive market, it is vital that the new, demilitarised components (enclaves) of an information economy should be built on the ruins of the military-industrial complex. The issue is how - without saving the organisational and technological structures of the many depressed enterprises - to avert the destruction of Russia's labour élite and the fall in potential for innovation, and how to forestall irreversible and potentially catastrophic consequences by developing high-tech industry.

It is vital to divorce the issue of preserving and developing existing enterprises (firms) strictly from the issue of preserving and developing the potential for innovation in the élite section of Russia's human resources. It has now become impossible to use inter-regional mobility as a solution to this problem. However, in many respects, it would be completely possible to stimulate solutions at a regional level. One effective way of tackling these problems might be the organisation of a national system of regional centres of innovation. The efforts of such centres could concentrate on preserving (and developing) the nation's labour élite. The main directions of their activities could be:

- the creation of a system of retraining and re-skilling for all categories of workers, including directors of enterprises;
- the organisation of a system of support to venture-capital SMEs, making use of the material bases of inefficient enterprises;
- the elaboration of basic channels for investment in regional programmes, which could ensure the preservation of potential for innovation.

Conclusion - realities and alternatives

Since the days of ancient Egypt and Babylon, every state has developed some kind of social policy: and, however ably a given policy is implemented, its scope and impact will depend on whose interests it represents. Whether defined by popular views or experts, social policy is intended to protect the interests of poorer citizens and to offer some kind of guaranteed education, health care, help for the unemployed, and so on. However, even if social policy does not include mechanisms to protect vulnerable social strata and groups, it does not cease to be social: it can, in fact, have an entirely different orientation - for instance, to support economically dominant groups, promoting growth in their education and the skills of government.

Under the conditions of a period of transition, the state becomes increasingly significant as social guarantor and organiser of social protection for the lowest social groups. A lightning transition to a new system and a new model of social policy is simply impossible - even more so given a situation of permanent economic crisis. There will have to be a significant passage of time for new mechanisms regulating the social sphere to take shape and new social policy actors to appear. In the meantime, old social policy mechanisms will be inadequate for a new economic system (in itself still in the making), while the new mechanisms and subjects of social policy are not fully formed.

In order to understand the general direction of social policy as it is actually being conducted by those in power in contemporary Russia, we should note that - in contrast to the expectations of many Russian intellectuals - both power and property have remained principally in the hands of the Soviet *nomenklatura*, which has turned the privatisation process and the formation of a new ruling élite to its own advantage.

Although the ownership of private property entails its responsible and efficient application in production, Russians who are owners 'of private property at society's expense' are free of responsibility and risk, and their wealth does not depend on their involving themselves in the business-like economic management of production. This is not, of course, only a matter of property ownership. In the past, Russia had neither a free market nor a democracy, and so, even in principle, personality types, ethics and all the main features of civilisation there differ from those in the capitalist world.

In order to achieve this 'success', Russia's ruling circles have broken any democratic activity on the part of the masses, and have restrained the country from achieving a democratic revolution anything like those which have taken place in Hungary, Poland and the Czech Republic - countries which have managed to get onto the path of capitalist and democratic development. As Boris Yeltsin has frankly and accurately stated:

> In September and October (1991), we literally went to the edge, but we were able to protect Russia from revolution. (*Rossiiskaya Gazeta* 20 August, 1992).

Real policy has developed on two levels. First was a relatively high proportion of expenditure on social protection in the official budget. But this was accompanied by low social expenditure in the real budget and as a proportion of real GDP; widespread corruption; the fiction that scales of unemployment among working people were modest; and the destruction of the existing systems of medical assistance and of education. Thus, it is becoming increasingly clear that to compare social policy in the USSR or in post-Soviet Russia with a welfare state is similar to comparing serf-based manufacturing under Peter the Great and Catherine the Great with 18th-century English capitalist manufacturing.

It is important to note that the radical neo-liberals who have - until recently - controlled the real administration and the real ideology, as well as the pragmatics of the situation, are members of the forming *haut-bourgeois* class and, as such, many of them have not bothered to conceal the value system that they are really defending, their own personal interests or their manifest indifference towards the interests of ordinary people. As Poptsov, political commentator and member of the first post-Soviet Russian government, has written:

> Chubais did not trouble himself very much with moral agonies when he was doing all he could to promote a new stratum (*bankers and large entrepreneurs*) to the top of political life, seeing this as his main source of public support. Let

us not forget the privatisation voucher fund institutions or the financial pyramid frauds. So it is hardly reasonable for Chubais to get apoplectic when his old adversary Berezovsky says : 'We own half the country and intend to rule it' (*Moskovskiye Novosti* (1998), 4, 2-8 February). And, in reality, one or two of Russia's 10 major companies and banks control about 70 per cent of the economy. (*Izvestiya* (1998), 17 March).

The ruling élite of Russia has spent and continues to spend the maximum possible of the country's limited resources on protecting the interests of leading financial and industrial groups. For example, in tackling the issue of repaying tax assessment debts, the specially created Extraordinary Commission for Tax Collection, headed by the then Russian Federation Prime Minister, Viktor Chernomyrdin, which was set up in October 1996, was extremely circumspect in its approach to major non-payers. As the Parliamentary Accounts Office has established, the net profits of Gazprom (a Russian joint-stock company) for 1996 were 33,200 billion roubles (about $6.5 billion). As 40 per cent shareholder, the state was supposed to receive 12,000 billion roubles, but received only 20 billion roubles. As a result of this and other similar government inaction, total losses for the period 1995-7 were 65,800 billion roubles (*Novaya Gazeta* (1998), 10, 16-22 March, p. 1-2).

Calculations by the Russian Academy of Sciences' Institute for National Public Forecasting have shown that, although the 85 per cent of the population with incomes below 400,000 roubles a month are paying income tax in full, those with an income of over 3 million roubles per person (15 per cent of the population) have paid only a tenth of their share of taxes (2 per cent of their aggregated income instead of the statutory 20 per cent). In the end, the amount that came into the public purse in 1996 did not add up to even 100,000 billion roubles (*Russkii Telegraf* (1997) 11 November). Proposals that an inventory of Federal property should be made, that there should be some kind of public monitoring of the incomes and outgoings of the largest natural monopolies, and that there should be a move from tax assessment on the basis of incomes to a system of property assessment plus rental payments to the state, meet stubborn resistance from oligarchical groups.

Professor Jeffery Sachs sees foreign trade as fertile ground for corruption, adding one further 'field' from which people can get rich illegally - low-interest Central Bank credits to private banks. Sachs, who can hardly be blamed for the rejection of neo-liberal economic principles, argues that the situation in Russia is fundamentally caused by the corruption which has penetrated everywhere, the constant companion of the reform process. He considers that guilt for this lies at the door of the West which, in 1992, neglected a historic opportunity to exert real influence over the situation in Russia. The developed countries did not give financial assistance to the young, and for the most part honest, reformers under the leadership of Gaidar. Because of the absence of external support, under the pressure of economic circumstances, Yeltsin was forced to conclude a 'pact with the devil', in the person of the former Party *nomenklatura*. The young reformers were, by and large, driven out of government, and the old apparatchiks seized controlling positions in the country's administration. Western leaders reassured themselves that people who did not have completely clean hands were better than out-and-out extremists.

This Western position was one of not opposing evil with force. In the case of Russia in 1992-3, Western policy entailed rejecting the active stimulation of democratic and liberal transformations in a large country which finds it difficult to operate on a non-aggressive, non-militaristic footing. In this context, it becomes easier to understand the lack of resources for social policy and the absence of any kind of opportunities to form a social state (*Moskovskiye Novosti* (1995), 87, 24-31 December).

Regardless both of broader circumstances and of the particular features of the political and economic situation, the real distribution of national income has always been and continues to be concealed. This is a result particularly of the fact that information about 'the real wealth of the rich' or about the discrepancy between the official and the real budget which the ruling political stratum has at its disposal does not appear in print. This is still *terra incognita*. Thus, more and more often, arguments arise amongst specialists about the degree of transparency or non-transparency of the Federal and regional budgets, and about the financial accumulations of companies. It remains completely unclear why, at a time when there is such a huge contraction in military spending, in expenditure on supporting 'friendly' regimes abroad, subsidies to former Soviet republics, and so on (in other words priorities that the country used to spend most of its money on), Federal and regional budgets for social expenditure look so pitiful. Surely Russia is a country with an unparalleled volume of natural resources which could be used in its economic life? Analysis of this kind has never been carried out - and obviously that is no coincidence. Whenever such data do appear in print, they are always somehow incomplete.

The largest energy, fuel and financial monopolies have come to form the core of an oligarchical regime that tends towards becoming a criminal one, and attempts on the part of the more judicious members of the ruling élite to curtail favouritism towards them have hardly been crowned with success. The issue here is not the redistribution of property, but the willingness of neo-capitalists to share their incomes with the national budget and thereby give the state the opportunity to make concrete efforts to extend its own social base and to alleviate the difficult position of substantial sections of the population. As Luzhkov, the Mayor of Moscow, has said:

> no one has ever denied in principle the long-standing assertion that rich people should take on some serious social functions and share their wealth with the poorest section of society... the practice of income redistribution is an essential condition for the stable development of society... (*Moskovskiye Novosti* (1998), 10, 15-22 March).

All this makes it obvious why Russia today has no resources to devote to the social protection of groups affected by the reform crisis, including the unemployed. Social policy in practice is characterised by a constant squeeze on social expenditure.

What are the alternatives? Even within the narrow limits of this system, there is still potential for adjusting social policy or seeking different policy variants from the one the government is currently conducting. Given this, it is worth looking at those variants which have been the subject of discussion within the country's élite.

At the moment, in Russia, three approaches to social policy can be distinguished: the first is the *oligarchy-capitalist model* of limited social policy. This approach has already dominated ruling circles for a number of years and is the one that actually determines the social policy of the present government. It is consistent with liberalism and monetarism. We have already outlined this variant of social policy above; the second approach is being developed by adherents of *administrative bureaucratic capitalism* - for example, the 'municipal capitalism' of Luzhkov in Moscow. This direction corresponds in principle to the Keynesian approach to running the economy and attaches great importance to harmonising social relations and taking account of the interests of the middle and lower sections of the population. Finally, a third model of social policy has been proposed by Nemtsov, a distinguished figure in Yeltsin's government who joined the country's leadership in 1997. It is a model which gained popularity in the public consciousness of Russia's democratic forces after the end of the 1980s. This policy could be characterised as the ideal model for the future, and might be formulated as being to create a *Russia with neither poor nor super-rich.* In practice, there is no actual example of this policy in operation.

The variety of possible scenarios for developing social policy is predetermined by the outcome of the confrontation, which has already begun, between comprador and national capital, or - using another measure - between the Latin American and Japanese paths along which capitalism could develop. This confrontation will provide the background to any developments that may unfold in the life of Russian society. At the moment, comprador capital is dominant, in co-operation with corrupt officialdom; while this tendency persists, Russia can only expect to follow the Latin American - in particular, the Argentinean, as it is often known - path of development. And even what economically useful national capital there is, is for the most part concentrated in the provinces.

When considering the potential role of national capital in the battle against comprador (oligarchy or *nomenklatura*/criminal) capital, we should especially note that, in November 1997, 12 million people were working in the small business sector, generating 7 per cent of the national product and 15 per cent of tax receipts. At the same time, 86 per cent of the taxes due from small businesses were being collected - a lot higher than the average for Russia. This shows the place of this sector of business - and the role of small-scale national capital - in the system of social and economic variables operating in Russian society (*Izvestiya* (1997) 12 November).

The academic and scientific intelligentsia and highly-skilled workers are, largely speaking, taking steps to preserve their own potential future; they are very well aware of their community of interests and they understand that they have little future within the framework of 'Latin American'-style development. They represent the broad mass of people, concentrated in military-industrial organisations and in high-tech production. So it is not impossible that Russia will succeed in shifting its trajectory of change and getting onto the path towards the formation of an information economy, information capitalism and intensive development of a middle class. In that case, the nature of social policy will also change; Russia will gradually become a real social state - the most appropriate future for a country with strong community consciousness and traditions of mutual aid.

But what can be done now? There is a real scarcity of resources in Russia today, and it is practically impossible to get money out of the large monopolies in the short term, to change the disposition of forces or the system of privilege at the top of the civil service, and so on. Consequently, it is not a question of introducing revolutionary measures into the economy or social policy; there have already been too many of these in Russia's bloody and tragic history. It is obvious enough by now that there will be no spasmodic shift that can successfully resolve the country's existing social problems, no dramatic switch from an oligarchical system to a system of competitive, democratic capitalism (even of a West European type). So, this is really a case of 'something is better than nothing'. In other words, all that can be done within the scope of social policy as it is now being conducted and mooted, is to define a number of elements contained in the policy more precisely - for example, defining the nature of taxation policy more precisely and then adjusting it, or adjusting the number of people in receipt of various goods from the state.

The authorities in some regions have already begun this evolutionary movement to find the antidote to a concoction unprecedented in history - *nomenklatura* liberal social policy. Even in Moscow the Mayor, Luzhkov, has argued that:

> Russia will never reach the end of the road to reform if it does not ensure that the population is protected. We need a firm system for social transformation, that can be clearly understood by every inhabitant of Russia... It would be a great pity to waste our energy and resources on overcoming the consequences of imbalances that affect the Russian state as a whole. But in future, we do want to try to demonstrate the justice of these proposals, with our region offering a separate example. (*Moskovskii vestnik* (1998) 24 April).

The key to the basis for change in Russia's trajectory of development is that capitalism (especially the form of it run by neophyte, Soviet-issue capitalists) requires firm, rational state control. The government could and should have preserved the competence to influence business through the only real stimulus - profitability. The experience, under the great American President, Franklin D. Roosevelt, of state intervention in the economy (which had nothing in common with Soviet totalitarian statism) may also now serve as a model for transitional economy countries. This adds to the normal orientation of business towards profit, the principle of social responsibility, guaranteeing society relative economic stability and, more especially, social stability through state regulation of private ownership.

In other words, we should not admit that there will, as the radical liberals preach, be some kind of spontaneous momentum in the development of the country, through the free play of market forces. A society which has lived for decades in a centrally planned economy and under conditions of paternalism cannot, by natural means and in an inconceivably short period of time, adapt to abrupt changes in its environment by merely and spontaneously initiating processes of social self-regulation and self-organisation. To ensure Russia' stable development while emphasising changes in the quality of life and in human responsibilities and duties, we need a combination of market-based self-regulation and state regulation.

Bibliography

Abalkin, L.I. (1998), 'Unavoidable changes' in Institute of Economics of the Russian Academy of Sciences, *Social and economic transformation mechanisms in Russia,* Moscow.

Aborieva, O. and Remizov, D. (1997), 'Small-scale enterprise in Voronezh Province (problems of setting up and expansion)' *Predprinimatel'stvo v Rossii,* no. 2, pp. 44-48.

Abrahamson, P. (1999), 'The Welfare Modelling Business' *Social Policy and Administration,* vol. 33, no. 4, pp. 394-415.

Adirim, I. (1989), 'A note on the current level, pattern and trends of unemployment in the USSR', *Soviet Studies,* vol. XLI, no. 3, pp. 449-461.

Aganbegyan, A. (1988), *The Challenge: Economics of Perestroika,* Hutchinson, London.

Akopyan, A. (1994), 'The patient pays three times' *Literaturnaya gazeta,* September 21st, p. 11, in *Current Digest of the Post-Soviet Press,* vol. 46, no. 38, pp. 7-8.

Alesia, A. and Perotty, R. (1997), 'Democracy, political stability and growth' *Problemes economiques,* no. 2, pp 510-11.

Allen, S. (1986), *The Experience of Unemployment,* MacMillan, Basingstoke.

Andrusz, G. (1984), *Housing and Urban Development in the USSR,* Macmillan, Basingstoke.

Andrusz, G. (1990), 'A note on the finance of housing in the Soviet union' *Soviet Studies,* vol. XLII, no. 3, pp. 555-570.

Andrusz, G. (1994), 'The causes and consequences of homelessness in Moscow and Sofia', paper for the ESRC East-West Workshop on the *Social Consequences of Marketisation,* London, 9-10th December, 1994.

Argyle, M. (1990) *The Psychology of Interpersonal Behaviour,* 4th ed., Penguin Books, Harmondsworth.

Ashwin, S. (1997), 'Shop floor trade unionism in Russia' *Work, Employment and Society,* vol. 11, no. 1, pp. 115-132.

Baglioni, G. and Crouch, C. (1991), *European Industrial Relations: the Challenge of Flexibility,* Sage, London.

Baranov, A. (1994), 'The housing situation in St. Petersburg' in *St. Petersburg in the Early 1990s: Crazy, Cold, and Cruel*, Charitable Foundation 'Nochlezhka', St. Petersburg.

Barr, N. (1992), *Income Transfers and the Social Safety Net in Russia*, World Bank, Washington.

Barr, N. (ed) (1994), *Labor Markets and Social Policy in Central and Eastern Europe, the Transition and Beyond*, Oxford University Press, Oxford.

Bessonova, O.E. and Krapchan, S.G. (1994), 'The public's participation in housing privatization' *SOTSIS*, nos. 8-9.

Bettleheim, C. (1978), *Class Struggles in the USSR, 2nd Period 1923-1930*, Harvester, Brighton.

Birman, I. (1997), 'Superficial knowledge can lead to anomalies' *Svobodnaya mysl'* , no. 9, p. 87.

Boron, A. (1995), *State, Capitalism and Democracy in Latin America*, Lynne Rienner, London.

Bourdieu, P. (1993), 'Social Policy', in Bourdieu, P. (ed) *Social Space and the Genesis of Classes*, Moscow, pp. 53-87.

Bovt, G. (1996), *Kommersant-Daily*, December 20th.

Brasier, M. (1990), 'Soviets hurtle towards abyss' *Guardian* , November 6th, p. 14.

Buckley, M. (1990), 'Social policies and new social issues', in S. White, A. Pravda, and Z. Gitelman, (ed) *Developments in Soviet Politics*, Macmillan, Basingstoke.

Burtin, Y. (1997), 'Getting out of the crisis: taking stock of illusions' *Oktyabr'* , no. 8.

Callan, T., Nolan, B., and Whelan, C.T. (1993), 'Resources, deprivation and the measurement of poverty', *Journal of Social Policy*, vol. 22, no. 2, pp. 141-172.

Castells, M. (1998), *The Information Age : Economy, Society and Culture, volume 3 - End of Millennium*, Blackwell, Oxford.

Castles, F.G. and McKinlay, R.D. (1979), 'Public Welfare Provision, Scandinavia, and the Sheer Futility of the Sociological Approach to Politics' *British Journal of Political Science*, vol. 9, pp. 157-171.

Champagne, P. (1996), 'Double dependency. Some remarks on the interrelationship between the fields of policy, economics and journalism' *Socio-Logos* (Almanac of the Russo-French Centre for Sociological Research at the Russian Academy of Sciences) Institute of Sociology, Moscow.

Chernina, N.V. (1994), 'Poverty as a Social Phenomenon in Russian Society' *SOTSIS*, no. 3.

Chernina N.V. (1996), 'The social problems of the unemployed (Novosibirsk Province)' *SOTSIS* No. 11.

Chetvernina, T. (1997), 'Forms and main features of hidden unemployment in Russia' in T. Zaslavskaya (ed) *Kuda Idet Rossia*, Intertsentr, Moscow.

Chetvernina, T. and Lakunina, L. (1998), 'Tension in the Russian labour market and mechanisms to overcome it' *Voprosy ekonomiki*, no. 2.

Chichkanov, V. (1987) *Izvestia*, September 4th, p 2.

Chinn, J. (1977), *Manipulating Soviet Population Resources*, Martin Robertson, Oxford.

Clarke, S. (1996), 'Structural adjustment without mass unemployment? Lessons from Russia', in *The Restructuring of Employment and the Formation of a Labour Market in Russia*, Centre for Comparative Labour Studies, University of Warwick, Warwick.

Commander, S. (et al) (1995) 'Russia' in S. Commander & F. Coricelli (eds) *Unemployment, Restructuring, and the Labour Market in Eastern Europe and Russia*, World Bank, Washington.

Dakhin, V. (1997), 'Discussing the formation of regional elites' in T. Zaslavskaya (ed) *Kuda Idet Rossia*, Intertsentr, Moscow, pp. 148-153.

Davidova, N. (1998), 'Regional specifics of Russian mentality' *Social Sciences*, Quarterly Review of the Russian Academy of Science, no. 1, pp. 36-48.

Davis, C. (1989), 'Priority and the shortage model: the medical system in the socialist economy' in C. Davis, and W. Charemza, (eds) *Models of Disequilibrium and Shortage in Centrally Planned Economies*, Chapman and Hall, London.

Davis, C. (1990), 'National health services, resource constraints and shortages: a comparison of Soviet and British experiences' in N. Manning, and C.J. Ungerson (eds) *Social Policy Review 1989-90*, Longman, London.

Davis, K. and Moore, W.E. (1945), 'Some Principles of Stratification' *American Sociological Review*, vol. 10, pp. 242-249.

Dean, H. and Taylor-Gooby, P. (1992), *Dependency Culture*, Harvester Wheatsheaf, London.

Denisovsky, G.M., Malkina, A.N. and Nazimova, A.E. (1992), *Post-totalitarian Society on the Cusp of the Centuries: the Dynamics of Change in Social Structure and Value-Orientations*, Moscow.

Dmytriev, A. (1997), unpublished report for Annual International Symposium, 17-19 January, Moscow, Inter-Disciplinary Academic Centre for Social Sciences, Moscow.

Doktorov, B.Z. (1994), 'Russia in the European socio-cultural space: discussion – value dimensions of Russian society' *Sotsiologicheski zhurnal*, no. 3, pp.4-26.

Dondurei, D. (1997), 'Who gains from hopelessness?' *Znaniye-sila* September.

Dossett-Davies, J. (1988a), 'Where Glasnost has not yet arrived' *Community Care*, May 5th, pp. 19-20.

Dossett-Davies, J. (1988b), 'Glasnost and mental health' *Community Care*, May 12th, p. 27.

Doyal, L. and Gough, I. (1984), 'A theory of human needs' *Critical Social Policy*, no. 10, pp. 6-38.

Due, J., Madsen, J., and Stroby-Jensen, C. (1991), 'The Social Dimension: Convergence or Diversification of IR in the Single European Market', *Industrial Relations Journal*, vol. 22, no. 2, pp. 85-102.

Economist (1990), September 22nd, pp. 25-28.

Ellman, M. (1989), *Socialist Planning* (2nd ed), Cambridge University Press, Cambridge.

Ellman, M. (1990), 'A note on the distribution of income in the USSR under Gorbachev' *Soviet Studies*, vol. XLII, no. 1, pp. 147-148.

Ellman, M. and Layard, R. (1993), 'Prices, Incomes and Hardship' in A. Åslund and R. Layard (eds) *Changing the Economic System in Russia*, Pinter Publishers, London.

Eratova, M. (1994), 'Viruses feast in a poor country' *Pravda*, April 13th, p. 8, in *Current Digest of the Post-Soviet Press*, vol. 46, no. 15, p. 24.

Esping-Andersen, G. (1990), *The Three Worlds of Welfare Capitalism*, Polity Press, Cambridge.

Esping-Andersen, G. (1999), *Social Foundations of Postindustrial Economies*, Oxford University Press, Oxford.

Evans, A.B. (1977) 'Developed Socialism in Soviet Ideology' *Soviet Studies*, vol. 29, no. 3.

Eyal, G., Szelényi, I. and Townsley, E. (1999), *Making Capitalism Without Capitalists*, Verso, London.

Ferge, Z. (1979), *A Society in the Making*, Penguin, Harmondsworth.

Ferner, A. and Hyman, R. (1992), 'Introduction', in A. Ferner and R. Hyman, (eds) *Industrial Relations in the New Europe*, Blackwell, Oxford.

Gallie, D., Marsh, C. and Vogler, C. (1994), *Social Change and the Experience of Unemployment* Oxford University Press, Oxford.

George, V. (1973), *Social Security and Society*, Routledge, London.

George, V. and Manning, N. (1980), *Socialism, Social Welfare and the Soviet Union* Routledge & Kegan Paul.

Gerchikov, V. (1995), 'Russia' in J. Thirkell, R. Scase and S. Vickerstaff (eds), *Labour Relations and Political Change in Eastern Europe*, University College London Press, London, pp. 137-168.

Giddens A. (1973), *The Class Structure of the Advanced Societies*, Hutchinson, London.

Giddens A. (1984), *The Constitution of Society*, Polity Press, Cambridge.

Giddens A. and MacKenzie, G. (eds) (1982), *Social Class and the Division of Labour*, Cambridge University Press, Cambridge.

Gilison, J.M. (1975), *The Soviet Image of Utopia*, Johns Hopkins University Press, Baltimore.

Gimpelson, V.E. (1993), 'Labour market and employment in Russia: beginning of changes', in R. Weichhardt (ed) *Economic developments in cooperation partner countries from a sectoral perspective*, NATO, Brussels.

Gimpelson, V.E. and Magun, V. (1994), 'Nouvel emploi et mobilité sociale des travailleurs licenciés' *Cahiers Internationaux de Sociologie*, vol. XCVI, pp. 57-75.

Gitelman, Z. (1990), 'The Nationalities', in S. White, A. Pravda, and Z. Gitelman, (ed), *Developments in Soviet Politics*, Macmillan, Basingstoke.

Goldfarb, J.C. (1989), *Beyond Glasnost*, University of Chicago Press, Chicago.

Goldthorpe J., Lockwood, D., Bechhofer, F., and Platt, J. (1969), *The Affluent Worker in the Class Structure*, Cambridge University Press, Cambridge.

Golov, A. (1998), 'The public's assessment of problems in Russian society: the year's issues' *Novaya gazeta*, March 2-6, no. 8, p. 4.

Gorbachev, M. (1987), *Perestroika*, Collins, London.

Gordienko, A.A., Pshevnev, G.S. and Plyusin, Y.M. (1996), 'The structure of behaviour of the unemployed' *SOTSIS*, no. 11.

Gordon L.A. and Chertikhina E.S. (1983), 'An expert evaluation of hypotheses in the study of prospects for developments in lifestyles' *SOTSIS*, no. 2

Gorshkov, M. (1997), *Nezavisimaya Gazeta*, January 16th, p.5, in *Current Digest of Post-Soviet Press*, vol. 49, no. 3, pp.1-3.

Goryacheva, N. (1996), 'The government is trying to hold back unemployment' *Finansovye izvestiya*, October 1ˢᵗ.

Goskomstat (1997), *Socio-Economic State of Russia*, Moscow.

Gotting, U. (1994), 'Destruction, adjustment, and innovation: social policy transformation in East Central Europe', Centre for Social Policy Research, University of Bremen, Bremen.

Granovetter, M. (1973), 'The Strength of Weak Ties' *American Journal of Sociology*, vol. 78, no. 6, pp. 1360-1380.

Granovetter, M. (1995), *Getting a Job : a Study of Contacts and Careers*, 2ⁿᵈ edition, Chicago University Press, Chicago.

Gudkov, L.D. (1996), 'The erosion of identification and social tensions in the regions' *Where is Russia Going?* (3rd ed.), Moscow.

Gudkov, L.D. (1999), 'Russia amidst other countries: the issue of national identity' *Monitoring obshchestvennogo mneniya: ekonomicheskiye i sotsial'niye peremeny*, no. 1, pp.39-47.

Halleröd, B. (1995), 'The truly poor: direct and indirect consensual measurement of poverty in Sweden' *Journal of European Social Policy*, vol. 5, no. 2, pp. 111-130.

Harding, N. (ed) (1984), *The State in Socialist Society*, Macmillan, Basingstoke.

Harré, R. (1993), *Social Being*, 2nd ed., Blackwell, Oxford.

Harwin, J. (1988), 'Glasnost children' *Guardian*, April 6ᵗʰ, p. 23.

Hill, M.J., Harrison, R.M., Sargeant, A.V. and Talbot, V. (1973), *Men Out of Work, a Study of Unemployment in Three English Towns*, Cambridge University Press, Cambridge.

Huntington, S. (1991), *The Third Wave: democratisation in the late twentieth century*, University of Oklahoma Press, Norman.

Institute of Economics (1998), 'Social priorities and economic transformation mechanisms in Russia' *Voprosy ekonomiki*, no. 6, pp 46-7.

Institute of Sociological Analysis (1997), 'Public Opinion Foundation Nation-Wide Survey, 1996' in *Current Digest of Post-Soviet Press*, vol. 49, no. 1, p.4.

Ivanov, V. (1987), *Izvestia*, May 5ᵗʰ, p. 2.

Ivanova, Y., Nikonova, O. Mozgovaya, O. (1997), 'St Petersburg: five angles to housing reform' *Sotsial'naya zashchita*, no. 4, pp. 7-11.

Kabalina, V.I. (ed) (1997), *The enterprise and the market: the dynamics of management and labour relations in the transition period (from research monographs)*, Moscow.

Kachanov, Y. L. (1992), 'Agents in the field of policy: position and identity' *Voprosy sotsiologii*, vol. 1, no. 2. Pp. 61-81.

Kachanov, Y. L. and Shmatko, N.A. (1996), 'Base metaphor in the structure of social identity' *SOTSIS*, no. 1, pp. 61-71.

Kalashnov, Y. (1997), 'Moscow employment theory' *Den'gi*, no. 42, p. 24.

Kagarlitsky, B. (1990), *Farewell Perestroika*, Verso, London.

Kapeliushnikov, R. (1997), 'Job and labour turnover in Russian industry' *The Russian Economic Barometer*, vol.VI, no.1.

Keane, J. (1990), 'The Politics of Retreat' *Political Quarterly*, vol. 61, no. 3, pp. 340-352.

Khakhulina, L. (1997), 'Public opinion about benefits, pensions and privileges' *Information Monitoring Bulletin*, no. 6(32), pp.39-45.

Khakhulina, L. and Tuchek, M. (1995), 'Income distribution: poor and rich in post-socialist societies (some results of a comparative analysis)' *Where is Russia going?* (2nd ed), Moscow.

Kohn M. L., Slomczynski, K. M., and Schoenbach, C. (1990), *Social Structure and Self-Direction* Basil Blackwell, Oxford.

Komarsky, V. and Maleva, T. (1996), 'Social policy in Russia in the context of macroeconomic reform' *Obshchestvennye nauki i sovremmenost'*, no. 6.

Konstantinova, N. (1998), *Nezavisimaya Gazeta*, January 14th in *Current Digest of Post-Soviet Press*, vol. 50, no. 2, p.15.

Kornai, J. (1980), *Economics of Shortage*, North-Holland, Amsterdam.

Koval, T. (1996), 'Regional Typology of the Socioeconomic Situation', working paper, Moscow.

Kovaleva, N. (1997), 'Conflicts, trade-unions, social support: opinions of employees and employers' *Information Monitoring Bulletin*, no.5 (31), pp. 26-32.

Kozyreva, P.M. (ed) (1994), *The Structure of Society and Mass Consciousness*, Institute of Sociology, Russian Academy of Sciences, Moscow.

Krasil'nikova M.D. (1996), 'Who economizes on what?' *Economic and Social Change*, no. 4, pp.35-6.

Kudrin, A. (1997), 'St Petersburg's progress towards the market' *International Journal of Urban and Regional Research*, vol. 21, no. 3, p. 426.

Lang-Pickvance, K., Manning, N., and Pickvance, C. (eds) (1995), *Environmental and Housing Movements, Grassroots Experience in Hungary, Russia and Estonia*, Avebury, Aldershot.

Lapin, N.I. (1992), 'Russia's hard years: a turning point in history, a crisis of values, future perspectives' *Mir Rossii*, no. 1, pp. 10-11.

Layard, R. and Richter, A. (1994), 'Labour market adjustment in Russia' *Russian Economic Trends*, vol. 3, no. 2, pp. 85-104.

Ledeneva, A. (1997), 'Personal connections and informal associations' *Mir Rossii*, no. 4.

Lenin, V.I. (1965) *Collected Works*, Lawrence and Wishart, London.

Lesage, M. (1993), 'The crisis of public administration in Russia' *Public Administration*, vol. 71, nos. 1/2, pp. 121-133.

Lipset, M. (1960), *Political Man: the Social Basis of Politics*, Heinemann, London.

Lokshin, M. and Popkin, B.M., 1999, 'The Emerging Underclass in the Russian Federation: Income Dynamics, 1992-1996' *Economic Development and Cultural Change*, no.4, pp. 803-829.

Lonkila, M. (1997), 'Informal exchange relations in post-soviet Russia: a comparative perspective' *Sociological Research Online*, vol. 2, no. 2, http://www.socresonline.org.uk/socresonline/2/2/9.html

Mack, J. and Lansley, S. (1985), *Poor Britain*, George Allen & Unwin, London.

Magidson J. (1993), *SPSS for Windows. CHAID*, release 6.0., SPSS Inc, Chicago.

Magun, V. S. (1995), 'The labour values of the Russian population: socialist model and post-socialist reality' *Where is Russia Going?* (2nd ed) Moscow.

Mandel, E. (1989), *Beyond Perestroika*, Verso, London.

Manning, N. (1993), 'TH Marshall, Jurgan Habermas, Citizenship, and Transition in Eastern Europe', *World Development*, vol. 21, no. 8, pp. 1313-1328.

Manning, N. (1998), 'Patterns of environmental movements in Eastern Europe' *Environmental Politics*, vol 7, no 2, pp. 100-134.

Mason, D.S. and Sydorenko, S. (1990), 'Perestroika, Social Justice, and Soviet Public Opinion' *Problems of Communism*, vol. 39, Nov/Dec, pp. 34-43.

Matthews, M. (1986), *Poverty in the Soviet Union*, Cambridge University Press, Cambridge.

Merton R., Fiske M., and Kendall P. (1992), *The Focused Interview*, Free Press, Glencoe, Illinois.

Mezentseva, E. and Rimachevskaya, N. (1990), 'The Soviet Country Profile: health of the USSR population in the 70s and 80s - an approach to a comprehensive analysis' *Social Science and Medicine*, vol. 31, no. 8, pp. 867-877.

Mozhina, M.A. and Popov, R.I. (1994), 'Income dynamics of the Russian population for 1992-3' in *Poverty: expert views on the issue*, Moscow, pp 111-21.

Muzdybaev, K. (1995), *Changes in the standard of living in St Petersburg, 1992-4*, 'SMART', St Petersburg.

Navarro, V. (1977), *Social Security and Medicine in the USSR*, Lexington Books, Lexington, Massachusetts.

Nemtsov, A. and Shkolnikov,V. (1994), 'To live or to drink?' *Izvestia*, July 19th, p.4, in *Current Digest of the Post-Soviet Press*, vol. 46, no. 29, p. 13.

Nevler, L. (1997), 'Key arguments on a swindling economy' *Znaniye-sila* September.

Niit, T. (1997), 'Housing and Environmental Movements in Estonia', in K. Lang-Pickvance, N. Manning, and C. Pickvance (eds.) *Environmental and Housing Movements: Grassroots Experience in Hungary, Estonia and Russia*, Avebury, Aldershot.

O'Connor, J.S. and Brym, R.J. (1988), 'Welfare Expenditure in OECD Countries, 1960-1980' *European Journal of Political Research*, vol.39, no.1, pp.47-68.

OECD (1996), *Labour Restructuring in Russian Enterprises: a case study*, OECD, Paris.

Offe, C. (1993), 'The Politics of Social Policy in East European Transitions: Antecedents, Agenda and Agenda of Reform' *Social Research*, vol. 60, no. 4.

Orebro workshop, 1994, unpublished report, St. Petersburg.

Osadchaya G.I. (1997), 'Families of the unemployed and family policy' *SOTSIS*, no. 1.

Ovcharova, L. (1997), 'The definition and measurement of poverty in Russia' http://www.csv.warwick.ac.uk/fac/soc/complabstuds/russia/russint.htm

Oxford Review of Economic Policy, 1995, vol.11, no.1.

Parsons T. (1953), 'A revised analytical approach to the theory of social stratification' in R. Bendix and S.M. Lipset (eds) *Class, Status and Power: a Reader in Social Stratification*, The Free Press, New York, pp. 92-128.

Pascall, J. and Manning, N. (2000), 'Prospects and problems for social policy' in H. Ingham and M. Ingham (eds) *EU Expansion to the East*, Macmillan, Basingstoke (forthcoming).

Perera, J. (1990), 'The shrivelled sea' *Guardian*, November 9th, p. 29.

Piachaud, D. (1981), 'Peter Townsend and the Holy Grail' *New Society*, 10 September, vol. 57, no. 982, pp. 419-421.

Piachaud, D. (1987), 'Problems in the definition and measurement of poverty' *Journal of Social Policy*, vol. 16, no. 2, pp. 147-164.

Pierson, J. (1988), 'Back in the USSR' *Community Care*, July 14th, pp. 22-24.

Piirainen, T. (1997), *Towards a New Social Order in Russia*, Dartmouth, Aldershot.

Pinkevitch, A.P. (1929), *The New Education and the Soviet Republic*, John Day, London.

Popov, H.P., Sazonov, V.V and Reznikova, O.V (1993), 'Russian unemployed talk about themselves and their problems' *Economic and social change*, no. 4, p. 33.

Preker, A.S. and Feachem, R.G.A. (1994), 'Health and health care' in N. Barr (ed) *Labor Markets and Social Policy in Central and Eastern Europe, the transition and beyond*, Oxford University Press, Oxford, pp. 288-321.

Prokopov, F. (1998), 'The bases of funding employment policy' *Chelovek i trud*, no. 2.

Radayev V.V. (1998) *The Formation of New Russian Markets: Transaction Costs, Forms of Control and Business Ethics*, TsPT, Moscow.

Radayev V.V. and Shkaratan, O.I. (1996), *Social Stratification*, Nauka, Moscow.

Rhodes, R.A.W. and Marsh, D. (1992), 'New directions in the study of policy networks' *European Journal of Political Research*, vol.21, pp.181-205.

RIISNP (Russian Independent Institute for Social and National Problems) (1997), 'Monitoring results, 1992-1997', *Transition of Russia: Difficult Search For a Solution*, RIISINP, Moscow.

Rimashevskaya, N.M. (1997), 'The social consequences of economic transformation in Russia' *SOTSIS*, no. 6, pp. 59-60.

Ringen, S. (1988), 'Direct and indirect measures of poverty' *Journal of Social Policy*, vol. 17, no. 3, pp. 351-366.

Roberts, J. (1990), 'Winter in Leningrad' *The Health Services Journal*, January 4th, pp. 18-19.

Rogovin, V.Z. and Ivanov, V.N. (1989), 'Social Policy in the USSR', unpublished ms.

Roik, V. (1997), 'Social policy at a time of renunciation of paternalism and dependency' *Chelovek i trud*, no. 2, pp. 62-3.

Rose, R. (1992a), *Russians Between State and Market*, Studies in Public Policy no. 205, University of Strathclyde: Centre for the Study of Public Policy, Strathclyde.

Rose, R. (1992b), *Divisions and Contradictions in Economies in Transition*, Studies in Public Policy no. 206, University of Strathclyde: Centre for the Study of Public Policy, Strathclyde.

Rose, R. (1993a), *Is Money the Measure of Welfare in Russia?*, Studies in Public Policy no. 215, University of Strathclyde: Centre for the Study of Public Policy, Strathclyde.

Rose, R. (1993b), *How Russians are Coping with Transition*, Studies in Public Policy no.216, University of Strathclyde: Centre for the Study of Public Policy, Strathclyde.

Rose, R. (1996), *Evaluating Workplace Benefits: the Views of Russian Employees*, Studies in Public Policy, 277, Centre for the study of Public Policy, University of Strathclyde, Strathclyde.

Rose, R. and McAllister, I. (1996), 'Is money the measure of welfare in Russia?' *The Review of Income and Wealth*, vol. 42, no. 1, pp. 75-90.

Rose, R. and Tikhomirov, Y. (1993), 'Who grows food in Russia and Eastern Europe?' *Post-Soviet Geography*, vol. 34, no. 2, pp. 111-126.

Rowntree, B.S. (1901), *Poverty: a study of town life*, Macmillan, London.

Roxborough, I. and Shapiro, J. (1996), 'Russian unemployment and the excess wages tax' *Communist Economies & Economic Transformation*, vol. 8, no. 1, pp. 5-29.

Rubtsov, N.V. (1994), 'Speech by the Head of the Chief Directorate of the Russian Federal Committee for Municipal Services' *Social Security*, no. 4 (January).

Rukavishnikov, V.O. (1994), 'The sociology of the transition period' *SOTSIS*, no. 9.

Russia-1997: Economic Juncture (1997), Statistical Issue of the Governmental Centre of Russian Federation, Moscow.

Russia-Europe Centre for Economic Policy (1997), *Economic Policy Review; main trends of development*, Russia-Europe Centre for Economic Policy, Moscow.

Russia in Figures (1997), Goskomstat, Moscow.

Russian Economy in the first six months of 1997 (1997), Goskomstat, Moscow.

Russian Economy in 1996: trends and outlooks (1997), issue 16, Institute for Economy in Transition, Moscow.

Russian Federation State Statistical Committee (1997) *Socio-Economic State of Russia* State Statistical Committee of the Russian Federation, Moscow, January-August.

Russian Statistical Yearbook (1995) Goskomstadt, Moscow.

Ryan, W. (1971), *Blaming the Victim*, Orbach and Chambers, London.

Sainsbury, D. (ed) (1994), *Gendering Welfare States*, Sage, London.

Sen, A. (1983), 'Poor, relatively speaking' *Oxford Economic Papers*, vol. 35, pp. 153-169.

Shapetkina, Y. (1994), 'The drinking water situation in Russia is very bad' *Nezavisimaya gazeta*, August 2nd, p. 1, in *Current Digest of the Post-Soviet Press*, vol. 46, no. 31, pp. 17-18.

Sharonov, A. (1998), 'Social policy: moderate liberalism' *Chelovek i trud*, no. 4, p. 63.

Sheregi F.E. (1986), 'A method of expert evaluation', in F.E Sheregi and M.K. Gorshkov (eds) *Principles of Applied Sociology*, Moscow, pp 63-67.

Shkaratan, O.I. (ed) (1985), *Blue-Collar Worker and White-Collar Specialist; Social Factors of Efficient Labour*, Moscow.

Shkaratan O.I. and Fontanel J. (1998), 'Conversion and Personnel in the Russian Military-Industrial Complex' *Defence and Peace Economics*, vol. 9, no. 4., pp. 376-380.

Shkaratan O.I. and Galchin A.V. (1994), 'Human resources, the military-industrial complex and the possibilities for technological innovation in Russia' *International Journal of Technology Management*, vol. 9, nos. 3/4, pp 464-480.

Shkaratan, O.I. and Tikhonova, N.E. (1996), 'Employment in Russia: labour market stratification' *Mir Rossii*, no. 1, pp. 94-153.

Shlapentokh, V. (1989), *Public and Private life of the Soviet People*, Oxford University Press, Oxford.

Shmelev, N. (1998), 'A new stage in Russian reform: limits and possibilities' *Voprosy ekonomiki*, no. 1, p. 4.

Shomina, E.S. (1992), 'Enterprises and the urban environment in the USSR' *International Journal of Urban and Regional Research*, vol. 16, no. 2, pp. 222-233.

Sinfield, A. (1981), *What Unemployment Means*, Martin Robertson, Oxford.

Smirnov S.N. (1996), 'Russian social policy is becoming active: better that it were not' *Segodnya*, October 2nd.

Smirnov S.N. and Maleva T. (1997), 'Extra-budgetary social funds: variants of reform' *Chelovek i trud*, no. 5, p. 30.

Smith, A. (1776), *An Inquiry into the Nature and Causes of The Wealth of Nations*, Everyman Edition, J.M. Dent, London.

Sokolov, A. B. (1997), 'Regional problems in banking and prospects for resolving them' *Den'gi i kredit*, no. 1, p. 16.

Solovyev, A. (1994), 'The situation in St. Petersburg labour market' in *St. Petersburg in the Earl 1990s: Crazy, Cold, and Cruel*, Charitable Foundation 'Nochlezhka', St. Petersburg, pp.166-170.

Standing, G. (ed) (1991), *In Search of Flexibility: the New Soviet Labour Market*, International Labour Organisation, Geneva.

Standing, G. (1999), 'The babble of euphemisms', paper to the conference on 'Ten Years After the Fall of the Berlin Wall: Contemporary Change in Central and Eastern Europe', School of History, University of Nottingham, 29 – 31 October 1999.

Statistical Bulletin of the Federal Employment Service (1997), Federal Employment Service, Moscow.

Steele, J. (1991), 'Soviet disabled struggle for political recognition', *Guardian*, February 7th, p. 12.

Stetina, J. (1990), 'When hope hits zero' *Guardian*, November 30th, p. 28.

Stroyev, E. (1997), 'Social development and Russian federalism' *Chelovek i trud*, no. 5, p. 5.

Szelenyi, I. and Manchin, R. (1987), 'Social Policy under State Socialism', in M. Rein, G. Esping-Andersen, and L. Rainwater (eds), *Stagnation and Renewal in Social Policy*, M.E. Sharpe, Armonk, New York, pp.102-139.

Tajfel, H. (1981), *Human Groups and Social Categories: studies in social psychology*, Cambridge University Press, Cambridge.

Therborn, G. (1986), *Why Some Peoples are More Unemployed than Others*, Verso, London.

The socio-economic position in Russia in 1995 (1995), Goskomstadt, Moscow.

Thirkell, J., Scase, R. and Vickerstaff, S. (eds) (1995), *Labour Relations and Political Change in Eastern Europe*, University College London Press, London.

Tikhonova, N.E. (1995), 'The values of Russians and prospects for the political process in Russia' in *The Renewal of Russia: the difficult search for a solution*, part III, Moscow, pp. 96-119.

Tikhonova, N.E. (1996a), 'Transformation processes in the consciousness of Russians: axiological aspects' in *Transformation processes in Russia and Eastern Europe and how they are reflected in the public consciousness*, Moscow, pp 45-61.

Tikhonova, N.E. (1996b), 'Experiences and Opinions of the Market Economy' *Orientierungen zur Wirtschaft- und Gesellschaftspolitik* June, no. 68, pp. 28-30.

Tikhonova, N.E. (1997a), 'Social stratification factors in post-Soviet society' *Obshchestvennye nauki*, vol. XXVII, no. 5.

Tikhonova, N.E. (1997b), 'Weltanschauung, Values and the Political Process in Russia' *Obshchestvennye nauki*, vol. XXVII, no. 4, pp. 65-80.

Tikhonova, N. E. (1997c), 'Investigations into Small Businesses in Russia' *Orientierungen zur Wirtschaft- und Gesellschaftspolitik* December, no. 74, pp. 40-42.

Tikhonova, N.E. (1997d), 'Social values and the political process in Russia' *Sotsiologicheskiye issledovaniya* May-June, pp. 55-74.

Tikhonova, N.E. (1998), 'The unemployed in Russia: sketches for a portrait' *Mir Rossii*, no. 1-2, pp. 79-126.

Tikhonova, N.E. (1999a), 'Russlands Sozialstruktur nach acht Jahren Reformen' *Bericht des Bundesinstituts für ostwissenschaftliche und internationale Studien*, no. 31.

Tikhonova, N.E. (1999b), 'Self-identification of Russians and its dynamics' *Obshchestvenniye nauki i sovremennost'*, no. 4, pp. 5-18.

Tikhonova, N.E. and Shchepurenko, A. (1998), 'The Desire of Russians for a Social State' *Orientierungen zur Wirtschaft- und Gesellschaftspolitik* December, no. 78, pp. 53-56.

Titmuss, R.M. (1963), 'The Social Division of Welfare: Some Reflections on the Search for Equity' in R.M. Titmuss *Essays on 'The Welfare State'* Unwin University Books, London, pp. 34-55.

Toshchenko, Zh. (1987), *Izvestia*, June 16th, p. 2.

Touraine, A. (1993), 'Introduction to a method of sociological intervention' in L. Gordon and E. Klopov (eds) *New Social Movements in Russia: from Russo-French Research Materials* Progress-Komplex, Moscow.

Touraine, A. (1997), 'Conversation between Andrei Zdravomyslov and Alain Touraine' (Paris, 25 November 1996), *Vestnik professional'noi sotsiologicheskoi assotsiatsii*, no. 1, no. 7, Moscow, pp 6-8.

Townsend, P. (1979), *Poverty in the United Kingdom*, Penguin, Harmondsworth.

Townsend, P. (1993), *International Analysis of Poverty*, Harvester Wheatsheaf, London.

Townsend, P., Gordon, D., Bradshaw, J. and Gosschalk, B. (1998), *Absolute and Overall Poverty in Britain in 1997*, Bristol Statistical Monitoring Unit, Bristol.

Trehub, A. (1987), 'Social and Economic Rights in the Soviet Union', *Survey*, vol.29, no. 4, pp. 6-42.

Treml, V.G. (1982), 'Death from alcohol poisoning in the USSR', *Soviet Studies*, vol. 34, no. 4, pp.487-505.

Tsivilev, R. and Rogogin, V. (1990), 'Social assistance for the elderly and the disabled in the USSR' *International Social Security Review*, vol. XLIII, no. 2, pp. 180-188.

Turner, B. (1986), *Citizenship and Capitalism*, Allen and Unwin, London.

Ulyukayev, A. (1997), 'Democracy, liberalism and economic growth' *Voprosy ekonomiki*, no.11, p. 10.

UN (1995), *The Copenhagen Declaration and Programme of Action*, World Summit for Social Development, 6-12 March, UN Publications, New York.

UNDP (United Nations Development Programme) (1999a), *Human Development Report for Central and Eastern Europe and the CIS*, UNDP, New York.

UNDP (United Nations Development Programme) (1999b), *Human Development Report 1999, Russian Federation*, UNDP, New York.

UNICEF (United Nations Children's Fund) (1999), *Women in Transition*, International Child Development Centre, Florence.

Urban, G.R. (1987), 'Introduction - Social and Economic Rights in the Soviet Bloc', *Survey*, vol. 29, no. 4, pp. 1-5.

Vishnevsky A. (1998), 'Report for the International Inter-Disciplinary Academic Symposium of Social Sciences', School of Social and Economic Sciences, Moscow, January, 16-19.

Walker, R. (1987), 'Consensual Approaches to the Definition of Poverty: Towards an Alternative Methodology' *Journal of Social Policy*, vol. 16, no. 2, pp. 213-226.

Warner W., Heker, M., and Cells, K. (1949), *Social Class in America: a manual of procedure for measurements of social status*, Chicago.

Wedell, J. (1999), *Collision and Collusion: the Strange Case of Western Aid to Eastern Europe 1989-1998*, Macmillan, Basingstoke.

Wilensky, H. (1975) *The Welfare State and Equality*, University of California Press, Berkeley.

World Bank (1999), *Country Brief, Russian Federation*, World Bank, Washington, p. 2.

Yadov, V.A. (ed) (1993), *Social Identification of the Personality*, Institute of Sociology, Russian Academy of Sciences, Moscow.

Yanowitch, M. (1977), *Social and Economic Inequality in the Soviet Union*, Martin Robertson, Oxford.

Yavlinsky/EPICentre (1993) *Oktyabr'*, no. 3.

Yermakova, M. (1994), 'In terms of health we are in 68th place' *Rossiiskiye vesti*, April 29th, p. 3, in *Current Digest of the Post-Soviet Press*, vol. 46, no. 17, pp. 17-18.

Zajda, J. (1984), 'Recent educational reforms in the USSR: their significance for policy development', *Comparative Education*, vol. 20, no. 3, pp.405-420.

Zaslavskaya, T.I. (1984), 'The Novosibirsk Report', *Survey*, vol. 28, no. 1, pp. 83-108.

Zaslavskaya, T.I. (1990), *The Second Socialist Revolution*, I.B. Tauris, London.

Zaslavskaya, T.I. (1995), 'The socio-economic structure of Russian society', *Ekonomicheskiye i sotsial'niye peremeny*, no. 6, pp. 7-13.

Zaslavzkaya, T.I. (1997), 'Social Structure of Russia' in T. Zaslavskaya (ed) *Kuda Idet Rossia*, Intertsentr, Moscow.

Zaslavskaya, T.I. (1999), 'The process of transformation in Russia: the socio-structural aspect' in *The Social Trajectory of Russia Undergoing Reform*, Nauka, Novosibirsk.

Zaslavsky, I. (1998), 'Towards a new labour market paradigm' *Voprosy ekonomiki*, no.2.

Zubova, L.G. (1996), 'Conceptions of poverty and wealth; criteria and extent of poverty' *Economic and social change*, no. 4.,VTSIOM, Moscow.

Zubova, L.G. and Khakhulina, L.A (1991), 'Poverty in the USSR: the public's point of view' *Voprosy ekonomiki*, no. 6 .